CARL A. RUDISILL LIBRARY
LENOIR-RHYNE COLLEGE

WAR MEMOIRS OF DAVID LLOYD GEORGE

1917

Photo. by Vandyk, London

THE IMPERIAL WAR CABINET AT DOWNING STREET

WAR MEMOIRS

of

DAVID LLOYD GEORGE

★ ★ ★ ★

1917

WITH ILLUSTRATIONS

LITTLE, BROWN, AND COMPANY

BOSTON  1934

Published November, 1934

PRINTED IN THE UNITED STATES OF AMERICA

CONTENTS

WAR MEMOIRS OF DAVID LLOYD GEORGE

Volume IV. 1917

In this fourth volume Lloyd George carries his memoirs of the World War through the tragic year of 1917, from the formation of the Imperial War Cabinet in England to the setting up of the Inter-Allied Council at Versailles. He takes up successfully the story of the Allied struggle with the Turks, the creation of the British Air Ministry, the labor unrest which required the Premier's resourcefulness to terminate, and the various peace moves including those made by Austria, the Vatican and Kuhlmann.

Perhaps the outstanding feature of this volume is Lloyd George's controversy with the war lords over the frontal attacks in the West, particularly the third battle of Ypres, of which the story of Passchendaele forms a tragic part. His indictment of the British High Command for this costly military failure is supported by contemporary documentary evidence, lifting the curtain upon the drama which was being enacted in official quarters at that time. A chapter is devoted to the Caporetto disaster in Italy and its effect on England. This led to the establishment of the Inter-Allied Council, by which means Lloyd George hoped to avoid a repetition of the ghastly and futile battles of 1917 and the wanton sacrifice of human life.

As the only member of the British Cabinet who remained continuously in office throughout the World War, each successive volume of his War Memoirs contains heretofore unpublished data of great importance.

ILLUSTRATIONS

WAR MEMOIRS OF
DAVID LLOYD GEORGE

1917

CHAPTER I

THE IMPERIAL WAR CABINET AND CONFERENCE

Imperial contribution to war effort — Canada's prompt action — Botha's loyalty to the union — Rally of Indian native States — Value and limits of Imperial consultation — My announcement of Imperial War Conference — Terms of invitation to Dominion Premiers — Decision to invite Indian representatives — History of Imperial Conference movement — India not a member — Lord Willingdon's letters — Cabinet's suggestion for procedure — Dominion representatives — Australia's failure to send a representative — Cabinet and War Conference meet — Meetings and Composition of Imperial War Cabinet — Matters discussed — Curzon and Milner sub-committees set up — Territorial peace suggestions of Curzon committee — Disarmament and League of Nations — Lord Robert Cecil's view — Problems of disarmament — Value of international conference habit — Further discussion on the proposed League — British frame only definite proposals for League of Nations — Pros and cons of disarmament — Imperial development: Massey's resolution — Methods of preference: tariffs or transport — My contribution to the discussion — Transport development advocated — Revised resolution adopted — Experiment successful — Representation of India in future Imperial conferences — Constitution of the Empire — Appendix A: Prime Minister's statement on the military and naval position — Appendix B: Agenda for forthcoming Special War Cabinet meetings with representatives of the Dominions and India — Appendix C: Summary of Sir Eyre Crowe's Memorandum — Appendix D: Summary of report of Lord Milner's committee on economic desiderata in terms of peace.

BEFORE the end of October, 1916, the Dominions had raised 673,808 men for the service of the Empire in the War. India brought this figure to well over a million. Had it not been for the readiness with which Dominion and Dependency sprang to our aid in the lean years of 1914–1915, the Allies would have been hard put to it to pull through before Italy came in, and at a time when the forces at the disposal of the Central Powers were at their best. Apart from the contingents sent from the Indian Regular Army, this impressive Imperial contribution was voluntary. Not a squad would have appeared in response to any order issued from Downing Street. It was a spontaneous rally to the flag which was marching to battle in a war when the whole Empire felt our cause was just. The Dominions even anticipated every appeal for help. So did some of the Princes of India. These great countries had no responsibility for the policy or diplomatic methods that preceded the War. They were, therefore, free to judge for themselves whether they were under any moral obligation to risk the lives of their citizens in an active participation in the conflict.

The Canadian Government, watching events from thousands of miles away, foresaw that war was inevitable, and on July 31st, the day before Germany declared war on Russia, began to lay its plans for the mobilisation of its forces. On August 3rd, the enrolment of volunteers began. As soon as our ultimatum expired, a message was sent on behalf of the Canadian Ministry: "Canada stands united from the Pacific to the Atlantic in her determination to uphold the honour and traditions of the Empire." Party conflicts immediately ceased. Sir Robert Borden, the Premier, of British stock, and Sir Wilfrid Laurier, the veteran leader of the Opposition, of French lineage, joined hands. The official call for troops was promulgated throughout the Dominion on August 5th, and in one week recruiting had to be stopped because more than one hundred thousand men had already offered themselves. The alacrity and enthusiasm shown by the premier Dominion were repeated in Australia and New Zealand.

South Africa had difficulties of her own. It was only twelve years since the Boer War — a fierce struggle between two white races, which devastated South Africa — had been brought to an end. The defeated race were in power and their gallant Commander in the field was Premier of the new South African Commonwealth. Germany had sympathised openly with the Boers in their desperate fight against the British Empire. When war was declared by the Empire against Germany, General Botha had to cope with formidable dissensions amongst his own people. A rebellion led by some of the most cherished and trusted leaders of the Dutch population broke out against his decision to take sides with the Empire. I recollect a meeting I had with General Botha during the Imperial Conference of 1911 in London. He represented the South African Union as Prime Minister. One morning he breakfasted with me, and after some interchange of reminiscence about the old pro-Boer controversies, he expressed deep gratitude and admiration for the fullness with which the British Government had granted self-government and freedom to a people so recently in arms against them. He then expressed a very definite opinion that sooner or later there would be war with Germany. He thought everything pointed in that direction. I then said to him, "If there is trouble, what will you do?" He said, "I will keep my word and stand by the Empire. As soon as war is declared I will lead forty thousand horsemen into German Southwest Africa and clear out the Germans." I knew Botha meant it, and if the occasion arose, would do it. The occasion arrived sooner than most observers anticipated. When it came, Botha stood by his word in the letter and in the spirit. He did more than he had promised. He not only cleared the Germans out of Southwest Africa, but helped us in the campaign in German East Africa and sent a contingent to the battlefields of Europe.

As for India, as soon as war was declared, the twenty-seven larger native States, which maintained Imperial Service troops, tendered the help of their armies, and several Indian rulers offered to lead their troops in person.

During the four years of war they all had their full share of the hard fighting and privations. The Indians helped us to defend the waterlogged trenches of Flanders through the miserable winter of 1914–1915 and contributed to our victories in Mesopotamia; Canadians, Australians and New Zealanders took a valiant part in some of the bloodiest encounters of the War and they all suffered heavily. South Africans took an effective lead in the attack on the German Colonial Empire. They had all won their right, long before 1917, to an honoured seat at the War Council of Empire. Some of the most notable victories of the War were won largely owing to the dash and courage of the fine troops from the Dominions who had come voluntarily to our aid. They won a fame of their own, gratefully and proudly conceded by their British comrades, chivalrously acknowledged by their German foes. Had they stayed at home, the issue of the War would have been different and the history of the world would have taken a different course. It was a near thing with all the help we got. If a million men — and such men — had been detached from our armies in the first three critical years of the War, Britain would not have been beaten, but she would not have won. On the continent of Europe, Prussian military autocracy would not have finally been overthrown without them. On the contrary, it would have ended the War with the stride of a Colossus — a bleeding Colossus — with one foot firmly planted on a devastated France and the other on a prostrate Russia.

But the accession of these leaders to our Council in 1917 was not a recognition — least of all a reward; it was a distinct and special contribution to our usefulness as a War Directory. In the great experiment there were difficulties to be surmounted and dangers to be avoided. The Imperial Cabinet must be allowed to discuss every circumstance connected with the conduct of the War. On the other hand, we would have to steer clear of any decisions which would impinge upon the complete independence of any of the contributory States. For instance, no direction could come from this body to the United Kingdom or to any Dominion as to the contribution in men and money each had to make, and certainly not as to the best means of raising soldiers or funds. Then there was also the colour difficulty, which affected all the Dominions in a greater or less degree, with the possible exception of New Zealand.

But we had no desire to confine discussions to the War. Any question affecting Imperial relations should be examined if anyone raised it. The future constitution of the Empire and trade relations were subjects bristling with controversial possibilities. But obviously they ought not to be ruled out. We decided that rigid rules should not be laid down, but that the best thing to do was to meet on terms of perfect freedom and equality, and trust to the common sense and Imperial patriotism of the delegates, whether they came from Britain or elsewhere.

The first public mention of the decision to hold an Imperial Conference — in connection with which the Imperial War Cabinet ultimately took shape — was in my speech to the House of Commons of December 19th, 1916.

"We feel that the time has come when the Dominions ought to be more formally consulted as to the progress and course of the War, as to the steps that ought to be taken to secure victory, and as to the best methods of garnering in the fruits of their efforts as well as of our own. We propose, therefore, at an early date to summon an Imperial Conference, to place the whole position before the Dominions, and to take counsel with them as to what further action they and we can take together in order to achieve an early and complete triumph for the ideals they and we have so superbly fought for."

Previous to this there had been an exchange of correspondence between Mr. Walter Long, the Colonial Secretary, and myself, on December 12th, 1916.

Mr. Walter Long was rather piqued at his exclusion from

the War Cabinet. He was always conscious of the fact that he was regarded by a large section of the Conservative Party as the most eligible successor to the leadership vacated by Balfour. There is no greater calamity that can befall a public man than that he should be constantly aware of some personal achievement or position in the past which others have completely forgotten. Long was convinced that his resentment at being left out of the War Cabinet would be shared by the Dominions. Lest, therefore, irreparable harm be done, he felt I should send to every Dominion a telegram (of which he enclosed draft) assuring them that the establishment of a small Cabinet of five that did not include the Colonial Secretary would in no way prejudice the interests of the Dominions, and promising them a weekly letter that would give them confidential news of all important matters.

I thought a weekly report was by no means an adequate recognition of the magnitude of the contribution made by them to the effort put forth by the Empire in the War. I therefore had already decided to propose to the War Cabinet that we should set up an Imperial War Cabinet in which the Dominions and India should be represented. I sent the following answer to his suggestion:

"12th December, 1916.

"My dear Colonial Secretary,

"I propose to say something about the Empire in my speech on Thursday. The more I think about it, the more I am convinced that we should take the Dominions into our counsel in a much larger measure than we have hitherto done in our prosecution of the War. They have made enormous sacrifices, but we have held no conference with them as to either the objects of the War or the methods of carrying it out. They hardly feel that they have been consulted. As we must receive even more substantial support from them before we can hope to pull through, it is important that they should feel that they have a share in our councils as well as in our burdens. We want more men from them. We can hardly ask them to make another great recruiting effort unless it is accompanied by an invitation to come over to discuss the situation with us.

"Please let me know what you think about it.

"Thanks for inquiries. I hope to be all right by Thursday.

Ever sincerely,

D. LLOYD GEORGE."

"The Rt. Hon. Walter Long, M.P."

The first reference to the Imperial Conference in the discussions of the War Cabinet was on December 20th, 1916, when I informed the Cabinet with reference to the statement I had made to the House on the previous day that I proposed to ask the Dominions to send representatives as soon as possible.

On December 22nd the matter was further discussed, and it was agreed to send telegrams to the Dominion Premiers, inviting them to a gathering which should not be an ordinary Imperial Conference, but a series of Cabinet meetings of which they would form members with the British War Cabinet, to discuss urgent matters arising out of the War. On December 23rd the discussion was pushed further, and it was suggested that the Dominion Premiers might wish when they were together here to deal with other matters than those that would be laid before them in the War Cabinet. It was accordingly decided that if the Dominion Premiers wanted to raise other points they could have a separate conference to deal with these issues, but that the prime object of inviting them should be the constitution of an Imperial War Cabinet.

Accordingly, a telegram was sent to the Dominion Premiers in the following terms:

I wish to explain that what His Majesty's Government contemplate is not a session of the ordinary Imperial Conference, but a special War Conference of the Empire. They therefore invite your Prime Minister to attend a series of special and continuous meetings of the War Cabinet in order to consider urgent questions affecting the prosecution of the War, the possible conditions on which, in agreement with our Allies, we could assent to its termination, and the problems which will then immediately arise. For the purpose of these meetings, your Prime Minister would be a member of the War Cabinet.

In view of the extreme urgency of the subjects of discussion, as well as of their supreme importance, it is hoped that your Prime Minister may find it possible, in spite of the serious inconvenience involved, to attend at an early date, not later than the end of February. While His Majesty's Government earnestly desire the presence of your Prime Minister himself, they hope that if he sees insuperable difficulty he will carefully consider the question of nominating a substitute, as they would regard it as a serious misfortune if any Dominion were left unrepresented.

The Colonial Secretary had promptly sent a preliminary notification to the Dominion Premiers after the War Cabinet meeting of December 20th, but the above telegram gave authoritative definition of the nature of the consultation to which they were being summoned. It was important not to announce it as a regular Imperial Conference, since the constitution of such a conference was already firmly defined by precedent, and what was desired on this occasion was something definitely simpler and more direct in character.

On January 1st, 1917, the matter again came before the War Cabinet, when it was agreed that Dominion Premiers should be invited to bring with them any of their Ministers whose presence might be necessary in connection with discussion of special issues; such Ministers not to become actual Members of the War Cabinet, but to be available for consultation as wanted. It was reported at this meeting that the Australian Premier had sent word that he would not be able to come over, as the lack of settlement in Ireland was causing trouble in Australia.

A further telegram was sent to the Dominions in the following terms:

I wish to make it clear that if your Prime Minister desires the presence at the War Cabinet of colleagues, of whose special knowledge he wishes to avail himself, the latter will be welcome, though of course the Prime Minister alone will be a member of the War Cabinet. Further, if your Ministers should desire to discuss other questions of common interest not directly affecting the conduct of the War, or less appropriate for discussion at the War Cabinet, His Majesty's Government are prepared to arrange facilities for conferring on any other questions awaiting decision between the Imperial Government and the Dominions, although it may not be possible for the Prime Minister to preside.

The cautious wording of this telegram was dictated by the wish to give full opportunities for conference, while avoiding any appearance of summoning a normal Imperial Conference, and becoming subject to the technical limitations which the official constitution of an Imperial Conference would impose.

On January 10th, 1917, it was decided that the Maharajah of Bikanir should be invited to attend the Imperial War Cabinet gathering as a third Assessor to the Secretary of State for India, representing the Indian Native Princes.

This question was further discussed on January 19th, and the Indian Secretary was authorised to publish a statement about the Indian representation at the Imperial Cabinet in the following terms:

As already announced, the Secretary of State for India, when representing India at the special sittings of the War Cabinet, will have the assistance of two gentlemen specially selected for the purpose. In pursuance of this decision, the Secretary of State has, with the advice of the Governor-General in Council, selected Sir James Meston, K.C.S.I., Lieutenant Governor of the United

Provinces of Agra and Oudh, and Sir Satyendra Prasanna Sinha. In accordance with a further decision of His Majesty's Government, the Secretary of State for India will also have the assistance of one of the Ruling Chiefs of India. With the advice of the Governor-General in Council, he has invited His Highness the Maharajah of Bikanir, G.C.S.I., G.C.I.E., A.D.C., to accompany him, and His Highness has accepted the offer.

In noting the amount of care and caution bestowed on the question of Indian representation at this gathering, it must be borne in mind that hitherto India had not participated in the Imperial Conferences. The constitution of the Imperial Conference had been settled in 1907, when the first was held. Prior to 1907, there had been a couple of "Colonial Conferences", the last of them taking place in 1902, when the Colonial Prime Ministers had been invited to London to consult with the Imperial Government on colonial matters. In 1907, Sir Henry Campbell-Bannerman, when summoning a Colonial Conference, decided to take the step in advance of establishing this as a definitely constituted Imperial Conference, to be held every four years, and attended by the Premiers of the self-governing Dominions, under the presidency of the British Premier. A permanent Imperial Conference Secretariat was set up, as a department of the Colonial Office, to keep the records of the conferences and make the arrangements for them. But India, not being a self-governing Dominion, was at that time outside the purview of the Conference Constitution. She was not represented at the Imperial Conference of 1911, the first to be summoned under the new constitution.

There was, therefore, no authority by which India could be invited to an Imperial Conference, and no understanding with the Dominion Premiers to permit of such a new development. But India had made a large contribution of men and money to the carrying on of the War, and her troops were fighting alongside white soldiers and against white enemies. This fact had created a new self-consciousness among the Indians that showed itself in a demand for greater recognition, and it also made consultation with them about the further conduct of the War just and desirable. Hence the Imperial Conference of 1917 was summoned on a special basis, outside the official constitution. The representation of India in the Imperial War Cabinet was the beginning of the open recognition of India's new status. The precedent was followed in the conferences and discussions of 1919 regarding the peace settlement, and since then India has had her place in every Imperial Conference. The two Imperial Conferences of 1923 — the regular Quadrennial Conference and the special Imperial Economic Conference — found India's representatives at the table alongside the Dominion Premiers.

Two letters I received during the War from the present Viceroy, Lord Willingdon (he was then Governor of Bombay), give a new idea of the changes effected in enlightened British opinion by India's loyalty during the War.

The first I received in January, 1916.

"22/1/16.

"My dear Lloyd George,

"Can you, amid all your preoccupation, give a minute to this letter coming from one who is trying to do his bit out here and has after three years got a profound and certain belief in the necessity for a big and generous move in the way of legislation both in economic and administrative matters by the Home Government?

"I won't go into any details, but I wish to preface my remarks by saying that I have written to various of our leaders on this and either got no answer or no encouragement. What the position here wants is courage and the readiness to take chances. If this is done by some leader after this War is over, it is my conviction that

India will prove to be in every way one of the most loyal and productive parts of the Empire.

"The Indian's point of view is 'You English have educated us. You have brought us to an intense desire to look after ourselves: when you want us you call us fellow citizens of a Great Empire, but when it comes to business you give us nothing but "concessions." We love our country, we want you to give us a real chance of doing something for it.'

"The Englishman replies: 'You are not ready for any more. We must have efficiency in our administration, and you can't come in and really help us administer until you can show more character and honesty.'

"But the Englishman will not realise that the Indian can't learn unless he is given a chance to do so. Of course, it is true that the advance of the Indian means the gradual disappearance of this great Civil Service out here, but *that,* if the Indians are given a real chance to progress, is inevitable. I only write this outline of view to ask you to keep in mind this great country after the War is over. India has done her part nobly during the War, and while she asks for nothing *because of that,* I think she deserves to be generously treated. It is such an opportunity for a statesman to bind, I believe for long years, this great people in the bonds of amity and Imperial Unity, that I hope you may remember this outburst, for the question is one of real Imperial concern.

"I am afraid we are in for a bad time up the Gulf; why is it that somebody blunders so often? We want a victory badly out here — Gallipoli and this last business in the Gulf have unsettled people a bit, but I think that bar Bengal, India will be staunch.

"All good wishes to you, and all congratulations on your munition efforts. I only hope the result may be the pulverisation of our foe before long.

Yours sincerely,

WILLINGDON."

The next came to me immediately after my appointment as Premier.

"Bombay,
10/12/16.

"My dear Lloyd George,

"I must write you a line to congratulate you warmly on being Prime Minister and on taking over the greatest responsibility for the Empire that has ever been borne by a British Statesman. Here we have wondered for some time why our proceedings have been characterised by so much leisurely statesmanship. While the Germans push on and seem to achieve their purposes because they show force and determination, we want to get a move on, a move that will show the Germans we mean business, a move that will hearten us all out here, and make us all feel that we are not allowing the enemy to run rings round us in the way of making up our minds and on our decisions.

"I think you may be quite happy about the position in India on the whole, though until we have settled Turkey, the Mohammedan uneasiness is sure to continue. Personally, I have never liked the Government's action with regard to the Sherif of Mecca which has been resented out here and is, I think, not going to be of much value to us.

"It is, I know, impossible for you to have much time to consider the future policy of this country, but I do trust that you will call to mind a letter I wrote to you many months ago suggesting that our policy should be conceived in a really generous spirit, for India has done, is doing, and will continue to do her part. It is, I am certain, a magnificent opportunity for securing the faithful loyalty of India for all time, to give her substantial advance and to give it generously. We must run a certain amount of risk in so doing, but I believe the risk should be run and I am confident the result will be satisfactory. Forgive my bothering you, but I wanted to write you these few lines to wish you God's speed in your great task and to express a hope that politicians will put aside party and support you in your endeavour through thick and thin until you have achieved the great result.

With all good wishes,
Yours sincerely,
WILLINGDON."

These were the first communications I received from any authoritative source in India which definitely indicated that the time had arrived when Great Britain should contemplate an advance on the lines of self-government for the Indian people.

I had several discussions, more especially with Lord Milner, Mr. Philip Kerr (now Lord Lothian) and Sir Maurice Hankey, as to the Agenda for the coming Conference. As a result of these talks the Secretary prepared a Memorandum which appears in Appendix B. It gives a good idea of the wide scope which we had arranged for the proceedings and the importance we attached to this unique gathering.

Sir Maurice Hankey's note was considered at a meeting of the War Cabinet on February 15th, and the proposals as to information to be prepared in the various departments were generally approved. With regard to the procedure at the meetings, the War Cabinet inclined to the view that the proceedings should open by a general synopsis by the Prime Minister of the military effort made by the United Kingdom, which should include a general review of the naval and military situation, and that the First Sea Lord and the Chief of the Imperial General Staff should be prepared either to answer questions at the meeting or to give the representatives of the Dominions and India any special information that they might require. The War Cabinet further considered that the Secretary of State for Foreign Affairs should be prepared to give a general review of foreign policy.

The Imperial War Cabinet in its personal composition was the most remarkable Council of War in the whole vast battlefield.

Canada was represented by Sir Robert Borden, who was the very quintessence of common sense. Always calm, well-balanced, a man of coöperating temper, invariably subordinating self to the common cause, he was a sagacious and

MR. HUGHES AT A CABINET CONFERENCE, 1916

ASQUITH: "David, talk to him in Welsh and pacify him."

helpful counsellor, never forgetting that his first duty was to the people of the great Dominion he represented, but also realising that they were engaged in an Imperial enterprise and that an insistent and obstructive particularism would destroy any hope of achieving success in the common task.

South Africa was represented by General Smuts, the gifted and versatile Dutchman. He had made a study of war and had no mean experience of it. He had just conducted a successful campaign in the vast jungles of tropical Africa, where he fought the most resourceful of all the German Generals — Von Lettow-Vorbeck.

Smuts is one of the most remarkable personalities of his time. He is that fine blend of intellect and human sympathy which constitutes the understanding man. Although he had proved his courage in many enterprises which demanded personal valour, and although he had shown his powers in many a fight which had called for combative qualities, his sympathies were too broad to make of him a mere fighting man. His rare gifts of mind and heart strengthened those finer elements which are apt to be overwhelmed in an hour of savage temper and pitiless carnage. Of his practical contribution to our counsels during these trying years, it is difficult to speak too highly.

The Dutch statesman was a complete contrast to the pugnacious little Welshman — W. M. Hughes — who directed so effectively the contribution of Australia to the War, but who, having only just returned to Australia, was unable to attend the Imperial Conference. He concentrated the whole of his acute mind and of his phenomenal energy on beating down the foe. Smuts and Hughes had nothing in common except an indomitable courage. They were both essential to the tasks of Empire at this grave juncture in its history. Hughes had been to England in 1916, and then did his fiery best to stir things up. He and Asquith did not get on too well. They would not. They were antipathetic types. As Hughes was never overanxious to conceal his feelings or restrain his expression of them, and was moreover equipped with a biting tongue, the consultations between them were not agreeable to either.

Massey, the burly son of an Ulster stock, led the New Zealand delegation. Shrewd, sensible, direct and single-minded, his very appearance inspired a feeling of strength in the fight. He was a complete answer to the foolish notion inculcated by Carlyle, that strong men are always silent. Once he started, his speech was a rapid torrent, but the waters were clear and they always dashed along in the right direction. His partner, Sir Joseph Ward, was a more finished, if equally galloping speaker. But although neither of them had an oratorical speed limit, their contributions were lucid, invariably directed to the point at issue and had a note of practical good sense which was always helpful.

"Bikanir" as he was familiarly and affectionately called — the Indian Prince — was a magnificent specimen of the manhood of his great country. We soon found that he was one of "the wise men that came from the East." More and more did we come to rely on his advice, especially on all questions that affected India.

Apart from the aggregate numbers that these men represented, their very presence gave confidence in the most depressing and dreary moments. The Imperial Contingent came into our counsels with minds not staled and stunted by years of thinking and toiling in departmental dugouts and deep trenches where progress was barred by entanglements of all kinds. It was a distinct advantage to have these fresh and untrammelled brains and these virile personalities with whom to interchange ideas. They had an invigorating and emancipating effect on our worn nerves and shackled minds.

On March 2nd, the date for opening the Imperial War Cabinet Meetings and the sessions of the Imperial War Conference was discussed. By mid-March the representatives of India and of all the Dominions except Australia would be present. Mr. Hughes, of Australia, could not be expected before April 9th at the earliest. It was agreed that the meetings could not wait till that date, but that matters specially affecting Australia could be held up till Mr. Hughes' arrival. The ultimate decision of the Cabinet was that the Special Imperial Sittings of the War Cabinet should begin about March 20th, but the discussion of peace terms, and similar urgent matters of common interest, should be postponed until Mr. Hughes' arrival. Meanwhile a number of questions, such as, for instance, man power, timber supply, mineral production, etc., could be discussed before the 20th of March between His Majesty's Government and the Dominion representatives, either outside or at the meetings of the War Cabinet, on the distinct understanding, however, that no decision affecting the Commonwealth of Australia should be taken.

On March 17th, the War Cabinet discussed the failure of Australia to send a representative to the Imperial War Cabinet. General Smuts had urged telegraphing Hughes that an Imperial consultation would be unreal without Australia's participation. But in view of the extremely difficult political situation in Australia, it was felt that such a message could do no good and might only embarrass Hughes; and it was decided that the best thing would be to pass a resolution at the first meeting of the Imperial War Cabinet regretting Australia's absence. I dwell on this incident as it affords an illustration of one of the practical difficulties experienced by so far-flung an Empire in securing authoritative consultation leading to action.

The Imperial discussions began on March 20th. As has been indicated in some of the foregoing extracts, it had been arranged for them to take two concurrent forms. On the one hand, there were the meetings of the Imperial War Cabinet, at which the representatives of the Dominions and of India joined with the British Cabinet to handle the daily administrative Cabinet problems, and also to decide on executive measures for the Imperial conduct of the War; and on the other hand, there were the meetings of an Imperial War Conference at the Colonial Office, presided over by the Secretary of State for the Colonies, to discuss a number of problems which either arose out of the War or had been accentuated by it. The two series of meetings, in both of which the same representatives of the Empire overseas were taking part, were mainly held on alternate days.

I opened the Conference with a general exposition as to the progress of the War and the aims for which it was undertaken — aims which would have to be realised before a stable peace could be secured. I reproduce that statement in an appendix [1] as it indicates the view taken by the War Cabinet at that time of the military position and of the allied objectives. It was delivered in secret session and therefore the situation and prospect could be reviewed without the reticence necessarily imposed on public utterances in a state of war.

Altogether there were fourteen sessions of the Imperial War Cabinet, the first being on March 20th, 1917, and the last on May 2nd. There were fifteen sessions of the Imperial War Conference, the first on March 21st, and the last on April 27th.

At the meetings of the Imperial War Cabinet, those present in full session were:

THE PRIME MINISTER OF THE UNITED KINGDOM (*in the Chair*)

The Rt. Hon. A. BONAR LAW, M.P., Chancellor of the Exchequer

[1] See Appendix A.

The Rt. Hon. the EARL CURZON OF KEDLESTON, K.G., G.C.S.I., G.C.I.E., Lord President of the Council
The Rt. Hon. VISCOUNT MILNER, G.C.B., G.C.M.G.
The Rt. Hon. A. HENDERSON, M.P.
The Rt. Hon. A. J. BALFOUR, O.M., M.P., Secretary of State for Foreign Affairs
The Rt. Hon. W. H. LONG, M.P., Secretary of State for the Colonies
The Rt. Hon. A. CHAMBERLAIN, M.P., Secretary of State for India
The Rt. Hon. SIR ROBERT L. BORDEN, G.C.M.G., K.C., Prime Minister of Canada
The Hon. SIR GEORGE H. PERLEY, K.C.M.G., Minister of the Overseas Military Forces of Canada
The Rt. Hon. W. F. MASSEY, Prime Minister of New Zealand
The Rt. Hon. SIR J. G. WARD, Bt., K.C.M.G., Minister of Finance and Posts, New Zealand
Lt. Gen. the Rt. Hon. J. C. SMUTS, K.C., Minister for Defence, Union of South Africa
The Rt. Hon. SIR E. P. MORRIS, K.C.M.G., Prime Minister of Newfoundland

When the subjects under discussion made it desirable, the C.I.G.S. and Sir John Jellicoe attended the Imperial Conference. Occasionally the War Secretary, the Food Controller, Shipping Controller, the President of the Board of Agriculture and other Ministers were summoned.

At the subsequent meetings of the Imperial War Cabinet, in addition to dealing with immediate war issues which arose from day to day, the Cabinet discussed the broader aspects of the War and the problems arising out of it. At the second session on March 22nd, statements on foreign affairs were made by the Secretary of State for Foreign Affairs and the

Secretary of State for India. Shipping and food problems, finance, the war effort of the Dominions and India and their capacity for further effort, were dealt with on different days, as also the relations with Russia and Greece.

As regards peace terms, two sub-committees were set up under the chairmanship respectively of Lord Curzon and Lord Milner, to discuss territorial and non-territorial desiderata of a peace settlement. On each of these committees the Dominions were represented. They held prolonged sittings. Ultimately they came to conclusions as to the Peace aims of the British Empire. (The non-territorial peace terms are embodied in Appendix D.)

Lord Curzon's Committee dealing with territorial questions, recommended that so far as the British Empire was concerned, territorial settlement after the War should leave in British hands the German colonies and Turkish territory that we had captured or occupied. This was the first occasion on which any indication was given that Britain meant as a condition of peace to retain its conquests in the German Colonial Empire. So far the British Government had formulated no such demand. It was mainly due to the insistence of the Dominion representatives. They made it quite clear that they had no intention of restoring to Germany after the War the territories they had conquered. The British members of the sub-committees took the same view concerning German East Africa and Mesopotamia. It was agreed that British delegates to a Peace Conference should take these proposals as a guide, but it was pointed out that if peace were negotiated while Allied territory was still held by the Central Powers, it might prove necessary to hand back some of our gains to secure satisfactory terms for our Allies.

In its final decision the Imperial War Cabinet, whilst accepting the Report of the Committee as an indication of the objects to be sought by the British Representatives at the Peace Conference and of their relative importance, rather than as definite instructions from which they are not intended in any circumstances to depart, noted that the demands of the British Empire would require to be correlated at the Conference with those of our Allies.

Mr. Henderson dissented from this resolution, as he said that the Labour Party could not agree to any annexations after the War.

The report of Lord Milner's Committee on non-territorial peace issues raised much more far-reaching questions, such as disarmament, the League of Nations, indemnity, trade arrangements after the War. These provoked a remarkable discussion at two successive meetings of the Imperial War Cabinet and the summary of these discussions as recorded in the Minutes of the Cabinet is perhaps worth transcription. These deliberations have their special value at the present time as they indicate how the statesmen of the British Empire in their first collective examination of proposals for disarmament and the establishment of the League of Nations foresaw all the practical difficulties that have since arisen to thwart the exalted purpose of peace lovers throughout the world.

With references to conclusion Number 6 of Lord Milner's Committee (*vide* Appendix D), the Prime Minister expressed the view that the Committee had rather thrown cold water on the idea of a League of Nations, and had not dealt at all with the question of disarmament or limitation of armaments, or of the sanctions by which the conclusions of a League of Nations, or the provisions of any agreement for the limitation of armaments, should be enforced. He thought that there would be great disappointment if it were thought that at the end of the War nothing could be done in these directions.

With regard to the limitation of armaments, Lord Robert Cecil pointed out that he had submitted a memorandum in which this was advocated, but confessed that he had been driven out of his position by the criticisms contained in an examination of that memorandum by Sir Eyre Crowe. Crowe's powerfully written document took a pessimistic view of the prospects of post-War disarmament. It is summarised in Appendix C, and is worth reading as an accurate account of difficulties actually experienced.

In this discussion which ensued it was pointed out that one of the first difficulties in the way was that of the standard of armaments to be allowed for each nation. The existence of our own dominating sea power, coupled with the sea power of America, was undoubtedly the best guarantee for peace; but it was probably one of the very first things which the members of an international body would agree should be cut down.

Then, again, there was the difficulty of the manner in which any limitation could be prescribed. Napoleon's attempt to limit the Prussian Army to a definite numerical strength had been directly responsible for the creation of the Prussian military system.

Further, it was impossible to draw the line as to what constituted armaments. In the present War, Germany had been able for two years and more to hold her own against the rest of the world in armaments, owing to her effective industrial organisation. That organisation had not been purely planned for war; its adaptation to military purposes had been a matter of improvisation in Germany as well as in Allied countries. But the fact remained that it was an essential part of Germany's military strength.

Lastly, there was the difficulty that the Powers who were most likely to use their armaments in order to forward their ambitions were the ones who would be least willing to fall in whole-heartedly and honestly with any scheme of limitation of armaments that might be agreed upon.

With regard to the question of a League of Nations, Lord Robert Cecil pointed out that there were really two main alternatives, namely, an International Court of Arbitration or a system of International Conference and Consultation. He did not believe that matters affecting the vital interests of the British Empire could possibly be submitted to the decisions of an International Tribunal. On the other hand, he did believe that a great deal could be effected if the habit of conference and consultation could once be firmly established. He thought one of the chief causes of international conflict lay in the fact that treaty terms attempted to settle for all time matters that were inherently subject to variation and development. Under a system of International Conferences, the situation could be periodically reviewed. To begin with, at any rate, the most hopeful plan probably was to say that no one should declare war till a conference of all the Powers had been summoned, the summoning and decision of such a conference taking place within a reasonable time.

In the discussion which ensued, it was pointed out that a periodical conference to readjust the map of Europe might possibly create causes of friction as well as allay them.

There was the further difficulty that, under any procedure which could be suggested for a League of Nations, or for a Conference of Nations, called together to deal with such problems as those of nationality, a United Italy could never have come into being, or the subject races of the Ottoman Empire have been delivered from Turkish oppression.

Lord Milner said that he did not believe that any attempt to establish an International Court would be successful or be a good thing in itself; but he did believe that a great advance could be made if the nations who entered into the next Treaty of Peace bound themselves not to go to war without submitting their cause to a conference. Failure to do so should be a case of war for all the Powers who were party to the Treaty. The conference, however, could not be a court, binding nations who took part in it to enforce its decisions. Such a conference, in his opinion, would, in all probability, have prevented the outbreak of the present war.

Sir Robert Borden expressed the view that the real basis of future peace must be the public opinion of the world. The present war had demonstrated the futility of treaties and conventions when nations were determined to violate them. He laid particular stress on the last sentence in conclusion Number 6 of Lord Milner's Committee — that which referred to discussion with our Allies and with the United States. He considered that the United States and the British Empire in agreement could do more than anything else to maintain the peace of the world.

Such was, in sum, the nature of the discussion on April 26th, 1917. At the next meeting of the Imperial War Cabinet on May 1st, a further discussion took place with reference to a League of Peace and the problem of disarmament. With regard to the possibility of a League of Peace, Lord Milner again expressed the view that the most that could be done would be for the Powers concerned in the Treaty of Peace to bind themselves not to go to war without previous conference, and all to go to war against any Power that violated this agreement.

Lord Robert Cecil read to the Imperial War Cabinet a suggested clause in the terms of peace by which it was agreed that, in case of any difference or controversy, a conference should be forthwith summoned, and no action taken until that conference had considered the matter, or for three months after the meeting of the conference. Each of the high contracting Powers should bind itself to enforce this agreement by cutting off all financial and commercial intercourse from an offending Power.

General Smuts suggested that the precise nature of the sanction to be imposed would have to be worked out later. It would be sufficient if the Imperial War Cabinet expressed itself in general terms in favour of the principle of a sanction.

The Imperial War Cabinet concurred in this view.

This discussion has considerable interest as evidence of the way in which the scheme for a League of Nations was at this time beginning to take definite form. It has all the more importance because it was found at the date of the Peace Conference that the British Government alone had taken measures to work out a practical scheme for the constitution of a League of Peace. President Wilson had not gone beyond the vague idea and the striking phrase. He had not attempted to develop his thoughts into any concrete plan.

On the subject of disarmament, this meeting of the Imperial War Cabinet continued its discussion, and Lord Robert Cecil briefly explained to the Imperial War Cabinet the difficulties in the way of any agreement, either between the Powers collectively or between individual Powers, with regard to disarmament. These difficulties, as set forth in Sir Eyre Crowe's Memorandum [1] had convinced him that disarmament was not a hopeful line of progress. It is fair to point out that Sir Eyre Crowe's arguments made only a temporary impression on Cecil's opinions, and that he soon reverted to the conclusion he had formed that without disarmament there would be no secure peace.

In continuing the debate, I stated that I was not quite convinced that Sir Eyre Crowe's arguments had quite exhausted the subject. In my opinion, the War had been largely due to the existence of a great, highly trained and professionalised army exciting public opinion and eager to test its strength. I thought it might be possible to have an agreement in favour of setting up in place of this provocative sys-

[1] Summarised in Appendix C.

tem based on the spirit of offensive, a militia system essentially non-provocative, and based on the idea of defence.

Against this it was argued that it was extremely difficult to get rid of the professional element altogether, and that the conditions of different countries differed so widely that it would in practice be impossible to find a system on which everybody could be agreed. Moreover, the greatest existing guarantee of peace — the British Navy — was undoubtedly a highly professionalised institution, and it would be impossible to ask for a general reduction of military efficiency on land without raising the question of naval disarmament. It was, indeed, suggested by General Smuts that if the European Powers by agreement debarred themselves from spending money on their land defence they would have much more to spend on big navies.

Mr. Henderson considered that Lord Milner's Committee, in framing paragraph Number 6 of their report, while they had excluded complete disarmament as a counsel of perfection, were quite prepared to consider any reasonable means for reducing armaments and preventing the recurrence of war. Personally, he held very strong views on the subject of disarmament, but was convinced that it was necessary first of all to see what result could be achieved in the direction of a League of Nations. The policy with regard to disarmament would have to depend on the nature of the international relations set up after the conclusion of peace.

Mr. Chamberlain confessed to feeling that any attempt to lay down restrictions on armaments was bound to give rise to opportunities for fraud. Public opinion in this country would insist that any British Government should be bound, both in the letter and in the spirit, by the restrictions. In a country such as Germany, public opinion would be entirely in favour of the restrictions being tacitly broken or evaded. He considered, however, that the suggestion contained in

Lord Milner's report, of communications with America, might be followed up, and that we might endeavour to see whether Americans, who had given a great deal of time to discussing these subjects, could formulate any workable scheme.

Sir Robert Borden said he was certainly quite willing that the question of limitation of armaments should be included in the details for discussion with the United States, which had been suggested in the last sentence of paragraph Number 6 of the Committee's Report. He adhered to his opinion that really the public opinion of the world was the only sure guarantee of peace.

The Imperial War Cabinet were of the opinion that the question of the limitation of armaments should also be discussed with the United States in connection with any discussion of this question of a League of Peace.

In connection with Imperial development after the War, the Imperial War Cabinet discussed ways and means of linking the Dominions and Motherland more closely. Mr. Massey put forward a resolution in the following terms:

That the time has arrived when all possible encouragement should be given to the development of Imperial resources, and (consistent with the resolution of the Paris Conference) especially to making the Empire independent of other countries for the food supplies of its population and raw materials for its manufactures. With these objects in view this Conference expresses itself in favour of:

1. A system by which each country of the Empire will give preference through its Customs to the goods produced or manufactured in any other British country; and
2. An arrangement by which, in the case of intending emigrants from the United Kingdom, inducements may be offered to such emigrants to settle in countries under the British Flag.

In the discussion on this resolution, Sir Robert Borden urged that Customs Preference was not only an Imperial, but also a domestic matter for Britain, and "no one in Canada would desire a Preference that was felt to be oppressive or unjust by the population of these islands. Any such feeling would injure the Imperial aspect of 'Preference.' " But the Empire could produce all its own food, if the cost of transport were reduced, and he suggested that "it might be possible for the United Kingdom and the Dominions to get together in some great enterprise which would restrict the cost of transportation within the Empire. Transportation was quite as important to all the Dominions as Customs Preference."

My contribution to the discussion was on the following lines: I began by saying that I was speaking not in my official capacity but as one who had taken a leading part in discussions on this question. My general attitude had been altered by things which had happened since the War. The War had undoubtedly revealed certain fundamental facts which it was necessary to take cognisance of in our Imperial and domestic arrangements. There were industries essential to defence which we had been compelled to build up at great cost in the middle of the War, and which might not be able to hold their own unassisted at the end of the War. It would be great folly, in view of the expenditure we should still have to incur upon the Army and Navy, if we neglected to maintain industries essential to the efficiency of those forces.

Again, there was the Imperial point of view. The value of cohesion and coöperation between the nations of the British Commonwealth had been revealed in an extraordinary way; it had been the great surprise of the War to our enemies and largely to ourselves, and had made us the most important factor in the War. Consequently, from the selfish point of view of the United Kingdom alone, the development of the Empire would be an essential motive in British policy. The figures Mr. Massey had quoted (about the direction of pre-War British emigration) showed that if more trouble had been taken over the development of the Empire in the past, the Dominions might possibly have had double their present population and proportionately increased the strength of the British contribution to the present war. These were fundamental facts which were bound to produce an essential change in the policy of the United Kingdom with regard to the Dominions, and vice versa.

With regard to the methods to be adopted, I wished to point out that the War had revealed, more particularly in the case of Russia, the peril which might arise from dear food. That issue was one which had somehow or other obsessed the minds of the working classes in the United Kingdom even since the Corn Laws, and the memories of the present War would revive that dread. I concurred in Sir Robert Borden's statesmanlike view, that it would not do for the prosperity of Canada to be based on the want of the workmen in England. I wished the working classes to regard the Empire as something that meant not only glory, but also material advantage.

I was all for Preference, and would personally assent to any resolution laying down the principle, but I asked Mr. Massey to leave out the three words: "through its Customs", which specified a particular method. I was inclined to consider that Sir Robert Borden's method of subsidised transit through the Empire would give a more substantial Preference. I was all for the old Roman method of binding an Empire together by its roads — in our case by shipping. Another argument in favour of this particular method was that the principal meat and wheat-producing countries besides the Empire were not our present enemies, but our Allies, Russia and the United States, and a declaration in favour of a customs preference might look as if we were attempting to do them an injury. It was quite true that improved shipping would also take trade away from them, but that was a matter which could be justified on grounds of Imperial defence, and was a recognised method of development employed by the United States, Russia and France.

I did not rule out the remission of dues on the Suez Canal, or the possibility of subsidy on the actual goods sent over, but trusted that for the moment the precise method should be left open for future discussion. The United Kingdom had got to consider the question of its own industries after the War. This was not a matter of Free Trade or Protection, but of stern Imperial necessity for defence. Subject to this, I would personally agree with the resolution.

After general discussion the Cabinet agreed in principle with the resolution, subject to elimination of the words about customs. As finally approved after a further discussion on April 26th, the resolution ran:

> The time has arrived when all possible encouragement should be given to the development of Imperial resources, and especially to making the Empire independent of other countries in respect of food supplies, raw materials and essential industries. With these objects in view this Conference expresses itself in favour of:
>
> 1. The principal that each part of the Empire, having due regard to the interests of our Allies, shall give specially favourable treatment and facilities to the produce and manufacturers of other parts of the Empire.
> 2. Arrangements by which intending emigrants from the United Kingdom may be induced to settle in countries under the British Flag.

At the concluding session of the Imperial War Cabinet I expressed the satisfaction of the British Cabinet with the experiment, and proposed that it should be repeated and incorporated in the machinery of the British Empire. To this effect they considered that sessions of the Imperial Cabinet, as distinct from the British Cabinet, should be convened

GENERAL THE RT. HONOURABLE J. C. SMUTS

annually, and that as an institution, the Imperial Cabinet should have an annual session, though that did not preclude the summoning of a special session if questions of urgency arose in the interval. While the War was in progress the main business of such a session would be to review the position of the War; apart from that, it would naturally review questions of foreign policy, Imperial defence, and other matters of common concern. It was to me inconceivable that in the future the Dominions should be neither fully informed nor consulted on questions which might lead to war.

This proposal was heartily endorsed by the Dominion representatives.

Concurrently with this Imperial War Cabinet, there took place at the Colonial Office a series of meetings of an Imperial War Conference. It was presided over by Mr. Walter Long, the Secretary of State for the Colonies, and attended by all the representatives of India and the Dominions that were in London for the Imperial War Cabinet. Leading Civil Servants were present for consultation, and when the subjects under discussion made it desirable, the Ministers of Departments concerned attended the sessions.

Discussion ranged at the Conference over a large number of topics connected with the War — equipment and training of men, care of soldiers' graves, demobilisation arrangements, naval defence, control of natural resources, munitions, post-War trade. Two of the resolutions adopted deserve mention as having a wider and more permanent bearing upon Imperial affairs. These were the resolutions upon Indian representation and upon the future Constitution of the Empire.

The resolution with regard to the representation of India at a future Imperial Conference ran as follows:

That the Imperial War Conference desires to place on record its view that the Resolution of the Imperial Conference of 20th April, 1907, should be modified to permit of India being fully represented at all future Imperial Conferences, and that the necessary steps should be taken to secure the assent of the various Governments in order that the next Imperial Conference may be summoned and constituted accordingly.

This resolution was important, not merely because it opened the door for the future appearance of India alongside the Dominions at Imperial Conferences, but because it marked the first Imperial recognition of the altered status of India. It was one of the preliminary stages of the reforms on Indian administration, which started that great country on the pathway towards full self-government within the British Commonwealth. And in view of the controversies that have arisen over the development of that idea, it is worth noting that its inception was not the whim of any individual, but was attributable largely to the cordial welcome accorded by the Heads of the Dominions to the representatives of India as equals in the Council Chamber of the Empire in its greatest emergency.

The Imperial War Conference also gave careful thought to the question of the Constitution of the Empire. The very grave issues which the War had brought to the fore, and the critical effects of partnership within the British Empire which it had demonstrated, made this a major problem. At the same time, it was not one to be dealt with hastily, and the resolution of the Imperial War Conference on this matter was as follows:

The Imperial War Conference are of opinion that the readjustment of the constitutional relations of the component parts of the Empire is too important and intricate a subject to be dealt with during the War, and that it should form the subject of a special Imperial Conference to be summoned as soon as possible after the cessation of hostilities.

They deem it their duty, however, to place on record their view that any such readjustment, while thoroughly preserving all existing powers of self-government and complete control of domestic affairs, should be based upon a full recognition of the Dominions as autonomous nations of an Imperial Commonwealth, and of India as an important portion of the same, and should recognise the right of the Dominions and India to an adequate voice in foreign policy and in foreign relations, and should provide effective arrangements for continuous consultation in all important matters of common Imperial concern, and for such necessary concerted action, founded on consultation, as the several Governments may determine.

This resolution was a formal interpretation of the meaning which underlay the convention and consultations of the Imperial War Cabinet.

Considerations of space have prevented me from doing more than summarise in the foregoing pages, a few of the outstanding matters of permanent interest which were dealt with in the course of this momentous and historic Conference. Every aspect of our far-ranging war interests came up for review before this, the first Empire Cabinet which ever assembled.

But the value of the Cabinet and Conference were vastly greater than their immediate utility as an instrument for discussing our common war problems, and with the extent and method of the help which the Dominions could supply. The meetings had an immense importance for the consolidation of the British Empire. The Imperial Cabinet did not end with a discussion of common problems; it directed common action in events of solemn magnitude which were shaking the earth and shaping the destinies of the people in every clime and continent. The fact bred alike a new individual dignity and a more conscious solidarity. In our discussions there was less concentration, in the minds of the Dominion Premiers, on the sectional interests of the part of the Empire which each represented, and more eagerness to pull together to secure the maximum achievement in our joint effort. We were partners, not only in a Commonwealth, but in a Crusade. And the fine spirit thus engendered proved to be of critical value when, after the War, we came to complete that review of the Empire's constitution which had received its preliminary survey while we were in such temper.

Nor was the work confined to our discussions round the conference table. The visiting Dominion Premiers took advantage of their presence here to travel round the country, to meet with the people of the Homeland, and deepen by speech and interview our sense of common purpose and Imperial unity. Mr. Hughes, of Australia, had done some invaluable work of this order when he was here in 1916. Meantime, his work was continued by Sir Robert Borden, of Canada, and Mr. Massey, of New Zealand.

So deep was the impression that General Smuts made at this time upon his colleagues, nay, upon the nation, that we would not let him leave us when the Conference was ended. We insisted on keeping him here to help us at the centre with our war efforts. In every aspect of our multifarious tasks he was a valuable helper. He took his full share of the numerous committees set up to investigate, to advise, and subject to Cabinet assent, to direct action on vital issues of policy and strategy. He became and remained until the end of the War, an active member of the British Cabinet for all the purposes of war direction.

APPENDIX A

PRIME MINISTER'S STATEMENT TO THE IMPERIAL WAR CABINET, ON THE MILITARY AND NAVAL POSITION

(MARCH 20, 1917)

You will permit me, on behalf of the British Government, to give the representatives of the great Dominions and of the Indian Empire welcome to the first Imperial Cabinet ever held in the British Empire. I need not dwell upon the essential distinction between this gathering and any other Imperial gathering we have ever held of representatives of the Empire. Previous gatherings were very properly characterised as Conferences, but this is a Cabinet in the real sense of the term, with power to take decisions and to give effect to them. And it is held to take counsel about the utilisation of the resources of the British Empire to the best advantage in the fulfilment of the most terrible duty ever imposed upon any Empire — a duty upon the proper and effective discharge of which not merely the destiny of the Empire depends, but, I think, the destiny of civilisation for many ages to come.

I do not know that it is necessary for me to say — because the fact is thoroughly well known to us all — that we were precipitated into this war before any opportunity could have been afforded us to consult first the Dominions or the Empire as a whole. A few days before war became inevitable, there were many well-informed statesmen in this country — I am not sure that it is not true of the majority — who thought it could be avoided; and even when a European war seemed to be inevitable, there were still very many statesmen peculiarly qualified by their knowledge to judge of events, who even then thought that we need not necessarily be involved in it. And it only became clear a very short time before the declaration of war that Germany meant deliberately to provoke it for sinister ends which have since become even more clear — to impose, first upon Europe, and, through Europe, upon the world, a military despotism; and I am sure that the representatives of the Empire will recognise that if they were not consulted before we had engaged ourselves in this war, it was due entirely to circumstances, not merely over which we had no control, but which many statesmen with an intimate knowledge of the facts did not at the time even foresee. However, we entered into it, as we conceived, for the defence of liberty, for the protection of weak nationalities who were threatened by a powerful autocracy, and we took for granted that the Dominions and the rest of the Empire would take exactly the same view as we did, that the very highest traditions of the British Empire made it imperative upon us to accept the challenge the moment it was thrown down. And the sequel proves that we were right in that assumption; for all parts of the Empire have nobly come to our aid — spontaneously and with a good heart, recognising that our quarrel in this is the quarrel of the whole Empire, and, through the Empire, the quarrel of humanity.

The Imperial Staff and the advisers of the great Navy of Britain will present their views as to the military and naval situation, and therefore it will not be for me even to attempt to give any sketch of the position from a military or naval point of view. The Foreign Secretary will, if not this morning, at any rate I hope to-morrow morning, give to the Cabinet a review of our foreign relations in respect both of our Allies and of neutrals, and also of the obligations into which we have entered. We shall have from the Chancellor of the Exchequer a review of the financial position in this country. The Minister of Blockade will give a summary of the actual position with regard to the blockading operations of Germany. The Secretary of State for India is here also, and will submit to the War Cabinet a document in which he will review the financial position, and the position in regard to military assistance and assistance in supplies — a most important matter for the consideration of this Cabinet. The Shipping Controller will also furnish us with a paper on the shipping position — a most vital element when we come to weigh and estimate the prospects of this country in the War.

I can only give a bare sketch of the task which I conceive is in front of us, and of the efforts which it will be essential for us to make in order to accomplish our purpose. We ought, in my judgment, to have, in the first place, a very frank discussion as to peace terms — such a discussion as would be impossible in public, and such a discussion as would not at present be possible in the first instance even with our Allies — a free, sincere, candid discussion amongst ourselves of what we conceive the peace terms ought to be. That is essential, not merely in order to equip those who will enter the Peace Conference, which will come sooner or later, with a knowledge of what the Empire as a whole desires to be achieved at that Conference. It is more than that. We cannot really measure the effort which we have still got to put forth until we have a clear comprehension of what we are aiming at, and what we conceive to be the essentials of any satisfactory peace. I think it is too early to lay down in rigid detail even our minimum demands. The War is not over, and although things for the moment may be going our way, the enemy is by no means exhausted. His army is greater than ever; he is in possession of hundreds of thousands of square miles of Allied territory; his power is still unbroken; he is still a very formidable, dangerous, and incalculable foe. And, therefore, whatever consideration, whatever attention we may give to the subject, however long we may deliberate, for us now to lay down, even in our own mind, in any rigid way, even the outlines of the terms without which we could not assent to signing a treaty of peace, is something, I think, which is beyond the determination of any human council at this stage. But we ought to have a very clear idea what it is we are aiming at, what we should like to achieve, what we hope to achieve. We ought to go beyond that: we should also dwell upon what we think we must achieve unless the blood which has been spilt is to be spilt in vain, and unless the world is to be plunged once more at no distant date into the same welter of destruction.

Let us then consider the things which surely must be essential to any rational, acceptable peace. In the first place the Germans must be driven out of the territories which they have invaded. They must abandon the lands which they have overrun — in France, Belgium, Russia, Serbia, Roumania, Montenegro. The freedom and independence of those countries must be restored, and Poland must not be merely restored, but restored under conditions which will give freedom to its oppressed population, and the events of the last few days in Russia have brought that possibility nearer to realisation than it ever was before. Compensation must be demanded for the damage done to these ravaged countries. It is undoubtedly desirable that there should also be such a geographical adjustment of the map of Europe, on the basis of recognising national rights, as will prevent trouble in future, secure a more permanent peace, and also make firmer and more solid the foundations of democratic freedom in Europe.

That surely is the very least which we ought to achieve in a peace. But if we only accomplish so much, we should have failed in some of the main purposes to which we have set ourselves in this terrible struggle. There are at least four or five other essential aims to be striven for, and the first is this: the conviction must be planted in the minds of the civilised world — a conviction that will ripen into an instinct — that all wars of aggression are impossible enterprises; that they accomplish nothing but the destruction of the aggressor. Men must in future be taught to shun war as every civilised being shuns a murder; not merely because it is wrong in itself, but because it leads to inevitable punishment. That is the only sure foundation for any league of peace. There has been a good deal of discussion lately about leagues of peace, and there is no doubt at all that we should endeavour to establish a league of that kind. But unless you drive that conviction into the human mind in every land, the league of peace will be built on a foundation of sand; and therefore the first thing to accomplish in this War is to make every country feel that in future, if it attempts to repeat the outrage perpetrated by Germany upon civilisation, it will inevitably encounter dire and destructive punishment. That, I think, is essential to the peace of the world. I will come later on to consider how far we have accomplished that.

The second aim which I hope will be achieved by this war is the democratisation of Europe. It is the only sure guarantee of peaceful progress. The menace to Europe did not come from its democratic countries; it came from a military autocracy. France, before the War, had just elected a peace Parliament. The majority had been elected on a peace ticket. It was the most peaceable and peace-loving Parliament that had ever been chosen in France. The election was fought on a military issue where the peace party won, because the French electors regarded the proposals that were set before them by the militarist party as provocative. It was essentially a peace Parliament. Rightly or wrongly, it was an extreme peace Parliament. In spite of dubious leadership, the French democracy were so bent on peace that they preferred choosing bad leaders who were for peace to choosing men of much greater power and genius who they thought were associated with militarist proposals. That was the case with France. Italy — well, Italy was so reluctant to wage war that she was months late in coming in, and it was with great difficulty that the most powerful statesman in that country was able to persuade the Italian Parliament, even in the end, to declare war. The Italian democracy was very loath to embark on war, and if it had not been for the appeal of their unredeemed territory in Austria, and the opportunity which presented itself of recovering it, they would never have come in. Then, as for ourselves, we have been reproached, and probably rightly reproached, for our unreadiness. That is a very different reproach from that of provoking war. The only rebuke which can be justly levelled against the British Government was that they were not ready for war. That, in effect, was the spirit that animated the democracies of Europe, and if Germany had had a democracy like France, like ourselves, or like Italy, we should not have had this trouble. Liberty is the only sure guarantee of peace and goodwill amongst the peoples of the world. Free nations are not eager to make war. The democratisation of Europe has come nearer within the last few days. In fact, if there is wisdom amongst the democratic rulers of Russia, not merely will Russia become a great democratic State, but Germany must follow her example inevitably; and the speech of the German Chancellor within the last few days indicates that clearly.

What is the third aim? The disruption of the Turkish Empire as an Empire. The Turks have been ruling, or rather misruling, the most fertile and the most favoured lands in the world. They have not ruled successfully any of the lands they have conquered, and I am not sure that they are not the only race in the world of whom that can be said. They are ruling lands which were the cradle of civilisation, the seminary of civilisation, the temple of civilisation, and, from the material point of view, lands which at one time were the granary of civilisation; and now those fair lands are a blighted desert, although once upon a time they were the richest in the world. The Mesopotamia expedition and its history is in itself the greatest reflection upon Turkish misgovernment. It proceeded through lands which were at one time about the richest under the sun, and yet we found them so swept of all fertility by hundreds of years of Turkish misrule that India had to supply practically everthing for our military expedition. We could only proceed slowly, after making railways and getting transport facilities for carrying there every provision for feeding an army. And yet this was a country that at one time maintained countless millions of people, and even countless armies. The history of the Mesopotamia expedition is the condemnation of Turkish misrule in that quarter of the world. The same applies to Syria, the same applies to Palestine, the same applies to Armenia — it applies to all those famed lands. The Turk must never be allowed to misgovern these great lands in future. We owe it to these countries, for the gifts with which they have enriched mankind, that we should do something to restore their glory. There have been many expeditions from Christendom into that part of the world to wrest them from the grip of the destroyer. I believe this will be the last, because it is the one which is going to be successful, and completely successful. It is impossible that we should permit these lands longer to remain under Turkish government. Under Turkish rule they have been a constant source of irritation and friction and war. There has been no one cause which has been more fruitful of bloodshed in Europe than the misgovernment of the Turkish Empire and its results. I am not sure that even this War had not something to do with German ambition in the East; in fact, as the Secretary for India was pointing out to us yesterday, there is a good deal to be said for the point of view that this was one of the main motives which inspired Germany in plunging the world into this chaos of blood. She had made up her mind to open up the road to the East, and probably to establish her dominion in the East. We are blocking that road, and the abolition of the Turkish Empire as an Empire will to a very large extent settle the European mind, and it will give the energies of these great nations something to operate on which will be beneficent to mankind as a whole. It will be a great achievement to restore these famous territories to the splendour they enjoyed in the past, and to enable them once more to make their contribution to the happiness and prosperity of the world. You will hear from the Staff, I hope, how far we have proceeded with this task. I believe we have advanced already about forty or fifty miles beyond Baghdad.

As to another war-aim which concerns ourselves alone, I shall be very disappointed if this War does not lead to a reconstruction of our own country in many respects, economic and industrial — local government, the relation of capital and labour, the conditions of life amongst the people, and generally in an improvement, in a raising of the standard of life of the vast multitudes of this kingdom; and finally, to a greater solidarity of aim and action as far as the British Empire is concerned. This War is already making of it a great and effective democratic commonwealth of nations which will exercise a real, a beneficent, and I think a permanent influence upon the course of human affairs. It is becoming more and more consolidated without in the least impinging on the freedom of the constituent parts.

I do not know that I should at this stage say anything about the German colonies which have been conquered so very largely, and in some cases entirely, through the efforts of our self-governing dominions. All I would like to say at this stage would be this — that I hope we will treat this question as part of the whole problem of the settlement of the War, and not consider it merely from the point of view of any particular part of the Empire. We shall consider it, I trust, not merely as members of the same Empire, but also in reference to the great Alliance into which the Dominions as well as ourselves entered when they embarked with us upon this war. The extent to which we can establish permanently our dominion in those colonies must depend very largely upon the measure of success we achieve in the War, because if the success were partial we could not expect our Allies to bear their share of the sacrifice whilst we were enjoying practically the whole of the advantage. That is all I would like to say at the present stage on that question.

I have only given a rough sketch of what I consider to be the main aims of this country and of the British Empire in the prosecution of this War. Are we anywhere near attaining these objects? We are getting nearer. No doubt the War has been a great disappointment to Germany — a very, very, great disappointment to Germany. She reckoned upon the knowledge that she had the most perfect military machine in the world. So she had. And she reckoned upon France being far inferior, not merely in numbers, but in equipment, in discipline, and in leadership. She regarded the Russian Army as an ill-equipped mob, very badly provided with transport, and therefore unable to bring up her millions to the point of conflict with Germany. As for us, they thought that, from a military point of view, we were contemptible, and they said so. And they calculated — and with some show of reason — upon being able to bring this War to a triumphant conclusion, in a very few months. There is no doubt about it — that was their reckoning, and there was a good deal to be said for their point of view. There were many soldiers to whom I had the privilege of talking before the War — not German soldiers, but soldiers in this country — who, looking at the condition of the French Army and contrasting it with that of the German, thought that Germany would just walk through it without the slightest difficulty, and for the first few weeks it looked as if that calculation was justified. Now all that has gone, and the result of the War has undoubtedly been a great surprise and a great disappointment to Germany. We know now that her casualties exceed the number of her army on a war footing before the War,[1] and I think if she could have foreseen what was going to happen she would have hesitated a good deal; and I think she would have hesitated long enough not to have taken the step which, in a fatal moment, she took when she declared war, first against Russia, and then against Belgium, thus bringing the British Empire into action against her. Still, her punishment is not sufficiently severe, even now, to create that essential conviction in the mind of all military autocracies without which peace is impossible.

I dwell on this because I want later on to come to the question of what is still left to be done, and that is the question to which I hope this Cabinet will address itself. Germany has failed, but we have not yet succeeded. She is retreating in the West, but she is retreating with a purpose.[2] All you can say is, she would not have retreated if she had been strong enough to hold her own, and she would certainly not have retreated if she had been strong enough to advance.

But let us look quite frankly at the position. She has more men in the field now than ever she had. Her equipment is more powerful. She is in possession of scores of thousands of square miles of Allied territory. She is in a very powerful military position, acting as she is on interior lines; and the enormous casualties which we have had to sustain before

[1] This estimate, based on figures supplied by the General Staff, was considerably exaggerated.

[2] I referred to the retirement to the Hindenburg line.

we could force Germany to take this last step show that Germany still possesses enormous resources. I would not like to embark upon a prediction, but looking at all these objects which, I have ventured to submit, constitute the main purpose of our engaging in this War, although I am very hopeful, I should still say it would be a fatal error to reckon upon our being able to so destroy the *military power of Germany as to be able to achieve those aims in 1917.* They are purposes which Germany cannot possibly assent to unless she feels thoroughly beaten. *It would be a mistake for us to assume that we can beat her in 1917.* If we can, all the better; *but for us to base the whole of our action, the whole of our arrangements, upon the anticipation that in 1917 we are going to inflict such a military defeat upon a Power which in 1917 is at its strongest, might be a miscalculation which would be fatal to the whole of our purpose.*

To attempt less than those aims which I have indicated would mean the renewal of the conflict at no distant date, the throwing away of the great sacrifices which have been made, and the postponing of the great struggle for the elimination of war and of the military autocracy which means war, until another generation arrives, perhaps sterner, more purposeful, more tenacious in the prosecution of its ideals than the one to which Providence has first entrusted the accomplishment of this great task.

The Allies are depending more and more upon the British Empire. Ministers who have visited other countries will bear me out in saying that each time they go to those countries they feel that there is on their part a greater and a greater dependence upon the strength of the British Empire. We started with one hundred thousand men, we have now three million in the field; but that is not all, as I shall point out. Lord Milner has just returned from Russia, and that is the tale he tells of it; they are all looking to Great Britain, and that is the case now more than ever, after this revolution. The autocracy there was probably looking to us less than the people; but now that the people are on top, their whole hope is centred in Great Britain. Lord Milner and I went to Rome, as you know, and we found exactly the same attitude of mind there. Many a time the Foreign Secretary and I have had to visit France, but invariably we have found, each succeeding time, a growing reliance on the strength of Great Britain. And that is inevitable, because it is not merely that we have increased thirtyfold, with the magnificent help which has been given us by the Dominions and by India, the numbers of our armies — they are depending upon us for other things which are just as essential to the waging of a successful war. Our finance is their very life-blood. They could not have tottered along and staggered so far on the way had it not been for the financial support which Great Britain had given them. Then there is our shipping — they would starve without it. It is not merely that they would not have their cannon and their shell, because we are bringing them steel and ore and material for both, but their people and their armies would actually starve. France, a great wheat-producing country, has to depend upon the fleets of Great Britain for her daily bread. The same thing applies to Italy; the millions of Italy would have died of starvation had it not been for the British Empire. Then there is coal — they have got to get their coal from here. The mines of France are in the hands of the enemy, and we have to supply French workshops and hearths with fuel. In men, in materials, in food, and I think I should add in morale, more and more they are depending upon the physical, the material, the moral support which the British Empire is giving to the whole of its Allies in this gigantic world struggle. The sense that we are getting more and more behind them is sustaining their courage, and that sense is increasing.

I say at once we could not have done it without the help the Empire has given us. It is impossible in words to describe our sense of gratitude and the thrill of pride with which we always think about the way in which the Empire came to our assistance when we risked the life of these islands upon the struggle for liberty in Europe. We could only spare one hundred thousand men to send to France at the beginning. The Dominions and India have practically given us a million already. It is very difficult to dwell upon what we feel about that; and the achievements of their valour — well, they are just a household tale on every hearthstone in these little islands. We know what we owe to the Dominions — how, in the first Battle of Ypres, when our little army had all been practically thrown in, and there was nothing left between the powerful military machine of Germany and our shores (and if they could have conquered the Channel, Heaven knows what would have happened then), the gallant soldiers who had come from India were thrown in and helped to turn the scale. And in the second struggle, when for a second time, by a diabolical device — we knew about poisoned gases too, but we disdained even to discuss them at this table, and when the matter was mentioned we said "No, we won't look at that" and we absolutely refused to debate it even in this room — when, I say, by a diabolical device the French lines were broken, and the Germans for a second time nearly succeeded in their attempt upon the Channel upon which we depend so much, we shall never forget how the valiant sons of Canada helped us. Australia last but not least — the glorious fights of the Australian troops in the Dardanelles and Pozières, and many another field where they sustained heavy casualties and achieved ringing triumphs by their valour.

And so I might go through the whole list; it is no use beginning to select instances; New Zealand, South Africa, Newfoundland, India, all have played their part, and here, last of all, we see how the brave sons of India are sweeping the Turks before them in the land of Mesopotamia. We all know these things, and it is the fact that the Dominions and India have come in, and come in not merely to show that they are contributing, but come in with the whole of their might and strength — it is that fact which has turned the scale in this great struggle. We wish to acknowledge that. It depends upon what we all continue to do together how this struggle is going to turn out; whether it is going to be a sort of half success which will mean a repetition of the struggle, or whether it is going to end in a victory which will create a new world such as has been the vision of many of us for years. Our army — a great citizen army — has become a veteran army. Its amateur officers are becoming skilful, trained leaders of men. But if this struggle goes on, we shall have to depend more and more upon the British Empire.

Now, what is it necessary for us to do? That is what I want to put before this gathering. What is it necessary for us to do in order to achieve the very sublime purpose which we have set before us? The first thing is this: we must get more men. Germany this year has put every available man into her army, relying undoubtedly upon our not being able to carry the conflict beyond 1917. She has therefore made the most amazing effort. She has called up men from unessential trades, she has organised the whole of her civilian population, and practically all her able-bodied men have been flung into the conflict in 1917. If the War goes beyond 1917, France has nothing to spare. France has already put one out of six of the whole of her population into this terrible conflict. It is a most wonderful effort, and she cannot do more. Next year she has got two hundred thousand or three hundred thousand coming on — boys of seventeen; she can do that next year, and that is about all she can do. Then Russia. Well, Russia is Russia. You never can tell what she can do; and the trouble of Russia is that if she could put men in, she has not got the lines of communication, the transport, which would enable her to make use of those men. And, therefore, the winning of this War in the real sense of the term, depends upon the efforts which the British Empire is able to put forward.

You will have figures circulated which will show exactly what we have all done — Great Britain, Ireland, and the rest of the Empire. We are relying upon getting a good deal more assistance from India, especially in the breaking up of Turkish power. I am sure that the resources of India, which have been willingly and enthusiastically placed at the disposal of the Empire in this struggle, will be available for any further efforts that it may be called upon to make; but undoubtedly it would enable us to concentrate far more upon the struggle in the West if India were to be able to undertake the larger share of the effort which is to be made in the fights in Mesopotamia and Egypt more especially. Efforts have been made to secure more labour from India — because in that respect we have a great scarcity. There is a great shortage of labour behind the lines in France, and this struggle is becoming very largely a matter of making roads, constructing railways, and generally making and improving the access to the front, so as to enable us to bring up our ammunition and men. There, undoubtedly, India could render us enormous assistance in the way, not merely of helping us with labour for that purpose, but, subject to what the War Office say, I personally think there are many men now engaged upon work behind the lines, and altogether right up to the lines, who I think might be replaced by men from India. I think we might incorporate into our armies men from the great Empire of the East who would release other men for other purposes — men not merely from the Army Service Corps, but I have also asked the War Office to consider whether even in the artillery it is not possible to utilise very large bodies of men from India for the purpose of bringing ammunition up and for other purposes. There are scores of thousands of men absorbed in these tasks in our artillery; they are not all gunners.

I have to apologise for taking up a very much longer time than I had anticipated in placing these considerations before the Cabinet. To be ready for 1918 means victory, and it is a victory in which the British Empire will lead. It will easily then be the first Power in the world. And I rejoice in that not merely for selfish reasons, but because with all its faults, the British Empire is the truest representative of freedom — in the spirit even more than in the letter, of its institutions. We are here representing a great many races. Even in the United Kingdom there are three or four different races, and the Dominions and more especially India, represent a considerable number of races. Of their free will they have come together to tender spontaneously their assistance to the Empire in this great struggle. That I regard as the triumph of the spirit and tradition of British institutions; and therefore, when I foresee that in 1918, with a special effort on the part of all of us, we shall be able to win not merely a great triumph, but to win it through the agency of the British Empire, I feel that it is worth our while to take steps to organise the Empire now, and to enable it to attain the heights of noble achievement and influence in the glorious task which is set before it.

APPENDIX B

AGENDA FOR THE FORTHCOMING SPECIAL WAR CABINET MEETINGS WITH REPRESENTATIVES OF THE DOMINIONS AND INDIA

Note by the Secretary

The Colonial Office telegrams indicate that the Special War Cabinet Meetings with representatives of the Dominions and India may commence about the second week in March. I venture to submit some preliminary observations for the consideration of the War Cabinet with a view, more particularly, to the preparation of materials required for the Conference.

1. The telegram sent by the Colonial Office and India Office on the subject of the Agenda is reproduced in the Appendix.

2. From this it will be seen that the Deliberations of the War Cabinet will fall broadly under three heads:

(1) Increased effort during the War.
(2) The Terms of Peace.
(3) *Post Bellum* Conditions.

3. As regards the first, it is presumed that the War Cabinet will, in the first instance, wish to place the representatives of the Dominions and India in full possession of all the facts regarding the Naval, Military, Political and Economic situation, both of the enemy and of the Allies. It is submitted, however, that a great deal of this information would better be communicated verbally rather than in the form of memoranda, partly owing to its secrecy and partly owing to the desirability of not flooding the Overseas representatives with a mass of literature which they will find it difficult to read and digest.

4. As a basis for this part of the discussion, it is sug-

gested that the memoranda should be confined in the main to questions of fact, which can be used, as it were, as works of reference during the Cabinet meetings. The information might be set forth under the following heads:

(1) The facts regarding naval coöperation rendered by the Dominions and India, with indications of further directions in which coöperation might be given. This would be prepared by the Admiralty.

(2) The facts regarding the military coöperation of the Dominions and India, with indications of any directions in which further coöperation might be given. This would be prepared by the General Staff.

(3) The facts regarding coöperation in shipbuilding, with indications as to further possible developments. This would be provided by the Shipping Controller.

(4) The facts regarding coöperation in the production of food, with suggestions by the Food Controller and the President of the Board of Agriculture and Fisheries.

(5) The facts regarding financial assistance given by the Dominions and India, with suggestions by the Treasury.

(6) The facts regarding coöperation by the Dominions and India in the provision of munitions, with suggestions by the Minister of Munitions.

(7) The facts regarding any other form of coöperation by the Dominions and India outside the above headings might be given by the Colonial Office and India Office respectively.

(8) The facts regarding the coöperation of the Crown Colonies, Dependencies, etc. This would be prepared by the Colonial Office.

It is for consideration also whether, conversely, the facts under each heading regarding Imperial assistance to the Dominions and India should not be given.

5. It is suggested that, following the highly successful precedent of the meetings at the Committee of Imperial Defence in 1911, the first meeting should open with a series

of general statements regarding the strategical, political, and economic situation, which might be made by the Prime Minister (whose statement might usefully include a recapitulation of the far-reaching economic and other measures taken in this country), the First Sea Lord, the Chief of the Imperial General Staff, the Secretary of State for Foreign Affairs, and the Minister of Blockade, respectively. Perhaps also Lord Curzon would make a statement on such matters as mercantile shipping, restriction of imports, and aërial warfare, and Lord Milner might say something about Russia. These statements might be followed up by a summing-up by the Prime Minister of the particular questions which on our part we wish the Dominions to consider; and an invitation for them to offer suggestions to us, after which, no doubt, a general discussion would ensue.

6. Probably a large number of the suggestions would have to be remitted, either to Special Sub-Committees or Conferences, or to the Parallel Conferences proceeding at the Colonial Office and the India Office.

7. With regard to the second group of questions relating to Peace, it is suggested that the only memoranda to be furnished should be the following:

A translation of the reply by the Allies to President Wilson.

Sir Louis Mallet's Interim Report and Final Report on Territorial Changes outside Europe.

The Board of Trade Memorandum on Economic Desiderata in the Terms of Peace, and Professor Ashley's Memoranda on Indemnities.

The Report of Lord Balfour of Burleigh's Economic Sub-Committee of the Reconstruction Committee.

The Reconstruction Committee's Report on Germany's after-war policy.

8. It is suggested, however, that early in these discussions the Prime Minister or the Secretary of State for For-

eign Affairs should make a full verbal statement covering the following subjects:

The Agreements made in regard to Constantinople and Turkey.

The Agreement with Italy.

The Agreement with Roumania.

The desiderata of the Allies, so far as they are known, and of ourselves in regard to territorial and economic changes, more particularly those affecting Belgium, Alsace-Lorraine, Poland, and the Balkans.

9. There are several matters which the Government itself has not yet considered in relation to the terms of peace. For example, there is the big question of policy as to whether we are to aim at some sort of international organisation, such as a league to enforce peace, or a league of the character of the Concert of Europe formed after 1815; or alternatively, something in the nature of a balance of power; the financial arrangements between the Allies and ourselves, and the question whether we should use these as a lever to bargain for territorial or other advantages; the question of ton for ton, and any naval desiderata. It would seem very probable that some of these questions will be raised at the Conference. I should like the instructions of the War Cabinet as to whether any material should be prepared in connection with any of them.

10. As regards the third group of *post bellum* problems, it is understood that they will probably, to a large extent, be discussed outside the Imperial War Cabinet, and that the Colonial Office have already been in communication with other Departments on the various subjects. Perhaps the most immediate of these is Demobilisation. The Demobilisation Sub-Committee of the Reconstruction Committee is, I understand, at present in abeyance, pending a decision on the future work of the Reconstruction Committee, but both

the Ministry of Labour and the War Office are actively at work. One question which may have to be discussed in the War Cabinet is that of the constitution of the British Empire, if it is raised by any of the Dominions and it is included in the general programme sent to the Dominions and India; but I would submit that, in the first instance, it would be more usefully raised at the Special War Conference at the Colonial Office, which is fully conversant with the past history of this question and its difficulties.

11. Other questions which would, in the first instance at any rate, fall rather within the scope of the Special War Conference at the Colonial Office would include: Commercial, industrial and shipping policy after the War, emigration (including coloured emigration), Imperial communications, All-Red Route, cables, etc., naturalisation, organisation of Consular and Intelligence Services, and any other subjects which the Colonial Office and the Dominion Governments may consider it desirable to raise, and finally the constitutional problem itself.

I have already written informally to the Chancellor of the Exchequer, Secretary of State for Foreign Affairs, Secretary of State for the Colonies, Secretary of State for India, Minister of Blockade, First Sea Lord, Chief of the Imperial General Staff, Minister of Munitions, Shipping Controller, Food Controller, and President of the Board of Agriculture and Fisheries, suggesting, for their consideration, the desirability of getting together the material for the various documents suggested in this note, and I should be glad to have the approval of the War Cabinet, in order to place the matter on a more formal footing, and also to receive any further instructions.

M.P.A.H.

2 Whitehall Gardens, S.W.
10th February, 1917

APPENDIX C

SUMMARY OF SIR EYRE CROWE'S MEMORANDUM

In a memorandum dated October 12th, 1916, Sir Eyre Crowe made a critical examination of the scheme which had been put forward by Lord Robert Cecil for a League to enforce peace.

Analysing this scheme, he noted that it proposed a joint association of all the Powers signing the Peace Treaty:

(1) To guarantee the territorial settlement it imposed;

(2) To settle in conference any question of modifying that settlement;

(3) To enforce their decisions by united action against a recalcitrant State;

(4) To carry out general disarmament under cover of the foregoing guarantees.

As regards the nature and constitution of the Conference of Nations which should be set up to deal with these issues, he observed:

(*a*) That it must include not only the Powers signing the Peace Treaty, but also the Neutral Powers; in fact, every Sovereign State would have to be included.

(*b*) That it would have to possess a permanent headquarters and organisation, so as to deal at once with every concrete issue arising.

(*c*) That it would work as a formidable means of obstruction and delay, but would be feeble in promoting definite progress.

(*d*) That the readiness of all countries to join in and pledge themselves to united action could not be taken as certain.

Assuming that all nations united in such a solemn league and covenant, would they keep it? Taking first the case of a violation or attempted violation of the territorial settlement, they would only be willing to enforce it as long as they felt it to be a just one. No territorial settlement could be permanently just, even if it was so at the outset. By degrees some Powers would feel it to be unjust, and there would be a division of Powers into two groups. If the revisionist group grew strong enough, it would force an alteration, whether the Conference approved as a whole or not. "When a combination of Powers commands a preponderance of force — using the word 'force' in its widest sense — and the necessary means of aggression, there can be no certainty that an effort on its part to alter the territorial settlement for its own benefit will be actively resisted by the rest of the world."

Failing active resistance, would the rest of the world impose a blockade and economic boycott? Probably not, if they were in any danger of being overrun in consequence by powerful neighbours. The economic as much as the military weapon would be powerless against a strong combination of Powers. At most, the proposed conference would be a mitigating influence against hasty aggression. It could not abolish it.

Further, wars do not always arise out of territorial disputes, even though they frequently end in territorial changes. Even the Great War did not so arise, for Austria explicitly disavowed any territorial ambition when she invaded Serbia. Even if the Conference could ensure counter-action against a war of territorial aggression, it could not compel nations to compromise on issues they felt vital to their national existence or interests. The only way in which agreement could be reached in a general conference would be by an evasion of the issue, or by accepting a majority vote. A majority vote on the vital issues would not be acceptable to a Great Power. "Great Britain in particular would be exposed to special and grave dangers; for a substantial majority among the Powers could at almost any time be found for measures ostensibly designed to favour the general cause of peace, but in effect calculated to curtail British supremacy at sea."

A settlement of a dispute means that either one party gives way to the other, or that a compromise is agreed upon. A satisfactory settlement means that both sides are satisfied as to the general justice of the solution agreed upon. Failing this, the issue is not settled; it is only postponed. Such postponement means that the unsatisfied side reckons it would lose more by going to war than the achievement of its aim is worth. This again means that it does not consider itself strong enough to win, or to win cheaply, in relation to the importance of the issue involved.

So to attain ends which a nation regards as vital, it will continue to seek alliances and to develop understandings with useful neighbours, as in the past. And when once it has secured sufficient backing for its side, a Conference cannot hold it back; a Conference would only reveal its strength and the measure of support it possessed. All that can be said in favour of the Conference is that it introduces a pause, and makes the issue clear, thus enabling outside nations to decide their verdict as to its justice.

But in the last resort, everything depends upon the "sanction" that can be applied; and this means military force. The forces of the League Powers must be such that in any dispute they can bring overwhelming pressure promptly to bear on any possible recusants before the smallest of their members can be overrun. If not, little Powers will not dare to act with the League in taking economic measures against a Great Power.

"The balance of power reappears as the fundamental problem. To prevent the possibility of any one State or group of States pursuing, through war and bloodshed, a policy of aggression and domination, nothing will serve but adequate force." The effectiveness of a League of Nations is ultimately a military problem.

This leads Sir Eyre Crowe to discuss the possibility of limitation of armaments as a means of reducing the horrors of war and increasing the power of a League of Nations as against any individual nation. Such limitation must be in terms of quantity of arms; kinds of arms; or expenditure of arms; or all three.

None of these methods is effective by itself. The possible size of armies is limited only by national man power. Lack of it can be met by using more potent weapons, and the prohibition of certain categories would only stimulate invention of new types; and even financial limitation may be defeated by discovery of cheaper and more deadly weapons.

Suppose all three were used together; even then certain further conditions are essential if genuine disarmament is to be carried out.

The first condition is confidence in the good faith of all parties. This does not exist and is not likely to. Any nation could evade disarmament agreements, and none will trust its neighbour not to attempt evasion.

The second and fundamental condition is for each State to accept for itself a standard of force which it will not exceed. Since nations differ widely in size, defensibility of frontiers, and responsibilities, the standard must be different for each. What shall the comparative standard be? Not that existing before the War, which has proved itself a danger to world peace. Not that which we can impose on the Central Powers after the War, if we defeat them, for they will not submit permanently to helpless inferiority. We cannot stereotype the relative armament strength of nations because they grow and decline and change, as do their relations with each other. "Who will undertake to fix the standard of armed strength for China, for Holland, for Mexico, for the United States? Can it be seriously believed that standards so fixed now could survive a general revolution in China, a quarrel over the Dutch Indies between Holland and Japan, or an American invasion of Mexico? Such events — none of them improbable — would scatter to the winds the papers on which the agreements for fixing the proportionate amount of armaments had been written."

Finally, Sir Eyre Crowe examined the prospects of an agreement about arms limitations between a few countries only. This, while apparently the simplest, he held to be really the most dangerous, because any alteration in the armament of other powers standing outside the agreement would upset its basis and stimulate a new armament race between its signatories.

In a footnote to Sir Eyre Crowe's Memorandum, Lord Robert Cecil said:

The objections to any attempt to limit armaments are very powerfully put. On the whole I agree that nothing can be done at present. But it is possible that in future ages a public opinion will develop so strong against the settlement of disputes by war that armament will be reduced by common consent. The history of feudalism in England illustrates my meaning. The catastrophe of the Wars of the Roses led to the supremacy of the law.

R.C.

APPENDIX D

SUMMARY OF REPORT OF LORD MILNER'S COMMITTEE ON ECONOMIC DESIDERATA IN TERMS OF PEACE

The findings of the Committee were set out under the following seven heads:

1. Paris Resolutions.
2. Control of Imperial Resources.
3. Renewal of Treaties.
4. Indemnities.
5. Settlement of private claims arising out of the War.
6. The League of Nations.
7. The Freedom of the Seas.

The Committee held that the Paris Resolutions were no longer applicable to the situation, but they commended that feature in them which supported a refusal to grant the enemy countries a renewal of most-favoured-nation treatment when making peace. The peace terms should impose no limits on the freedom of the governments within the Empire to develop their natural resources for national purposes. No general renewal of pre-War treaties and conventions with the enemy Powers should be made.

On indemnities the Committee felt unable to prophesy just how much we could hope to get. Indemnities in kind would probably be more practical than money, though this also should be exacted as far as feasible. Shipping, railway material and natural products like potash, the last over a period of years, might be claimed; and money payments should also be spread over some years.

"The greatest difficulty connected with an indemnity is to determine which are the parties possessing the strongest claim to the benefit of it, having regard to the fact that even all justified claims cannot possibly be satisfied." Belgium should be given priority, and after her, France in respect of her northeastern provinces, and Serbia. Britain had an equal claim with these in respect of her shipping. If France secured the rich iron fields of Lorraine, it would go some way to compensate her for the destruction wrought in her territory. The Committee doubted whether the transfer of the German Navy would have much practical value.

For the settlement of private debts the Committee suggested that each government should pay to its creditor citizens the sums due to them from enemy nationals, and collect from them debts they owed. Any balance could be settled between the Governments. The validity of action taken under Emergency Acts and regulations with respect to enemy property should be insisted on by us in the peace settlement.

The conclusion on the League of Nations ran as follows:

> The Committee were deeply impressed with the danger of the complete destruction of civilised society which threatens the world if the recurrence of a war like the present cannot be prevented, and with the necessity of devising means which would tend, at any rate, to diminish the risk of such a calamity. They felt, however, that any too comprehensive or ambitious project to ensure world peace might prove not only impracticable, but harmful. The proposal which seems to promise the best results proceeds along the path of consultation and conference for composing differences which cannot otherwise be adjusted. The Treaty of Peace should provide that none of the parties who are signatories to that Treaty should resort to arms against one another without previous submission of their dispute to a Conference of the Powers. The Committee think that the details of such a scheme should be discussed with our Allies and especially with the United States of America, before the conclusion of the War.

No fundamental change was thought to be necessary in the British policy regarding the Freedom of the Seas.

CHAPTER II

THE STRUGGLE WITH THE TURK

Palestine and Mesopotamia

Near East Front the one bright spot — Strategic value of attack on Turkey — Turkey in vulnerable position — Pan-Turanian outlook of Turks — Russians command the Black Sea — Review of fronts attacked — Position at end of 1916 — Turkish strength in Palestine — War Office instructions to Maude and Murray — Arab support for the British — Our responsibility for three fronts — Lawrence of Arabia — Maude's successes in Mesopotamia — Maude asks permission to advance — Robertson's objections overruled — Capture of Baghdad — Russian coöperation breaks down — Maude's brilliant campaign — Death of Maude — Defence of Egypt and Suez Canal — My advocacy of Palestine campaign — Murray's instructions extended — Robertson cannot spare reinforcements — Murray's instructions watered down — Sinai Peninsula cleared of Turks — Robertson's memorandum on Palestine campaign — Cabinet accepts advice of General Smuts — More troops ordered from India — Sykes-Picot Agreement — First Battle of Gaza — Murray invited to capture Jerusalem — Second Battle of Gaza — Change in Egyptian Command: Smuts approached — Smuts declines command — Protests at Smuts' inclusion in War Cabinet — Appointment of General Allenby — His preparations for advance — Beersheba and Gaza captured — Fall of Jerusalem — Effects of our victory — Disputes as to Allenby's reinforcements — Smuts sent to investigate the position — Smuts recommends Aleppo campaign — Allenby's final advance — Importance of Turkish Front proved.

If the year 1917 was one of difficulty and disaster for the Allies on the battlefields of Europe, it witnessed some striking and heartening successes for our cause in the Near East. Here was the one bright spot in our land operations. And we needed the encouragement; for nearer home we had the failure of the Nivelle offensive, the mutiny of the French troops, the breakdown of Russia, the massacres of Passchendaele, and the Italian collapse of Caporetto. The "Western Front" strategy had once more turned out to be a bloody repulse, bloodier than ever. That failure had reacted on the position in the Near East, for before the close of the year it had rendered inevitable the conclusion of armistices with the

Central Powers by both Russia and Roumania, and their exit from any further military service on the Allied side.

There was no period in the War when the overthrow of the Turkish Empire could not have been accomplished by the joint action of the British and Russian Governments, with an effort well within the compass of their resources. There was no period, certainly during the first three years, when that overthrow would not have produced a decisive effect on the fortunes of the War.

As a feature of the general strategy of the War, the elimination of Turkey from the ranks of our enemies would have given us that access to Russia and Roumania which was so disastrously lacking, and without which they were driven out of the War. It would, in 1915, have given us the control of the Balkans; afterwards it would have enabled us to recover the control we lost in September, 1915, and thus have put us in a position to join forces with the Roumanians and the Russians. The Allied spear could have been thrust under the fifth rib of Austria, the Danubian flank which was her weakest side geographically and ethnographically. It would have saved Britain over a quarter of a million troops from Egypt and Mesopotamia, and Russia one hundred and fifty thousand men from the Caucasus. The course of the War would have been altered and shortened. Further, for the British Empire, the fight with Turkey had a special importance of its own. The Ottoman Khalif was the religious head of the Moslem world, and there were more Moslems in the British Empire than under any other ruler, which made our conflict with Turkey a very delicate problem. The Turkish Empire lay right across the track by land or water to our great possessions in the East — India, Burma, Malaya, Borneo, Hong Kong, and the Dominions of Australia and New Zealand. Egypt, through which the Suez Canal — the "jugular vein" of the Empire — ran, was under

Turkish suzerainty. It was thus vital for our communications, as it was essential for our prestige in the East, that once the Turks declared war against us, we should defeat and discredit them without loss of time. A final defeat of the Turkish armies by overwhelming numbers, after they had on equal terms beaten us in battle after battle for three campaigns, left a bad impression on the Oriental mind. The importance of a speedy victory over the Turks for the security of the British Empire was undeniable.

Could such a defeat have been inflicted on the Turk in 1915 or 1916 as would have forced him to make peace with the Allies? No one who takes the trouble to master the elementary facts can for a moment doubt the feasibility of achieving such a result early in the War. The Turkish Army was in such a bad state in 1912 that it was easily defeated by the Balkan States. Most of its useful guns had been either captured or destroyed in that conflict. The Arab population, which constituted twenty per cent. of the population of the Turkish Empire, was disaffected. The Anatolian peasant, who had always proved himself to be a good fighter when well led, was war-weary. His unbroken defeats during the Balkan War had for the time being taken the spirit out of him. Nearly half of this ill-equipped and dispirited army was sent to face the Russians in Armenia.

As regards the general disposition of the Turkish military forces in 1915–1916, it must be borne in mind that the real political aims of Turkey at this time were Pan-Turanian. They particularly wished to expand in Trans-Caucasia and Cis-Caucasia, regions inhabited by kindred tribes; and to assert and maintain hegemony over Persia. Pan-Turanianism having replaced the Pan-Islamism of Abdul Hamid, the Turks were comparatively little interested in the alien Arabs, and throughout the War they tended to direct their major efforts towards the Caucasus.

The fight against Great Britain made no appeal to the Turk. There was nothing in it to rouse him from his despondency and disillusionment. At the end of the War, in October, 1918, it was found that there were just as many deserters as there were men in the field. The total ration strength of the Turkish Army at that date was two hundred and fifty thousand. The number of deserters had then reached the figure of two hundred and twenty-five thousand. Wounded soldiers, when they were discharged from the hospital, mostly walked home and never returned to the colours. Except at the Dardanelles, the Turkish Army was a lame bluff. Even at Gallipoli it could easily have been overcome, had the attack been properly organised and directed and made in good time. In Palestine and Mesopotamia nothing and nobody could have saved the Turk from complete collapse in 1915 and 1916 except our General Staff. The real citadel of the Ottoman Empire was neither at Achi Baba, Baghdad nor Jerusalem — but in Whitehall. For three years this redoubtable garrison of the effete beat off every attack made on the attenuated armies of the Turk. The War Office saved Gallipoli from falling: for two years it protected the feeble garrison of Palestine from meeting its doom. It did what it could to avert the capture of Baghdad.

As early as the winter of 1914–1915, Enver Pasha collected an army of one hundred and fifty thousand men to attack the Russians in the Causasus. But they attempted an impossible movement through the snows of the high mountain passes, and were defeated with heavy losses by Yudenitch's Russian Army, which numbered one hundred thousand at that time. Nearly a third of the Turks must have perished in the snow, and one of the four Corps employed was enveloped and destroyed by the Russians. The rest of the Turkish Army was scattered around and about Mesopotamia,

Palestine, Syria, the Hejaz, and the Marmora. Asia Minor and Palestine had a long coast line which laid them open to attack at many vulnerable points from the sea. This menace alone would have absorbed many of the Turkish troops. The Turkish Empire was therefore specially vulnerable to attacks from a power that had a complete command of the sea. In the early stages of the War, the Turks had no through rail communicating with their territories beyond the Taurus Mountains. Had there been during the first three campaigns a resolute and well-directed attack either on Alexandretta, Palestine or Mesopotamia, the wretched force on the eastern side of the Taurus could have been swept up with the greatest ease.

A considerable force was kept at Alexandretta to prevent the possibility of a landing. Smyrna for the same reason absorbed a certain number of troops. The Russian Navy had complete command of the Black Sea. The Russians claim that up to the end of February, 1916, they had sunk about four thousand Turkish schooners and feluccas. The sea communication via the Black Sea to victual, munition and reinforce the Turkish Army in the Caucasus was cut off by the Russian Navy. The land route from the Bosphorus took about thirty days. On the other hand, on the Russian side the railway came down through the Caucasus and the railhead was only eighty miles from the great Turkish fortress of Erzerum. In addition to this handicap, the fact that the command of the Black Sea was in the hands of the Russians exposed the whole of that coast to the danger of a sudden attack at many points. The roads to Syria and Mesopotamia were bad, and the railway would not enable the Turks to send the necessary supplies to any point east of the Taurus Mountains, had there been a serious attack. The lack of communications would have been fatal to the Turkish defence, had there been a concerted attack pressed with determination, by the Russians from the Caucasus and by the British from Egypt or Alexandretta and Mesopotamia. The Turkish Armies could have been crumpled up in a single campaign. Even if the supplies and reinforcements had been available in the Constantinople area, they could not have been transported to that distance in time to avoid disaster.

The map (page 72) shows the Turkish rail equipment in Asia Minor during the War. The line from Haidar Pasha Station at Scutari to Riyak, twenty-five miles from Damascus, was a single-track standard-gauge branch of the Anatolian-Baghdad Railway. But it had two serious gaps — one in the Taurus Mountains, twenty miles long, and the other in the Amanus Mountains five miles long. In these gaps there were twenty tunnels waiting to be completed. The Amanus gap (at Baghche) was covered early in 1917, and a light line run through the Taurus tunnels at the same time; but the standard-gauge line was not carried through till almost the end of the War. The first through train from Haidar Pasha to Riyak did not run till September, 1918. Up to Muslimie, north of Aleppo, this line also had to carry the traffic for the Turkish forces in Mesopotamia. The rolling stock was also deficient.

Troops and supplies for Palestine and the Hejaz had to be detrained at Bozanti, and were moved down by road to Tarsus, whence they were railed to Alexandretta. From there they went by road again to Aleppo to rejoin the railway. All supplies had to rely on mule, camel and motor for these two considerable treks — and the routes had to carry the Mesopotamian as well as the Palestinian and Arabian supplies.

From Riyak, north of Damascus, the further railway connection was by a light, 1.05 metre-gauge line, which ran down to Medina in the Hejaz, with a branch running to Haifa. From this branch an arm ran down through the plain of Sharon and connected with the Jerusalem-Jaffa light railway — a French line with a different gauge (1 metre). These light systems were prevented by the British Navy from getting any coal, and of course it was practically impossible to send them any across the Taurus. So during most of the War they had to rely on wood fuel. This muddled, gapped, and at its best, single-line system was obviously unsuited for the movement, provisioning and munitioning of any large forces.

The war against the Turks was carried on by the Russians across the Caucasus, and by the British at Gallipoli, in Mesopotamia and across the Suez Canal. This is hardly the place to recount in detail the course of the campaigns against Turkey. In previous volumes I have made some reference to the Gallipoli muddle and sketched the gruesome story of the first advance in Mesopotamia. In Egypt we had proclaimed a British Protectorate as soon as war with Turkey broke out, deposed the pro-Turkish Khedive and appointed his pro-British uncle as Sultan, and made Egypt an important military base. During the first two years of the War we stood on the defensive behind the Suez Canal against small and ill-equipped Turkish forces. They bluffed us by feeble assaults, which they had no means of pushing further. It took us twenty-one months to muster sufficient courage to attack a much inferior army and drive them some way back into the peninsula of Sinai. When I became Premier at the end of 1916, we were still maintaining a defensive attitude on all the Turkish Fronts, although we had overwhelming forces at our disposal in these areas.

In a telegram to the C.I.G.S. on December 13th, 1916, General Murray said:

Enemy can now bring 25,000 against me: in a month's time 40,000: if he abandons Hejaz, another 12,000. Any further additions must come from Europe, Mesopotamia or Caucasus.

The Turkish forces were seriously ill-nourished, for there was not enough corn in Canaan to feed them, and their transport mules were half-starved.

A considerable proportion of their troops were drawn from the Arab population, which was against Turkish rule. This disaffection culminated in a serious revolt in the Hejaz in the summer of 1916.

The "Official History" also notes that the Historical Section of the Turkish General Staff gives the strength of the Turkish forces which took part in the first Battle of Gaza, on the 27th of March, 1917, including one regiment of the 53rd Division which advanced from the north to intervene in the battle, as 16,000 rifles.[1]

Reinforcements were hurried down after that battle, and at the time of the second Battle of Gaza, Turkish sources state that the ration strength of their force was 48,845: including 18,185 rifles, 86 machine guns, 101 guns: but only 68 guns were in action at Gaza II. and only 12 of these were above field-gun calibre. On these figures, the "Official History" notes that "the rifle strength is so small in comparison with the ration strength that the latter probably applies to all troops in Southern Syria."[2]

The volume of Military Statistics gives the total strength of the British Expeditionary Forces in Egypt and Palestine on February 1st, 1917, as over 158,000, including 7,500 Indians. Upwards of fifty per cent. of the total were infantry. Not all of these, of course, were up on the Palestine Front; at the second Battle of Gaza, three British infantry divisions and two mounted divisions were in action.

General Maude in charge of our Mesopotamian forces, had been told by the C.I.G.S. at the end of September, 1916, that he must expect no further reinforcements, and must

[1] "Official History of the War" (Military Operations, Egypt and Palestine), Vol. I, p. 280.

[2] *Ibid.* P. 379.

TURKISH RAILWAYS IN ASIA MINOR

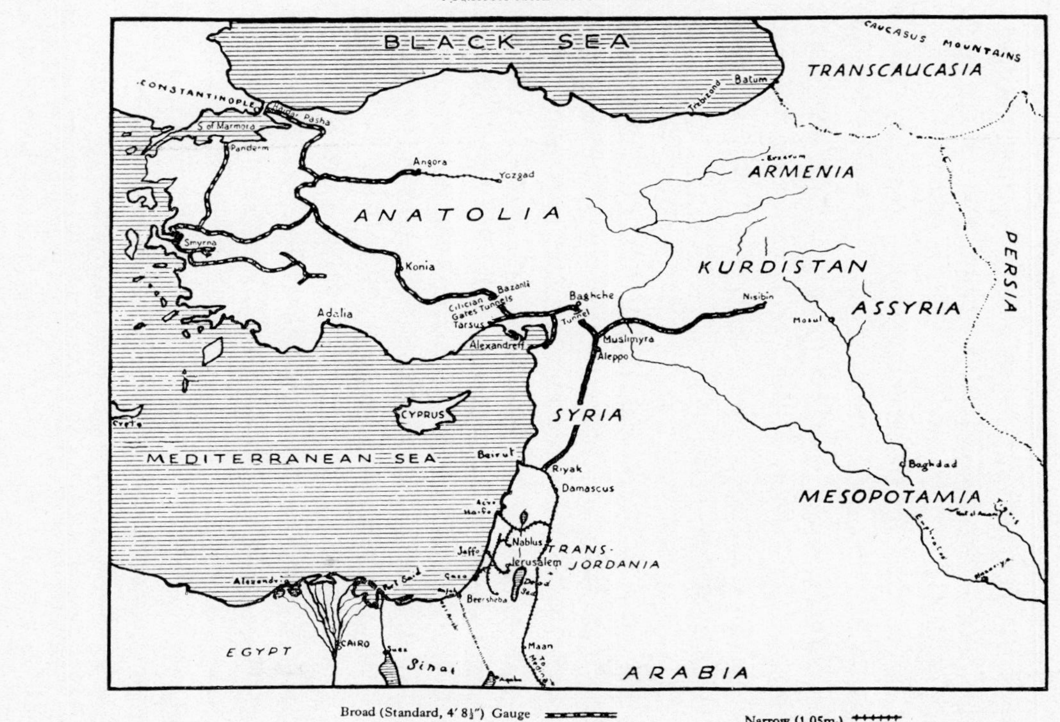

Broad (Standard, 4′ 8½″) Gauge

Narrow (1.05m.)

confine himself to defending the oilfields and pipe lines of the Anglo-Persian Oil Company, and holding the Basrah Vilayet. At the end of October, on the intercession of General Monro, the new Commander-in-Chief of India, Sir William Robertson relented to the extent of giving Maude permission to maintain an aggressive front, and exert local forward pressure against the Turks, but only within the four corners of the general instructions for a defensive policy by which he had been limited. In Egypt, Sir Archibald Murray had similarly been instructed to pursue a mainly defensive policy. He was a General well adapted to the faithful conduct of a timorous policy. Such a message from the War Office read by him on the balcony of his hotel at Cairo would be as welcome as a cool breeze in the sultry desert air. It was suggested that his best line for defence of the Suez Canal would be at El Arish, on the eastern side of the Sinai Peninsula, which meant advancing over his front some distance. He asked for a further division to give him an adequate force for this operation, but when it was not forthcoming, he agreed to attempt the advance with the forces at his disposal.

One other factor — a vitally important one — in our conflict with Turkey must be mentioned. As I have already pointed out, the Arabs of the Arabian Peninsula were no lovers of the Turks and were much more inclined to friendship with the British. When hostilities opened between Turkey and the Allies, and the Ottoman Khalif proclaimed a Holy War against us, the rulers of the Arabs refused to accept and publish his proclamation, and on the contrary, watched for an opportunity to throw off the Turkish yoke. Our agents among them, who included men long skilled in the arts of Oriental diplomacy, encouraged this attitude and promised them arms and ammunition. The issue was precipitated by the Turks, who got wind of the Arab disaffection and decided to suppress it by the traditional Turkish method of massacre and brutality. Their policy succeeded further north, in Syria, for the time. But in Arabia the Sherif of Mecca, who ruled the Hejaz — the part of Arabia containing the Holy Places of Mecca and Medina — and was of the Quraish, or tribe of the Prophet, decided to strike first, before the Turkish reinforcements coming to the Arabian garrisons could arrive. He revolted against the Turks in June, 1916. One of his sons, the Emir Feisal, attacked Medina, the terminus of the Hejaz Railway, while another, Ali, broke the line further north, and Sherif Hussein himself overwhelmed the Turkish garrison of Mecca.

We promptly sent to their aid rifles, ammunition and stores, which were landed at the port of Rabegh in the Hejaz, halfway up the Red Sea. We also sent two mountain batteries, manned by Egyptian gunners. Throughout the autumn of 1916, when the situation in the Hejaz was reported to be very uncertain, and a danger existed that the Turks might advance on Rabegh, *en route* for Mecca, and capture the stores there and cut the connection between the Sherif and ourselves, there was frequent debate in the War Committee whether a strong detachment of British forces should not be landed at Rabegh, to fortify that port and hold it secure against the feared Turkish advance.

Thus we had to take action in regard to three different campaigns against the Turks: the British expedition in Mesopotamia; the Suez Canal Front; and the Arab revolt. I was anxious myself to see real pressure being exerted against the Turk. But the War Office was strongly opposed to increasing our commitments on any of these fronts. In the circumstances, it was fortunate for us that our long connection with India and Egypt had resulted in the possession by us of many capable officers experienced in the kind of desert warfare which these campaigns afforded, who knew how to get the maximum effect with comparatively small forces; and that we could command agents with a close knowledge of Oriental people and their ways.

Of all issues, the most immediately urgent appeared to be that of ensuring the safety of our Arab allies in the Hejaz.

In January, 1917, we sent a small military Mission to assist Lieutenant Colonel Wilson, our representative with the Sherif. One of the men included in this Mission was a young archæologist, Captain T. E. Lawrence, who had prior to this been doing intelligence work for us in Cairo. Lawrence actually arrived, ahead of the Mission, in December. He had made a preliminary visit in October, when his report, after a meeting with Feisal, had considerable influence on our subsequent action. He is one of the few romantic figures of this mechanical war. On land, most of the romance of such a war is in the dauntless movements of masses marching through Hades. Two or three hypnotic personalities alone appeared. Lawrence of Arabia was one of them. In the Hejaz he got on amazingly well with the Arabs, whose confidence he was able to win in the fullest measure, and he became an adviser and military leader among them in a series of intrepid adventures which harassed and embarrassed the unorganised, ill-equipped Turk. Without any military training, like Clive, he developed a remarkable military flair. Largely owing to his inspiration, a mobile force of irregular cavalry was raised among the Arabs who had rebelled against Turkish rule. Although the force raised was a small one, compared with the enormous numbers of men engaged on both sides on the Palestine Fronts, it is difficult to overestimate the value of the service they rendered in the attack upon the Turkish positions. The Arab horsemen belonged to the same race and were men of the same type and training as the great cavalry which swept the remnants of Roman civilisation from the whole of North Africa, conquered Spain, crossed the Pyrenees and challenged Christendom on the plains of Western Europe. Their numbers were not great: the swarms of dashing riders who successfully fought the Crusaders in Syria and Palestine can no longer be levied in these depopulated lands. But their daring was as great as that of their forefathers, and their mobility as baffling to their foes. Under Lawrence's guidance, the Arabs made a flank move up the Red Sea, whence they operated against the line to Medina. They made many breaks in this line, but they did not cut it. They also captured Wejh on the Red Sea, some way north of that town — this last with the aid of the British Red Sea patrol. The Turkish forces in Medina, far from being able to advance on Rabegh and Mecca, were thenceforward in a state of siege. A guerilla warfare was waged on their communications, and early in July the Arabs defeated the Turkish forces in a desert battle near Ma'an, and captured Aqaba, which latter port was to serve them for their base throughout their successful campaign in 1918. The capture of this valuable maritime place removed all danger to the British communications in the Sinai Peninsula, and enabled the Arabs to threaten the flank of the Turkish forces which were opposing ours. The result was that there were more Turks occupied in guarding the long line of the Hejaz Railway, and the territory south of it than were opposing the British in Palestine.[1] These masterly tactics demonstrated the real use which could be made of the mobility of mounted troops in this way. Up to the present, the sole use for which cavalry had been designated was to charge barbed entrenchments, whilst Lawrence's strategy showed that if the fine cavalry divisions which were wasted in Flanders had been put to proper use, they could have achieved the overthrow of the Turk without diminishing by a single unit forces which were essential for siege operations on the Western Front. In Palestine they

[1] See Liddell Hart. "Lawrence of Arabia."

would have been in the right place: in Flanders they were in the way.

While the desert tribes were thus being helped to revolt against the Turk, we were pursuing our own campaigns against the enemy. In Mesopotamia, General Maude had been given permission to exert such pressure as he safely could with the forces at his disposal. He knew that these forces were more than sufficient to sweep away the remnant of Turkish resistance, and that there was no justification for the palpitations that seized the General Staff whenever a fez appeared anywhere along the parapet. He realised that the new Government at home viewed an active policy with favour. This stimulated and encouraged his efforts. By the end of January, he had cleared the right bank of the Tigris, driven the strong Turkish forces out of Kut with heavy loss, and sent them and their reinforcements flying helter-skelter back towards Baghdad. He followed them up, inflicting further losses on them, and by the end of February, 1917, he had put about three quarters of their force out of action, taking forty-five hundred prisoners. The remnants had retreated in disorder on Baghdad, flinging guns and howitzers into the Tigris as they fled.

General Maude was anxious to follow up this success and confident of his ability to do so. On February 24th, 1917, he cabled the C.I.G.S. asking for permission. His previous instructions, in September, 1916, had told him that no advance on Baghdad was to be contemplated, and he now asked:

In view of the change brought about in situation by recent successes on Tigris Front, I shall be glad to learn whether His Majesty's Government in any way desire to modify their instructions. . . . Until I get your reply I do not propose to delay, but intend to follow up retreating enemy closely, being careful however, to do nothing which will prevent me from *adjourning* my position readily according to your further orders. Enemy has suffered very severely during past 2½ months and his losses have been out of all proportion to his strength. Also we have captured over 4,500 prisoners besides guns and machine-guns, rifles, ammunition and material. This series of reverses would have completely broken troops possessed of less fighting qualities than Turks. Opportunity would, therefore, seem favourable for further advance if this accords with policy of His Majesty's Government. Scope of such advance would depend on information received as to further enemy reinforcements being diverted in this direction. Owing, however, to heavy losses already incurred by Turkish forces as above, these, unless considerably more than we anticipate at present, have now lost much of their value.

I was very anxious that Maude should now press on and capture Baghdad. Sir William Robertson viewed that proposal with instinctive disfavour and raised various objections to it in the War Cabinet. There was the difficulty of maintaining the force. Baghdad was a difficult place to hold. There was the shipping shortage to consider, and the possibility of Turkish reinforcements. But on the admission of the General Staff as to the relative strength of the opposing forces on the spot, I felt there was no risk with such a competent leader as General Maude, and the War Office could not ignore the fact that it would be a very valuable success, wiping out the shame of our defeat at Kut a year before and encouraging both our own people and our friends in the East. Nor could they ignore the further fact that General Maude was confident of his ability to achieve this success, and was pressing on a defeated enemy with troops flushed with victory, whom he had led with consummate ability. The C.I.G.S. admitted that Maude could probably raid Baghdad successfully, though he might not be able to hold it permanently until reinforcements reached him. He agreed with our decision that Maude might be told to establish British influence in the

Baghdad Vilayet, and that subject to the security of his force he might exploit his success in this sense as fully as possible. The instructions sent to Maude were therefore liberally drafted, and the daily reports coming from him of more successes and prisoners captured made it impossible for the War Office to veto his victorious march on Baghdad. On March 11th, the British forces captured Baghdad — a stroke which at once rehabilitated our prestige in the East and cheered our people at home, much in need just then of some bright news, while it was disheartening for the enemy, and cast the first shadows upon the Berlin-to-Baghdad ambitions of Germany.

A proclamation, prepared by the War Cabinet, was issued by General Maude to the people of Baghdad, announcing the liberation of the Mesopotamian Arabs from Turkish misrule, and summoning them to coöperate in the development of a sound civil administration. The language of the proclamation was guarded, as while we had no desire to annex Mesopotamia, we could not yet be sure what its ultimate form of government would be. For the time being, Maude was advised to retain the existing governmental machinery, substituting Arab for Turkish personnel and spirit.

Thereafter, Maude proceeded to extend control over the whole Vilayet and clear it of enemy troops. We had hoped to join forces, north of Baghdad, with the Russian Army of the Caucasus, and press forward jointly against the Turks. But as a result of the Russian Revolution, the Caucasus Army began to suffer the same demoralisation as overtook the Russian forces on other fronts. A year earlier the junction could have been effected and the Turkish Armies finally overthrown. On April 2nd, our Mesopotamian force made contact with the Russian Army, but it was too late then, for the Russians fell back before the end of the month, and in spite of our offer to provision them, they abandoned the struggle by degrees and withdrew from the ground they had won. The Turks were thus left free to send more forces against us, both in Mesopotamia and in Palestine.

Fortunately, General Maude's force was both well equipped and well led. There was no repetition, now that it was in charge of the home Government, of the neglect and cheese-paring which the Indian Government had practised so disastrously on the first Mesopotamian expedition. The Turks were determined to recover their lost position, and General von Falkenhayn was sent by Germany to assume charge of their operations. He made his headquarters at Aleppo, and reports reached us that considerable Turkish reinforcements were being mustered by him, supported by German troops, for an advance against us. But his railway communications were unequal to an effective effort and our advance on the Palestine Front forced him to weaken his concentration. General Maude carried out a series of brilliant operations by which he defeated every Turkish force within his reach, and so broke their morale that they deserted freely and would not stay within striking distance of our army.

On November 18th, 1917, General Maude died at Baghdad, stricken down by cholera. It was a great blow, for he was a most able General, sure-footed as well as dashing in his conduct of operations. His campaign up the Tigris had been a series of masterpieces of efficient strategy. After the capture of Baghdad, he had established the British position there very firmly, and consolidated our authority throughout the area. Announcing his death to the House of Commons, on 19th November, I said of him:

Sir Stanley Maude, after a very distinguished career in subordinate positions in the early part of the War, assumed supreme command in Mesopotamia at a time when our arms were still under the stigma of the failure at Kut, and of the break-down of our transport organisation. By his power of organisation, his indefatigable energy, and his personal influence he not only overcame all the difficulties which had hitherto paralysed our efforts, but raised to the highest pitch the fighting spirit and enthusiasm of his men. He then led his armies to a series of victories which thwarted the enemy's ambition and safeguarded our position in the East, and in the fighting which led up to the capture of Baghdad, and secured the town after it had fallen into our hands, Sir Stanley Maude displayed qualities of resource, decision and enterprise which marked him out as a great leader of men and as a commander of the first rank. Now, in the hour of his triumph, he has been stricken down by a fell disease, and the country mourns the loss of one of its most valued sons.

General Maude is one of the established military reputations of the War. His fame is rooted firmly in achievement of a high order.

Of all the points at which the Turkish power could be assailed, the most vital for us was the Egyptian Front. We had been in practical, if not theoretical charge of the administration of Egypt since the suppression of Arabi Pasha's revolt in 1881. And the Suez Canal was the gateway of the East. So our campaign across the Canal in the direction of Palestine was a highly important offensive-defensive, so far as the interests of the British Empire were concerned. Since the abandonment of the Gallipoli adventure, it was the front on which we stood the best chance of striking a serious blow at Turkish power and compelling it to sue for peace.

Since it was my constant wish to strike the enemy as far as possible where he was weakest, and where the British military experience in open warfare could secure its fullest utility, I was anxious, as soon as the Balkan gate was slammed in our face, that we should exploit as fully as possible the opportunities which a campaign in Palestine could offer. But that view was not shared by our military advisers. Sir William Robertson records his view in his book "Soldiers and Statesmen" that the Egyptian campaign was useful so long as it went no further than the defence of the Suez Canal, but that these operations later "became objectionable, for they absorbed troops which should have been sent to the Western Front, where every available man was needed to assist in the great struggle then approaching its decisive phase."

"Decisive phase" is hardly an accurate description of the mud-crawling strategy of the Flanders campaign. If one fifth of the men sacrificed in a venture which every General in the British Army (except Haig) condemned had been sent to Allenby, the Turk would have been so completely crushed that he would gladly have accepted peace terms.

But Sir William Robertson's resistance delayed and hampered the campaign which gave us the capture of Jerusalem, the triumphal advance to Damascus, and ultimately the overthrow of Turkey and her withdrawal from the War. This would have ensured the collapse of the Central Powers on the Balkan Front. And that would have accelerated the end. The Palestine campaign, like that in Mesopotamia, was one essentially suited to the special abilities and experience of British generals. It was the kind of warfare in which our army excelled, and in which we could reasonably hope to deal smashing blows on our enemies and to knock away the props by which the German power was sustained.

When I formed my Government, the instructions under which Sir Archibald Murray was operating charged him to confine himself to the defence of Egypt and the Canal, in maintaining which he was recommended to advance, if possible, as far as El Arish on the eastern side of the Sinai Peninsula — still within the Egyptian frontier — and maintain his front there. I at once raised with the War Office the question of allowing him to embark on a further campaign into Palestine when El Arish had been secured, and on my instructions Sir William Robertson wired to Murray on December 9th, 1916, asking him to submit plans for an advance beyond El Arish, and state what additional troops he would require to execute them. The text of the telegram was as follows:

> To-day Prime Minister mentioned to me desirability of making your operations as successful as possible. I am in entire agreement. Wire précis of action proposed beyond El Arish, stating what additional troops you would require for advance, if any. I cannot help thinking that in view of importance of achieving big success on Eastern Front, and the effect this will have, you might risk having fewer troops on Western.[1] A success is badly needed, and your operations promise well.

Sir Archibald Murray, who was at that time making a careful preparation for an advance upon El Arish, replied giving an account of his prospective movements, and saying that after taking El Arish he proposed to advance to Rafah, on the Syrian frontier, complete the clearing of the Sinai Peninsula, and then, if circumstances permitted, move against Beersheba, where the enemy's main concentration appeared to be. He asked if he could have two divisions from Mesopotamia and any spare mounted troops there were in Mesopotamia or India, assuming that nothing could be spared from France.

The C.I.G.S. answered saying:

> Your telegram, 10th December, has been seen by Prime Minister, who wishes you to make maximum possible effort during the winter. Until the spring we cannot send any troops from Mesopotamia, and if you need reinforcements before then they must be drawn either from France or Salonika. . . .

He went on to ask when the two extra divisions would be needed; could Murray water so large a force as six divisions

[1] The Western frontier of Egypt.

and cavalry, and what enemy forces did he expect to meet?

Sir Archibald Murray replied that he would have liked one division at once, for his advance on El Arish, but would carry on without it. He would want the second division by February 15th for the advance to Beersheba. He did not expect that the hot weather would bring his operations to an end.

This last prospect alarmed the War Office. They had been prepared to acquiesce in a winter campaign, for which any extra troops needed could be released without impairing the supplies for a summer campaign in France. But if the fighting in Palestine were to involve a permanent call on further divisions, and on drafts and supplies to keep them in full fighting form through the summer, it would encroach on the troops intended for General Haig. He would have fewer men for the swamps of Passchendaele. So Robertson wired to Murray:

> In order that any possibility of misunderstanding may be removed, *I wish to make it clear that notwithstanding the instructions recently sent to you to the effect that you should make your maximum effort during the winter, your primary mission remains unchanged, that is to say, it is the defence of Egypt.* You will be informed if and when the War Cabinet changes this policy.

Sir Archibald Murray went ahead with the forces at his disposal, pressing forward to El Arish on December 21st, to find it already abandoned by the Turks. He then carried out two highly successful attacks upon their forces at Magdhaba and Rafah. By the first, fought on December 23rd, 1916, he virtually cleared the Sinai Peninsula of the enemy. He captured 1,282 prisoners. By the Rafah victory he established himself on the Palestine frontier. Enemy killed and prisoners totalled over 1,800. Our own killed and wounded were 487.

At both of these actions we also secured a considerable military booty in the shape of guns, rifles, ammunition, stores, horses, mules and camels. The whole operation proved with what a miserable bluff we had been held in impotent futility on the Canal for over two years, whilst our troops in the Dardanelles and Mesopotamia were being defeated by the real Turkish Armies.

Sir William Robertson was most anxious to avert the danger of any troops being sent from France to Palestine, and on December 29th, 1916, he submitted a memorandum to the War Cabinet, in which, referring to my proposal for a Palestine campaign, having for its object the capture of Jerusalem, he urged:

> In the opinion of the General Staff, an offensive in Syria should not be undertaken until next autumn, and in the meanwhile our commitments in the minor theatres should be reduced to the minimum in order that our maximum effort may be made in France. At the same time, we should complete our preparations in Egypt for an offensive in Syria in the autumn of 1917.
>
> If the War Cabinet approves this policy, Sir A. Murray will be directed to establish himself in such a position as can be held defensively during the summer with the minimum force and is at the same time suitable as a starting-point for an offensive campaign in the autumn. He should be told that as many troops as can be spared from India, Mesopotamia and East Africa will be sent to him as soon as circumstances permit, and instructed to be ready to send such white troops as he can spare, after the beginning of March, to France.

This memorandum was considered by the War Cabinet on January 2nd, 1917, and we decided to accept, in principle, the recommendation of the General Staff. The French were at the time pressing us to take over more of their line, to set their troops free for the Nivelle offensive, and while Sir Archibald Murray had set his requirements at two more divisions, the General Staff estimated that he would need three, which could not be spared if the plans agreed for the summer offensive on the Western Front were adhered to. It was part of Sir William Robertson's strategy to exaggerate the numbers of the Turkish forces opposed to us in Palestine and Mesopotamia in order to deter us from ordering an advance in that quarter. As a matter of fact, it was within his knowledge at that hour that the forces at Murray's disposal considerably exceeded those of the Turks, both in number of men and equipment. This knowledge he withheld from the Cabinet.

There were at this time, as I have already stated, about thirty thousand Turkish troops in Southern Syria. Their force which took part in the first Battle of Gaza, in March, 1917, numbered sixteen thousand rifles.

As regards the proposal for more troops from India to reinforce the Egyptian Army in the autumn, the War Cabinet decided that the Secretary of State for India and the Secretary of State for War must make all necessary arrangements for pressing forward the raising of the new Indian battalions, so that they might be ready by August for the operations mentioned in the Note of the Chief of the Imperial General Staff.

The situation was somewhat complicated by the desire of the French to put a finger in any Palestinian pie that might be baking. They had an interest in Syria and North Palestine. The agreement as to respective spheres of interest in Asia Minor, prepared by Sir Mark Sykes under Sir Edward Grey's instructions, and M. Georges Picot, under orders from the Quai d'Orsay, and confirmed by the British Government in May, 1916, had placed the region from Acre to Aleppo in the French sphere. It was a fatuous arrangement judged from any and every point of view. Under this Sykes-Picot Agreement, Russia was to push her frontier southwestwards into Asia Minor, taking in Armenia, Erzerum, Trebizond and northern Kurdistan. France was to be allowed to annex a strip of Asia Minor west of the new Russian frontier, running down to Adana and the Gulf of Alexandretta, and continuing along the Syrian coast to the north of Palestine. Britain was to be given Mesopotamia from the Persian Gulf to north of Baghdad; also the ports of Haifa and Acre in Palestine. France was to set up an Arab Kingdom or group of kingdoms in the Syrian hinterland, over which she would establish a sphere of influence, and Britain was to do the same in Transjordania, southern Palestine and Arabia. Palestine was cut up into sections, the centre to be placed under a special régime established by an arrangement between France, Russia and Britain. This impracticable plan was at first kept carefully secret from Italy, but when she learned of it she promptly put in a claim for the remainder of southwest Asia Minor, including Smyrna. Sir Mark Sykes never approved of the plan. It was forced upon him by the Foreign Office. Needless to say, the proposed partition could not be adhered to when the Peace Treaty was being prepared. But it warranted the French claiming a special interest in Syria, so that when we proposed an advance in that direction, the French suggested that they had better coöperate. But our General Staff were opposed on principle to involving us in the complexities of yet another composite expedition, with the resulting problems of plurality of command and discipline, and in any event we did not want a French Army in Egypt, as this might have induced political complications. On December 15th, 1916, the War Cabinet, discussing the proposed campaign, decided to notify the French of our intention to press on with operations which might involve tribes within their sphere of influence, and at the same time to assure them that our sole object in this was the defeat of Turkey, and that we should welcome their political coöperation in any negotiations which might arise affecting that sphere. At the Anglo-French Conference held in London on December 28th, 1916, M. Ribot offered to attach a French battalion to our force, so as to show the French flag. I postponed the acceptance of this offer until our troops should be entering Palestine. I also agreed that a French Political Mission should then join our force. In due course both of these steps were taken. An Anglo-French Political Mission, under Sir Mark Sykes and M. Picot, joined our expedition in April, 1917, and small detachments of French and Italian troops were added to it in May. In the following year, when the campaign through northern Palestine to Damascus and on to Aleppo was in prospect, the French force was considerably increased. But in 1917, it was little more than a "token" force.

The decision that troops for an advance on Jerusalem could not be supplied to him until the autumn was telegraphed to Sir Archibald Murray by the C.I.G.S. on January 11th, 1917. Eleven days later, he was ordered to give up one of his four divisions and send it to France. With his depleted army, he kept up his pressure against the Turks, but found it hard to get them to join action against him. The War Office doubtless hoped that he would be unable to launch any operation which would involve us in further commitments to this "side show." On January 30th, I asked the C.I.G.S. how his arrangements were progressing for the autumn campaign and instructed him to report to the War Cabinet "as to the preparations that were being made for operations from Egypt against Turkey as soon as local climatic conditions render them feasible." Robertson records in his book "Soldiers and Statesmen" the grumble which this request provoked. His view was that we could not make plans so long ahead.

Sir Archibald Murray, who was running a railway line

across the desert of Sinai and bringing a pipe for water, wished to defeat the enemy forces in front of him, to ensure the safety of his railhead from an attack by them. So, in the latter part of March, he pressed forward towards Gaza, and on March 26th he launched an attack on the Turkish forces in that town. The attack, which was directed by Sir Archibald Murray from his headquarters at Cairo, was badly fumbled so that the troops were withdrawn without capturing the town, though it was practically within their grasp. But the operation showed that definite successes were possible for us on this front, on a scale which we could hardly hope for anywhere else. More resolute and skilful leadership would undoubtedly have realised a success, which might have had a decisive influence on the Palestine campaign, and in conjunction with Maude's victory might have ended in the collapse of Turkey in 1917. With an unimaginative and stubborn soldier at the centre and a nervous and overcautious soldier in Egypt, the opportunity was missed. Had Maude been in Egypt, he would have broken the Turkish lines and captured Jerusalem by Easter, 1917.

On April 2nd, the War Cabinet devoted the afternoon to an examination of the prospects in Palestine. We realised the moral and political advantages to be expected from an advance on this front, and particularly from the occupation of Jerusalem. After full discussion, we passed a resolution that the Chief of the Imperial General Staff should inform the General Officer commanding the Egyptian Expeditionary Force that we were very anxious to exploit the successes already achieved to the utmost possible extent, and to capture Jerusalem; that he should ask Sir Archibald Murray to state definitely whether he intended to advance along the route of the existing Turkish railway direct on Jerusalem, or to proceed by the coast route to Jaffa, or to utilise both routes; and that he should invite Sir Archibald Murray to give a full estimate of his requirements in men, guns and transport, in order to ensure the occupation of Jerusalem.

This resolution clearly indicates a readiness on the part of the War Cabinet to give Murray further reinforcements for his task. But the C.I.G.S., in communicating our decision to him, appears to have informed him that no more reinforcements would be forthcoming. Sir Archibald's dispatch records in regard to this communication:

> I was informed that the War Cabinet relied on me to pursue the enemy with all the rapidity compatible with the necessary progress of my communications, and was anxious that I should push my operations with all energy, *though at the same time no additional troops were to be sent to me,* since it was considered that, in view of the military situation of the enemy, my present force would suffice.

The Minutes of the War Cabinet at this time contain no suggestion that we took that view of his forces.

However, he continued with his offensive plans, and having failed to carry Gaza by his surprise attack, he made careful preparations for a further assault, which took place on April 17th. But meantime the Turkish forces had been reinforced, and the action had to be broken off on April 20th without achieving its object.

In reviewing the course of this campaign on April 23rd, the War Cabinet came to the conclusion that it was desirable to introduce more resolute leadership into the command of the Egyptian Expeditionary Force, and with the concurrence of the War Secretary and the C.I.G.S., decided to make a change in the Chief Command of this Army. In regard to the choice of a successor to Sir Archibald Murray, it was pointed out that General Smuts had expressed very decided views as to the strategical importance of Palestine to the future of the British Empire. He would therefore be likely to prosecute a campaign in that quarter with great determination, and there was a strong feeling that he would be one of the most suitable selections for the Chief Command of the Egyptian Expeditionary Force.

On the other hand, the War Cabinet were aware that there was a growing opinion in favour of the retention of General Smuts in a central position in this country, with a view to the utilisation of his great qualities in the higher conduct of the War.

General Smuts was a standing disproof of the theory tenaciously held by the British War Office (despite the classic example of Oliver Cromwell to the contrary) that no one was competent to hold high military command without long training in the regular army.

The career of General Smuts furnishes a practical demonstration of the absurdity. He was a lawyer by profession. But in the Boer War he was able with untrained troops to hold at bay for years the best military brains that our War Office could find to put against him, with the resources of the Empire behind them. In British East Africa he showed himself a brilliantly efficient, resourceful and energetic Commander-in-Chief of our forces. Had he consented to take in hand the Palestine campaign, I have not the least doubt that it would, under his charge, have been one of our most successful efforts.

The Imperial War Cabinet concluded its meetings on May 2nd. As I have already related, I had asked General Smuts to stay on for a time in this country, as I felt he was too useful a man to be let go. Arising out of our Cabinet discussion, I asked him if he would undertake the High Command in Palestine. He asked for time in which to consider the matter, but eventually on May 30th, he wrote to me declining the post. His own account of this incident is as follows:

> The Prime Minister was immensely interested in this war front. He was strongly under the impression that Palestine might

be made a decisive feature of the War; that Turkey might be broken and sent out of the War, and that this might be the beginning of the end for the whole German Front. He was very anxious that a determined offensive should be made in Palestine, and it was with that object in view that he offered me the command. I considered the matter carefully at the time, and then consulted with Sir William Robertson, the Chief of the Imperial General Staff, about the offer that had been made to me. I asked Sir William what he thought about the matter, and he said to me, quite frankly, that if I were to accept the offer under the impression that something first-class could be done in Palestine, I would be making a great mistake, and he would dissuade me from accepting the command under such an impression. He said that it had been an obsession with Mr. Lloyd George for a long time that the War was to be won on one or other of the minor fronts and not on the Western Front. Mr. Lloyd George, he said, was forever talking of concentrating on some other front in order to win the War, but the Military Authorities were entirely opposed to that view, and every first-class soldier was agreed that the War could only be won on the main front, *i.e.*, the Western; and he thought it would be a great mistake to weaken our effort on that front in order to make a splash elsewhere. He thought that Palestine could at best remain only a "side show", and whatever success I could achieve there would not materially affect the fortunes of the War.

The impression Sir William Robertson made on my mind was that I would not have the support of the War Office in getting the necessary men and material that would be wanted to make a first-class push in Palestine, and that if I went there I would probably be shut up there for the rest of the War. Mr. Lloyd George would have the full obstruction of the War Office in any of his efforts to help me, and I might be left stranded there. In view of the attitude of the War Office, I finally declined the offer. Mr. Lloyd George often afterwards told me that I had made a great mistake, and it is a question whether he was not right, because I saw afterwards how tremendously keen he remained on this Palestine question; and it is quite possible that if I had undertaken the job in May, 1917, something quite spectacular might have been done long before it was actually done by Allenby in the autumn of 1918, and it is quite conceivable that the War might have been shortened appreciably by a breakdown of the Turkish forces on the Palestine Front.

General Smuts' letter to me, dated May 31st, 1917, declining the Palestine Command, explained that:

The most careful consideration has only strengthened my first impression that the Palestine campaign will be a mistake unless at least the capture of Jerusalem is made a reasonable certainty, and all the reinforcements necessary for that purpose are assured. A limited advance, which stopped short of the capture of Jerusalem, would serve no particular purpose, and might easily be a disappointment to the public and appear as a fresh failure. . . .

I retained General Smuts here by making him a member of the War Cabinet — a step which secured general approval, though it called forth some indignant protests from members of my Ministry, who were horrified at the unprecedented step I was taking.

Mr. Walter Long deemed it necessary to enter a protest as Colonial Secretary. In his opinion "it was quite clear that Smuts could only join for Military questions. This appears to raise all sorts of difficulties."

He suggested that "the simplest and best plan would be to make him a Member of the Imperial General War Staff. You could then arrange for him to attend whenever you like, or indeed, always and there could be no difficulty. It is obvious you can't give him a voice in the settlement of general questions affecting, as they all do, Canada, Australia, New Zealand. . . ."

Meantime, in view of Murray's second failure in front of Gaza, Sir William Robertson secured the consent of the War Cabinet to a modification of the instructions sent to him.

Murray was no longer required to press on at once towards Jerusalem, but merely to take every favourable opportunity of defeating the Turkish forces opposed to him, and to follow up with all the means at his disposal any success gained, with the object of driving the Turks from Palestine as and when this should become practicable. I however came to the conclusion that with Murray in command no results could be expected and I pressed Robertson to find a more enterprising commander. He recommended General Allenby. I heartily concurred in his recommendation. I felt that his experience and qualities as a cavalry leader specially fitted him for the Palestinian campaign.

On June 5th, 1917, the War Cabinet decided, in view of General Smuts' rejection of the offer of the Command, that General Allenby should be appointed as Commander-in-Chief of the British Forces in Egypt, and that arrangements should be made for him to take over the Command as soon as possible. The policy to be adopted in that theatre of war would not be settled until General Allenby had assumed control.

Before Allenby left for Egypt, I had an interview with him and impressed on him that we wanted a determined attack to be pushed against the Turks, with the object of driving them out of Palestine. They were known to be getting war-weary, and a succession of defeats might well drive them out of the War altogether. I told him in the presence of Sir William Robertson that he was to ask us for such reinforcements and supplies as he found necessary, and we would do our best to provide them. "If you do not ask it will be your fault. If you do ask and do not get what you need, it will be ours." I said the Cabinet expected "Jerusalem before Christmas."

There is one further incident in connection with this interview which is worth recording. The late Sir William

Robertson Nicoll had presented me with a copy of Sir George Adam Smith's volumes on Palestine. I had read these with absorbing interest, and I was struck by his detailed survey of the country from the point of view of the geographical difficulties it presented to an invader. I was convinced that this work was a better guide to a military leader whose task was to reach Jerusalem than any survey to be found in the pigeonholes of the War Office. Allenby afterwards acknowledged that it was invaluable to him for the accuracy of its information about the contour of the country.

On reaching Egypt, Allenby obtained an "appreciation" of the position from General Chetwode which showed that the enemy had now under Falkenhayn's direction strongly fortified Gaza, reinforced their army, and were holding a front from that place to Beersheba. As the Turks had now upwards of five divisions defending the front, an attacking force would need a definite superiority if it could hope to break through and follow up its success. So that we required seven infantry divisions and three cavalry divisions for an offensive. We were not informed that the Turkish divisions were considerably inferior in numbers to ours.

Allenby wired to the War Office on July 12th for two further divisions and further artillery to bring his force up to this standard. At the moment we could not send these as all the available troops at home were stuck in the mire in and around Passchendaele. But we asked him to reckon the 75th Division — then being gradually formed in Egypt — as one of the two, and on August 10th were able to inform him that we had the consent of the French to withdraw a division from Salonika and send it to Egypt. In any case, July and August were very hot months in Palestine, when military operations had to be virtually suspended. General Allenby was also informed on August 10th that his instructions were to strike the Turks as hard as possible during the coming autumn and winter, no geographical objective being set as the limit for his advance.

The spirit of the troops in Palestine had been greatly improved by Allenby's arrival. They knew that he had been sent for the purpose of breaking the deadlock before Gaza and pressing forward to victory. He decided that in order effectively to organise and direct the attack it was necessary that he should himself be at the front with the Army, instead of directing them from Cairo, where Sir Archibald Murray had kept his headquarters, and he established his G.H.Q. near Khan Yunis, between Rafah and Gaza. Throughout August and September he was completing the very elaborate arrangements necessary for furnishing supplies — particularly water — to the troops in their advance, and moving them into position. Best of all, perhaps, Allenby was not wedded to the fantastic obsession which dominated the War Office and Headquarters in France, that the best place to attack the enemy was at his strongest point. In the Turkish Front from Gaza to Beersheba, Gaza itself had now become a formidable fortress, on which a frontal attack could only be made with very heavy casualties, and Allenby decided to strike instead at Beersheba, the most distant but weakest part of the line, and turn Gaza, instead of sacrificing men in an effort to capture it by direct assault. It is characteristic of a certain type of military mind that in spite of the success of his plan, he has been severely blamed for this strategy in some military quarters, and the "Gaza school" have insisted that his proper course was to attack on that nearest and strongest point.

Towards the end of October he started to move his troops eastward in earnest; and as he had previously carried out sundry reconnaissances in force, the Turks did not realise that he was really preparing an attack on the remote Beersheba end of their line — they still expected it to fall on

Photo. by Dudley Glanfield

FIELD MARSHALL VISCOUNT ALLENBY, G. C. B.

Gaza. He feigned preparations in that direction, which misled the Turks. On October 31st, Beersheba was carried by assault, and the eastern end of the Turkish Front turned. Then, while this end of the enemy line was being rolled back, Allenby pressed up on Gaza, which the enemy abandoned on November 7th, and after a couple of days' fighting broke into rapid retreat, pursued by the British forces, till they were driven behind the Jaffa-Jerusalem line. Allenby avoided a direct assault on Jerusalem, which he captured by encircling it. When they found the city was doomed, the Turkish defenders hastily evacuated it, and it surrendered on December 9th, 1917.

The achievement was of immense importance, alike on military and on sentimental grounds. From a military standpoint it disintegrated the Turkish concentration at Aleppo, which had been intended to carry out, under Falkenhayn's direction, a great campaign for the recovery of Baghdad and the restoration of Turkish and German control of the pathway to Persia. Thereafter the Turks did some successful campaigning in Trans-Caucasia against the disorganised relics of the Russian forces, but they were unable to regain a foothold in Mesopotamia, or in southern Palestine. They were in fact so much broken by defeat that if we had been able to follow up our victory with larger forces we might soon have driven them out of the War. Our six hundred thousand casualties in the fiascos on the Western Front had so depleted our resources in men that we could no longer exploit victory on any front, but the moral effect of the victory was tremendously important. It cheered our own people at a critical time, when defeatist elements were making their influence felt among us. It greatly encouraged our American Allies. And among that great international fraternity, the Jewish race, it was an earnest of the fulfilment of the Balfour Declaration, made on November 9th, 1917, that we favoured "the establishment in Palestine of a national home for the Jewish people."

The attitude of the War Office towards this historic triumph is exemplified by the fact that whereas they ordered all the bells of London to ring out chimes of joy over the muddled tank attack of Cambrai, not a flag was hoisted to call attention to the capture by British troops of the most famous city in the world which had for centuries baffled the efforts of Christendom to regain possession of its sacred shrines.

The question arose as to how far and how promptly this success could be further exploited. The War Office, which objected to this "side show", had all along tried to discourage it by suggesting that we could not spare any more troops for it, and that with the troops at his disposal, Allenby could not meet the possible concentration of the enemy. Somewhat before this, on October 5th, Sir William Robertson had telegraphed to Allenby, saying that the War Cabinet would like him to advance to the Jaffa-Jerusalem line, and asking him what troops he wanted for the operation, bearing in mind that two German Divisions were reported to be preparing to join the big Turkish concentration at Aleppo. Apparently this warning, and the other information supplied to Allenby by the War Office and other intelligence sources, gave him the impression that he would have twenty divisions against him, and he asked for his own force to be made up to a similar strength — *i.e.* by a further thirteen divisions. That was a reinforcement which we could not just then provide for him, and I also felt certain that the demand had been elicited by a War Office exaggeration of the strength of the forces he would have to meet — as events proved to be the case. We know now that the forces at Allenby's disposal were overwhelmingly superior to any the Turks could muster, and that if he had pressed forward, there was no Turkish Army that could offer any substantial resistance. The German General who was Chief of the Staff of the Turkish Army facing Jerusalem, reported to Liman von Sanders, who took over the supreme command of the Turks in Palestine early in 1918, that there were only thirty-nine hundred rifles available for the defence of a sixteen-mile front. Most of the divisions were reduced to an average strength of about fifteen hundred rifles. If these facts were known to Allenby at that time, it is incredible that he should not have taken full advantage of the Turkish right without any loss of time. I cannot however help conjecturing that his caution was not due to any fear of being beaten by this miserable remnant of a defeated army, but rather to his dread of the consequences of brushing aside the restraining hand from Whitehall. Valuable time was lost, and it took nine or ten months to accomplish what could have been achieved in two or three. It enabled the Turk to last out almost to the end, and to hold up hundreds of thousands of British troops.

After the fall of Jerusalem, the War Cabinet decided to send the following message to Allenby:

> In view of the change in position created by your recent victory over Turks, and by revised information as to enemy's strength and breakdown in his transport, War Cabinet would like to have your opinion by telegram as soon as possible as to the manner in which, and extent to which, it is possible to exploit your success in Palestine with forces now under your command, plus the division under orders for Mesopotamia.

On the following day, December 13th, we instructed the General Staff to submit for consideration a project for carrying out the following alternative policies:

(*a*) Complete the conquest of the whole of Palestine, and hold the country for the remainder of the War.

(*b*) Continue the advance through Palestine and Syria to the vicinity of Aleppo, so as permanently to interrupt railway communication with Mesopotamia.

This request was also passed on by the C.I.G.S. to Allenby for his comments.

General Allenby sent back word that for the moment he could do little on account of the rains, which that winter were particularly heavy in Palestine, and which caused serious difficulty to the transport. If limited to his existing force, he expected to have cleared the whole of Palestine and established his line well on the way to Damascus by June or July, 1918. To advance to Aleppo, if it were strongly held by the enemy, would necessitate a force of sixteen divisions in addition to his cavalry.

The War Office was very much opposed to any such extension of our Turkish campaign, and mustered all the arguments it could find against it. On the other hand, the Supreme War Council at Versailles favoured the plan of acting on the defensive in the West until the American Army was ready, while we proceeded to knock out the Turks, and thus make a breach in the front of the Central Powers. In order to get an independent view, the War Cabinet decided, on January 28th, 1918, to depute General Smuts to proceed to Egypt with full power on their behalf to confer with Generals Allenby and Marshall, or their representatives, the Naval Commander-in-Chief in the Mediterranean, the Government of Egypt, and any other authorities, in regard to the military situation in the Middle East, and to advise the War Cabinet as soon as possible on the best use and coördination of all our resources in that theatre, with a view to the most vigorous prosecution of the War against Turkey.

General Smuts proceeded to the East and after holding consultations with our leaders there, reported on February 15th in favour of making the Mesopotamia force act on the defensive, and concentrating on a thrust by Allenby up towards Aleppo. The Cabinet agreed to adopt this policy. But before it could be carried into effect, the German break-through on the Western Front compelled us to muster all our available forces to resist their attacks there. General Allenby had captured Jericho in February, 1918, and in March and April he carried out a couple of raids into Trans-jordania. Thereafter the lack of reinforcements and the hot weather brought operations to a standstill until September. In September and October he made a brilliant sweep through Damascus and Aleppo, which knocked out the Turks and brought them to sue for an armistice.

Had this offensive been undertaken at an early stage in the War and properly supported from home, the Turkish collapse would have come sooner, and the repercussions in Europe would have been shattering.

It may however be remarked here with regard to the 1917 campaigns against the Turks, that their success proved to the hilt that the Turkish sector of the defences of the Central Powers was by far the most vulnerable point, and that it was the one where the training and experience of the British military forces could be put to much their best use. Yet the stubborn refusal of our military advisers to take advantage of the remarkable opportunities which were thus open to us, and their insistent concentration upon the most impenetrable fortresses of the Western Front, prevented us from scoring such a decisive success until the last moment.

CHAPTER III

CREATING THE AIR MINISTRY

Aviation before the War — Swift progress in the war years — Post-War services — Naval Air Service undertakes home defence — Lord Derby's Air Committee — Admiralty crushes the committee — Curzon appeals for better air organization — An Air Board appointed — Its first report: persistent opposition by Admiralty — The Curzon-Balfour duel — Draft conclusions of War Committee — Proposed distribution of authority — War Cabinet's discussion — I closure the dispute — Lord Cowdray appointed: his first report — Constitutions and functions of new Air Board — Our serious state vis-à-vis Germany — Rapid progress under new system — Growing dimensions of air warfare — Output still inadequate — Policy of reprisal raids postponed — Daylight raid on London, July 7, 1917 — Defence measures adopted — My statement at the secret session — General Smuts examines the problem — Proposals for London's air defence — Reorganization questions — Smuts' second report: lack of air policy — Independent Air Ministry proposed — Summary of conclusions — War Cabinet discussion: Admiralty still obstructive — Air Policy Committee set up — Air Ministry Bill — Lord Northcliffe's breach of confidence — Cowdray's difficult position; resigns from Air Board — Lord Rothermere appointed Air Minister — My letter of appreciation after his resignation — Haig's Testimony to work of Ministry — Continuing value of Air Ministry.

PROMINENT among the contributions which the Great War made to technical progress was the immense development of the art and practice of flying which it fostered. When the War broke out, flying was still in its infancy. The first cross-Channel flight by an aeroplane had been made only five years before by Blériot; and no British airman had yet covered two hundred miles in a single flight. I witnessed one of the first flying exhibitions at Reims in the summer of 1909. The most famous airmen of France and America took part in the show. It was a beautiful summer's day, but a slight breeze was blowing most of the day, so that no aeroplane could fly. In the cool of the evening, the movement of the air subsided, and there was a complete calm. The aeroplanes took advantage of this atmospheric improvement to circle round. The Royal Flying Corps was only established in 1912, with a military and a naval wing, and up to the outbreak of the War the military wing confined its studies to the use of aircraft for reconnaissance. The possibilities of aircraft as auxiliaries to our fighting services had been quickly recognised by ourselves, as they had been by all the other armed Powers. But in those early days the machines in use were primitive, insecure, and still very much in the experimental stage. They were being developed as ancillary aids to our forces on land and sea, mainly, if not entirely, for purposes of observation. Their organisation was not based on a recognition that to these age-old spheres of conflict there had now been added a third — the battlefield of the air.

To the infant invention of aviation, the War proved to be a forcing house of tropical intensity. Fertilised by a stintless outpouring of life, of treasure, and of technical research in every belligerent country, it progressed more rapidly in the four years of war than it might have done in a score of years of peace. As the War proceeded, its possibilities of independent use became steadily more obvious. And as in the West the deadlock of trench warfare on the ground developed, we came to devote increasing attention to a battlefield where no trenches could be dug, no minefields sown. Had the War persisted a few months longer, we should have hurled ruin from the air on to the chief cities of Central Europe. Doubtless our own capitals would also have suffered their share of disaster.

From that red sowing, the world has since reaped in peace the immense advantages of civil aviation on a wide commercial scale. (This, too, is still an infant, though a sturdy one.) And if the possibilities of aerial attack in time of war now add to life a new menace of incalculable horror, the developments of air transport are playing in time of peace a part in promoting international intercourse, in the overleaping of frontiers, in establishing new links between one country and another, which may help to avert those conflicts whose horrors they would so intensify.

I have here to sketch briefly the steps we took to establish in Britain an organisation which should be able to make the fullest use of the new weapon of aircraft in war, and should be adapted later on to the task of turning it to the arts of peace.

Even before the War, the naval and military wings of the Royal Flying Corps tended to diverge. There was no central policy for the air, and as the new arm was ancillary only to the established defence services, it was developed by them in terms of their conception of the help it could render their respective operations. The War Office saw chiefly the reconnaissance possibilities of aircraft. At the Admiralty, the fertile brains of Mr. Churchill and Lord Fisher conceived wider uses for it. Lord Fisher took an alarmist view of the ultimate possibilities of the Zeppelin. I recollect a paper written by him in 1915 in which he depicted the gruesome spectacle of a ton of explosives dropped from the clouds on to the Horse Guards Parade, and destroying in one shattering explosion all the historic buildings surrounding that square, with the Admirals, Generals, Statesmen, and Civil Servants under the ruins "in one red burial blent." He counselled anticipation of this fell blow.

In 1913, the Admiralty decided to adopt for the naval wing a threefold use of seaplanes — for coast defence and patrol, for scouting as eyes of the Fleet, and as attacking and bombing planes operating from battleships. So when the Expeditionary Force went across to France, it took all its military planes with it for scouting purposes, and we had to rely alike for the air defence of Britain and for raiding and bombing the air bases of the enemy, where their Zeppelins were housed, on the machines of the Naval Air Service — tasks which Mr. Churchill cheerfully undertook and vigorously pursued. He accepted on September 3rd, 1914, at Lord Kitchener's request, the charge of our Home Air Defence, and on the principle that attack was the best form of defence, he flung planes across to Dunkirk to raid enemy air bases. Out of this grew a large independent development of naval air activity, leading to the organisation of the Royal Naval Air Service as a quite distinct body from the Royal Flying Corps. To quote the first Report of the Air Board, in October, 1916:

> . . . Before the War, as is well known, there was no independent Naval Air Service or organisation at all. There were a military and a naval wing of a joint Service. Mr. Churchill took the Naval Air Service into his own hands, and, though the Fourth Sea Lord was nominally responsible, ran it himself on vigorous but unorthodox lines. When he resigned, it became for the first time a subordinate branch of the Admiralty, reorganised on naval lines, under an Admiral, with naval heads of the personnel and technical branches.

We soon found that there were several grave drawbacks to this aerial dichotomy. The two air services, naval and military, were competing with each other for the available supplies of aero engines — many of which were at that stage only procurable from France. They were competing rather than pooling their experiments and inventions in regard to technical improvements. The Navy, being at once the senior Service and an essentially mechanised service, started with a priority of claim on available resources, and a superior array of mechanical talent. There was a good deal of bombing by the naval aeroplanes on the Belgian coast. There was no authenticated record of any hits which demolished German craft or works, but Belgian towns were undoubtedly damaged, some Belgian civilians killed, and the rest terrorised.

The aviators of the Army were far more constantly and crucially engaged in vital operations of an obsessing kind. Concentration on the use of aeroplanes as handmaids to the operations of fleets and armies meant a failure to develop their possibilities as an independent arm, and even left it uncertain which of the two branches should properly undertake such tasks as the defence of London against attacks by Zeppelins and German aeroplanes, or the carrying out of reprisal raids on German towns. In short, the net result of this division of responsibility for our flying services was overlapping, inefficiency, and a seriously swelling casualty list.

The immunity with which the German airships rode across Britain, dropping destructive bombs exasperated public sentiment. There were ominous rumblings in Parliament and in the Press, and in February, 1916, Mr. Asquith sought to remedy the state of affairs by setting up a joint War Air Committee, presided over by Lord Derby, "to collaborate in arranging questions of supplies and design for the material of the Naval and Military Air Services, upon such points as will be referred to it by the War Committee, the Admiralty, the War Office, or any other Department of State." Shortly afterwards the strength of popular feeling on the need for a better development of our air services found vent in the return of Mr. Pemberton Billing as an Independent Member for East Herts, on the strength of his advocacy of more efficiency in the air.

The Joint War Air Committee had a short life. The Admiralty showed that it had not the slightest intention of permitting any interference by such a body with its independent control of the R.N.A.S. and its supplies. After a couple of months of disheartenment and frustration, Lord Derby, the Chairman, and Lord Montagu of Beaulieu, the independent member of the Committee, both resigned, and the Committee collapsed. Lord Derby stated as his reasons that the Committee had no executive power and no authority; that a fundamental difference was found to exist between the two branches of the air service, each having its own organisation, *esprit de corps,* and aspirations, and that the Committee was debarred by its terms of reference from discussing any question of policy.

Lord Curzon, in the spring of 1916, proposed the setting up of a more authoritative body. Something, he urged, must be done to improve the situation:

> . . . After nearly 21 months of war our fighting planes are inferior to German machines, and for the time we have ceased to hold the mastery of the air. Though we are now turning out some splendid new machines, we are still working at the front with a majority of old types, and our men are liable to be outclassed and outpaced by the enemy. . . . As regards the relations between the two branches of the service, so imperfect has been the coördination that, not merely are designs competed for and machines ordered, but operations have sometimes been undertaken without any intercommunication. Each service still claims the right to conduct long-range offensive operations, and therefore to acquire the high-power engines for the purpose. The evidence is incontestable that there has been a great lack of coöperation, and a competition, often the reverse of advantageous, between the two services. . . .

He urged that the proper course would be the establishment of an Air Ministry, but admitted that this would be resisted by the Admiralty, and might give rise to friction and ill will; and suggested as a secondary course the setting-up of an Air Board with real powers. Mr. Balfour, who as the spokesman for the Lords of the Admiralty, acted throughout this controversy as the persistent opponent of every proposal for coördination, retorted in a memorandum skilfully massing every possible argument against a change. But after further exchanges of memoranda and counter-memoranda, Mr. Asquith decided to set up an Air Board. Lord Kitchener stated that the Army Council "would welcome and would be prepared to support a Board constituted on the lines suggested" by Lord Curzon. Mr. Balfour on behalf of the Admirals reiterated his objections. The establishment of the Board was announced in the House of Commons on May 17th, 1916. Lord Curzon was appointed its chairman, and it consisted of two naval, two military representatives, Lord Sydenham as independent expert, and Major Baird as Parliamentary Secretary. It was empowered to discuss and make representations to the Admiralty and War Office in regard to air policy and combined operations, and the types of machine required; to organise and coördinate the supply of material and prevent competition; and organise a system for interchange of ideas on technical developments.

The first Report of the Air Board was issued by Lord Curzon on October 23rd, 1916. It detailed what they had done and attempted to do since their formation, and then proceeded to recount the hopeless difficulties they had encountered in carrying out their appointed tasks through the persistent opposition of the Admiralty, of which a detailed and documented account was given. This opposition was making their work impossible.

> . . . No expansion of the work of the Air Board, no complete fulfilment of the charge with which it was entrusted, and no adequate provision for the urgent necessities of the future, are, in our opinion, possible, so long as the Admiralty adopts its present attitude towards the Air Board, and so long as the administration of that branch of the Air Service which is in the hands of the Admiralty is conducted on the present lines. It is with no pleasure that my colleagues and I question the administration of a Department possessed of such splendid traditions, and with such a glorious record of service, as the Admiralty. But it is our pro-

found conviction, for which we shall proceed to state the reasons, that the addition to the Navy of responsibilities for the air — not in itself necessarily impracticable — has, in the manner in which it has been carried out, been attended with results that have been equally unfortunate to the Navy and the Air Service, and, if persisted in, will be incompatible not merely with the existence of an Air Board, but with the immense and almost incalculable development that ought to lie before a properly coördinated and conducted Air Service in the future. . . .

As I have mentioned in a previous Volume,[1] this Report gave rise to what in other circumstances might have been viewed as a highly entertaining series of dialectical exchanges between Lord Curzon and Mr. Balfour. Lord Curzon was proposing that the Air Board should take charge, for both air services, of invention, research, experiment, design, production, inspection and finance. Mr. Balfour wanted to retain at the Admiralty the responsibility for all these functions so far as the R.N.A.S. was concerned. Mr. Montagu proposed that production for both services should be taken over by the Ministry of Munitions. After several meetings of the War Committee on the 27th and 28th of November, 1916, we reached the stage of putting down *draft* conclusions, but these were not finally confirmed when the Asquith Coalition fell. The substance of these draft conclusions was as follows:

The Ministry of Munitions should undertake design and supply of aeroplanes for both the Army and the Navy.

The Air Board should be definitely responsible for allocating our available aerial resources between the Admiralty and the War Office.

A Fifth Sea Lord should be appointed and added to the Air Board, which should also have a representative of the Ministry of Munitions.

[1] Vol. II, Chap. XVII, pp. 381–383.

The distribution of responsibility between the various authorities should be as follows:

(*a*) The Admiralty and War Office will concert their respective aerial policies in consultation with the Air Board.

(*b*) The Admiralty and War Office will formulate the programmes of aerial production required for the fulfilment of the approved policy, and will submit these programmes to the Air Board.

(*c*) The Air Board will decide as to the extent to which it is possible to approve the departmental programmes, having regard to the possible rate of production, the needs of the other Department, and the respective urgency of the demands.

(*d*) The Air Board (Admiralty and War Office) will place the order with the Ministry of Munitions.

(*e*) The design of the machines and commodities ordered will be undertaken by the Ministry of Munitions, working in the closest possible association with the Department for whom the order is placed.

(*f*) The Ministry of Munitions will give every facility for direct communication on all matters of detail between the representatives of the Admiralty Air Department and the Department of the Director-General of Military Aeronautics respectively and the actual manufacturers.

(*g*) Any of the Departments represented on the Air Board, and the Air Board itself, will have the right of appeal to the War Committee in case of dispute.

This scheme proposed a very considerable move forward from the disorganised and unsatisfactory condition which was then obtaining. But Mr. Asquith's failure to clinch the issue at the War Committee by giving his final decision on the issue raised meant that we had still to settle it afresh under the new Government. On December 15th, Lord Curzon expressed in the War Cabinet a hope that the question might soon be settled. He was still acting as Chairman of the Air

Board on its old basis, and wished to be relieved by its reconstitution with a fresh Chairman holding new powers. But the First Sea Lord, Admiral Jellicoe, objected that he was still discussing the matter with the new First Lord, Sir Edward Carson, and would let us know as soon as they were ready for us to thrash it out.

We dealt with it on December 22nd, 1916. By this time the Admiralty had succeeded in kneading its new First Lord into full acceptance of its attitude, and the results of his education were shown in a long memorandum, arguing the utter impracticability of any attempt to coördinate the R.N.A.S. and R.F.C. under the supervision of the Air Board, and urging that the proposed steps in this direction should be limited to the fewest and smallest possible.

In the Cabinet discussion, there was an attempt to lure the Government into the old maze of arguments. Jellicoe "desired to express in the strongest terms his opinion that the policy of making the Admiralty dependent on another Department for the design and supply of aircraft would be disastrous." But I refused to allow the reopening of a question which had so exhaustively been examined by the late War Committee, and the Draft Conclusions were formally approved, Lord Curzon registering his dissent. The Air Board, Admiralty, and War Office were instructed to work out the details of the new arrangements in consultation with the Ministry of Munitions.

Lord Curzon's duties as a member of the War Cabinet made it impossible for him to continue to act as Chairman of the Air Board, and we appointed Lord Cowdray to this position. On January 19th, 1917, four weeks after our meeting of 22nd December, he was able to report a substantial measure of agreement, in a letter to me which ran as follows:

"Air Board,
19, Carlton House Terrace,
London, S.W.
19th January, 1917.

"Dear Prime Minister,

"To-day the four departments concerned — Admiralty, War, Munitions and this Board — have arrived at an agreement as to their varied functions in connection with the Air Service.

"I am thankful that I can thus report that the draft Charter, which will shortly be submitted to you for approval, will be an agreed document.

"The Admiralty have insisted upon the lighter-than-air craft remaining with them. To this we could make no valid objection for the time being as it does not involve any conflict with the aeroplanes and seaplanes — and these are enough to occupy us for some time. The chances are that lighter-than-air craft will come our way shortly.

"No time has been lost in getting on with the preliminaries for expediting and augmenting the supplies of aircraft.

"Munitions Department have allotted two fine men (Weir and Martin) to these supplies.

"I must express to you my appreciation of the help and support that Lord Derby and Dr. Addison have given me. The Admiralty have also assisted (always subject to their predisposition) in a way that deserves acknowledgment.

Believe me,
Yrs. v. sincerely,
COWDRAY."

A Technical Committee was to be set up under the Air Board to deal with design, thus eliminating the confusion and overlapping in this respect which had thus been described in the first report of the Air Board in October, 1916:

One of the first questions that attracted the attention of the Board was the unsatisfactory arrangement by which aeronautical inventions affecting the two Air Services are, under existing conditions, liable to be dealt with by one or other of five distinct bodies, namely:

The Royal Naval Air Service.
The Royal Flying Corps.
The Board of Invention and Research.
The Munitions Inventions Department.
The Advisory Committee on Aeronautics.

It appeared to the Board that this state of things presented a double defect. In the first place it led to the same experimental work being undertaken twice over on behalf of the two departments; and, secondly, it involved the risk of a valuable invention being brought to the notice of only one of the two Departments whom it might interest.

The Royal Aircraft Factory at Farnborough was to be placed under the Ministry of Munitions for the manufacture of planes.

This scheme was duly adopted by the War Cabinet, and on February 6th, we were able to announce the composition of the reconstituted Air Board.

The little wars conducted behind the front between Departments, of which this is a sample out of many, caused serious delay and damage to our interests in the War. When I witnessed the energy and manœuvring displayed by those who were engaged in these internecine conflicts, I often wished it could have been concentrated and directed against the enemy.

At last peace was established and coöperation substituted for contention. Under the new arrangement, the design and production of aircraft were greatly improved and expedited — not before it was time, for at this period of the War the Germans were getting dangerously ahead of us in the mastery of the air. On February 15th, Sir Douglas Haig wrote warning us that the deliveries of aircraft promised by the

Director of Air Organisation at the War Office were not being made, and that he was faced with a serious shortage.

> The position as regards fighting squadrons in particular is most serious. *Our fighting machines will almost certainly be inferior in numbers, and quite certainly in performance, to those of the enemy.* In view, therefore, of the marked increase in the number and efficiency of the German aeroplanes, it appears that we cannot expect to gain supremacy in the air in April, and it is even possible that it may pass to the enemy.
>
> The seriousness of this situation cannot be over-rated, and its possible effect on the results of our operations will no doubt be fully realised by the War Cabinet.

This was the situation in which months of futile wrangling and competitive organisation had landed the air force. The military and naval authorities respectively had had things in their own hands, with this result. Once again we had to call in civilian aid to clear up the muddle.

The improvement which this new body effected is shown by the fact that two months later, on April 17th, 1917, they were able to report that the arrangements they had now set in operation were assuring a rapid multiplication of the output of improved types of aeroplane. The monthly deliveries of aero engines would be nearly two and one half times as many as they were in 1916 and during the next four months, July–October, the monthly production would be more than three and one half times that of 1916. The new Air Board pointed out that such an increase had not been possible under its predecessor, as the old system of divided responsibility between the naval and military air arms had prevented proper organisation of the national resources in this field.

Through the summer of 1917, the Air Board worked hard and efficiently at its tasks. At this time aircraft were assuming an importance far greater than they had hitherto possessed and coming rapidly to be regarded as formidable weapons of war. The Army in the field clamoured insatiably for larger supplies. At home, the German air raids on London and the southeastern counties grew very frequent, and the damage and loss of life caused by them assumed serious proportions. There was no way of preventing these enemy planes from coming over. The most effective measure that could be taken was to furnish a powerful air fleet for home defence, which might make air raids by the enemy too expensive in casualties by destroying large numbers of the invading planes; and to carry out reprisal raids on enemy cities on a scale which would convince them that this form of warfare was bad business. For both of these purposes, large numbers of planes were needed, independently of the requirements of either the Army or the Navy.

On June 9th, 1917, Lord Cowdray reported to me:

> The Air Board to-day is now turning out each week as many aircraft as were turned out in a month this time last year. By the end of the year it will be turning out fully ten times as many aircraft as it was doing in the summer months of 1916.

In addition to the increase in numbers there was a marked improvement in power and efficiency.

But even this increase, creditable as it was, we felt to be inadequate to our growing needs, and on June 14th, the War Cabinet decided that a much increased programme of construction must be put in hand. The Air Board was ordered to prepare a scheme for this in consultation with the Ministry of Munitions and War Office, even at the expense of other important supplies of munitions. At this meeting we also decided, in view of the fact that a serious air raid had taken place on the previous day over Woolwich and Poplar, to concentrate for a short time a strong force of the best planes and pilots in this country, in order to give the next raiders a hot reception. Two squadrons were accordingly recalled temporarily from the Western Front and stationed near Canterbury and Calais respectively.

We carefully investigated the question of reprisal raids, but after full examination of the matter by experts, it was decided that we had not as yet a number of machines available of sufficient power and range to be able to embark upon a regular programme of long-distance bombing raids on German towns. And to carry out an isolated raid would only exasperate the German people and lead to an intensification of their attacks.

The two squadrons that had been temporarily withdrawn for home defence from the Western Front remained on guard for about three weeks, during which period the country was free from air attacks, except for one raid in Harwich. In point of fact, the weather was unsuitable for raids during this period, apart from the one day when the Harwich raid was carried out. On July 6th, Sir Douglas Haig recalled his two squadrons, as had been arranged. The next day was fine and clear, and in the middle of the morning a large fleet of German aeroplanes reached central London and dropped a number of bombs on the City and south of the Thames, killing and wounding numbers of people and causing a great deal of material damage. There was grave and growing panic amongst the population in the East End where the attack had taken place. At the slightest rumour of approaching aeroplanes, tubes and tunnels were packed with panic-stricken men, women and children. Every clear night the commons around London were black with refugees from the threatened metropolis. It is right, however, to record the fact that the undoubted terror inspired by the death-dealing skies did not swell by a single murmur the demand for peace. It had quite the contrary effect. It angered the population of the stricken towns and led to a fierce demand for reprisals.

As a result of this last raid on the metropolis, the Cabinet decided to recall two squadrons from the Western Front for home defence, and to ask Sir Douglas Haig if he could arrange a reprisal raid on Mannheim.

The figures which Sir William Weir was able to give us as to the rate of production of aero engines showed that we should soon possess an air fleet much in excess of the necessary demands of the Army and Navy. But it would be some weeks before these would begin to take shape as additional trained squadrons. We decided to improve the arrangements for dealing with fires resulting from air raids, but in view of Sir Douglas Haig's protest against the withdrawal of two squadrons, we resolved to withdraw only one, and to abandon the proposal of raiding Mannheim for the present. We also decided to hold a secret session of Parliament that afternoon, at which we could lay the facts before the Commons and tell them our intentions.

At this secret session I explained to the House how matters stood. I gave them figures to show the way in which aeroplane construction was now being expedited, so that before long we should have an adequate supply both for our military operations and for home defence and independent attack. But until that time, I made it clear that our military requirements must have priority.

The first consideration before the Government is to see that the Army in France is sufficiently supplied with aeroplanes. A sufficiency of aeroplanes means everything to that Army. They are the eyes of the Army, which cannot advance without them. By their means the Army discovers the enemy's trenches, guns and machine-gun emplacements. To photograph these requires air supremacy, and without that air supremacy it is sheer murder to allow troops to advance. . . . The slightest deficiency in the work of observation from the air, a single machine-gun emplacement overlooked, might in a few minutes mean the loss of thousands of gallant lives. The first duty of the country is to protect these men. The Germans realise the importance of this question quite as much as we do. The second means by which they are attempting to diminish our superiority is by trying to force us to withdraw our machines from France in order to protect our own towns. If the Germans know that by bombing English towns they can force us to withdraw fighting squadrons from France, there could be nothing which would encourage them more. . . . If the aeroplanes can be provided for the Front and for our defence against raids, that will, of course, be done. If not, the Army must come first, and it is vitally important that the Germans should know it.

This statement satisfied the House.

But while the arrangements we made were as effective as our expert advisers could suggest, in terms of our existing organisation and resources, I felt that we must go far more thoroughly into the matter, with a view to ensuring the best possible use of the air weapon, alike for attack and for defence. It was a question that called for examination by a fresh and able mind, free from departmental prejudices. Fortunately such a mind was available. I asked General Smuts to investigate the problem of the air on behalf of the Cabinet. He consented, and on July 11th, the War Cabinet agreed that a Committee should be set up, consisting of myself and General Smuts, in consultation with:

A representative of the Admiralty,

A representative of the General Staff,

A representative of the Field Marshal Commander-in-Chief, Home Forces,

and such other experts as we might desire.

Its terms of reference were:

To examine (1) the defensive arrangements for Home

Defence against Air Raids, and (2) the existing general organisation for the study and higher direction of aerial operations.

As I was myself unremittingly busied with every phase of our national activities, I had to leave the chief burden of the work to General Smuts, and I kept in constant touch with him.

General Smuts went first of all into the question of the defence of London, on which he submitted his report to the War Cabinet on July 19th. He found that the success of the German raids was due in no small measure to causes which could be remedied. In the first place, although we really had a very large number of machines and personnel in the Air Services available to defend London, they were not unified, but were independently controlled by three or four different authorities, so that there was no organised coöperation between them, and the Germans could attack us without serious risk of counterattack. The measures recommended by General Smuts and adopted by the War Cabinet were, in the first place, to secure a unified command under a first-class officer of the whole defence forces against air attacks on London. General Ashmore was appointed for the purpose and proved a most efficient officer. The available planes were combined into proper units, trained for fighting in flight formation, so as to meet the German attack in that form. Three or four squadrons were recommended for formation, which could deal with the enemy, not only over London, but also before London was reached. This was done, and the Germans, when next they attacked, found themselves opposed by forces equal to their own, in mass formation, before they reached London, and only isolated machines reached the metropolitan area at all. The anti-aircraft guns were also placed outside London in such a way as to meet the advancing planes with their fire before they reached London. Under the new organisation developed from General Smuts' recommendations, our air defences of London were rapidly transformed in strength and effectiveness. Daylight raids became too dangerous for the Germans to attempt, and night raids grew steadily more difficult and costly.

The second matter referred to this Committee — the question of air organisation generally and the higher direction of aerial operations — took longer to examine. In consultation with me, General Smuts set himself to consider the questions:

1. Shall there be instituted a real Air Ministry responsible for all air organisation and operations?
2. Shall there be constituted a unified Air Service embracing both the present R.N.A.S. and R.F.C.?
3. If so, how shall the relations of the new Air Service to the Navy and Army be determined so that the functions at present discharged for them by the R.N.A.S. and R.F.C. respectively shall continue to be efficiently performed by the new Air Service?

The second and final report, presented by General Smuts on August 17th, 1917, contained an examination of these questions and a series of recommendations for their solution.

The report noted briefly the controversies which had raged round this issue in the former War Committee. It paid tribute to the excellent work of the reconstituted Air Board, but pointed out that this body was really a Conference rather than a Board, being a consultative association of representatives of the Fighting Services and Ministry of Munitions, without a technical and advisory personnel of its own. Hence it could never form an independent air policy, but only one subordinated to military and naval strategy. The time was now rapidly approaching when such subordination could no longer be justified.

This passage from the report has an important bearing on one of the most difficult problems of Disarmament:

Air Service . . . can be used as an independent means of war operations. Nobody that witnessed the attack on London on the 11th July could have any doubt on that point. Unlike artillery, an air fleet can conduct extensive operations far from, and independently of, both Army and Navy. As far as can at present be foreseen, there is absolutely no limit to the scale of its future independent war use. And the day may not be far off when aerial operations, with their devastation of enemy lands and destruction of industrial and populous centres on a vast scale, may become the principal operations of war, to which the older forms of military and naval operations may become secondary and subordinate. . . .

In our opinion there is no reason why the Air Board should any longer continue in its present form as practically no more than a conference room between the older Services, and there is every reason why it should be raised to the status of an independent Ministry in control of its own War Service.

. . . Next spring and summer the position will be that the Army and Navy will have all the Air Service required in connection with their operations; and over and above that, there will be a great surplus available for independent operations. Who is to look after and direct the activities of this available surplus? . . . The necessity for an Air Ministry and Air Staff has therefore become urgent.

. . . It requires some imagination to realise that next summer, while our Western Front may still be moving forward at a snail's pace in Belgium and France, the air battle front will be far behind on the Rhine, and that its continuous and intense pressure against the chief industrial centres of the enemy, as well as on his lines of communication, may form an important factor in bringing about peace. . . .

The further argument was also adduced that with the progressive exhaustion of man power on both sides, the importance of mechanised warfare would increase and that the air arm multiplied immensely the potency of the individual combatant.

The report emphasised the chaos which would result from continuing the R.F.C. and R.N.A.S. independently of a new Air Force, and urged that it would suffice if the needs of the Army and Navy were specially studied by the Air Force, and those units attached to them were seconded to them and placed under their orders while operating on behalf of the older Services. It summed up its conclusions in eight recommendations:

1. That an Air Ministry should be instituted forthwith, to administer all matters connected with aerial warfare.
2. That it should have an Air Staff to make plans, direct operations, collect intelligence and train personnel.
3. That the Ministry and Staff should arrange for the amalgamation of the R.N.A.S. and R.F.C.
4. That the personnel of these services should only be transferred to the new force with their own consent.
5. That close liaison should be established and maintained between the Army, Navy and Air Staffs.
6. That the Air Staff should provide air units for service with the Army and Navy, to act during such attachment under naval or military control, and with such types of machine as those services desired.
7. That regular officers of the Navy and Army should be seconded to the Air Force for fixed periods for employment with the naval and military air contingents.
8. That officers and other ranks should be able to transfer permanently to the Air Force if they wished.

This report was considered at length by the War Cabinet on August 24th. The official view of the Board of Admiralty, voiced on this occasion by Sir Eric Geddes, the new First Lord, was still doggedly opposed to any interference with the

R.N.A.S. They suggested that the new Air Ministry should take over the R.F.C. and leave the R.N.A.S. alone.

Ultimately the War Cabinet, after the most careful consideration, decided to accept in principle the recommendations made in the Second Report of the Prime Minister's Committee on Air Organisation, as summarised in paragraph Number 10 of the Report.

This was the beginning of the Air Ministry. The first big fence had been cleared on the way to the setting up of such a Ministry, and the pressing forward of the scheme was recommitted to the capable hands of General Smuts. In the meantime we approved General Smuts' suggestion that a Committee should be appointed to assemble at once, composed as below, to advise the War Cabinet on all questions relating to Air policy:

General Smuts (in the Chair),
The First Lord of the Admiralty,
The Secretary of State for War,
The President of the Air Board.

This was in order that we should not be held up, pending the carrying of legislation, in the adoption of measures to put our growing air strength to its fullest use. The Air Board, as Lord Cowdray stated at this meeting, had no policy beyond supplying the needs of the Army and Navy. By this time Sir Douglas Haig had fifteen hundred machines, besides the reserve of machines on the Western Front. The Admiralty also had fifteen hundred naval machines, with five hundred seaplanes. A policy was needed for use of the surplus machines which might presently be available.

The announcement of our intention to establish an Air Ministry was made in the House of Commons on October 16th, and the Bill itself was given a first reading on November 8th. It had in the meantime been very carefully examined by the Departments concerned, and revised in consultation with them by the Air Committee under General Smuts, and by the War Cabinet. The almost impossible feat had been accomplished of securing substantial agreement with its terms by the Admiralty and War Office. It passed through Parliament without difficulty, and obtained the Royal Assent on November 29th, 1917.

A most unfortunate *contretemps* marred the peace of the Administration in connection with the setting-up of this new Ministry. At this time, Lord Northcliffe had just returned from his Mission to America, and I was anxious to make the best use of his great driving power in the national interest. It seemed to me that there would be remarkable scope for this in the new Air Ministry, where the two existing wings of our flying services had to be welded together, and the new air weapon — a weapon of vast and undeveloped possibilities — employed to the fullest extent along lines still to be planned. Lord Cowdray, the Chairman of the Air Board, had done very sound and successful work in that post, and was quite naturally expecting to pass on to be Minister for Air in the new régime. But Lord Cowdray's health was not such as to permit him to give the necessary ruthless drive, the untiring leadership and energy which would have been essential to the new Ministry in the urgent circumstances of the moment. It was my intention to invite Lord Cowdray to take charge of a department where his great business experience and his ripe judgment would have been valuable, and to choose a younger and physically fitter man for the post of Air Minister. At a luncheon in Downing Street, in the course of conversation with Lord Northcliffe, I sounded him on the subject without making any definite offer. Before doing so I had intended to offer Lord Cowdray another and equally honourable position in the Ministry which would not put upon him such an exceptional nervous and physical strain. For the moment I did not discuss the matter with Lord Cowdray. The Air Ministry Bill was not yet through and in any event I did not propose to disturb Lord Cowdray unless Northcliffe was prepared to take the post. Northcliffe said he would let me know his answer when he had thought over the matter. In lamentable breach of my confidence, and with one of those lapses into blundering brutality to which his passion for the startling gesture sometimes led him, he proceeded to write me a letter declining the post, and embarking on a series of quite irrelevant criticisms of the Government in respect of the Censorship, our moderation in dealing with conscientious objectors, our inferiority to the Americans in fervour and enthusiasm, and such matters; and published this letter in full in the *Times* before I ever received it.

The text of this letter was as follows:

"15th November, 1917.

"Dear Prime Minister,

"I have given anxious consideration to your repeated invitation that I should take charge of the new Air Ministry. The reasons which have impelled me to decline that great honour and responsibility are in no way concerned with the office which is rightly to be set up. They are roughly as follows:

"Returning after five months spent in the virile atmosphere of the United States and Canada, I find that, while those two countries are proceeding with their war preparations with a fervour and enthusiasm little understood on this side of the Atlantic; while the United States has instantly put into operation Conscription, over which we wobbled for two years, and is making short work with sedition-mongers; while Canada has already given such proofs of thoroughness as the disfranchisement of conscientious objectors and the denaturalisation of all enemy aliens who have been naturalised in the last fifteen years; while we, for our part, are asking immense sacrifices from those peoples — there are still in office here those who dally with such urgent questions as that of the unity of war control, the eradication of sedition, the mobilisation of the whole man and woman power of the country, and the introduction of compulsory food rations. I have had personal experience myself, while in America, of the obstruction and delay in certain Departments in London, which, for example, postponed the sending of Lord Reading's vital and most successful Mission. I find that the Censorship is still being misused, and that men in various positions of authority, who should have been punished, have been retained and in some cases elevated. The spirit of the men and women of Great Britain is clearly as eager and as splendid as ever. We have, in my belief, the most efficient army in the world, led by one of the greatest generals, and I am well aware of the fine achievements of many others of our soldiers, sailors and statesmen; but I feel that in present circumstances I can do better work if I maintain my independence and am not gagged by a loyalty that I do not feel towards the whole of your Administration.

"I take this opportunity of thanking you and the War Cabinet for the handsome message of praise sent to me as representing the five hundred officials of the British War Mission in the United States, many of them volunteer exiles. Their achievements and those of their ten thousand assistants deserve to be better known by their countrymen. The fact that their work is not known is due to the absurd secrecy about the War which is still prevalent. Everything that these officials are doing is known to our American friends, and of course to the Germans. I trust I make no breach of confidence in saying that some of the documents which have passed through my hands as Head of the Mission are such as if published would greatly increase our prestige in the United States and hearten our people at home.

"May I also take this opportunity of giving a warning about our relations with that great people from whom I have come? We have had the tragedy of Russia, due partly to lack of Allied propaganda to counteract that of the Germans. We have had the tragedy of Italy largely due to that same enemy propaganda. We have had the tragedies of Serbia, Roumania and Montenegro. There is one tragedy which I am sure we shall not have, and that is the tragedy of the United States. But, from countless conversations with leading Americans, I know that, unless there is swift improvement in our methods here, the United States will rightly take into its own hands the entire management of a great part of the War. It will not sacrifice its blood and treasure to incompetent handling of affairs in Europe.

"In saying all this, which is very much on my mind, believe me that I have none but the most friendly feelings towards yourself, and that I am greatly honoured by your suggestion.

Yours sincerely,

NORTHCLIFFE."

The publication of this letter in such a manner, or at all, was characteristic of Lord Northcliffe's worst side. It was what made it so difficult to have confidential dealings with him. Where either his vanity or temper was implicated, he had no regard for the decent behaviour which bound average men of honour. There was of course nothing unusual in the procedure by which he had been sounded as to his willingness to take the Air Ministry. Such soundings always have to be made before any reshuffling of offices in a Government takes place, and obviously it is taken for granted that persons so approached shall treat the matter in strictest confidence pending the completion of the other arrangements involved in the shuffle. Unless and until Northcliffe let me know that he would undertake the Air Ministry, I clearly could not approach Lord Cowdray with a proposal that he should transfer to another ministerial post.

Thus the publication by Lord Northcliffe of the statement that I had offered him the Air Ministry placed Lord Cowdray in a very humiliating position. Not unnaturally, he took bitter offence at learning for the first time through the columns of the public Press, and not from me, that such a change of Ministers was being contemplated. He promptly sent me his resignation from the chairmanship of the Air Board, in a letter of strong protest. He never forgave me the affront. The ranks of the Anti-Lloyd George Liberals received an influential recruit, and in post-War years the Press, which he controlled, became a vehicle of his implacable resentment and hostility, which helped to widen and deepen that schism in the Liberal Party that has led to its crumbling and collapse.

The result was that while Parliament was duly carrying the Air Force Bill, we had lost our Air Minister. However, before the end of November, I succeeded in persuading Lord Rothermere to accept this post. He held it for the very difficult first five months of the new Department, during which time he succeeded in carrying through the task of blending the Royal Naval Air Service and the Royal Flying Corps into a single new service — the Royal Air Force. On April 1st, 1918, their fusion was formally accomplished. Lord Rothermere was working under grave handicaps, for the War had inflicted upon him two tragic bereavements, under which his health eventually gave way. Certain changes which he found it desirable to make in the Air Staff in April, 1918, provoked a fresh outburst of the criticism from which the new Ministry constantly suffered, and on April 23rd, 1918, he resigned his office. The last straw had been when he found that Members of Parliament who had been enrolled in his Headquarters Staff were using the information they thus acquired to lead attacks upon him in the House of Commons. In his letter of resignation, dated April 23rd, 1918, Lord Rothermere urged this as a final reason for his resignation:

> Another and more decisive reason [he wrote] is that this young force after all the publicity it has received during the last few weeks requires a rest from comment and criticism. So far no harm has been done. I feel, however, that continuance during the next few months might impair discipline and prejudice efficiency.
>
> With myself as Secretary of State there is every reason to suppose that comment and criticism will continue. . . . The

danger to discipline through constant publicity is well illustrated in the report in this morning's newspaper of yesterday's proceedings in the House of Commons. Two of the three Members of Parliament pressing Mr. Bonar Law to give an early day for a debate on Air Ministry affairs are officers of the Royal Air Force holding junior Staff appointments under me in the Hotel Cecil. . . . Why in the House of Commons should they flout disciplinary codes where elsewhere similar conduct by any other Staff Officer would form the subject of enquiry by his superior officers?

Sequestered in the Hotel Cecil, Major Sir John Simon has acted as an assistant secretary or clerk to Major-General Sir H. Trenchard, late Chief of the Air Staff. Two months ago I mentioned to you the extreme unsuitability of this arrangement with its possible dangers. As events have proved, I was not wrong. . . .

My reply, which was sent after it had been shown to and approved by my colleagues in the War Cabinet, was as follows:

"10, Downing Street,
Whitehall, S W.1.
25th April, 1918.

"My dear Rothermere,

"I have received your letter tendering your resignation as Secretary of State for the Air Force with the deepest regret. Your work there has been of inestimable service to the nation, and time will bring with it a full recognition of your achievement. It is no small thing to have taken over the conduct of an entirely new arm of the Service in the middle of a great war, to have extricated it from the difficulties which surrounded it, coördinated the two services which made it up, and bestowed on its administration an initiative which has given the new force a real supremacy at the front. And all this has been done in such a brief period of time.

"It is the more to be lamented that, having set the Ministry on its legs, you cannot remain to enjoy the fruition of your own brilliant work. But I feel on reading your letter that I cannot press you to stay, much as the Government must suffer from your retirement.

"Your sacrifices to the National cause have been so heavy, and the strain imposed on you so cruel, that it would be impossible to deny you the right to some repose. Sympathy in these matters is generally best given by silence, but I am sure that you know without my telling you how much I sympathise with you in your losses and in the way in which you have continued your public duties in spite of everything.

"No minister ever had greater difficulties to contend with than you had in effecting the fusion of the two Services, and the Air Force has every right to be proud of its First Secretary of State.

"I am authorised by my colleagues to state that they share fully the views I have expressed in this letter.

Yours very faithfully,

D. LLOYD GEORGE."

Testimony to the success which had been achieved in reorganising our air arm is supplied by Sir Douglas Haig's dispatch (dated July 20th, 1918) describing the German offensives of March and April, 1918. He says:

> Throughout the period of active operations our airmen have established and maintained a superiority over the enemy's air forces without parallel since the days of the first Somme battle. Not content with destroying the enemy in the air, they have vigorously attacked his infantry, guns and transport with bombs and machine-gun fire, and in the fighting south of the Somme in particular gave invaluable assistance to the infantry by these means on numerous occasions. In addition, the usual work of reconnaissance, photography, artillery coöperation and bombing has been carried out vigorously and with remarkable results.

Sir William Weir was appointed to the post vacated by Lord Rothermere and held it until the end of the War. During these concluding months our Air Force further developed the marked superiority over the enemy which Lord Rothermere's Administration had so conspicuously established.

During 1918, thirty thousand aeroplanes were manufactured and forty thousand more were on order. Preparations were made for devastating aerial warfare against the chief cities of Germany by the spring of 1919. Happily, the signing of the Armistice averted the necessity for carrying out this programme.

In recording the achievements of our Air Service, I may be allowed to quote the tribute I paid to it in the course of a speech in the House on October 29th, 1917, when I said:

> I am sure the House would like special mention to be made of our Air Service. The heavens are their battlefield; they are the cavalry of the clouds. High above the squalor and the mud, so high in the firmament that they are not visible from earth, they fight out the eternal issues of right and wrong. Their daily, yea, their nightly struggles are like the Miltonic conflict between the winged hosts of light and darkness. They fight the foe high up, and they fight him low down. . . . Every flight is a romance, every record is an epic. They are the knighthood of this war, without fear and without reproach. They recall the old legends of chivalry, not merely by daring individually, but by the nobility of their spirit, and, among the multitudes of heroes let us think of the chivalry of the air.

Peace came, but the Ministry of Air has survived. It is a permanent contribution to our national organisation which we have inherited from the War. It is remarkable among Ministries in that it is concerned no less with the arts of peace than with those of war. On the military side it administers a third fighting service, which ranks alongside the country's forces on land and on water, and in days to come might well prove even more crucially important than they for national defence. But equally it controls on the civil side the development of aviation as a new servant of commerce and amenity, and its utility for this purpose will persist if war should finally and fortunately disappear from the future activities of mankind, and warships and cannon rust away.

CHAPTER IV

STOCKHOLM AND MR. ARTHUR HENDERSON

Social disturbance caused by War — Difficult problems for the Government — Medley of forces which effected Russian Revolution — Sir George Buchanan's report of March 15, 1917 — Message to Russia from British Labour — French and British Labour send deputations — A Stockholm Conference proposed by Neutrals — Fresh Labour deputation to Russia — Soviet invites Socialist deputations — Consultation with French and Italian Governments — Series of conversations at Stockholm — Suggestion to replace Buchanan at Petrograd — M. Albert Thomas' success in Russia — Henderson to visit Russia — Confusion in Russia — Buchanan's dislike of Socialists — Henderson unable to replace Buchanan — Passports granted to minority Socialists for Russian visit — British anger at Socialist sedition — Sailors' and Firemen's Union refuse to take MacDonald to Russia — Mr. Henderson returns — Consults with Labour Party Executive — Stockholm project revived — Kerensky's limitations — Henderson's blunder in going to Paris — Asked for explanation — He defies the War Cabinet — His activities in Paris — "Doormat" incident — Cabinet anxious to retain Mr. Henderson — Mr. Henderson's defence in the House — My defence of Henderson — Conflicting tendencies in Russia — Message from the Embassy — Kerensky takes charge — Cabinet opposed to Stockholm Conference — Henderson urges participation in Labour Conference — Russian Embassy's letter — Henderson's stubborn persistence — Cabinet maintains its attitude — Mr. Henderson's resignation — Cabinet reviews the situation — Definition of its attitude — Kerensky's difficulties with Soviet — Debate in the Commons — Labour support for Stockholm fades — Reasons for Mr. Henderson's blunder.

The Russian Revolution provoked repercussions far and wide in the political ideas and movements of other countries. For that matter, it is still doing so, and in many lands it has proved and is proving the stimulus, by attraction or by repulsion, for revolutionary and counter-revolutionary upheavals which are bringing about great constitutional changes. When revolution fails to spread, it hardens into reaction.

The war conditions which made the unrest particularly dangerous, fomented by the Russian eruption, at the same time favoured the flow of its fiery streams. The social conditions and conventional restraints, inbred through generations of peace, had been unloosed. Men, torn from their homes, from their work, from all the training and habits of a lifetime, were being thrown together with strange companions from unfamiliar social orbits to be trained to destroy, or set to new tasks of munition manufacture or departmental duty. Women and girls were being emancipated at a stroke from the hobble skirts and chaperonage of the pre-War era, and sent forth, often in man's attire, to do work hitherto reserved for men only. The Government was perforce taking powers over men's lives, properties and businesses on an unprecedented scale. It was dictating as to wages, rates of profit, and the use to which industrial machinery and organisation were to be put. The break with the past seemed final, and every political theorist was stimulated to speculate what shape the new order could or should assume. So when Russia suddenly flung away her ancient Czarist régime, and embarked on a great Socialist experiment, numbers in this country were eager to emulate her example. That the movement of liberation which Russia was then beginning with such hopes and amid such an atmosphere of good wishes would rush headlong into the Red Terror, and complete the upheaval and uprooting of the existing social and economic order, was not then foreseen.

As the year 1917 advanced, therefore, we were faced, in addition to our darkening war anxieties, with the necessity of handling with a wise admixture of firmness and moderation the domestic situation that arose from industrial and political unrest, aggravated to an acute degree by the forces released through the Russian upheaval. The shock that came from Petrograd passed through every workshop and mine, and produced a nervous disquiet which made things difficult in recruitment and munitionment. To maintain our national unity and pursue steadily our national purpose, it was vital that the members of the Government should keep their heads and handle the labour situation prudently as well as firmly. That was by no means easy. In this part of the struggle, Mr. Arthur Henderson became a war casualty.

Because so many differing and indeed violently opposed forces generally have a share in bringing about revolutions, the Russian, like all others, was a confused business. There were Army generals who wanted to make the Czar abdicate, and secure a regency under which they would be free from Court intrigues and interference. There were democratic leaders in the Duma who sought to establish responsible constitutional government. There were Nihilists and anarchists whose chief purpose was utter revolt against the existing order, and international communists who desired to establish the Marxist State and the Third International. It could not be foreseen which of these various forces would finally triumph and grasp the steering wheel of the revolution. The vast mass of the people in Russia just wanted to be released from their distresses. They needed food and fuel. They were looking for efficient and clean government. Most of all, they were tired of bloodshed and wanted peace. They were not concerned as to the group from which deliverance came as long as they got it. Which of the rival factions won depended on the qualities of leadership and organisation they could respectively produce.

On March 15th, 1917, our Ambassador at Petrograd, Sir George Buchanan, sent us a telegram which reflected the uncertainties of the situation:

Open opposition is likely to develop very shortly between parties of the Social Revolution and of the Duma. The latter is for war, and should it prevail quickly, Russia will be rendered stronger than in the past. Peace at any price is the object of the former party, and military disaster would follow its advent to power. Could English Labour leaders be induced to send a telegram to Duma Labour leaders (Kerensky and Chkheidze) expressing their confidence that Kerensky and Chkheidze and their comrades will support free peoples fighting German despotism, pointing out that every idle day spells disaster to their brothers, fighting in the trenches, and that victory to Germany would bring disaster to all classes of the Allies? The telegram might also refer to the unity of all classes in Britain, and especially to what the working classes are doing. Inasmuch as advice from England at present moment carries great weight, I attach great importance to immediate dispatch of telegram on above lines.

A telegram was accordingly drafted by Mr. Henderson, the representative of Labour in the British War Cabinet, and sent off to the Labour leaders in the Duma:

Organised labour in Great Britain is watching with deepest sympathy the efforts of the Russian people to deliver themselves from power of reactionary elements which are impeding their advance to victory. Labour in England and France has long realised that despotism of Germany must be overthrown if way is to be opened for free and peaceful development of European nations. This conviction has inspired them to make unprecedented efforts and sacrifices, and we confidently look forward to assistance of Russian labour in achieving the object to which we have devoted ourselves. Earnestly trust you will impress on your followers that any remission of effort means disaster to comrades in trenches and to our common hopes of social regeneration.

A few days after this, on March 26th, Mr. Henderson reported to the War Cabinet that representatives of the French Socialist Party — who stood for war *à outrance* — were, with the authority and consent of the French Committee of Foreign Affairs, shortly arriving in England en route to Petrograd, whither they were going on a Mission to the Russian Socialist Party, their object being to persuade that party to do all in its power to bring the War to a satisfactory conclusion. The War Cabinet decided that Mr. Henderson should use his influence to secure that a suitably composed

British Labour Deputation should accompany the French party with the same object. This was done, and Will Thorne and James O'Grady joined the Mission.

Their prospects of success in Russia were not improved by the action of some of their colleagues at home. British Socialism was then divided in opinion, the majority supporting the War, while the pacifist minority, strongly represented in the Independent Labour Party, whose leading figure was Mr. Ramsay MacDonald, devoted itself to criticising and creating difficulties and generally weakening the morale of the nation. When the delegates of the Labour Party were in Russia, a member of the I.L.P. sent a message to a Russian Socialist, asserting that they were the paid emissaries of the British Government, and not real representatives of British Labour. This gave rise to violent attacks on them in the Russian Socialist Press — a dangerous effect in a country where discipline had vanished and murder by a suddenly excited mob was a commonplace occurrence. As Sir George Buchanan records in his book, "My Mission to Russia": "The matter was eventually put right by Mr. Hyndman, who requested Kerensky by telegraph to 'contradict most emphatically lying statement of the I.L.P.' "

Meantime, discussion was on foot as to the holding of an international Socialist Conference at Stockholm. This suggestion had arisen as follows: the international confederation of the Socialist organisations in various countries — known as the Second International — which existed before the War and had its headquarters at Brussels, had been temporarily scattered by the German invasion of Belgium. Its offices were abandoned, and its chief officials escaped to The Hague. But efforts were made to revive it by the Dutch and Scandinavian Socialists, and in April, 1917, a joint Dutch-Scandinavian Committee, presided over by the Swedish Socialist statesman, Mr. Branting, issued an invitation to all the Socialist parties of the world to attend an international Socialist Conference at Stockholm to discuss ways and means of bringing about peace.

The proposal was not one likely to find wide acceptance. Belligerent governments would clearly refuse to have terms of peace dictated to them by a Party Conference. The same observation would apply if the international conference had been Liberal or Conservative. Most of the Socialists in the belligerent countries supported their governments in carrying on the War. The Executive of the French Socialist Party decided at the end of April by thirteen votes to eleven not to go to Stockholm, while the Russian extremists led by Lenin reached a similar decision for opposite motives, being contemptuous of the bourgeois mentality of the Second International. On May 11th, Mr. Henderson reported to the War Cabinet that the Executive of the British Labour Party had decided not to take part in the Stockholm Conference.

The proposal therefore seemed dead. But it was known that in Russia there was considerable division of opinion among the Socialists about the issue of continuing the War or trying to make a separate peace, and Mr. Henderson told us that the British Labour Party Executive proposed to send a Mission to Petrograd, consisting of himself, Mr. G. Roberts, M.P., and Mr. Purdy, to strengthen the war purpose of the Russian Socialists. We decided that in view of industrial conditions here, it would be better for Mr. Henderson not to go, but we were willing for Mr. Roberts to be given permission to join such a deputation. At that time Russia was being administered by a provisional government based on the Duma. But much of the real power was in the hands of the Petrograd Council of Workmen's and Soldiers' Delegates — the Soviet. This body decided to invite representatives of both the majority and the minority Socialist movements in the Allied countries to come and discuss the situation with it. News of this reached us in a telegram sent on May 10th, by M. Miliukoff, the Russian Foreign Minister, through the Russian Embassy in London:

The Executive Committee of the Council of Workmen's and Soldiers' Deputies have asked me to forward to the Governments of Great Britain, France and Italy the following telegram:

"The Executive Committee express the hope that the Governments of Great Britain, France and Italy will not refuse to grant facilities for the journey to Russia to the delegations of the Italian Social Democratic Party, the British Independent Labour and Social Democratic Parties, and of the Opposition Group of the French Socialist Labour Party who have been invited to Petrograd. The Executive Committee would be grateful for a favourable reply."

Please convey this message to His Majesty's Government.

We decided before answering this message to send a telegram to the French and Italian Governments in the following terms:

His Majesty's Government have received through the Russian Embassy here a formal invitation from the Executive Committee of the Workmen's and Soldiers' Deputies to grant facilities for the journey to Russia of representatives of the Independent Labour and Social-Democratic Parties. These Parties form a small fraction of the Socialist movement in Great Britain, and their opinions are of a pacifist complexion. His Majesty's Government understand that a similar invitation has been issued to the French/Italian Government. To reply by a direct refusal would irritate the Russian extremists and perhaps discourage their moderate colleagues. On the other hand, in view of the resignation of M. Gutchkoff, and the reports of the growing disorders in Russia, it seems impossible to accept the invitation without reserve. His Majesty's Government therefore propose to reply stating that, owing to submarine warfare, the means of communication between Western Europe and Russia are very much restricted, and only those persons can be allowed to travel in that direction who wish to do so for business of National importance. No intimation has yet reached His Majesty's Government from any section of the Socialist Party expressing their desire to go to Russia. But it is impossible for His Majesty's Government to give a definite reply on the subject until they know what persons wish to go to Russia and what is the object of the proposed journey.

His Majesty's Government would be glad to know if the French/Italian Government concur in the action proposed.

On the following day, May 16th, 1917, Mr. Henderson told us that the British Labour Party was not proposing to send any delegates in reply to the Soviet's invitation until further information had been received from the Russian Socialist Party as to the nature of their proposals.

The Dutch-Scandinavian Socialists had not entirely abandoned their idea of a conference at Stockholm. They had proceeded to arrange a series of separate and successive conversations between themselves and representatives of the various belligerent nations' Socialist Parties. M. Vandervelde, the Belgian Socialist leader, took part in one such conversation at Stockholm in early May, and we learned that the arrival there of German and Russian delegations was expected shortly. The British Labour Party had put out the suggestion of an Inter-Allied Socialist Conference in London; but the Russians had not yet consented, as they were now in favour of holding an International Conference in some neutral country. In these circumstances, the Foreign Office arranged that the Labour delegates who had been visiting Russia should stop at Bergen on their way back, so as to be available if it were decided to send British representatives to any of the conversations that might take place at Stockholm.

The matter was discussed at a meeting of the War Cabinet on May 21st, 1917. In view of the prospect of German Socialists going to Stockholm and fraternising there with the

Russians, it was suggested that there might be an advantage in sending a strong British delegation, even one headed by Mr. Arthur Henderson. Alternatively, it might be worth while to send Mr. Henderson to Petrograd on a special Mission, similar to that being carried out for the French by M. Albert Thomas. We were told that Mr. Ramsay MacDonald and Mr. Jowett of the Independent Labour Party, and Mr. Inkpin of the British Socialist Party, had now applied for passports to Petrograd, and presumably had the intention of stopping at Stockholm en route. This was a development arising from the invitation extended by the Russian Soviet to the Minority Socialist movements.

It was not at this stage clear whether the various conversations proceeding at Stockholm were likely to be followed by a formal conference. If so, it was agreed that while there was a good case for having British representatives there to watch proceedings and put the British case, it would be very difficult for Mr. Henderson, as a member of the War Cabinet, to attend. If Mr. MacDonald and his pacifist friends were going, we felt that a strong delegation of the British Labour Party ought to go as well.

We decided to cable Mr. Albert Thomas at Petrograd that we thought it dangerous for Russian and German Socialists to confer without any British representatives being present, and ask for his views on the matter.

Two days afterwards, on May 23rd, we further considered the question of our representation in Russia. Our Ambassador there, Sir George Buchanan, had rendered very fine service, but the very fact that he had established excellent relations with the Imperial Government, and with the Provisional Government which replaced it, made him an object of suspicion and distrust to the new Administration which had now been set up under Kerensky, with the support of the Soviet. It was urged by the Foreign Office that he should be supplemented or replaced by someone whose known sympathies with Labour and Socialist movements would ensure him the confidence of the Russian Government.

The War Cabinet was also impressed with the success achieved in Petrograd by M. Albert Thomas, the French Socialist leader, whose services had been publicly recognised in an interview granted by M. Terestchenko, the new Russian Foreign Minister. As the continued coöperation of Russia was clearly of great importance to us in the War, we decided to invite Mr. Arthur Henderson to make a personal sacrifice and to go to Petrograd on a similar footing to that of M. Albert Thomas.

No immediate decision was considered necessary as to how long Mr. Henderson should stay, but he was advised to make his political arrangements on the assumption that the visit would be temporary. It was decided that, in the event of Mr. Henderson's accepting the invitation, Sir George Buchanan should be retained in Petrograd for a short time in order to post Mr. Henderson up on matters of detail. At the end of a few weeks, subject, however to Mr. Henderson's concurrence at the time, Sir George Buchanan should be recalled to London for purposes of consultation. It was generally agreed that it would be desirable for Mr. Henderson to leave for Petrograd at the earliest possible date.

Mr. Henderson read a telegram he had received from M. Thomas to the effect that the Workmen's Council was awaiting the arrival of a British Delegation, and that he attached great importance to the presence of Mr. Henderson himself.

There were clearly a number of very strong reasons for sending Mr. Henderson on this Mission, and even for arranging that he should for a short time replace Sir George Buchanan at the Embassy in Petrograd. Things in Russia were in a state of great confusion and uncertainty, and in the medley of competing forces between which its Government was divided, it was very important to reinforce those elements that were favourably disposed to continuing the War. It was becoming more and more doubtful whether Russia would carry through with the Allies right to the end. The demand for peace was becoming more and more imperative. The speeches delivered at the endless meetings held at street corners in Russian cities were a prolonged keen for peace. Albert Thomas described them to me on his return. His account reminded me of the meetings I had witnessed in the Welsh Revival. The excitement was not violent, but deep. An eerie emotion, more religious than political, seemed to have possessed the Russian workers. With a nation in such a mood, anything was possible. But its temper did not conduce to an effective prosecution of the War. The best we could hope for was that the Russian Armies would defend their trenches, and thus hold in front of them a million or two Germans and Austrians until the Americans were ready to fight. In this task M. Albert Thomas, a Socialist speaking to fellow Socialists, had achieved marked success. It was not a part that Sir George Buchanan was fitted to play, for he never concealed the fact that he had no sympathy whatever with Socialists. In his book he tells how M. Albert Thomas had dinner with him one day at Petrograd, along with Henderson, and two Russian leaders — one of them also a Socialist leader — and how: "talking to me after dinner, he asked: 'What would you have said had you been told five years ago that I and two other Socialists would one day be guests at your table?' 'The very idea of such a thing would,' I replied, 'have appalled me.' " The Russians could not but be aware of this covert antagonism behind the suavity and polish of the expert diplomat, and its existence discounted for them the value of any advice he gave them. He belonged so essentially and obviously to the old order that was passing away — that had already passed away beyond recall in Russia.

Mr. Arthur Henderson duly went to Russia. But when he acquainted himself with the range and difficulty of the tasks which Sir George Buchanan was carrying out, he decided that he could not undertake to relieve him of them even temporarily. He was an experienced political organiser, in fact he proved himself to be the greatest political organiser of his day. But this job called for different qualities and he had the good sense to realise they were not his best. He spent six weeks there, and early in July decided to return home.

Meantime there were further developments in regard to Stockholm. Following the Soviet's invitations to the Minority Socialist Parties, we had decided to grant passports to Mr. Ramsay MacDonald and his party to proceed to Russia, with the prospect of their calling in at Stockholm to take part in the conversations that were being held there. But we learnt a little later that the French Government had refused similar permission to its Socialists, and that the Government of the United States was perturbed at our decision to allow representatives of our pacifist element to proceed to Stockholm. It was urged that these conferences might have an injurious effect on the morale of the soldiers — this was said to be General Pétain's view — and might force the Allies into a premature and unsatisfactory peace.

There was also a growth of feeling against our decision in this country, owing to anger at the action of seditious elements. This hostility was fostered by the Labour, Socialistic and Democratic Conference held in Leeds on June 3rd, with the object of establishing in Great Britain a Council of Workmen's and Soldiers' Delegates, on the lines of the one now in existence in Russia. The immediate effect of the speeches delivered and the resolutions passed at this meeting was to rouse strong indignation against the revolutionary and pacifist agitators who were stirring up trouble in many important munition centres throughout the country. Whether the promoters of the gathering contemplated revolution or not, depended, I think, in their minds on the response given to their appeals and the measure of support accorded to their policy. Had the workmen rallied to their proposal of establishing a Soviet in Britain on Russian lines, then the Leeds meeting would have inaugurated a British Revolution and Mr. MacDonald would have been our Kerensky. That is why public opinion took alarm. There were in particular, strong protests from the Sailors' and Firemen's Union and from the British Workers' League against allowing Mr. Ramsey MacDonald and his fellows to go to Russia or to Stockholm.

On the whole, however, we decided that it might give offence to the Russian Socialists if we withdrew the passports. The general body of opinion in this country was entirely sound, and we considered that if Mr. Ramsay MacDonald went to Stockholm and there adopted a German point of view, he would be absolutely discredited in this country. On the other hand, if he adopted the Allied point of view about Belgium and Alsace-Lorraine, the Germans would see that even extreme Socialistic opinion was against them. In either event we stood to gain. We wired to Mr. Henderson in Russia for his views, which were favourable to allowing Mr. MacDonald to proceed to Russia. At the same time, and especially in view of the French and Russian attitude, we felt we could not grant him permission to take part in a conference at Stockholm, with enemy subjects. Our attitude was explained to the House of Commons by Lord Robert Cecil on June 8th, 1917, when in reply to a question he said:

The War Cabinet, after very careful consideration, decided that it was desirable to issue these passports if applied for, because

THE RT. HONOURABLE ARTHUR HENDERSON, M. P.

the Russian Government had strongly and repeatedly expressed the desire that the representatives of the minority as well as of the majority of working-class opinion should be allowed to visit Petrograd, and have expressly mentioned the Independent Labour Party as one of the bodies which they desire to have that opportunity.

The War Cabinet were advised by those most qualified to express an opinion, including our Ambassador, Sir George Buchanan, and Mr. Henderson, that a refusal would lead to very serious misconception among our Russian Allies, and would cause great discouragement to those in Russia who were most anxious to carry on the struggle for freedom with the fullest energy. If the passports are issued, they will be for Petrograd.

They are not intended to enable the holders to attend or take part in any international Conference at Stockholm, and still less to communicate directly or indirectly with enemy subjects at Stockholm or elsewhere, and it is only on this express understanding that the passports will be issued. I understand that representatives of the views of the great majority of the working class may also apply for passports to go to Petrograd, and these also will be issued if asked for.

Mr. Ramsay MacDonald thereupon asked if he would be allowed to talk with such men as Mr. Branting, and Lord Robert Cecil said that Mr. Branting was a highly respected statesman in Sweden, and by no means hostile to the Allied cause; but that the prohibition would apply to communication, direct or indirect, with the enemy.

Further responsibility was however taken out of our hands by the action of the Sailors' and Firemen's Union, which decided to refuse to convey Messrs. Ramsay MacDonald and Jowett to Russia.

One Sunday afternoon Mr. Ramsay MacDonald rang me up from Aberdeen. The telephone for long distances is still a school of patience; it was then an instrument of torture. Conversation was faint, disjointed, disrupted and incoherent.

I did ultimately gather that Mr. MacDonald was experiencing difficulty in getting on board the ship that was to carry him to Russia, and that the sailors were giving him some taste of what a general strike, such as he subsequently advocated in 1926, would be like. I promised to see what could be done. I asked Mr. Barnes to interview Mr. Havelock Wilson for us, and try to persuade him to use his influence with the Sailors' and Firemen's Union with a view to inducing them not to persist in their embargo on Mr. MacDonald's visit to Russia. Havelock Wilson was obdurate. I knew that his influence with the sailors was paramount.

At the beginning of July, Mr. Snowden wrote to me pleading with the Government to take some action to facilitate the journey of Messrs. MacDonald and Jowett, and again Mr. Barnes undertook to use his good offices on their behalf. But on July 17th he had to report to us that in his opinion the matter should be dropped. The Sailors' and Firemen's Union had proved adamant. There would be grave difficulties in prosecuting them for their attitude. To attempt compulsion would have been worse than futile, for the feeling throughout the country was one of unqualified approval of the action of the sailors. It was suggested that we might have sent a cruiser. Had we done so, it might have led to a serious mutiny. We had plenty of troubles without provoking fresh ones. The Labour Unions of the country expressed no resentment at Mr. MacDonald's failure to secure transport for Russia. He was barred by his own comrades in the Labour movement from carrying out his purpose of visiting Russia, despite the readiness of the Government to let him go there, and our utmost efforts of persuasion on his behalf.

Mr. Henderson arrived back from Russia on June 24th. I was not in England when he returned, as I had gone to Paris on the 23rd for an Inter-Allied Conference, accompanied by Mr. Balfour, General Smuts, Admiral Jellicoe and Sir William Robertson. I cannot help regretting that I was not on the spot when Mr. Henderson reached England, as had I been able to talk things over with him immediately, I might have been able to avert the very unfortunate conflict which arose between him and his colleagues in the War Cabinet.

Mr. Henderson brought back with him four members of the Russian Soviet, who had been appointed to visit the Socialist Parties of the Allied countries. Without first meeting his colleagues of the War Cabinet, and ascertaining the attitude that was being adopted toward current problems, he proceeded to attend a meeting of the Executive of the Labour Party, of which he was still Secretary. They had before them an invitation from the French Socialists to send some representatives to accompany the Russian Soviet delegates to Paris, to discuss with them the proposals for an Inter-Allied Socialist Conference and for an Internationalist Socialist Conference at Stockholm. This latter proposal had been revived by Mr. Branting and the Dutch-Scandinavian Socialist Committee, at the instigation of the left-wing Socialists of Russia. When Mr. Henderson was in Russia, Kerensky had told him he fully supported the plan. This is understandable in view of Kerensky's position at the time. Though not at the head of the Government, he was a leading member of it, and he also was a member of the Soviet, thus keeping a foot in each camp. This bifurcation, which at the time gave him his power, was also ultimately the cause of his downfall and of the collapse of Russia into Bolshevism; for Kerensky could never bring himself to take sufficiently rigorous measures against the extreme left, even when they resorted to violent measures to achieve their objects. He was a master of the eloquence that stirs masses, but he trusted too much to his remarkable gifts in that direction, and ignored the fact that there comes a time when words must be translated into action. Able to sway the Duma, the Soviet or the crowd triumphantly with a speech, he relied on his oratorical arts. The man who mattered — Lenin — was not within the sound of his voice, and had he been, it would have made no difference to that ruthless fanatic. He despised the Kerensky type.

Lenin was also a great speaker. Orators are divided into two classes. There is the orator for whom effective speech is in itself the aim and also the end. The emotion he rouses is the measure and attainment of his success. But there is the other type for whom oratory means persuading and stirring his hearers to definite action in which the orator leads. The fact that Kerensky hovered and hesitated between these two types, but that Lenin belonged to the latter class, made the entire Bolshevik Revolution.

Fresh from the glow of that atmosphere of emotionalism and exaltation which great revolutions excite, Mr. Henderson was out of tune with the stern but rigid sense of responsibility and self-control which was dominant here. When he came back from Russia the fine steel of his character was magnetised by his experiences. He was in an abnormal frame of mind. He had more than a touch of the revolutionary malaria. His temperature was high and his mood refractory. The Executive of the British Labour Party offered to nominate him, as its Secretary, to go along with its chairman, Mr. Wardle, and its Treasurer, Mr. Ramsay MacDonald, as their delegates to Paris with the Russian Soviet emissaries. He accepted the nomination. It was a profound blunder. As a Member of the British War Cabinet, he had no right to go off to Paris without even consulting his colleagues in the Cabinet, arm in arm with Ramsay MacDonald, who was openly opposed to the War and to all measures for its effective prosecution, and had been organising pacifist propaganda, to talk over with French Socialists the arrangements for an International Conference of which his own Government did not approve, and to which our Allies, the French, the Italians and the Americans, were strongly opposed.

Mr. Henderson failed to put in an appearance at the meetings of the War Cabinet on the 25th and 26th of July. At the latter meeting, the question was raised of his proposed visit to Paris, which had come to the knowledge of the Foreign Office through the application of the Labour Party delegates for passports. Mr. Henderson had not notified the War Cabinet of his intentions, though he cabled me in Paris where I was at the time, stating that he was coming to Paris with four Russian delegates and Messrs. Wardle and MacDonald — not, however, stating their business.

The War Cabinet was naturally a good deal perturbed at the news of Mr. Henderson's intended trip and decided that Mr. Henderson should be asked to confer with his colleagues in the War Cabinet at 7.30 P.M. that evening, with a view to their ascertaining from him how far the proposed action committed His Majesty's Government to the meeting of British Socialist representatives with enemy Socialist representatives at Stockholm; and whether the inclusion of Mr. Ramsay MacDonald among those chosen to proceed to Paris implied official recognition by the British Government of Mr. Ramsay MacDonald's status as a representative of British Socialists.

This conference with Mr. Henderson was duly held, and the Members of the War Cabinet told him clearly how thoroughly they disapproved of the course he had decided to take. He intimated to them that he had made up his mind and his arrangements for the visit, and could not and would not draw back. Mr. Bonar Law and his Cabinet colleagues were in a difficult position, for they could hardly prohibit Mr. Henderson from going, nor yet demand his resignation from the War Cabinet as a condition of his action; and yet it was clear that they would be blamed by Parliament and the country for allowing the Cabinet to be mixed up, through one of its members, in a discussion between Mr. Ramsay MacDonald and French and Russian Socialists, about arrangements for a World Socialist Conference where Germans would discuss with British pacifists how to end the War and on what terms to arrange peace. Mr. Henderson was in an aggressive mood and informed them that it was on his advice that the Executive of the Labour Party had now decided in favour of sending delegates to Stockholm. This met with unanimous disapproval from the Cabinet, and Mr. Henderson told them that if they insisted he was willing to tender his resignation from the War Cabinet. Naturally they could not press him to do this, for they knew that I greatly valued his membership and appreciated the help he had rendered the Government in our relations with Labour. So amid this atmosphere of disapproval he went off to Paris.

His behaviour at Paris was hardly of a nature to reassure public opinion here. Along with Mr. Ramsay MacDonald, he became a member of a small sub-committee to examine and revise the proposed arrangements for the Stockholm Conference. The other members were a left-wing and a right-wing French Socialist, and two of the degates from the Russian Soviet — Messrs. Ehrlich and Goldenberg, from the right and left wing respectively of Russian Socialism. On this committee Mr. Henderson tried hard to secure agreement that the Stockholm Conference should not go further than mutual consultation as to the war aims of the respective belligerent countries, and the lines on which they might be willing to make peace, and that it should not proceed further to pass binding resolutions on these matters, where neutrals and the enemy might outvote British Socialists upon issues vital for this country. He had some success in this effort, but the fact that then and subsequently this question seems to have been unresolved, and that there was a strong wish on the part of a number of the national Socialist groups proposing to attend Stockholm to make it the occasion for authoritative pronouncements, shows how recklessly Mr. Henderson was plunging in supporting the scheme.

He returned to England on August 1st, and had an interview with me at which he recounted his proceedings. I could not disguise the unpleasant character of the situation which he had created by his action. At the same time I was extremely unwilling to lose him from the Government. He had been a loyal and courageous colleague. He had done some very fine work for the country as a member of my own Cabinet and of the preceding one, in helping us to keep in touch with Labour and in getting the Trade Unions to coöperate with us in necessary war measures. I also had a warm personal esteem for him. So I decided to talk the whole thing over with the rest of the War Cabinet and seek their agreement with the course of retaining him with us, if at all practicable. I asked him to come round to the Cabinet that afternoon at half-past four, to discuss matters with us.

It was of course inevitable that the other members of the War Cabinet would wish to express their views in this discussion with considerable frankness, and we decided to get this part over before asking Mr. Henderson to join us. As a result, he was asked on his arrival to wait a while in my Secretary's rooms. This was the famous "doormat" incident. Unfortunately the delay, which was designed solely to spare him personal unpleasantness, lasted about an hour, and when at the end of that time Mr. Barnes went out to speak to him about what had been taking place, he found Mr. Henderson in a highly resentful frame of mind. There was no longer any question of his offering to resign, as he had done at the Cabinet meeting before he left for Paris. On the contrary, he challenged us to demand his resignation — which, as I have said, was the last thing I wished to do. He recounted the circumstances of his decision to visit Paris, and urged that his course there had been on wise lines, particularly in regard to making the Stockholm Conference a consultation and not an assembly at which binding decisions should be taken. As to whether he himself would propose to go to Stockholm if invited by the British Labour Party, he declined to give a definite answer. "He had always realised that it would be very difficult for him to proceed to Stockholm as a Member of the British War Cabinet. Consequently, if he should receive a nomination for the Conference, he would have to reconsider the whole position according to circumstances."

We made it clear to him that we wanted to retain him in the Cabinet, and examined with him how the case could best be stated in Parliament, which wished to discuss the matter that evening on the adjournment. It was generally agreed that Mr. Henderson could dispose of criticism in the House of Commons by pointing out that the difficulty had arisen from the fact that he held a dual position as a Member of the War Cabinet and as Secretary of the Executive Committee of the British Labour Party. It might frankly be admitted that, on the present occasion, this had entailed some misunderstanding, but it must be borne in mind that it also possessed great advantages. It had enabled Mr. Henderson in the past to keep in the closest possible touch with the views of the Labour Party, and so, by first-hand information, to assist the Government in preparing its war measures on lines which would be acceptable to Labour. Moreover, it had enabled Mr. Henderson to attend the previous Conferences of Allied Socialists with good results. For example, only last Christmas he had attended a Socialist Conference at Paris, where he had met with considerable opposition, but had eventually induced the Conference to take the view which he shared with the British Government in regard to the prosecution of the War. Further, he could point out that members of the French and other Allied Governments occupied a position similar to his own. On balance, therefore, the dual nature of his position had been an advantage.

We recognised that the House of Commons was less concerned at the moment about Stockholm than with the fact that Mr. Henderson, a Member of the War Cabinet, had gone off to this Paris meeting in company with Mr. Ramsay MacDonald, who only a day or two earlier had been making himself conspicuous as the leader of the pacifists in a debate on war aims in the House of Commons and who, in the Manifesto of Aims of the Leeds Conference, which he had a leading part in summoning, had declared that its purpose was to make this country like Russia. But we suggested that Mr. Henderson could remind Parliament that this was not the first conference to which he had gone in MacDonald's company. Their association on such occasions was inevitable, since one was Secretary and the other Treasurer of the British Labour Party. If he also reaffirmed his war attitude on the lines of some of his recent speeches, he should satisfy the House.

Mr. Henderson had to face a rather unfriendly Chamber that evening, when on the motion for the adjournment he was called to give an account of his conduct to the House of Commons. In his defence he urged that one important part of his Paris visit had been to make arrangements for an Inter-Allied Socialist Conference; that, as to the Stockholm proposal, he had found, when in Russia, that the Russians were strongly in favour of it, so he had willingly accepted the invitation of the Labour Party to be a member of the Delegation to Paris to make arrangements for it; that the anomaly of his doing so while a member of the War Cabinet was inherent in his dual position. He had accompanied Mr. Ramsay MacDonald to Paris and on to the sub-committee there, because he wanted to keep him in order. "I deemed it of the highest importance that I should go on the sub-committee to assist in keeping my Hon. Friend the Member for Leicester right. . . . If there had to be a representative of the Minority, and if that representative was elected by the Executive of the Party, then I was not going to demur. I was going to accept the position, and do what I could, if I found him going astray. . . ." And apart from his duty of chaperoning Mr. MacDonald and keeping him out of mischief, Mr. Henderson urged that if there was going to be a Stockholm Conference, it was his duty to see that it was held at a date when the Americans could be present if they wished, and that it was a consultative, not a binding assembly. He suggested that there might be considerable advantages in the holding of such a conference, but at the same time made it clear that his own views on our war aims and the need of fighting till we could win them were unaltered.

A little later in the debate I myself spoke warmly in Henderson's defence. I paid a tribute to his war services to the Government and justified the anomaly of his dual status as Member of the War Cabinet and Secretary of the Labour Party on the ground of its proved practical utility. In France, M. Albert Thomas occupied an analogous position. I promised that the Government would give this problem its careful consideration and would consult about it with France. The Government was not committed to Stockholm. The Inter-Allied Conference in London was a different matter, and we thought this very desirable. In conclusion, I begged the House not to take a line which might increase the troubles of the Russian Government, which was just then facing extraordinary difficulties.

My speech had the desired effect of moderating the temper of the House. The motion for adjournment was talked out and the difficult corner safely rounded. But the affair left Mr. Henderson in a stubborn and defiant temper which was before long to cause further trouble. A combination of pugnacity and sensitiveness is not easily appeased.

At this time the situation in Russia was causing us grave anxiety. For a good while past, its government had borne a most indefinite and unreliable character. While the official Executive was preaching a continuance of the War, it was allowing the utmost civil and military disorder. Bolshevist Commissars, representing the left wing of the Soviet, incited the troops to abandon the War and shoot their officers. They persuaded workmen to leave their tasks in munition factories. There was no certainty who was really governing Russia. At the beginning of August, the whole government fell into chaos, and on August 4th, Sir George Buchanan told us in a cable "We are at present without a Government, so that there is no one to whom I can speak." A telegram of the same date from the Military Attaché at Petrograd informed us:

> As things stand at present, this country is travelling straight to ruin. No real measures have been taken during the last fortnight to reëstablish among the troops in the rear, either the authority of the officers or discipline among the ranks. Until discipline in the rear has been established and the troops are made to fight, there is not the slightest hope of an improvement in the conduct of the Army at the front. And while there is no discipline in the Army, the men in the railway repair shops and in the mines cannot be made to work.
>
> If things are allowed to go on as at present, there will be a general breakdown of railway transport in the winter, and that will result in a famine in Petrograd and in the Army. The only man at present with any magnetic influence among the Ministers

is Kerensky, and he does not yet understand the necessity of discipline. Among his immediate military advisers, none are men of character. The Socialists would prefer to run a class war rather than the national war, and to the mass of the soldiers this appeals as being not so dangerous. . . .

A few days later, Kerensky formed a coalition government in which the Soviet was only one of the groups represented. Its influence was to some extent overpowered and held in check by the other groups.

At the meeting of the War Cabinet on August 8th we discussed once again the question of the Stockholm Conference. We had learnt both from the United States and the Italian Government that they were not going to allow representatives from their countries to go to Stockholm. We were also opposed to the Conference, as was France. The Attorney-General had circulated to the Cabinet on the previous day the information that it would be illegal for any British subject to engage in conference with enemy subjects except with the authority of the Crown. Mr. Henderson was at first inclined to urge that this decision should be forthwith published, but after consulting with his Labour colleagues, he found that they were unanimously opposed to this being done before the Labour Party conference, which was to take place on August 10th, and he informed me that he agreed with this decision. He suggested, however, that instead of the Government announcing its opposition to the Stockholm Conference, we should wait until after the Labour Party meeting, for if this turned down the proposal, nothing further would be necessary. This idea was discussed with him at our Cabinet meeting on the 8th, and it was felt that it would be much more convenient to the Russian Government, and more conducive to the maintenance of good relations between the British Government and the Labour Party, that the working men themselves should refuse to attend rather than that the Government should announce their decision and thereby appear to dictate to the Labour Party. This course, it had been ascertained by personal enquiry, was also acceptable to the French Government. From this point of view the best course appeared to be to leave the final decision until after the meeting of the Labour Party on Friday, August 10th.

We decided that in replying to any questions on the matter in the House of Commons, Mr. Bonar Law should confine himself to stating that:

(*a*) The attendance of British delegates at the Conference would be illegal.

(*b*) Such a Conference could not be attended by British delegates without the permission of the Government.

(*c*) The whole question was being examined by Government.

(*d*) It was obviously one which concerned not this Government alone, and

(*e*) A full statement would be made on Monday, the 13th August.

Mr. Henderson was present at this Cabinet meeting, and took part in the discussion which ended in the decisions which I have here set out. Apart from him and myself, there were also present the other members of the War Cabinet — Lord Curzon, Lord Milner, Mr. Bonar Law and General Smuts — and in addition, Mr. Balfour, Lord Robert Cecil, Lord Derby and Sir William Robertson. I am not speaking alone from my own recollection, but from that of all these eight responsible statesmen, when I say that the impression we all had was that Mr. Henderson at this discussion recognised the impossibility of pressing the Stockholm Conference and agreed with us that it must be abandoned. Indeed, he assured us that he expected the Labour Conference would turn it down "by a fair majority."

Our surprise therefore may be judged when in the Press

on Friday morning there appeared the statement that Mr. Henderson was still in favour of sending British delegates to Stockholm, and would urge that view in the Labour Conference to be held that day. We were of course aware that Mr. Henderson held to the idea that Stockholm was greatly desired by the Russians, particularly by Kerensky. But it so happened that the last few days had seen a considerable change in the Russian situation. The power of the Soviet for the time being had been greatly reduced, and Kerensky's need to conciliate it by supporting its desire for the Stockholm Conference was now far less urgent. This fact, and the circumstance that the Russian Government was no longer concerned about the holding of the Conference, were communicated in a letter from the Russian Embassy which we received on Thursday morning, and which was promptly circulated to members of the Cabinet. It was in Mr. Henderson's possession on Thursday evening, by his own subsequent admission, when he was preparing his speech for the Friday meeting of the Labour Party. The letter was critically important for the issue, and I give it in full:

"Russian Embassy, London,
8th August, 1917.

"Your Excellency,

"In a telegram I sent to the Russian Foreign Minister three or four days ago I gave him an account of the statements made in the House of Commons by the Prime Minister and Mr. Henderson concerning the latter's visit to Paris, as well as of Mr. Bonar Law's statement regarding the Stockholm Conference and of the discussions which were taking place in the different Labour organisations of Great Britain as to the desirability of sending delegates to Stockholm. I also drew the Russian Foreign Minister's attention to the reply given by the American Federation of Labour to the French Confédération Générale du Travail.[1] In conclusion

[1] The American Federation had declined to send delegates to Stockholm.

I said the following: 'I consider it absolutely necessary, with a view to safeguarding the stability and closeness of our union with Great Britain, where the majority of public opinion is adverse to the Conference, that I should be in a position to declare most emphatically to Mr. Balfour that the Russian Government, as well as His Majesty's Government, regard this matter as a Party concern and not a matter of State, and that the decisions of the Conference, should it be convened, would in no way be binding on the future course of Russian policy and of Russia's relations with her Allies.'

"In reply to this message I have just received the following telegram: 'I entirely approve of the declaration to be made to His Majesty's Government in the sense suggested by you, and you are hereby authorised to inform the Secretary of State for Foreign Affairs that, although the Russian Government do not deem it possible to prevent Russian delegates from taking part in the Stockholm Conference, they regard this Conference as a Party concern, and its decisions in no wise binding upon the liberty of action of the Government.'

"I hasten to lay before you the above information, as I fear that the impression has hitherto prevailed that, in the words of one of the London newspapers, 'Russia ardently desired the Stockholm Conference,' and this argument has been put forward in order to influence British public opinion in favour of the Labour and Socialist Parties of Great Britain participating in the Conference.

I have, etc.,

C. NABOKOFF."

The importance of this statement was obvious, in view of the fact that the argument which weighed most strongly with Mr. Henderson, and on which he was going to lay most stress in the Friday Labour Conference, was the unpleasant effect on the Russian Government which our refusal to send delegates to Stockholm would entail. On the contrary, the Russian Government was now no longer under the heel of the extreme Socialists of the Soviet, by whom the renewed move for a Stockholm Conference had been fathered, and was striving to shake free from their domination still more. The holding of the Stockholm Conference at their instigation would not strengthen Kerensky's hands in his struggle with them.

Knowing this; knowing too, that the War Cabinet of which he was a member was definitely opposed to the Stockholm Conference, and that it would be illegal for British subjects to attend it, Mr. Henderson went to the Labour Conference on Friday morning and delivered a passionate oration in favour of British Socialists sending representatives there. News of this was brought to me, and I promptly sent him round a further copy of M. Nabokoff's letter with a request that he would communicate it to the Conference. He did not do so, holding apparently that he had sufficiently covered the ground in his speech when he stated that there had been a tremendous change in the position in Russia since he was there, and that "Such evidence as we have, though it is slight, suggests that there has been a modification in the Government's attitude towards the Conference."

On leaving the morning session of the Conference, he wrote me the following letter:

"Offices of the War Cabinet,
2, Whitehall Gardens,
London, S.W.1.
10th August, 1917.

"My dear Prime Minister,

"Mr. Sutherland forwarded me the telegram signed by Nabokoff on your instructions. I had already seen it and in the course of my speech, I took the opportunity of intimating that there had been a modification in the attitude of the new Government as compared with the old to the proposed Conference.

"The Conference has adjourned till two o'clock with no debate, in order that the different sections can take counsel as to the course they are prepared to support when we resume this afternoon.

"I think I ought to inform you that after the most careful consideration, I came to the conclusion that I could take no other course than to stand by the advice I had given the day after my return from Russia. I endeavoured to make a statement of the position as I found it in Russia and since my return, both pro and con. It is absolutely impossible to estimate what decision the Conference will reach. If you would like to see me at its conclusion, I shall leave myself at your disposal for an appointment.

Yours sincerely,

ARTHUR HENDERSON."

In the voting at the afternoon session the effect of Mr. Henderson's plea was to persuade the British Labour Party to reverse its previous decision and resolve by more than three to one in favour of being represented at Stockholm.

The War Cabinet considered this situation the same evening. Mr. Henderson was not present. He had avoided the meetings of the Cabinet since the one on Wednesday, August 8th, to which I have referred, when he had learned that no delegates could legally go to Stockholm, and that the Cabinet was opposed to British representation there. In face of the report of the Labour Conference vote, the Cabinet renewed their determination not to allow British representation at Stockholm, and decided to approach the French, Italian and United States Governments informing them of our decision.

At this meeting a communication was read from M. Albert Thomas, stating that a telegram had been received from Petrograd to the effect that the Provisional Government had disinterested itself in the Stockholm Conference, and that M. Kerensky desired that it should not meet.

There remained to be considered the position of Mr.

Henderson. Feeling in the War Cabinet was very strong as to his action in thus publicly urging upon British Labour the adoption of a course to which we were definitely opposed, and one which we considered, in common with our Allies, to be detrimental to our position and war interests. Although I was profoundly unwilling to ask for his resignation, it seemed in the circumstances impossible to avoid taking firm action. We decided that I should send him a letter of remonstrance, the terms of which were agreed by the War Cabinet, and that for the time he should not be summoned to Cabinet meetings nor have Cabinet documents circulated to him. Before actually dispatching the letter, however, we agreed to make further enquiry from the Russian Embassy about the use which could be made of M. Nabokoff's communication of August 8th.

When we met again on Saturday morning, August 11th, there were two new factors in the situation. Mr. Henderson had tendered his resignation, at the same time informing me that he continued to share my desire that the War should be carried to a successful conclusion, and that he trusted to be able to still assist us to this end in a non-governmental capacity. And M. Nabokoff had given us full permission to publish the communication from the Russian Government, so long as his name was not mentioned.

I replied to Mr. Henderson's letter of resignation as follows:

"11th August, 1917.

"My dear Henderson,

"I am in receipt of your letter of this morning, tendering your resignation of your position as a member of the War Cabinet, and have received the permission of His Majesty, to whom I submitted your resignation, to accept it. My colleagues and I have received with satisfaction the assurance of your unabated desire to assist in the prosecution of the War to a successful conclusion, and they greatly regret that you can no longer be directly and officially associated with them in that enterprise. There are, however, certain facts with which it is essential that the public should be acquainted in order that they may form a correct appreciation of the events that have led to this regrettable conclusion.

"The first is that your colleagues were taken completely by surprise by the attitude which you adopted at the Labour Conference yesterday afternoon. You knew that they were, in the present circumstances, unanimously opposed to the Stockholm Conference, and you had yourself been prepared to agree to an announcement to that effect some days ago. At your suggestion however, and that of your Labour colleagues, it was decided to defer any such announcement until after the meeting yesterday. I was under the impression, after several talks with you, that you meant to use your influence against meeting enemy representatives at Stockholm. What has happened in Russia during the last few weeks has materially affected the position in reference to that Conference. You admitted to me that the situation had completely changed even within the last fortnight, and that whatever ground you might have thought there was for delegates from Allied countries attending such a Conference a fortnight ago, the events of the last few days had shown you the unwisdom of such a course. That was clearly what you led me to believe; it was also the impression left on the minds of your colleagues in the Cabinet and of your Labour colleagues in the Ministry. It was therefore with no small surprise that I received a letter from you yesterday afternoon stating that you 'ought to inform me that after the most careful consideration you had come to the conclusion that you could take no other course than to stand by the advice you had given the day after your return from Russia,' and that your colleagues subsequently read the speech which you had delivered.

"Surely this was a conclusion of which you ought to have informed the Cabinet before you entered the Conference. When you spoke at that Conference you were not merely a member of the Labour Party, but a member of the Cabinet, responsible for the conduct of the War. Nevertheless, you did not deem it necessary to inform the Conference of the views of your colleagues, and the delegates were accordingly justified in assuming that the advice you gave was not inconsistent with their opinions.

"The second point is this. Yesterday morning we received a most important communication from the Russian Government, in which we were informed that 'although the Russian Government did not deem it possible to prevent Russian delegates from taking part in the Stockholm Conference, they regarded it as a Party concern and its decisions as in no wise binding on the liberty of action of the Government.' And further the covering letter which accompanied this communication contained these words: 'I hasten to lay before you the above information, as I fear that the impression has hitherto prevailed that, in the words of one of the London newspapers, "Russia ardently desired the Stockholm Conference," and this argument has been put forward in order to influence British public opinion in favour of the Labour and Socialist Parties of Great Britain participating in the Conference.'

"Immediately on receipt of this intimation, I sent it over to you with a request that you should communicate it to the Conference. You omitted to do so. It is true that in the course of your speech you made a very casual reference to 'some modification' in the attitude of the Russian Government; but there is a manifest difference between the effect which would necessarily be produced upon any audience by an indifferent summary of that description and the communication to them of official information showing that the attitude of the Russian Government towards the Stockholm Conference was very different from what had been supposed.

"In these circumstances, your action does not appear to have been fair either to the Government or to the delegates whom you were addressing. They were left in ignorance of a vital fact which must necessarily have affected their judgment.

"I am sending a copy of this correspondence to the Press.

Yours sincerely,

D. Lloyd George."

It was of course inevitable that the Parliament should discuss the situation which had arisen, and a debate upon Mr. Henderson's resignation took place as soon as the House of Commons began its Orders of the Day on Monday, August 13th. In preparation for this debate the Cabinet reviewed the situation that morning, and decided that Mr. Balfour should have a personal interview with Mr. Henderson before he made his statement, to arrange with him how far he could make public use of the private official information concerning the issue. We felt that Mr. Henderson, being on his defence, should be given all facilities for utilising as much of the information as was necessary to his case and compatible with the public interest.

In the course of our Cabinet discussion, we reviewed the circumstances which had brought it about that while in May we were prepared to consider allowing delegates to go to Stockholm, in July we were definitely opposed to the Conference. We noted that the reason for this change of attitude was that in May the Russian Government were in the hands of the Workmen's and Soldiers' Committee, and, under its influence, were then inclined strongly in favour of the Stockholm Conference, and that the British Government were, in this matter, to a great extent influenced by their desire to support the authority of a newly formed body which had not yet firmly established itself. The consequence of the influence exerted by the Soviet, however, had been to shatter the discipline of the Russian Army and the organisation of the nation, and the Russian Government were at the moment taking measures to reëstablish discipline in their forces by means which were absolutely contrary to the principles of the Soviet, and showed that the policy of the extreme revolutionaries had been discredited.

To permit the attendance of British representatives at the Stockholm Conference, which was tantamount to countenancing fraternisation between one section of the Allied British public and one section of the enemy public, would be very prejudicial to the policy which the Russian Government were engaged on and were pressing forward, the very first item of which was the prohibition of fraternisation between Russian troops and those of the enemy.

It was recognised that no difficulty would be found in proving, on the above lines, that the conditions had completely changed since May, 1917, but that there would be considerable difficulty in doing so without embarrassing M. Kerensky.

This last point was the really difficult aspect of the problem. M. Kerensky was still struggling with the power of the Soviet, and to some extent dependent on its good will. He dare not announce his open opposition to it without putting himself in the gravest peril from a body which was always rousing the mob with the cry of a danger of counter-revolution, and used bomb and revolver freely to dispose of opponents. Indeed, he found it necessary to declare an interview published a few days later by the *Daily News* that he was not opposed to the Stockholm Conference, and in fact that he thought it of great importance. Any other statement would probably have shortened his life.

The debate in the House on the Monday afternoon added little fresh to the story. The chief fact that emerged from Mr. Henderson's statement was that evidently he had stubbornly made up his mind to press through the decision in favour of the Stockholm Conference, and that the various contretemps, such as the friction with his Cabinet colleagues before he went to Paris, and his detention on the doormat of the Cabinet room after his return thence, had only stiffened his determination. He failed to make it clear why he had lain low and said nothing of this resolve at the Cabinet meeting, where it had been clearly settled that delegates would not be allowed to go to Stockholm. He suggested that if we had forced him to resign on the issue of Stockholm before the Labour Conference on Friday, it would have made the vote in favour of Stockholm only more emphatic.

My own speech was carefully restrained, for I did not want to add any avoidable bitterness to the situation. I expressed regret that Mr. Henderson had left his colleagues in ignorance of his real attitude on the issue. I regretted that he had seen fit to slur over the important communication from Russia, despite my request to him to communicate it to the Conference, and I hinted the strong reasons, based on the Russian situation and the attitude of our other Allies, for abandoning the Stockholm proposal. Mr. Asquith followed me with a tactful speech, appreciating Mr. Henderson's past services but agreeing that an impossible situation had now arisen, and expressing his confidence in the fundamental soundness of Labour in regard to the War, despite this momentary discord.

About a week later, on August 21st, the Labour Party resumed its Conference and took a fresh vote on Stockholm. It is significant of the lack of enthusiasm for Stockholm amongst the rank and file of organised Labour that whereas on August 10th they had voted in favour of participation by 1,846,000 to 550,000 — a majority of 1,296,000 — on this occasion, despite whatever feeling was roused by the circumstances of Mr. Henderson's resignation in the meantime, the vote was 1,234,000 to 1,231,000 — a majority of only 3,000 in favour of Stockholm. This was in spite of a powerful and aggressive speech at the Conference by Mr. Henderson, defending his attitude and reaffirming the desire of M. Kerensky for the Stockholm Conference to take place.

The whole story is an unhappy one. Of Mr. Henderson's fundamental good will and sound patriotism there was never any question. When he left the Government all his colleagues profoundly regretted that he found it necessary to depart. But they realised that it was inevitable, in view of the complicated situation in Russia and its disturbing effect on the attitude of Labour throughout the Allied countries.

The revolutionary movements which sprang up here in 1917 caused us for the time a good deal of anxiety and made urgent demands on our powers of statesmanship and tact.

CHAPTER V

PROBLEMS OF LABOUR UNREST

British industrial restlessness in 1914 — Fresh disturbances created by War — Contrasting conditions of soldier and civilian — All-round conscription impracticable — Immense development of state and industrial control — Private enterprise still normal method in industry — Emergency regulation of labour essential — Labour grievances increase — Russian Revolution stimulates sedition — The Shop Steward movement — Attractive job to agitators — Defects of Trade Union organisation — Rank and file movement — Position in regard to strikes — Engineering strike at Barrow — Cabinet's firm action — May engineering strikes — Government stands firm: ringleaders arrested — Cost of the strikes — Workers sound at heart — Danger of leaving grievances without remedy — Letter of Master of Balliol — Commission on industrial unrest — Terms of appointment — Conscription dodgers — Leeds Socialist Conference — Four resolutions — My refusal to suppress conference — Its principal outcome — Seamen's attitude justified — Work of Commissions on Industrial Unrest — Food shortage and high prices — Restrictions on labour — Combing-out causes trouble — Blunders of recruiting officers — Local grievances — Summary of commissioners' recommendations — Steps taken to deal with food problem — Wage rate difficult — Munitions of War Act, 1917 — Birth of Whitley Councils — Reconstruction Committee appointed. Proposals of Whitley sub-committee — General approval by employers and Trade Unions — First Whitley Council — Industrial unrest abroad — Influence of the King in preserving industrial peace.

Of all the problems which Governments had to handle during the Great War, the most delicate and probably the most perilous were those arising on the home front. The issue in prolonged wars has always depended largely on the spirit of the peoples who waged them. That axiom was more applicable to this struggle than to any other war of which records exist, for the whole manhood — and womanhood — of the belligerent nations were organised for war and had been drawn into the war machine. Armies might gain successes or meet with reverses; but once great nations had become thus mobilised for war, they could not be forced to surrender unless their home front broke down. That happened to Russia. In the end it befell Bulgaria, Austria and finally Germany. To guard against it happening to Britain was the most anxious preoccupation of statesmanship here.

In a modern industrial State, the vast bulk of the population consists of wage earners and those dependent on them. Since Britain is the most highly industrialised State in the world, the contentment and coöperation of the wage earners was our vital concern, and industrial unrest spelt a graver menace to our endurance and ultimate victory than even the military strength of Germany. In this respect we started the War under a heavy handicap. Its outbreak came at a time when disturbances in the ranks of British labour were more serious and widespread than they had been at any time since the rise of large-scale industrial organisation. The old industrial tyranny of the nineteenth century was breaking up. A new and hopeful spirit of justifiable discontent was abroad, fostered by the spread of education. It was accorded sympathetic treatment by the Government of the day in their attitude to social questions and the ameliorative legislation they had enacted. But this did not satisfy the new spirit of dissatisfaction with economic conditions. Workers were agitating for a higher standard of life and a more dignified status than they had endured in the past. From 1911 onwards there was a steady development of strike action, and in the summer of 1914 there was every sign that the autumn would witness a series of industrial disturbances without precedent. Trouble was threatening in the railway, mining, engineering and building industries. Disagreements were active, not only between employers and employed, but in the internal organisation of the workers. A strong "rank and file" movement, keenly critical of the policy and methods of the official leaders of Trade Unionism, had sprung up and was gaining steadily in strength. Such was the state of the home front when the nation was plunged into war.

Happily for us, the shock of the national peril brought about a prompt and hearty truce between these warring interests. The Trade Union leaders proclaimed an industrial peace for the duration of the conflict. Strikes then in progress were brought quickly to an end. The autumn programme of labour disturbances was abandoned, and the trade unions decided to postpone for the time being their demands for higher wages and altered conditions. There was a higher rate of recruitment amongst the workers in some of the disturbed areas than even in districts which knew nothing of strikes and lockouts.

But if the immediate threat of unrest based on peacetime issues was thus dissolved in the waters of world conflict, there were new troubles and problems of infinite complexity created for us by the conditions under which industry had to be carried on in a world war. Its peacetime structure was shaken to chaos. There was a general post among the workers. Wages, hours, trade-union customs and regulations went by the board. The population was violently redistributed and set to unfamiliar tasks. How to control this shifting confusion, to force it into orderly channels, to seek out and eliminate the manifold discomforts, grievances, injustices and anomalies which it produced before they bred disaffection and revolt, were tasks that exercised our unremitting attention.

One main root of the problem was the circumstance that war divided the nations into two sections. On the one hand were those millions of men who had volunteered or been conscripted for the armed forces of the Crown. On the other, were the millions left in civil life. The recruits were drawing the slender Army pay, were subject to rigorous military discipline, and were called on to face danger, death and limitless discomfort in a service where working hours might extend all round the clock, and where an attempt to strike work might be dealt with by a firing squad. The Revolutionary Government of Russia resorted to this ultimate sanction of military discipline just as ruthlessly as the "bourgeois" Governments of the West. The civilians could enjoy domestic comfort and personal freedom, and make excess profits or earn extra wages too, that were often far bigger than anything they had known in peacetime — and certainly much greater than the pay drawn by their comrades who were fighting in the trenches. Between these two sections of the nation it was impossible to hold the scales even and impose on them an equality of sacrifice. The full use made of the voluntary system before we imposed conscription had the result that in the later years of the War an increasingly high proportion of those still in civil life were men who were averse to military service, so that our measures to secure further recruits from them to maintain the strength of our Armies encountered an ever-stiffening resistance.

Theoretically, no doubt, the logical solution of the difficulty would have been to conscript the whole nation at a blow and place alike the military and the civil sections under the same kind of control. But a moment's reflection will show that this logical solution was utterly impracticable. We had not the Continental tradition and habitude due to a century of conscription. Our civilian structure, industrial, commercial, professional, counting occupations which ran into many thousands of different classes and varieties, from the great factory to the village carpenter, could not have been brought under the rigid discipline that was possible and necessary in trenches within range of the enemy's gunfire. The ideal of nation-wide conscription for the varied tasks of national defence could be adopted as a principle which would justify all useful and feasible measures of Government control. But it could not be applied in the sense of enforcing a genuine equality of sacrifice and sanction as between those who went out as soldiers and those who stayed at home in civilian life. Nor could you equip those who were in charge of the operations of industry at home with the autocratic authority vested in officers in the field. Civilian occupations continued to be on the peacetime basis of employer and wage earner.

But they were brought under governmental supervision to an unprecedented and revolutionary extent. The State arrogated to itself the supreme right to direct, control, divert, restrict, or even suppress industry, wherever the national interest called for any such action. Sometimes it exercised all these powers. Direct production in old, extended, and improvised arsenals increased enormously, and the numbers of State employees multiplied manifold. Woolwich spread and extended by square miles. New factories and workshops employing scores of thousands of workers were set up by the State to produce guns, shells, explosives, bombs, aeroplanes, and every kind of war material. In most of these the management was under the direction of State officials, and incidentally, in economy and efficiency these men were an acknowledged success. Hundreds of other factories and workshops were commandeered by the State for war work, but neither the ownership nor the management was changed. The railways were placed under Government control without any change in ownership or staff. The same thing applied to the shipping of this country. The general policy of these concerns was subordinated to the decision of the Government to place the interests of State and war first and foremost. Subject to that principle, the owners retained the management of their businesses. The same policy was pursued with the production and distribution of food. The means of production and distribution were left in private hands so long as the owners conformed to the demands and orders of the State. The system was neither Stalin nor Roosevelt. It fell short of the former's ideas, but went beyond those of the latter. Many still think that it was more practical than either. It certainly produced prompter results, and that is what matters most in war.

Subject to these modifications, private enterprise was left to carry on its business during the War in accordance with its peacetime practice. Even in those concerns owned and run by the Government, the State was an employer, not a commanding officer. The result was that while the enlisted man was translated into direct and whole-time Government service, the civilian worker remained a more or less independent wage earner, and was still in most cases employed by a firm operating for private profit, even when its output was required by the Government. The soldier, however small his pay, had no sense of being exploited to provide wealth for a profiteer. The worker, even though his wage was much larger, felt himself a unit in a system which made profits for employers and dividends for shareholders, and suspected that if to help his country he put forth an extra effort, some capitalist would skim the cream of recompense from the increased output.

That extra effort was vitally needed. The War made unprecedented and insatiable demands upon our industrial capacity. The utmost possible production was required from field and factory and mine to supply our needs. At the same time, the fittest and ablest men were being drafted into the Army. Five million of them were withdrawn in the course of the War from civilian occupations; and although a million women were recruited to industry, the country was left woefully short-handed. A definite quickening in the application of labour-saving devices did not supply the deficiency. Under this stress we had no alternative but to adopt an emergency organisation of the labour available; and that meant calling on the workers to abandon for the time being many rights and privileges in regard to hours of work and division of labour which they had won by generations of slow struggle from their employers. Something of this process I have recorded when telling about the development of the Ministry of Munitions.

It was far from easy to achieve that object. The workers had already agreed, for patriotic reasons, to lay aside for a time their campaign for better conditions. On top of that, they were asked to renounce some privileges and protections already won. We had to secure their consent and coöperation by persuasion, not compulsion, for so long as the system of private enterprise prevailed, a worker could not be ordered to his task in the service of a profit-making employer as a soldier could be ordered to the trenches in the service of his country, even though the worker's task might be as vital for the national safety. The pecuniary rewards of the most exalted Generals did not amount to one tenth the profit earned by a successful employer of labour. Those who waxed impatient at times with the difficulty we experienced in our dealings with labour during the War, and who thought the Government too lenient and timorous in its methods, ignored this difference, which was the essence of the problem. Our workers were resolute, and quite justifiably so, however ready they were to do their bit for their country, to submit to no regulation which would make them mere platoons of industrial mercenaries under the command of private employers.

Throughout the War, this problem of the wise handling of labour was one that gave the Government constant anxiety. But by 1917, several causes combined to make it more than ever acute.

Conscription, which had been adopted in the spring of 1916, was now in full operation. The country was being rapidly denuded of its able-bodied manhood, and to supply the insatiable demands of the Army, inroads had to be contemplated on those workers who had hitherto been privileged and exempt by virtue of the national importance of their occupations. Dilution — the substitution of a proportion of unskilled workers in jobs previously reserved exclusively for trained craftsmen — had to be correspondingly extended. Grievances multiplied in regard to wage rates. The growing shortage of food and the difficulty of ensuring a really equitable distribution of the limited supplies, was the most serious grievance of all. The growth of munition works led in some districts to housing shortages and congestion. The meagre supplies of beer and the lightening of its gravity caused much ill feeling. "Swipes", as it was contemptuously called, was doubly unpopular. It was lacking in kick and in quantity. The brewers had not yet had time to make up in quality for the diminution in alcoholic content. The presence of the additional water was too obvious. Owing to heavy taxation, the consumer had to pay more for this poor stuff. Whiskey was very expensive and the districts that drew inspiration from that fountain complained of the drought. Then among the officials appointed by the Government to carry out its measures, not all were competent and tactful; for the Government, too, had to do the best it could with such people as it could get among a population from which most of the fit and eager men had been skimmed, and the immense tasks of the War compelled the creation of great new departments and staffs. In short, there was an array of causes, great and small, which combined with the general upset of the old order and the griefs and anxieties of the War to breed a spirit of irritation and annoyance.

In this condition the body corporate of the nation was assailed by a new infection. The coming of the Russian Revolution lit up the skies with a lurid flash of hope for all who were dissatisfied with the existing order of society. It certainly encouraged all the habitual malcontents in the ranks of labour to foment discord and organise discontent. Fishers in troubled waters, they did not create the unrest, but they took full advantage of it. Their activities sprang into special prominence in 1917 and seriously added to our difficulties. In Russia, they pointed out, the workmen formed a separate authority coördinate with the Government. There, they were more powerful than the peers in England. Their veto was effective in the administrative as well as in the legislative sphere. They dominated the military activities of the nation. Why not in Britain? That was the question asked in every workshop and at every street corner. The questioners left no doubt as to the answer they would give; and although the common sense of the British workmen provided them with good reasons for a different reply, still the Russian example had its allurements and was therefore disturbing.

This propaganda became closely associated with the Shop Steward Movement, which rose to prominence during the War, and was the active agency in most of the strikes and disturbances with which we had to deal. Of this movement, the development and aggressiveness of which caused acute trouble, a word of explanation is perhaps needed.

Before the War, a number of Trade Unions had begun the practice of authorising their district committees to appoint a representative member of the Union as shop steward in any workshop where a number of members of the Union were employed. These shop stewards were the lowest grade in the Trade Union hierarchy. The following passage from Rule 15 of the pre-War rules of the Amalgamated Society of Engineers, as revised in 1913, may be taken as describing their functions. Other Trade Unions appointing shop stewards adopted rules substantially similar:

(5) Committees may also appoint shop stewards in workshops or departments thereof in their respective districts, such stewards to be under the control of the Committee, by whom their duties shall be defined. The stewards shall report at least once a quarter on all matters affecting the trade, and keep the Committee posted with all events occurring in the various shops, and they shall be paid 3s. for each quarterly report; namely, 2s. for duty performed, and 1s. for attendance and report to Committee, these to be payable by the District Committees, and should a shop steward be discharged through executing his duties he shall be entitled to full wage benefit. . . .

(6) District Committees shall also have power to call aggregate meetings, or shop meetings, upon trade questions. . . .

The job was not an attractive one to the average efficient workman. The remuneration was negligible. The shop steward was liable to lose time by going round to investigate alleged grievances and infringements of trade-union rules and practices, and most men who took on the job lost money by so doing. But it was largely seized on by young men who had become imbued with ideas of increasing the power of the workers as a means of acquiring local influence and carrying on propaganda.

They were a miscellaneous array. Most employers in the early days refused to recognise them and would only deal with district committees of Trade Unions. Some shop stewards were appointed by authority of the committees. Some were elected by their fellow members of a union in a shop, but their appointment was never confirmed by the district committee. As the War went on and non-union diluted labour penetrated the shops, numbers of shop stewards were appointed by these new bodies of workers, to watch their interests. In some shops the stewards representing the different craft unions worked for their own men only, even in opposition to stewards of another union. Elsewhere they formed workshop organisations in which the interests of all the crafts employed would be considered jointly. This was particularly developed by those stewards who advocated the amalgamation of the craft unions in large combinations representing the whole body of skilled workers in an industry — as, for example, the National Union of Railwaymen incorporates the various grades of railway workers.

Before the War, neither shop stewards nor workshop organisations had any power as negotiating bodies with employers. But some of them were feeling after that power, and thus rousing the suspicion and antagonism of the established hierarchy of the Trade Unions. It must be admitted that the machinery of Trade Unionism was at the time in need of serious overhaul. One can have the heartiest sympathy with the aims of Trade Unionists, and yet recognise that the forms of organisation they had developed haphazard in their fights of the nineteenth century, and the principles they had sought to lay down for the government of workshop activity, were not always ideal in the interests either of workers or employers. The movement for reform of the system was interrupted by the War. The emergency legislation which restricted the use of the strike weapon still further impaired the authority of the Trade Union leaders, and gave local agitators opportunities of seizing the reins. These opportunities were increased by the introduction of dilution. For dilution was essentially a workshop problem, and whatever bargain might be come to with Trade Union officials, the actual arrangements for the introduction of diluted labour had to be made separately in each workshop, by agreement with the skilled workers there. In practice, that meant that they had to be made with the shop stewards, who thus became the key men in negotiations with labour.

In districts where the shop stewards were imbued with syndicalist notions of "workers' control" of industry, they tended to organise themselves together in a "rank and file" movement, hostile alike to employers and to official Trade Unionism. The first marked symptom of this new form of labour trouble was shown in the shipbuilding strike on the Clyde, in the winter of 1914–1915, where the shop stewards formed a "Central Withdrawal of Labour Committee." As time went on, the tendency grew for the shop stewards in a district or a large works to associate together for common action in local or works organisations which cut horizontally across the structure of official Trade Unions. From this there spread the "rank and file" movement, of which the prime agitators were in many cases associated with the I. W. W.,[1] a revolutionary syndicalist organisation founded in America, which sometimes did not hesitate to employ the weapons of arson, sabotage and seditious conspiracy to wage war on capitalism. The rank and file movement was antagonistic to the higher ranks of official Trade Unionism, and sought to go behind it and educate the rank and file in class consciousness, stirring them up "to force up wages, force down hours, and insist on such improved conditions of employment that the capitalists will find it cheaper to retire." It found sympathy and support in a powerful section of the British Socialist Party and the Independent Labour Party, which were opposed to the War.

This was the movement which, in 1917, fomented many of the labour troubles with which the Government was faced. It held its first Conference at Leeds, in November, 1916, when delegates attended from twenty-eight towns. At the second conference, in March, 1917, they came from thirty-six towns, and at the third, at Manchester, in June, 1917, from seventy-two towns. The movement caught on especially among the workers in the engineering industry and seriously increased the difficulty of munition production.

[1] Independent Workers of the World.

The position at this time was that strikes and lockouts in the industries concerned with munitions had been prohibited by the Munitions of War Act, 1915, and a system of compulsory arbitration substituted. While that measure did not actually prevent any strike from taking place in such works, its effect was that no official strike could be ordered, and any stoppage that occurred was local and unofficial. For some time it did in fact succeed in settling most disagreements and prevent a stoppage. In 1916, the number of working days lost through labour disputes was the lowest for nine years. But with the growth of power of the shop stewards, there was a marked increase during 1917 in the extent of labour stoppages. During the year there were 688 disputes, affecting 860,727 workpeople, and causing the loss of 5,966,000 working days. This total, though still well below those of the years 1912–1914, showed how serious was the problem, when every day lost diminished the means of effective prosecution of the War on land and sea and in the air.

Symptomatic of the kind of trouble we now had to face was the strike of engineers engaged on munition work at Barrow, which broke out on March 21st, 1917, over a grievance in regard to wage rates. The strike was discountenanced by the leaders of the Amalgamated Society of Engineers and its allied unions, who instructed the men to resume work at once, pending an arbitration upon their claim. But the men held a mass meeting at which they rejected this advice. Neither the unions, the employers, nor the Ministry of Labour were able to bring about a settlement, and finally on April 2nd, the War Cabinet considered the matter further and decided that the time had come to take strong measures. We resolved that a Proclamation, calling on the Barrow workmen to return to work within twenty-four hours, should be issued that afternoon (April 2nd). If the men did not return, the shop stewards who brought the men out on strike should be arrested under Regulation Number 42 of the Defence of the Realm Act for the impeding of the production of war material. When the men had returned, negotiations should at once be opened for settling their grievance as to piece rates.

The Barrow workers immediately responded to this by offering to send a deputation of their shop stewards to London to discuss their grievances; and the Minister of Labour agreed to receive them on condition that the men first resumed work. This they did, and a settlement was duly reached on the issues in dispute. But a fortnight's work had been lost.

Far more serious was the series of engineering strikes which broke out in April and May, 1917. These were in the first instance precipitated by the stupid and improper action of a Rochdale firm, which turned some women munition workers on to commercial work, for which the principle of dilution had not been accepted by the Trade Unions. It ignored a warning protest from the Ministry of Munitions and followed up its action by dismissing some of its men, while retaining the women. The directors were of that stubborn, autocratic type that was in its way at least as dangerous to industrial peace as the worst communist agitator. They would not deal with the Trade Unions. They informed the representative of the Ministry of Munitions, when he called to expostulate and bring about a settlement, that "as they had run their own business for many years themselves, they did not intend to alter their methods for the Ministry or anyone else; if they were to be forced to give way to the Trade Unions, they would close the works."

Eventually there seemed no other course but to prosecute the firm for breach of the Munitions of War Act. But action was delayed by the Ministry as long as possible, in the hope that the firm would respond to appeals made to it to modify its attitude. Meantime the workers of the firm had handed in their notices and on April 29th, a mass meeting at Rochdale decided to strike in sympathy with them. Next day the shop stewards in Manchester induced the workers in the engineering shops there to join the strike. By May 5th, sixty thousand men were on strike in Lancashire, and in the course of the next few days the strikes spread to Sheffield, Rotherham, Derby, Crayford, Erith, Woolwich and through the London district. While the original strike in Lancashire was based on opposition to dilution in non-government work, elsewhere the shop stewards seized the moment to protest against the withdrawal of the Trade Card system.

Although the Government brought the Rochdale firm to heel and made satisfactory terms with the authorities of the A.S.E. regarding the conditions under which the Trade Card was to be superseded, the strikes persisted. The Ministry could not negotiate direct with the shop stewards without betraying the recognised officials of the Trade Unions, who were being defied by the ringleaders of the strikes. The grievance of the workers was removed by the peremptory action of the Ministry and the stoppage at Rochdale ended on May 8th. But in Manchester, Merseyside, Sheffield and the London district it continued, and attempts were made to stop the power houses. The situation was repeatedly considered in the War Cabinet. On May 16th, we decided that the Government should adhere to its policy of recognising only the constituted authorities of the Trade Unions, and that no deputation from the shop stewards should be received except at the request of the executive of the Union.

On the following day we had a conference at Downing Street, at which we decided to take action against ten of the most violent ringleaders of the strikes. Eight of them were promptly arrested and placed in Brixton jail. The other two went into hiding. Consultations followed immediately between the officials of the A.S.E. and a conference of the unofficial strike committees, then gathered at Walworth, which resulted in a joint deputation from both bodies to the Ministry of Munitions, at which agreement was reached for the conclusion of the strikes. In most centres work was resumed forthwith, and after the arrested shop stewards had been released on May 23rd, giving an undertaking to abide by the agreement, the remaining men went back to work.

The strikes were ended. But they had caused a serious setback to our production of munitions. They had spread to the engineering shops of forty-eight towns; they had involved nearly two hundred thousand men, and caused the loss of one and a half million working days — more than the total of men affected and days lost in the engineering and shipbuilding trades between the outbreak of the War and the eve of the strike. It was useless to put the blame for these troubles merely on syndicalist agitators. The agitators had played their disastrous part; but they would have been powerless unless there had been genuine discontent among the workers, and unless here and there some employers, like the ones to which I have already alluded, gave provocation by arrogant unwisdom. I recognised that the only way to ensure peace was to remove the real causes of grievance and ill feeling. The workers were sound at heart. This had been clearly shown at the Annual Conference of the Labour Party, held in January, 1917, at Manchester. At that assembly, a resolution approving the action of the Party leaders in joining the second Coalition Government was carried by 1,849,000 votes to 307,000. Another, declaring in favour of a fight to a finish against German domination, was carried by 1,036,000 votes against 464,000. While, on the other hand, a resolution breathing class antagonism and distrust, and calling for the reconstitution of the Socialist

International with a view to controlling the peace settlement, was rejected by 1,498,000 to 696,000 votes.

The majority of workers were opposed to any weakening of the national unity or authority. But there was a real danger that the hardships, anomalies and annoyances of the times might be worked up by trouble-makers to wear down their sense of patriotic duty. Some of their grievances might be trivial; but a succession of pinpricks can be more exasperating than a violent blow. Information was reaching me from a different quarter about the growth of industrial discontent. The late Master of Balliol, A. L. Smith, who was very much in touch with Labour, wrote warningly to one of the Ministers on the subject of working-class discontent, and said of the men from whom he had gleaned his information:

> They are men with exceptional opportunities of judging, and none of them are alarmists, and all deeply uneasy about the situation. "A spark may make an explosion" as they put it. "Neither class knows how angry the other is."
>
> Meantime the talk about following the example of Russia is being heard everywhere. All agree that the right man sent down at once on the spot to hear both sides and give some real guarantee and not mere promises would settle matters.

Another correspondent, a prominent business man, wrote to one of my ministerial colleagues about the prevalent unrest, stating in the course of his letter:

> At the present moment a very large number, if not the majority of the firms who are working for the Ministry of Munitions are seething with discontent. . . .
>
> When Mr. Lloyd George first instituted the Ministry of Munitions, he stated that it was to be a Ministry without red tape, and the success of the Department in its early days was extraordinary. Every contractor was intent only on giving his best, and one of the marvels of the War was the wonderful response and the rapidly in-

creasing output from contracting firms under his sympathetic handling. But unfortunately . . . red tape is now rampant . . .

I determined to have a careful and sympathetic examination carried out to find what real and justifiable causes of unrest were present. This intention I announced in the course of a speech which I made in the House of Commons on May 25th, 1917, when I said:

"The termination of the strike affords a very good opportunity for reviewing the whole of the labour position. . . .

"I trust that as far as the particular dispute which occasioned that strike is concerned, it has been happily terminated, but I agree that there is a good deal of matter for further investigation. There has been great unrest in some quarters. The Government have their views as to how that has been fostered, but at the same time there are some genuine grievances which have assisted the designs of those who have got ulterior motives which have no special reference to the Labour situation, and therefore the Government have decided to appoint a Commission of Enquiry into the industrial unrest, to enquire and report upon the operation of all the war emergency legislation of the Government and its administration in regard to labour, and to make recommendations which will tend to minimise industrial unrest, especially in the shipbuilding and engineering trades, during the continuation of the War. It is proposed to divide the country into something like seven areas, and to appoint separate Commissions to investigate the causes of unrest in each of those various areas. An effort will be made to secure the services of a labour representative and of an employer, with an impartial chairman in each case. We thought it was better to divide the country into seven areas, inasmuch as it would be impossible for any Commission to cover the whole ground in anything like reasonable time; and to investigate the industrial unrest in each of those areas, with a view to advising the Government whether it is desirable to make any alterations either from the administrative point of view or to recommend legislative changes in this House.

As a matter of fact, the Area Commissions appointed were ultimately eight in number. Each of them had an experienced and responsible man of independent standing as chairman, and supporting him, an employer and a labour representative. Their Minute of Appointment was signed on June 12th, 1917. I urged them to do their best to carry out their investigations and complete their reports in a month, and gave them a completely free hand to adopt whatever procedure they should each consider best calculated to enable them to discharge their task as quickly and efficiently as possible.

By this method I hoped to get the information which would help us to deal with real grievances. It would not, of course, remove the troubles arising from the intrigues of deliberate mischief-makers. On May 26th, 1917, I received from a colleague a letter which he said had come from a man "whose information about the state of feeling in the labour world I have always found very reliable." This correspondent said:

> During the last few weeks the Independent Labour Party in conjunction with the Union of Democratic Control, have made a very big stride forward, and we are finding it extraordinarily difficult. . . . Their immediate object has been to bring about a strike, followed by rioting of such a nature that troops would be obliged to fire, and from this they hoped to evolve a general strike, which would bring the whole War up with a jerk here, in much the same manner as the revolution has stopped all military proceedings in Russia. . . .

The writer went on to attribute the recent success of Mr. Ramsay MacDonald and his allies in working up discontent to the fact that over one hundred thousand young unmarried men, who had taken shelter in reserved occupations, were now afraid of being combed out, and were strenuously supporting the U.D.C and the I.L.P. in every revolutionary measure likely to hamper the Government and stop the War, in order to save themselves from the trenches.

Confirmation as to the attitude taken up in this quarter was promptly supplied by the action of the Independent Labour Party and the British Socialist Party (from which the pro-War members had recently seceded) in summoning a joint convention to meet at Leeds on Sunday, June 3rd, 1917, "to hail the Russian Revolution and *to organise the British Democracy to follow Russia*", as the *Labour Leader* described it in headlines. A letter summoning this Convention, signed on behalf of "the United Socialist Council" by Mr. Ramsay MacDonald and other leaders of left-wing Socialism, was addressed on May 23rd, 1917, to Trades Councils, Trade Unions, Local Labour Parties, Socialist Parties, Women's Organisations, and Democratic Bodies. It announced that the Convention would "begin a new era of democratic power in Great Britain. *It will begin to do for this country what the Russian Revolution has accomplished in Russia.*"

Four resolutions were propounded for this Convention. The first was designed to hail the Russian Revolution. The second, on foreign policy and war aims, called on the British Government "immediately to announce its agreement with the declared foreign policy and war aims of the democratic Government of Russia." The third, on civil liberty, demanded, among other things, a general amnesty for all political prisoners and the release of labour from all forms of compulsion and restraint. The fourth, which attracted most attention, *called for the establishment, in every town, urban and rural district, of Councils of Workmen's and Soldiers' delegates, and proposed "that the conveners of this Conference be appointed a Provisional Committee, whose duty shall be to assist the formation of local Workmen's and Soldiers' Councils and generally to give effect to the policy determined by this Conference."*

Nervousness was expressed in some quarters as to the possible outcome of the Leeds Conference and I was urged to prohibit it, but I thought that it would be a mistake to treat it too seriously. The only measure taken by the Government was to support the War Office in its ban on soldiers in uniform attending. Events proved that we had gauged it aright. The Conference was largely attended and seemed imposing, and its resolutions were carried by sweeping majorities. But as very many of the "delegates" attending it were individual enthusiasts who came without authority or instructions from any organised bodies, their votes bound no one but themselves. The leaders were mostly men of the type which think something is actually done when you assert vociferously that it must be done. The most important result of the Convention was the irritation it roused among the members of the Sailors' and Firemen's Union, who were indignant that it had declared against demanding any compensation from the Germans for sailors murdered in the U-boat campaign. They held a protest conference of their own in the course of the following week, and resolved not to man any vessel on which peace delegates should sail who adhered to this attitude. Mr. Ramsay MacDonald was himself the chief sufferer from this. He thought it would be better for him to be out of England when the Leeds resolutions to set up revolutionary machinery on the Russian model were put into operation. His part of the business was accomplished. He had helped to summon the meeting. He had delivered a resonant speech to the delegates. Action was not in his line. So he decided to be out of the way. He resolved to visit Russia and Stockholm. As I relate elsewhere, the seamen refused to take him there, despite the request of the Government, and insisted on keeping him in England, where, knowing him better than I did, they felt certain he would be harmless. He must surely be grateful to them to-day.

The sailors were risking their lives to help the country through its agony. The Russian convulsion had undoubtedly upset the equilibrium of the worker everywhere. We felt it in our coal mines and in our munition works when everything depended upon whole-hearted energy and coöperation. There were disputes and misunderstandings which had a perceptible effect upon the output of material essential to victory. Mr. Ramsay MacDonald had done his best by speeches, by writings, by clandestine manœuvring and stimulating organisation to accentuate difficulties. The sailors knew there were men of like mind and purpose in Russia who were striving to persuade their fellow countrymen to break faith with the nations which had come to the aid of theirs at a critical moment. And quite frankly, the seamen thought they were serving their country by preventing people of this sort from coming together to foment mischief at this critical hour. They did not trust Mr. Ramsay MacDonald's patriotism. Can you blame them?

The English Revolution on Russian lines which was to start up passed off thus with little damage done. The Commissions on Industrial Unrest made rapid progress with their investigation into the genuine causes of uneasiness, and by or before the 12th of July, the reports of all the eight commissions had been completed, though a further supplementary report by the Northwestern Area Commissioners on the Barrow-in-Furness District could not be sent in until the 16th. On July 17th, Mr. George Barnes, the Minister for Labour, was able to submit to me all these nine reports, together with his summary of their contents.

A reassuring feature of these was their agreement that:

There is a strong feeling of patriotism on the part of employers and employed throughout the country, and they are determined to help the State in its present crisis. Feelings of a revolutionary character are not entertained by the bulk of the men. On the contrary, the majority of the workmen are sensible of the national difficulties. . . .

Mr. Barnes in his summary analysed the main causes of industrial unrest, as revealed in the reports. Some of these were universal; others were prominent only in certain localities, and did not appear to be serious elsewhere.

Among the universal causes of unrest, the most serious was agreed by all the Commissioners to be the high food prices in relation to wages, and the unequal distribution of food. While it was true that certain grades of munition workers were earning far more than they could have hoped to do in peacetime, the general level of wages throughout the country had not risen as rapidly as the general cost of living. Indeed, Mr. J. H. Thomas had declared that the railwaymen would be willing to forego the increases in wages they had received if they could be placed back on the old price level for the living costs. When to this was added in the workers' minds a suspicion that someone was profiteering at their expense, and the fact that sometimes they could not obtain needed articles of food even if they had the money, while they knew that others were getting them, the food grievance became not only a leading cause of unrest in itself, but "its existence in the minds of the workers colours many subsidiary causes, in regard to which, in themselves, there might have been no serious complaint."

The operation of the Munitions of War Acts, and in particular the restriction upon the mobility of labour through the system of the leaving certificate, was another universal cause of unrest. A worker engaged on munitions production could not leave his employer to take up work with someone else unless the employer gave him such a certificate, consenting to his leaving; if he left without this, no one else could employ him for six weeks. "Workmen have been tied up to particular factories and have been unable to obtain wages in relation to their skill. In many cases the skilled man's wage is less than the wage of the unskilled." The leaving certificate had been adopted to deal with a special emergency. It had already served its purpose. When conscription had been brought into force for the Army, there was no further need for the leaving certificate, and the Government had already decided to abolish it. Complaint was also made that the conditions laid down by the Munitions of War Acts in regard to the introduction of dilution and the altering of working conditions were not being observed by some employers, who played fast and loose with the regulations, and failed to consult their workers as they were required by the law to do, when making such arrangements.

A third general grievance was the way in which the Military Service Acts were being operated. It illustrates the difficulties which a country not accustomed to universal military training is bound to experience in war. It was of course inevitable that as the demand for recruits grew, men previously exempted by virtue of their occupation should be called up. At one time all the men engaged in certain essential forms of work such as munitions, shipbuilding, mining, railways and agriculture had been exempt. When it became necessary to claim some of the younger men for the army, taking them from safe and well-paid jobs in which they had thought themselves to be secure for the duration of the War, to the dangers and discomforts of the trenches, they were not only disgruntled; they felt that a kind of government promise was being broken.

The annoyance caused by the necessity of calling up some of the young, fit men engaged in the less skilled operations

Reproduced by courtesy of "Punch"

THE SAILORS REFUSE TO TAKE MR. RAMSAY MACDONALD TO THE STOCKHOLM CONFERENCE

"Hoist with his own Petard."

MR. RAMSAY MACDONALD (*Champion of Independent Labor*)
"Of course I'm all for peaceful picketing — on principle. But it must be applied to the proper parties."

of industries formerly exempted was unavoidable. But it was aggravated by a conviction, based on glaring if exceptional instances, that the wrong men were in some cases being taken, and that pledges given to the Trade Unions in respect of the calling-up diluted labour before skilled members of the crafts were taken, were not being faithfully kept. High-handed action by officers in charge of recruiting were reported, and there was widespread complaint that when grievances were referred to tribunals and arbitration boards or the Government departments, the delay in settlement was intolerable, and could only be cut short by a strike.

Further, there were other serious causes of unrest found in some, though not all areas, among which were mentioned:

The want of sufficient housing accommodation in congested areas;

The liquor restrictions;

Industrial fatigue, due to Sunday and overtime work;

Want of confidence in the fulfilment of Government pledges;

Lack of consideration by some employers of their women workers;

Delays in granting pensions to soldiers;

Inadequacy, at present price levels, of the compensation payable under the Workmen's Compensation Act.

The recommendations of the Commissioners were summarised by Mr. Barnes as follows:

(1) Food Prices. — There should be an immediate reduction in price, the increased price of food being borne to some extent by the Government, and a better system of distribution is required.

(2) Industrial Councils, etc.—The Principle of the Whitley Report should be adopted; each trade should have a constitution on these lines.

(3) Changes with a view to further increase of output should

be made the subject of an authoritative statement by the Government.

(4) Labour should take part in the affairs of the community as partners, rather than as servants.

(5) The greatest publicity possible should be given to the abolition of Leaving Certificates.

(6) The Government should make a statement as to the variation of pledges already given.

(7) The £1 maximum under the Workmen's Compensation Act should be raised.

(8) Announcements should be made of policy as regards housing.

(9) A system should be inaugurated whereby skilled supervisors and others on day rates should receive a bonus.

(10) Closer contact should be set up between employer and employed.

(11) Pensions Committees should have a larger discretion in their treatment of men discharged from the Army.

(12) Agricultural wages in the Western Area, now as low as 14s. to 17s. a week, should be raised to 25s. a week.

(13) Coloured labour should not be employed in the ports.

(14) A higher taxation of wealth is urged by one Commissioner.

In addition to the above recommendations, the recruiting system is universally regarded as requiring most careful handling. In some areas an increase in the supplies of alcoholic liquor is demanded. The coördination of Government Departments dealing with labour is reported as an urgent matter; and an appeal for increase of publicity and fuller explanation of Government proposals is made in several of the reports. . . .

The findings of these commissions proved invaluable to the Government in its task of dealing with the grievances of the workers, and allaying industrial discontent.

The problem of the distribution and price of food was of course the special preoccupation of the Food Ministry, the activities of which I have described in another chapter. Food remained a grave and difficult issue throughout the War. Not until a general system of compulsorily rationing the consumer was introduced, were we able to surmount the difficulties of securing an approximately fair distribution of the available supplies. When compulsory restriction of food supplies was first suggested in the early spring, Labour resistance was so strong that we decided on the recommendation of Mr. Henderson to postpone it. By fixing a maximum price for bread we were able to limit to some extent the mounting cost of living, and something was done for the munition workers by pressing forward the extension of canteens for them, where they could be sure of getting good food at reasonable prices. So successful were we in this that we actually had a complaint by a Member of Parliament on October 24th, 1917, that in one munition area, "the excellence of the arrangements . . . in providing high-class but economical meals to the public is a menace to the existence of privately owned restaurants and cafés"! The objector was informed, in answer, that "we shall certainly do nothing to interfere with the proper provision of food for our munition workers."

The most immediate industrial problem was that of the anomalies in the worker's wage. To secure the acceptance of dilution by the Trade Unions, the Government had promised that the extra hands introduced should be paid the same piece rates as had formerly been received by the skilled Trade Union workers. The result was that as improved processes and mass-production methods were introduced, many piece workers earned a very considerable wage, while the experienced skilled men who had trained them, and who were themselves employed on more difficult operations of craftsmanship, paid at time rates, earned much smaller sums. This was a galling situation for the skilled and experienced worker, particularly as the system of the leaving certificate prevented him from throwing up his skilled job and going off to take up a semi-skilled job where he could earn as much as a less highly skilled worker.

On July 18th, Dr. Addison left the Ministry of Munitions to become Minister for Reconstruction, and was replaced by Mr. Winston Churchill. Action was immediately taken by him to carry out the recommendations of the Commission. He introduced an Amending Act to give him the necessary authority to deal with the difficulties. Gradually there was a perceptible improvement in the Labour situation. The feeling of malaise evaporated and a healthier atmosphere was restored.

The satisfactory results of the Munitions of War Act, 1917, were shown by the fact that on November 6th, 1917, the Labour member for Attercliffe, Mr. Anderson, could state in the House of Commons that:

"We have at this moment a much better atmosphere, in which there is far less industrial tension than there was sometime back. . . . I hold no brief for the present Minister of Munitions. I believe he has his personal and political detractors — I am not concerned with them one way or the other — but in my opinion he has brought courage and a certain quality of imagination to the task of dealing with labour questions since he became Minister of Munitions. Because of that, the situation has perceptibly improved, and I hope he will go on in the same direction. . . ."

The shop steward movement, which continued to cause us trouble throughout the year, had indicated that there was need for a revision of the machinery of negotiation between employers and workers. In this connection an important development of 1917 was the birth of the "Whitley Council." A Reconstruction Committee had been set up in 1916 by Mr. Asquith, primarily with the object of making preparations for the restoration of peacetime conditions on a sound system when the War ended. I decided that it was desirable to extend considerably its terms of reference. On February 15th, 1917, I announced to the War Cabinet the names of a new Reconstruction Committee, the terms of reference of which should be:

(1) To consider the Terms of Reference and composition of the existing Sub-committees of the Reconstruction Committee.

(2) To consider what further enquiries should be made in connection with reconstruction.

(3) To consider reports made to the Prime Minister from the Sub-committees.

(4) To recommend to the War Cabinet what immediate action should be taken in connection with the reports of the Sub-committees.

One of these sub-committees, under the chairmanship of the Rt. Hon. J. H. Whitley, M.P., was charged with the study of Relations between Employers and Employed. On March 8th, 1917, it produced a report in which it proposed the setting-up of "Joint Standing Industrial Councils" in the better-organised industries. The report had a mixed reception from the members of the Reconstruction Committee. Mr. Montagu, the vice-chairman, was in favour of the proposal. Mrs. Sidney Webb, on the other hand, subjected it to a torrent of destructive criticism, and concluded with the assertion that such Councils could only be set up in the Railway and Postal services; and declared:

> "I cannot imagine that it would be worth while the Government committing itself to such a harmless but insignificant project, or that it could be, with any wisdom, separately promulgated apart from other items in the Government Reconstruction Programme on the Relations of Employers and Employed."

Mr. Whitley's Committee made prompt rejoinder to her criticisms, and it was eventually decided by the War Cabinet on June 7th, 1917, to circulate the Report to the leading Trade Unions and Employers' Federations, and to the Commissioners on Industrial Unrest, for their views. On June 19th we took the further decision to publish the Report.

The Commissioners on Industrial Unrest took a warmly favourable view of the proposals of the Whitley Committee. Their attitude is well expressed in the following extract from the Report of the Commission on the Northwestern Area, which included the very disturbed districts of Lancashire:

> We have been very much impressed by the report of the Reconstruction Committee on the "Relations between Employers and Employed." We have had the opportunity of putting before important deputations of employers and men these proposals, and asking their opinion on them. Although they all expressed a natural desire to consider them more fully, yet the principle at the bottom of them was received with cordial approval. This principle, which seems to us to be a statesmanlike proposal of the best method of dealing with unrest, and includes within its scope much that we have already said about the necessity for decentralisation and local control, is set out in Section 14, which, to our mind, is exactly what is needed in this area to allay many causes of Industrial Unrest.

It was not until the autumn that we had collected from Trade Unions and Employers' Associations a sufficiently large number of replies to satisfy us that there was general approval of the Whitley Report. When this was assured, we announced, on October 25th, 1917, our official adoption of the Report, and expressed our hope that its recommendations would be carried into effect. The Ministry of Labour proceeded to invite employers and workers into conference, in suitable industries, with a view to the setting-up of Joint

Industrial Councils. The First National Whitley Council, that for the pottery industry, was announced on December 21st, 1917. In May, 1918, the Whitley system was introduced into the shipbuilding industry. Engineering held aloof, but continuous efforts throughout 1917 resulted in an agreement on December 20th, 1917, between the Engineering Employers' Federation and a number of Trade Unions, by which arrangements were made for discussion and negotiation between the employers and works committees of shop stewards. During the latter part of the War and the immediate post-War period, some seventy-three joint councils were set up in various industries and civil administrations, and they served a very valuable purpose in helping the country through the difficult period of readjustment after the War, though many of them functioned only for a short time, and then fell into abeyance. While a number of industries failed to adapt the system successfully to their particular conditions, Whitleyism has worked admirably in others, and has made a real contribution to industrial harmony.

As one reviews the various causes which led to industrial unrest in 1917, the bewilderments and hardships of the time, war-tiredness, the ghastly losses, the deepening and intensifying horrors of the struggle, the receding horizon of victory, and here and there the clumsiness and arrogance of employers and managers which all helped the insidious efforts to preach sedition and promote disturbance by which the workers of the country were assailed, one is not so much surprised at the extent of trouble which the Government had to face, as at the fact that it was no greater. Russia collapsed altogether in this year. France suffered a mutiny of her troops, a great deal of violent Socialist agitation, and in the last six months of the year was buzzing with rumours of treasonable plots, which culminated in the arrest of certain prominent journalists, and the levelling of a charge of high treason against M. Malvy, the former Minister of the Interior, and M. Caillaux, an ex-Premier. Italy was seething with disaffection and sedition, which brought about the outbreak of food riots in the autumn and contributed in a measure to the collapse of the 2nd Army at Caporetto. Germany had a crop of strikes, and in July a mutiny broke out in the navy, of which the object was to force an immediate peace. The Imperial Government only succeeded in keeping the nation quiet by promising very far-reaching constitutional reforms. The same situation developed in Austria. There also a promise of far-reaching reforms had to be made. This undertaking and the victory of Caporetto quieted temporarily the discontent in that Empire.

There can be no question that one outstanding reason for the high level of loyalty and patriotic effort which the people of this country maintained was the attitude and conduct of King George. I have already referred in an earlier volume to the way in which he encouraged the work of the Ministry of Munitions in its early days, and interested himself in the actual processes of the arsenals and factories, and the well-being of those engaged in them. In 1917, the King not only maintained but greatly intensified his efforts to come into personal contact with the workers on the home front, and to encourage them in their tasks. The mere list of the visits which he paid to munition factories, shipbuilding yards, and other centres of industrial and social activity would fill several pages of this book. Wherever sorrow fell or trouble threatened, the King made it his business to look into the matter personally. On February 4th, 1917, for example, he went down to Silvertown, where a disastrous explosion had just occurred in a munition works, and visited the bereaved and homeless workers. In March and April, he paid a series of visits to Projectile and Filling Factories in the Home

Counties and London district. In May, when the dangerous series of strikes broke out in Lancashire, the King arranged to spend a week touring the areas where the trouble was most acute — Merseyside, the Manchester district, Morecambe and Barrow, and proceeding on to Workington and Gretna, visiting the leading munition factories and shipyards. Doubts were expressed in the War Cabinet as to the wisdom of his action, but I was confident that he would be safe among his own people, and authorised Mr. Arthur Henderson to make arrangements for the King to meet personally the leading Trade Unionists in each place that he visited. It is significant that the strikes broke down the day after he completed this tour.

In mid-June the King again made an extended tour — this time of the shipyards of the northeast coast, Tyne, Tees and Humber. He visited some two dozen shipbuilding and marine engineering works at Middlesbrough, Stockton-on-Tees, the Hartlepools, Sunderland, North Sands, Howden, Wallsend, Walker-on-Tyne, North Shields and Hull. We were straining every nerve at that time to expedite shipbuilding in order to make good the disastrous losses we had suffered in the submarine campaign, and the King's visit was of the utmost value in stimulating the shipwrights in their urgent task.

The Clyde was always a danger spot for labour trouble. In mid-September the King spent four or five days there, and visited more than two dozen shipyards and steelworks. So far as I can recall, neither these nor any other of the innumerable visits he paid during the year to places where industrial unrest was present or threatening were marred by any kind of unpleasantness. On the contrary, the loyalty of the people was heartened to new vigour by the presence of their Sovereign in their midst, and by the warm personal interest he showed in their work and their anxieties. In estimating the value of the different factors which conduced to the maintenance of our home front in 1917, a very high place must be given to the affection inspired by the King, and the unremitting diligence with which he set himself in those dark days to discharge the functions of his high office.

CHAPTER VI

ELECTORAL REFORM

Outstanding electoral problems — General election during War undesirable — Life of Parliament prolonged — Power to consult country essential for democratic Government — A second prolongation — Special Register Bill — Controversy over issues raised — Position in December, 1916 — Striking report of Speaker's Conference — Biennial revision of Register — Electoral qualifications revised — Women's suffrage — Decision to sound the Commons — Tory revolt: Sir Edward Carson's letter — Cabinet attitude to Report proposals — Further reprieves of the Parliament — Changed views on Women's suffrage — My support of the motion — Big majority for the resolution — Progress of the Reform Bill through Parliament — House of Lords fights for proportional representation — Mr. Bonar Law's candour — A remarkable progressive achievement.

THERE were three fierce party conflicts being fought out in Parliament and the country, when the great guns of war roared out their "Halt." Irish Home Rule, Welsh Disestablishment and the abolition of the plural voter. The two first were suspended until the War was over. There was a practical difficulty which forced us to deal with the third during the War.

Plural Voting was in terms of political partisanship the most controversial of the issues involved in electoral reform. Women's Suffrage, no less controversial, cut across the lines of party division. As to the need for reform of registration and franchise qualifications, and for a redistribution measure, there was fairly widespread agreement. And the support for alterations in the voting system by adoption of proportional representation, second ballot or alternative vote, did not follow strict party alignments. The terms of the resolution under which the Lords first rejected the Plural

Voting Bill showed that there was general recognition of the need for some comprehensive revision of the existing system.

The issue was forced to the fore by the circumstance that Parliament was already three and one-half years old when the War broke out. It had been elected, under the Septennial Act, in December, 1910, and had met for the first time on January 31st, 1911. But its first step had been to carry the Parliament Act into law, thereby limiting its own life and that of future parliaments to five years, and it was thus due to end not later than January 31st, 1916.

It was most undesirable, at a moment when it was essential for the nation to hold together and maintain a united front, that an election should be held at which the conflict of rival candidates would bring to the surface every point of difference between groups of citizens upon which an electoral fight could be based. To introduce these divisions into the trenches might have been fatal to the discipline and cohesion essential to an army.

Accordingly, in July, 1915, the Elections and Registration Act was passed, which postponed the holding of municipal elections due to take place that year, and authorised the abandonment of the compilation of a new Register. Mr. Long, when bringing in this Bill, stated on behalf of the Asquith Coalition Government that we were of opinion that elections should if possible be avoided till the War was over.

In accordance with this attitude, when December, 1915, came and Parliament had by the terms of the Parliament Act only another month to live, its life was prolonged for another year — a period cut down in Committee to eight months, *i.e.* until September 30th, 1916.

The situation which resulted in 1916 from these steps was in some respects profoundly unsatisfactory. There were few people either inside or outside of Parliament who wished to plunge the country into the distractions and divisions which a General Election would evoke. But on the other hand, acute divisions of opinion on certain important issues were developing between Ministers within the Government, and both in the House and in the country a good deal of dissatisfaction was manifesting itself with the way in which the War was being conducted. Should matters become critical, it was essential that the Government should have in reserve the power to appeal to the country for a verdict on its policy and a fresh mandate for its course. Should hostilities suddenly terminate, it would be necessary to consult the country as to the line to be taken in making peace. But if for either of these causes an election were to become necessary at short notice, there was no Register available, later than that compiled in 1914, which had come into force in January, 1915. There was no arrangement for enabling men in the Army and Navy who might still be on that register to record their votes, if they were out of the country, or for tracing and polling the votes of munition workers. It was generally conceded that no men had a better right to be consulted as to the future of the country than those who had risked their lives for its defence. There was also a growing feeling that the manner in which the women of the country had come forward to work on its behalf, taking the places of men who went to the front, ought to remove the last prejudice of those people — among whom I was not numbered — who had formerly opposed Women's Suffrage.

The approach of September made it necessary for us either to face the prospect of a General Election or to take further action for prolonging the life of the existing Parliament.

Accordingly, on the 14th of August, 1916, two Bills were brought before the House of Commons. The first, the Parliament and Local Elections Bill, proposed to extend the life of the existing Parliament for a further eight months — a period later cut down in Committee to seven months. The second, the Special Register Bill, provided for the compiling of a new Parliamentary Register, to be ready in May, 1917, the ordinary statutory dates for sending of precepts, preparation of lists, etc., being varied for this purpose; and further made an extension of the usual provisions for the removal of electoral disabilities, to the effect that soldiers, sailors and munition workers, who would have qualified for inclusion in the Register if they had stayed at home, should be duly entered on it.

The first of these two measures was duly carried by both Houses, and the life of Parliament extended until April 30th, 1917. But the second measure called forth a lively controversy. It was felt that something rather more far-reaching than the actual provisions of the Bill was wanted to ensure that all men who were risking their lives in defence of their country should be entitled to vote for the Parliament that would not only determine the terms of peace but the conditions under which the Britain for whom these men had fought should henceforth be governed. But the recognition of this principle raised the further question of women's suffrage, with which the Bill as originally drafted failed to deal. So after some debate had taken place, Mr. Walter Long proposed that the Bill should be dropped, and the Speaker asked to summon a conference, representing as far as possible all sections of political opinion, to examine the whole question of the Franchise and Electoral Reform, and see whether an agreed settlement of these issues could not be found.

Mr. Lowther accepted this task, and invited some thirty-two men representing the most varied angles of political thought on the issue in question, and including five members of the House of Lords, to serve in his Conference. It held its first meeting on October 12th, 1916, and promptly got down to a close study of the problems it had been invited to review.

When therefore I became Prime Minister in December, 1916, I had to count among my inheritances a Parliament whose lease of life, already twice extended, ran till the end of the coming April, a Speaker's Conference busily engaged in reviewing the electoral system, and as the only means of electing a new Parliament — if such a step became necessary for any sudden reason — a Register compiled in 1914, which omitted the names of hundreds of thousands who had the best of all titles to be electors, and an electoral law which made no provision for recording their votes when they were overseas on their country's business. Clearly it was a state of things which could not be allowed to continue.

On December 14th, 1916, a few days after I had taken charge of the Government, the Speaker approached me to tell me the stage which had been reached in the work of the Conference, and to ask whether we wished them to proceed. I asked him to be good enough to complete the task with all dispatch.

This he did, and the Speaker's Conference held its final meeting — the twenty-sixth — on January 26th, 1917. On the following day Mr. Lowther forwarded to me the report of its findings.

It recommended alterations which would have been regarded as sweeping and sensational even by the Liberal Party as a whole in pre-War days. But there can be no more striking evidence of the change effected in public opinion by a colossal struggle for freedom, which united all classes in one fraternity of effort and sacrifice, than the fact that the great bulk of the revolutionary changes had been approved unanimously by an assembly which included politicians of the most diverse possible views — extreme Tories, rigid Liberals, advanced Socialists. The possibilities of the future can never be accurately judged except by those who have seen mankind operating under the impulse of an intense exaltation of spirit.

The chief of these unanimous recommendations were the following:

The Register of voters should be revised and brought up to date every six months. The Clerk to the Local Authority (Borough or County Council) should be Registration Officer, and the cost of registration should be borne equally by the rates and the Exchequer.

The ordinary qualification for a vote should be six months' residence in the constituency. Plural voting was not to be altogether abolished, but closely cropped. One vote in a second constituency (apart from the residence vote) might be exercised, in respect either of a qualification as a University voter, or of the occupation of business premises in a constituency other than that where the voter resided.

Proposals were made for a redistribution of seats, and for their grouping as far as possible in constituencies of between three and five members, in which elections should take place by the method of Proportional Representation. The representation of Universities was to be retained.

All elections should take place on one day. Returning officers' expenses should be paid by the Exchequer. Candidates should be required to make a deposit of £150, liable to forfeiture if they polled not more than one eighth of the votes cast. A reduced maximum scale of candidates' permissible expenses was laid down, and other suggestions made for amending the Corrupt Practices Act.

Men serving with His Majesty's Forces should be entitled to registration as voters in the constituency where they had their home.

In addition to these unanimous recommendations, there were a few on which unanimity could not be attained, but which were adopted by a majority. Among them were the partial removal of disability for electors who had received Poor Law relief; the proposal that in single-member constituencies the election should be by the Alternative Vote; and the making of provision for an Absent Voters' List.

But by far the most important of the issues on which the Conference failed to reach agreement was the question of votes for women. On this, the Speaker reported that:

The Conference decided by a majority that some measure of woman suffrage should be conferred. A majority of the Conference was also of opinion that if Parliament should decide to accept the principle, the most practical form would be to confer the vote in terms of the following resolution:

Any woman on the Local Government Register who has attained a specified age, and the wife of any man who is on that register if she has attained that age, shall be entitled to be registered and to vote as a parliamentary elector.

Various ages were discussed of which 30 and 35 received most favour.

The Conference further resolved that if Parliament decides to enfranchise women, a woman of the specified age, who is a graduate of any University having parliamentary representation shall be entitled to vote as a University Elector.

We now had to face up to the question whether or not it was feasible for us, struggling as we were at that moment in the darkest epoch of the War, to dedicate the thought, the labour and the parliamentary time necessary to carry through legislation based on this report. I have already given some indication of the immense variety of new tasks on which we were just then engaged. From this point of view, the time might well seem the least propitious that could be found for the consideration of a far-reaching measure of domestic legislation and constitutional reform. But on the other hand, we had to consider that the continuing Party Truce gave us a unique opportunity of carrying through an agreed measure; that the remarkable degree of unanimity reached by the Conference augured well for our success; and that in any event some legislation would have to be passed shortly, either to renew the old system of registration or to impose a fresh one, in preparation for the next election.

We felt that before undertaking any large-scale legislation on the basis of the Report, we must be assured that the general opinion of the House of Commons was in favour of such a course being pursued. On February 6th, 1917, the matter was discussed in the War Cabinet, and we decided with one dissentient that the House of Commons should be informed that the situation with regard to Franchise and Registration had obviously been changed by the holding of the Speaker's Conference; that the House of Commons would have a very early opportunity of considering the question, but the exact method must be left for further consideration by the Government, which had during the past week been occupied with business of urgent necessity.

On 20th February, in reply to a question in the House, Mr. Bonar Law stated:

"It is clear that the House ought to have an early opportunity of deciding what action should be taken in connection with the Report of the Conference over which you, Sir, presided.

"After endeavouring to ascertain by unofficial enquiries what course would be most acceptable to the House, the Government have come to the conclusion that the best method of procedure would be that a Resolution or Resolutions embodying its decisions, should be moved on behalf of the Conference.

"If a motion to this effect be placed upon the Order Paper, the Government will give an early opportunity for its discussion."

By agreement with the Government, Mr. Asquith put down a resolution, approving the Report. Time was allotted for the debate to take place on March 28th.

As was to be expected, there was no unanimity amongst the Conservative supporters of the Government on the recommendations of the Speaker's Report. The opposition was essentially one of right-wing Tories. I had been warned to expect it. As far back as March 8th, I had received a communication from Sir Edward Carson in which he sent me a resolution signed by over 100 Unionist M.P.'s denouncing the suggestion of electoral reform. His letter was as follows:

"Admiralty, Whitehall.
8th March, 1917.

"My dear Prime Minister,

"The enclosed resolution signed by over 100 Unionist Members of Parliament was handed to me to-day and I think it right to bring it to your notice.

"Personally I was never in favour of the Speaker's Conference, and declined to have any share in it.

Yours sincerely,
EDWARD CARSON."

The enclosure was in these terms:

SPEAKER'S REPORT ON ELECTORAL REFORM

The undersigned members, having considered this Report, desire to represent to the Government:

(1) That the time is not opportune to consider proposals involving so many and great changes in the Electoral and Registration Law of the country.

(2) That the present Parliament has been prolonged beyond its legal term for the sole purpose of enabling it to deal with questions strictly pertaining to the prosecution of the War, and that it should confine its energies within those limits.

(3) That certain of the proposals must inevitably prove to be of a highly contentious character.

(4) That there has been no sufficient enquiry as to the expediency or practicability of many of the proposed changes.

(5) That no proposals for Franchise Reform and Redistribution which do not include Ireland should be submitted to the Parliament of the United Kingdom.

It was a disconcerting letter to receive from the First Lord of the Admiralty in my own Ministry. But despite this warning, I obtained the support of the Cabinet for the resolve to proceed with legislation to enact the recommendations of the Conference. The fact that only a hundred members could be found to sign a protest, proved that five sixths of the House of Commons (including a majority of the Conservative Party) were in favour of action on the lines of the Speaker's Conference.

On March 26th, the War Cabinet considered the issue, and resolved to go forward with the proposals including Women's Suffrage in spite of the formidable opposition which had developed amongst their supporters. We decided to recommend the House of Commons to adopt the Speaker's Report on Electoral Reform, and to introduce a Bill to carry it out, subject to the following exceptions:

(*a*) The question of Women's Suffrage, which should be included in the Bill, but as to which amendments should be left for decision by Parliament in accordance with the views of Members, without putting on the Whips;

(*b*) The question of Proportional Representation which the Speaker's Conference should be invited to reconsider.

Meantime it was clear that, whatever decision the House of Commons should reach in regard to the proposals of the Speaker's Conference, it would not be possible to carry legislation providing for a new electoral Register, and effect the compiling of such a Register, in time to elect promptly a new Parliament, if the existing House were dissolved on April 30th. So on March 27th, 1917, a further "Parliament and Local Elections Bill" was given a first reading, for the purpose of extending the life of Parliament until November 30th, 1917. This was duly carried in the course of April. I may here anticipate subsequent developments by saying that two further reprieves of a similar nature had to be secured for

Parliament before the War was over. In November, 1917, its life was extended until July 31st, 1918 — a further eight months; and in July it was given six months more. Before that last extension was exhausted, the War was over, and as the new Register was complete, there was no justification for further prolonging the life of a Parliament elected on a limited franchise which had already exceeded the term of its constitutional existence by three years. It is one of the little ironies of history that the very Parliament which enacted a shortening of parliamentary duration from the seven-year period imposed two hundred years before by the Septennial Act, should have reprieved itself by successive stages until its own life was longer than that of any since the Long Parliament of 1640.

The debate on the Conference Report was opened on March 28th, 1917, by Mr. Asquith, who moved a resolution in the following terms:

> That this House records its thanks to Mr. Speaker for his services in presiding over the Electoral Reform Conference, and is of opinion that legislation should promptly be introduced on the lines of the Resolutions reported from the Conference.

Since Mr. Asquith had himself appointed the Conference, it was eminently suitable that he should move this resolution. He recapitulated the circumstances which had led to its appointment, and the problems with which it had been invited to deal. And he expressed his enthusiastic welcome for its conclusions.

"That result is that we have in this Report what I confess I was hardly sanguine enough to hope for — 37 resolutions dealing with all the thorniest problems which have divided Parties and been the subject of embittered controversy during the lifetime of a generation. Of these 37 resolutions, no less than 34 were passed with unanimity. That is one of the most remarkable concordats in our political history. In my opinion it would not only be folly, but it would be something like criminal folly, if we were to throw away such a unique opportunity."

Before the War Mr. Asquith was one of the most inveterate opponents of Women's Suffrage. It was the only controversial topic that stimulated him to bitterness. His admission, therefore, that the work accomplished by women in the War had led him to change his views on the question of Women's Suffrage, and abandon his opposition to granting them the vote, constituted one of the most dramatic incidents in the Debate.

"During the whole of my political life I have opposed the various schemes which have been presented from time to time to Parliament for giving the Parliamentary vote, whether piecemeal or wholesale, to women. . . . My opposition to woman suffrage has always been based, and based solely, on considerations of public expediency. I think that some years ago I ventured to use the expression. 'Let the women work out their own salvation.' Well, Sir, they have worked it out during this War. How could we have carried on the War without them? Short of actually bearing arms in the field there is hardly a service which has contributed, or is contributing, to the maintenance of our cause in which women have not been at least as active and as efficient as men, and wherever we turn we see them doing, with zeal and success, and without any detriment to the prerogatives of their sex, work which three years ago would have been regarded as falling exclusively within the province of men. . . . I therefore believe, and I believe many others who have hitherto thought with me in this matter are prepared to acquiesce in the general decision of the majority of the Conference, that some measure of women's suffrage should be conferred. . . ."

An Amendment was moved by Mr. Salter, a respected Conservative Member who afterwards became a judge of the High Court, which would have confined our legislative action to a measure to prepare a new Register and secure the inclusion of soldiers and sailors in it, with means to record their votes if abroad on service. His attitude represented the point of view of those who did not welcome domestic reforms in wartime, either because they regarded them as an undesirable distraction from our main concern, or because they were opposed to the suggested reforms themselves.

Speaking in support of Mr. Asquith's motion, I gave a review of the electoral situation, and urged that it was of vital importance that we should make a provision whereby the next parliament, which would have to settle the problems of peace and reconstruction, should be really representative of the men and women who had by their effort and suffering made the new Britain possible. The moment a Franchise Bill was brought in, such questions as Plural Voting, University Representation and Women's Suffrage were bound to arise. Since the majority of the House would be on the side of such reforms as were outlined by the Speaker's Conference, the only result of bringing in such a measure as Mr. Salter proposed would be to have the majority in opposition to its limits, instead of in favour of its provisions.

On the question of votes for women, I reminded the House that I had always supported this, and that the heroic patriotism of the women workers during the War had now made their claim irresistible. Further, the domestic problems which would have to be faced after the War would intimately concern them, and to exclude them from a voice in choosing the parliament that would deal with these issues would be an outrage.

I admitted that the question of Proportional Representation was in a different category. It was not an integral part of the reform of the franchise or of redistribution. Whether it should form a part of the whole scheme was for the House to say. The other measures need not stand or fall by their verdict on it.

After a full debate, Mr. Asquith's motion was adopted

by 341 votes to 62. Thus, by a most emphatic majority, we were encouraged to put our hands to this very important constitutional reform.

It is hardly necessary here to recapitulate the long debates and controversies to which the new Reform Bill gave rise. It was brought in under the title of the Representation of the People Bill, and passed its second reading on May 23rd, 1917, by 329 votes to 40. Discussion in Committee lasted nearly until the end of the year. The clause according the vote to women was carried by a seven-to-one majority, but Proportional Representation was struck out of the Bill, and the Alternative Vote in single-member seats was carried by a majority of one. The third reading was passed on December 7th, 1917, and the Bill went to the House of Lords.

There the chief conflict centred round the issue of Proportional Representation, which their noble Lordships wished to insert in the Bill. With the Alternative Vote they would have nothing to do. For a few days the Bill became a shuttlecock between the two Houses, till a stage was reached where the Commons were being called on to consider the Lords' Amendments to Commons' Amendments to Lords' Amendments to Commons' Amendments to Lords' Amendments to the Bill. By that time the Lords had finally quashed the suggestion of the Alternative Vote, and in regard to Proportional Representation were contenting themselves with insisting that the Boundary Commissioners under the Act should prepare a scheme for a limited experiment of P.R. in one hundred constituencies, which should come into force if adopted by both Houses of Parliament. Pleading with the Commons to accept this compromise, Mr. Bonar Law, that sometimes disconcertingly candid Conservative, said:

"Any Second Chamber, at all events the House of Lords, is naturally a Conservative institution. We admit that. We agree also, I think, that except in time of war, and the unity with which

Parties were acting, it would have been utterly impossible to get the Second Chamber to adopt this Bill at all. It could only have been done after a big Party conflict, in which the whole feeling of the country was roused against the House of Lords. In no other way could it have been done. . . . I do not believe that the country cares twopence one way or the other about either proportional representation or even the alternative vote, but I do say that the country does care about the passing of this Bill. . . . If the Bill fails to go through now it will produce a feeling in the country which I am afraid to contemplate."

This was a striking admission. The leader of the Tory Party acknowledged that the country profoundly desired the Bill, and at the same time owned that in ordinary times nothing but a desperate conflict in which the whole country was roused against the House of Lords would have availed to carry it.

In the heart of a cyclone there is a patch of calm. It is with some satisfaction that I can recall how we took advantage of that vortex of domestic peace to carry through this great progressive measure. It was by far the biggest advance since the Reform Bill of 1832, and in some respects was even more revolutionary. It redistributed seats on a uniform basis throughout the kingdom. It reduced plural voting to its lowest limits. It gave manhood suffrage, and most revolutionary of all, it opened the doors of the polling booth to women for parliamentary elections. It increased the total electorate from about 8,350,000 (all males) to over 20,000,000, including about as many women as the total electorate prior to the Bill. It provided an efficient system of registration and various provisions for checking extravagance and corruption at elections. We had long called ourselves a democratic country. Not until this measure was passed into law could it be truly said that our parliamentary representation was elected on a basis really democratic.

CHAPTER VII

THE AUSTRIAN PEACE MOVE

Austrian Emperor's death; character of his successor — Dismal prospect for the Empire — Karl's anxiety for peace — Allied friendliness to Austria — Rumour of Austrian peace move in Scandinavia — Count Mensdorff's visit to Norway — Prince Sixte — Karl's envoy brings peace terms — Count Czernin's unpromising note — Attempt to divide France from England — Attitude of French Government to the notes — Prince Sixte's reply to Karl — Karl's attitude to Allied peace aims — No concessions to Italy — Karl's autograph letter — French Government favourably impressed — Secrecy of negotiations vital — Difficulty of discussion with Italy — Austro-Italian hostility — My interview with Prince Sixte — Conference at St. Jean de Maurienne — Sonnino opposes peace negotiations with Austria — Austro-Italian agreement impossible — Sonnino's large ambitions for Italy — Independent peace approach to Austria by Italy — Another interview with Prince Sixte — French answer to Karl's letter — Fresh peace offers from Austria — Record of the Emperor's verbal message — Italian demands unwarranted — Confused Italian situation — Karl's second letter — Details of Italian offer — A greaseless Germany — Sixte has unsatisfactory discussion with French Government — I urge Ribot to take action — Text of Karl's second letter — Count Czernin's four points — Italy the main stumbling block — My letter to Ribot — Anglo-French Conference in London — Cambon's suspicion of Italy — His amazing lack of judgment — Quality of French patriotism — Sixte *pourparlers* neutralised — Italy announces annexation of Albania — Conflict of French and Italian policy — Leakage in France — Ribot denies secret diplomacy — Ribot shows Sonnino the correspondence — Negotiations fall through — Danger of disloyalty between Allies — France utters a final negative — Karl's melancholy fate.

Now we come to an episode which furnishes a new illustration of an old historical fact that, where you are working with allies, it is just as difficult to negotiate an honourable peace as to wage successful war. Personal and national susceptibilities and jealousies cloud judgment and impede united action in both cases.

As the Great War dragged on through its third year, the strain came to be felt acutely in a number of ways by Austria-Hungary. The Dual Monarchy had with difficulty been held together in peace, and was very ill-adapted to resist the stress of prolonged hostilities. I once characterised it as "the ramshackle Empire", and the event of the War proved how apt was the description.

While the aged Emperor Francis Joseph lived, the anxieties of the Austrian Government could not become vocal in any appeal that hinted at concessions to the enemy. Dyed deep in the purple traditions of his Imperial pride, he upheld that pride of Empire with his last breath — his own and that of myriads of his devoted subjects. During the last year of his reign he was too feeble in mind and body to be told the truth as to the state of his country. But on November 21st, 1916, he breathed his last, and was succeeded by the Archduke Karl, who was his heir by virtue of a succession of tragedies that had one by one removed those nearer to the throne. Karl was of a liberal and pacific disposition. The Empress was a Bourbon. Her brother, Prince Sixte, served in the Belgian Army and regarded himself as a Frenchman. She had no love for Prussia and certainly no hatred of France. She possessed a strong personality and her influence over an amiable and amenable husband was considerable. She saw only too clearly the dangers to the Hapsburg dynasty of a further prolongation of the War. Personal devotion to a monarch who had become a legendary figure to his people kept together an assembly of antagonistic races in a semblance of Imperial unity. Karl possessed no personal attribute nor had he acquired any popular affection that would prevent the rival tribes of his Empire from falling away from his throne or even fighting each other. The Empress was more acutely alive to this fact than the Emperor, and she disliked the idea of risking her husband's throne and that of her son for the doubtful chance of humbling France and exalting the Prussian Kaiser.

It was no enviable heritage to which Karl succeeded.

The Austrian Empire was being dragged along remorselessly by its dominant partner in a ruinous struggle, the end of which was not in sight. The military party in Germany had vast ambitions of territorial aggrandisement which they still cherished some hope of achieving through the War, but their success would almost certainly lead to the subordination of Austria to Prussian overlordship. Once or twice already Austrians had been saved from disaster by the timely assistance of the Germany Army. If the Central Powers were ultimately victorious, Austria might expect to become, for all practical purposes, a vassal of Germany. During the War, she could not hold her frontiers without German help. After the War, she could not hope to keep her unruly subjects together without the same powerful aid. If the Central Powers were defeated, inevitable ruin, revolution and a break-up awaited the Empire of the Hapsburgs. It is not surprising that Karl and his intelligent consort looked out longingly for an early peace without victory or defeat, which might give him some prospect of holding together the shaky Empire over which fate had enthroned him.

His first act on succeeding to the Crown was to publish an address to his peoples in which he declared:

> "I desire to do all in my power to end, as soon as may be, the horrors and the sacrifices of the War, and to restore to my Peoples the vanished blessings of Peace, so soon as the honour of my Arms, the vital interests of my States and their faithful Allies, and the malignity of my Enemies will allow."

This declaration was in marked contrast to the tone of the German Peace Note, issued three weeks later. It sounded no note of bombast and triumph, and hinted nothing of a purpose of annexations or other war gains. It was the utterance of one who wished himself safely out of the War, on any terms he could honourably accept.

In the following months, persistent rumours gained currency that Austria was on the lookout for an opportunity to make a separate peace with the Entente. And in fact we learnt later that as early as December 5th, 1916, Karl was party to an approach being made through his mother-in-law to his wife's brother, Prince Sixte of Bourbon, who was then serving as an artillery officer in the Belgian Army, for the purpose of voicing his desire for peace negotiations.

Although Austrian statesmen had been primarily responsible for plunging Europe into the carnage of a World War, there was no feeling of antipathy towards Austria, either in Britain or in France. Germany was regarded as the real culprit. This was not altogether a just appreciation of the origin of the War. But it would be fair to say that, without the guaranteed support of Germany, Austria would not have struck the blow that precipitated universal war. British and Austrian swords had never clashed, and British and Austrian interests had not hitherto come into conflict in any part of the globe. And although French and Austrian soldiers had fought against each other on many a famous battlefield, still there was no feeling of rooted hostility on either side. They had in recent times been equally the victims of Prussian militarism. That gave them a certain comradeship in misfortune. The aged Austrian Kaiser was regarded as a genial and well-meaning potentate who wished to end his days in peace with all mankind. The names of Austrian statesmen conveyed no significance to the general public outside Austria. The French view of the origin of the War was that Germany engineered it, and when the suitable moment arrived put the pistol in the hands of the venerable Emperor and urged him to pull the trigger that not only gave the signal, but fired the powder magazine of Europe. At any time, therefore, when Austria was prepared to restore Serbian independence and emancipate its Italian population, Britain and France would only too gladly make peace and shake hands with the Hapsburgs.

In January, 1917, a story reached Sir M. Findlay, the British Minister at Christiania (now Oslo), to the effect that Austria was anxious to feel her way to peace negotiation. Baron Franz, who had been Austrian Chargé d'Affaires at Copenhagen, and was still attached to the Legation, was said to have discussed the matter with the King of Norway, and there were certain persons in Copenhagen who declared themselves to be instructed to make arrangements for a diplomatic talk, strictly secret, about the possibility of peace with Austria. Sir M. Findlay informed our Foreign Office in a series of telegrams about these reports, and it sounded serious enough for us to decide to send Sir Francis Hopwood (now Lord Southborough) to Scandinavia on February 1st, 1917, to investigate the story. Sir Francis visited Christiania, Copenhagen and Stockholm, and had several meetings with the alleged agents of Austria, but they failed to arrange a meeting between him and any authorised Austrian diplomats. Count Mensdorff was the last Ambassador of the Austrian Empire in London. His attractive personality and his obvious friendliness towards Britain made him a popular figure in political and social circles in London. The break with Britain filled him with genuine sadness; but he did not possess sufficient influence in Vienna to modify the wild counsels of the Austrian Foreign Office. Count Mensdorff visited Scandinavia at this time. It is not clear why he went there at this juncture. At any rate he and Sir Francis Hopwood did not meet. The "agents" suggested that the Austrian peace move must have been quashed by the Kaiser, who had just been paying a visit to Vienna, and that the Mensdorff Mission was countermanded. Probably, however, the Austrian Emperor had decided against attempting to open negotiations via Scandinavia, preferring to make use of his brother-in-law, Prince Sixte. Hopwood had an audience on March 6th, 1917, with the King of Norway, who told him that Count Mensdorff, "who was *triste,* very worried, and much fatter", had discussed with him the desire of Austria for peace and had hinted at proposals. He had said, however, that the Austrian Government was deeply disappointed with the Allies' reply to the German Peace Note, especially with that part of it dealing with the rights of small States and various nationalities. Count Mensdorff had pointed out that Austria was made up of small nationalities and of various races, and said that the Austrians had read the Note as an incitement to their people to rebel and bring about the break-up of the Austrian Empire. This is an indication of the practical difficulties which stood in the way of making peace with Austria. It could only have been achieved at that time by perpetuating the subjection of four fifths of the population of the Hapsburg Empire to the Teutonic yoke.

Sir Francis Hopwood was thus forced to return without making any direct contact with Austrian diplomats, or even securing incontrovertible evidence that a peace move was being sought from that quarter. But although his mission was nugatory, I felt we ought not to neglect any opportunity which seemed to offer itself for detaching any of our enemies from the powerful combination we were fighting.

We were shortly to learn through another channel that the Emperor Karl was sincerely desirous to open negotiations with the Allies.

Prince Sixte of Bourbon, the son of the Duke of Parma and brother of the Empress Zita of Austria, was a member of the former Royal House of France, and for ten years before the War he had been settled in Paris, and regarded himself as a Frenchman. Such was the prejudice in France against the Royalist connection that when war broke out, Prince Sixte found himself unable to join the French Army; but through the intervention of his cousin, the Queen of the Belgians, he and his brother found work with the Belgian Army, at first in the Red Cross, afterwards in the artillery.

Princess Zita had married the Archduke Karl of Austria at a time when there seemed no prospect of his becoming the heir to the Austrian throne. But the Sarajevo outrage unexpectedly left Karl heir-presumptive to Francis Joseph; and when at the end of 1916 he found himself perched precariously on the tottering throne of the Dual Monarchy, and looked round for some really trustworthy friend whom he could use to conduct secret negotiations with the Entente Powers, Karl naturally bethought himself of his brother-in-law.

A meeting was arranged in the first instance between Prince Sixte and his mother, the Duchess of Parma, who was with her daughter in Vienna. The meetings took place in Switzerland on January 29th, 1917. Very little appears to have passed then beyond a letter to Sixte from his sister, endorsed with a few lines from Karl, pleading that he would help them to make peace. Sixte told his mother the lines on which he thought any peace acceptable to France would have to run, and she brought this information back to her son-in-law.

On February 13th, 1917, Prince Sixte was again in Switzerland, to meet an envoy accredited from Karl, who told him that the Emperor was most anxious for peace, and would be prepared to consider it upon the following terms:

(1) A secret armistice with Russia in which the question of Constantinople would not be made an issue;

(2) Alsace-Lorraine and

(3) Belgium to be restored;

(4) The formation of a Southern Slav Monarchy, embracing Bosnia-Herzegovina, Serbia, Albania and Montenegro.

It is well to note that Italy is altogether ignored. The Emperor evidently contemplated a peace in which her claims were brushed aside, and to which therefore she would be no party. This attitude was maintained throughout the subsequent negotiations and was largely responsible for their failure.

Prince Sixte told the envoy that such a peace could not be negotiated openly, as both Germany and Italy would oppose it. If Karl wanted to make it secretly, he must send along some document which Sixte could pass to the French Government as a basis for diplomatic negotiations.

On February 21st, the envoy reappeared, bringing a minute that had been drawn up by Count Czernin, who had recently been appointed Foreign Minister by the Emperor Karl; and a secret and personal message written by Karl himself.

The note drawn up by Count Czernin was of a very unaccommodating nature, and would not by itself have served in the smallest degree to promote an early peace move. It was to the following effect:

(1) The Alliance between Austria-Hungary, Germany, Turkey and Bulgaria is absolutely indissoluble, and the conclusion of a separate Peace by any of these States is permanently barred.

(2) Austria-Hungary has never contemplated the destruction of Serbia. It is, however, necessary for her to be on guard in every possible way against the recurrence of such political activities as led to the outrage of Sarajevo. Otherwise, Austria-Hungary intends to renew her friendly relations with Serbia and to cement them by liberal economic concessions.

(3) Should Germany consent to relinquish Alsace-Lorraine, Austria-Hungary would, naturally, make no opposition.

(4) Belgium should be restored and should receive compensation *from all the belligerents.*

(5) It is quite wrong to suppose that Austria-Hungary is po-

litically subordinated to Germany; on the other hand, it is commonly believed in Austria-Hungary that France is completely under the influence of England.

(6) Similarly, Austria-Hungary has no idea of annihilating Roumania. She is, however, bound to retain that country as a pawn until she has obtained guarantees of the absolute integrity of the Monarchy.

(7) Austria-Hungary has publicly announced that she is at war in self-defence only, and that her object will have been achieved as soon as she is assured of the free development of the Monarchy.

(8) In Austria-Hungary there is no difference of privileges between the various subject races. The Slavs will ever enjoy the same rights as the Germans. Foreign nations have misinterpreted the feeling among the Slavs, who are actually most loyal to their Emperor and Empire.

The first paragraph of this memorandum seemed to bang the door against any hope of concluding a separate peace with Austria-Hungary. Its intention was, however, probably to protect the negotiators in case Germany should get wind of what was going on. They could also fall back on it if they found cause to suspect that the Entente were trying to use the negotiations not to make a genuine peace, but merely to split up the Central Powers.

The concluding paragraph was clearly intended as a retort to the remarks about the freedom and independence of small nations which had figured in the reply of the Entente Powers to President Wilson's Peace Note. Karl's notion of a Southern Slav kingdom was thrown over. As to Belgium, she was to be compensated out of a fund to which we were all to contribute.

The tone as well as the terms of Czernin's Memorandum would not have evoked on the Allied side any desire for further negotiations. A short personal note from the Emperor

Karl, by which it was accompanied, contained comments on Czernin's propositions intended to be of a more friendly character, although it did not advance matters much further. It ran as follows:

Secret —

To (3): We will support France, and bring pressure to bear on Germany with all our means.

To (4): We have the greatest sympathy for Belgium, and know that she has been unjustly treated. *The Entente and ourselves* will make good her serious injuries.

To (5): We are entirely uncontrolled by Germany, and indeed *against Germany's will* we have not broken off relations with America. We have the idea that France is completely under the influence of England.

To (7): Germany too [is at war for self-defence].

To (8): Among us there are no special privileges for particular races. The Slavs have full equality of rights. All races are united and loyal to the Dynasty.

—— *Our sole object is to maintain the Monarchy in its present dimensions.*

The suggestion in Czernin's fifth paragraph, and Karl's repetition of it in his note, that France was dominated by England, was an effort, though not a very subtle one, to engender distrust and dissension among the Allies, and rouse the pride of the French to assert and demonstrate their independence by giving favourable consideration to the Austrian proposals. It is clear that at this stage Austria hoped not so much for a separate peace as for an understanding with France about peace terms which might prove a lever to force general peace negotiations. It was an effort to detach France from the Alliance.

On March 5th, 1917, Prince Sixte laid these memoranda before President Poincaré. The President was not favourably impressed by Czernin's note, but saw in that of Karl a prospect of a basis for negotiations. He consulted with Briand, who agreed that the first step before approaching the Allies was to get a more explicit statement from Karl as to the terms he would make with France, Belgium, Russia and Serbia, and that then the allies of France could be cautiously informed as to what was on foot. Arrangements about Italy and Roumania could be left over for the moment. Both Poincaré and Briand were clear that only a separate peace with Austria alone should be considered, as there was no prospect of Germany at this stage consenting to any terms the Entente could accept.

Prince Sixte wrote at length to Karl, telling him of the reception by the French Government of his messages, and of the attitude they had taken up. He urged the Emperor to make a definite offer of peace in terms of the four main points that had been raised:

1. Restoration and independence of Belgium;
2. Reëstablishment of France's eastern frontier at the line of 1814 (*i.e.* including Alsace-Lorraine and the Saar);
3. Restoration and independence of Serbia;
4. Russia's right to obtain Constantinople.

The claims of Italy were not being pressed by France at this stage.

The outcome of this was that Prince Sixte and his younger brother, Prince Xavier, paid a secret visit to Vienna, which they reached on March 22nd, 1917, and on March 24th, had an interview with the Emperor Karl in his castle of Laxenburg, a few miles from the capital. Prince Sixte's account of this interview casts a sinister light on the German Peace Note and proves that the Allies had correctly interpreted it. He states that the Emperor told the brothers that he thought it essential to make peace without delay. He had tried without success to induce his German allies to agree to a peace of accommodation; but *"they were bent on exacting the terms of a peace of victory.*" If he (Karl) were finally unsuccessful in persuading them to accept just and equitable terms, he would be prepared to make a separate peace, rather than sacrifice the Dual Monarchy to Prussian ambitions.

The terms of a possible peace were discussed, and Karl showed himself quite willing to meet French wishes in regard to their eastern frontier, and the demilitarisation of the left bank of the Rhine. He also approved the restoration of Belgium. As to Serbia, the one point which stuck in his throat was the secret pan-Serbian societies, which had before the War been a constant source of anxiety and danger to the Government. If these were really suppressed, and Serbia would firmly discountenance any future efforts to foster revolutionary or Irredentist movements in the Slav provinces of Austria-Hungary, he would be willing to restore Serbian independence and give her the Albanian coast as an outlet to the sea. As regards Russia, the revolution there had made Russia's future war effort and war aims problematical, and he was inclined to say nothing definite about Constantinople. But the cynical selfishness which has thwarted every effort to establish world peace on just and therefore firm foundations was displayed in Karl's approach to the Allies. Whilst he showed the greatest readiness to give up Germany's conquests from 1870 to 1917, he was more reluctant to consent to surrender Austrian annexations of Italian territory. He was most unwilling to make any concessions to Italy. The younger Emperor felt bitterly about Italy's action in breaking away from the Triple Alliance and joining with Austria's enemies, and he despised the Italians for their inability to capture from his numerically inferior Army the Trentino and the coast line to Trieste, to which they laid claim. He told his brother-in-law that while the main forces of Austria had been engaged against Russia and Serbia, a few territorial battalions and his "gallant Tyrolese" had sufficed to hold all

Italy at bay along what had been originally designed in the Austrian plan of campaign as only an extreme line of outposts. Why should he, in the teeth of the strong anti-Italian feeling among his people, hand over to Italy a piece of Austrian territory which the Italians showed themselves quite unable to take?

This kind of talk was not very helpful. In view of the treaty under which Italy entered the War, we could not have deserted her now without being guilty of the greatest perfidy.

From his interviews with the Emperor, Prince Sixte returned to France, bearing with him an autograph letter written by Karl, which ran as follows:

"Laxenburg,
24th March, 1917.

"My dear Sixte,

"The third anniversary of a war which has plunged the world in mourning is now drawing near. All the peoples of my Empire are united more firmly than ever in the determination to preserve the integrity of the Monarchy, even at the cost of the greatest sacrifices. By virtue of their unity, of the generous collaboration of all the races of my Empire, we have been able to hold out for nearly three years, against the most serious assaults. No one can deny the military achievements won by my troops, especially in the Balkan theatre of war.

"France, too, has shown a strength of resistance and a vigour which are magnificent. We all admire without reservation the fine traditional gallantry of her Army and the spirit of self-devotion of the French people.

"And therefore do I note with special pleasure that although for the time being we are opponents, no real divergence of views or of aspirations separates my Empire from France, and that I am justified in hoping that my own lively sympathy with France, added to that which prevails throughout the Monarchy, will prevent the recurrence at any future time of a state of war for which the responsibility can be laid at my door. To this end, and in order to set out in a precise manner the reality of these sentiments, I request you to convey secretly to M. Poincaré, the President of the French Republic, the information that by every means and by the exercise of all my personal influence with my allies, I will support the just claims of France in regard to Alsace-Lorraine.

"As for Belgium, she must be fully reëstablished in her sovereignty, retaining the whole of her African possessions, without prejudice to the compensations she may receive for the losses she has sustained.

"As for Serbia, she will be reëstablished in her sovereignty, and as a token of our good will we are willing to grant her a just and natural access to the Adriatic Sea, as well as liberal economic concessions.

"In return, Austria-Hungary requires as a primordial and absolute condition, that the Kingdom of Serbia shall for the future abandon all connection with and shall suppress every society or federation of which the political object is the disintegration of the Monarchy, and particularly the 'Narodna Obrana'; that loyally and by all the means in her power she shall suppress every kind of political agitation, whether in Serbia or beyond her frontiers, that has this character, and that she shall give us an assurance to this effect, guaranteed by the Entente Powers.

"The events which have taken place in Russia compel me to withhold my ideas in regard to her until a legal and compact Government shall have been established there.

"Now that I have set forth my ideas for you, I will ask you to set out for me in your turn, after having discussed them with those two Powers, the opinions in the first place of France and England, so that a basis for agreement may thus be prepared, on the foundation of which official negotiations can be undertaken and concluded to the satisfaction of all parties.

"Hoping that we may thus be able soon to bring to an end the sufferings of so many millions of men and of their families, that now are in sorrow and anxiety, I beg you to be assured of my fraternal affection.

CHARLES."

Germany was to restore the independence of Belgium and to give Alsace back to France, Serbia was to be bribed at the expense of Albania, but not a word about Italy. Austria was to concede nothing in return for a peace her sovereign ardently desired.

Prince Sixte reached Paris with this letter on March 30th, 1917, and on the 31st he had a further interview with M. Poincaré, at which M. Cambon was present in the unavoidable absence of M. Ribot (Briand by this date had resigned and been succeeded by M. Ribot), and the Emperor's letter was laid before them. They were favourably impressed with its contents.

After some discussion, both Poincaré and Cambon were in favour of Prince Sixte proceeding to England and informing King George and myself of the proposals made by the Austrian Emperor. But in this they were reckoning without M. Ribot, who on learning later in the day what had taken place, insisted that he must himself play the part of the channel of communication with the British Government. He sent word to Sixte that he was inviting me to meet him in a few days' time at Boulogne, that he would inform me under a strict pledge of secrecy about the Emperor's letter, and make preliminary arrangements with me for the Prince to visit King George and inform him about Karl's proposals.

The matter of secrecy was vital at this time. For Karl had a well-founded fear that if it should get to the ears of the German Government that he was trying to negotiate a separate peace behind their backs, they would promptly take steps to render this impossible, by ordering him either to send Austrian troops to the Western Front, or to enter on an offensive against Italy, or otherwise destroy the atmosphere in which peace could be negotiated with the Entente; and even his life would be in grave danger. The fate of the heir to the Turkish throne, Prince Youssouf Yzzedin, was a significant object lesson of the peril anyone ran who proved himself inconvenient to the German authorities. It was perfectly obvious that any peace move carried through Austria would necessarily be a separate peace involving the abandonment of her alliance with Germany. No peace was possible between the Entente and the Prussian military clique that dominated Germany, until one side or the other was decisively defeated. Germany would therefore regard an Austrian peace as a gross betrayal and was likely to go to any length to avoid or avenge a desertion which would isolate her and trap her in a corner.

Actually M. Ribot's preoccupations as newly appointed Premier kept him from meeting me until the 11th of April, when we met by arrangement at Folkestone and he showed me the Emperor's letter under a strict pledge of secrecy. I have before me as I write the pencilled copy of the original French text which I made with my own hand at the time, on which I endorsed the fact that it had been handed to the President on March 31st, 1917. With it is a further pencilled note of the principal points which emerged in my discussion with M. Ribot about the offer. This runs as follows:

Wants separate peace.

Allies can prosecute War against Germany alone to complete victory.

Alsace-Lorraine

French Revolutionary Boundary — and get reparation, indemnity and guarantees on left bank of Rhine.

Suggests Cilicia for Italy instead of Trentino.

I considered that we ought to proceed with the negotiations but that we must avoid every appearance of a breach of faith with the Italians and must therefore carry them along with us. M. Ribot, however, was insistent that we should preserve complete secrecy about the Emperor's move. This, in his opinion, was rendered more difficult if another party were brought into the negotiations. I realised that it would add to our difficulty in preserving the secrecy which was essential to success in such confidential negotiations. But I urged that we must do our best to sound Baron Sonnino without betraying the Emperor's confidence, and we agreed that we should arrange a meeting with the Italian Premier and Foreign Minister at an early date to talk the matter over in so far as we could within this embarrassing restriction.

Next day, Prince Sixte had an interview with Poincaré and Ribot, and heard the result of the Folkestone meeting. He was gravely alarmed at the suggestion of telling Sonnino about the Emperor's letter, as he feared an indiscretion on the part of the Italian Government, which would assuredly have disastrous consequences for Karl. But his deepest apprehension arose rather from the fear that if Italy were brought into the negotiations, the Austrian Emperor could not obtain the consent of his people to satisfying Italian demands, and that the negotiations would therefore fail. There was a feeling of real hostility on the part of the Austrian ruling classes towards Italy. The fact that Italy was accused of betraying the Triple Alliance and taking advantage of her ally's difficulties in order to annex her territory, created an exasperation towards Italy which would make a separate peace with her almost impossible. It was for this reason that the Emperor's letter offered the Italians nothing in the deal. On the other hand, once the Italians realised that Austria was not contemplating any territorial concession to them they would deliberately give away the secret of these separate talks to Germany, in order to put an end to conversations which might leave Italy in the lurch. Sonnino himself was trustworthy, but this could not be said for some of his colleagues, and he might feel himself bound to tell them about the matter. M. Poincaré was of the Prince's way of thinking, as were the two Cambons, Jules and Paul. M. Ribot also reluctantly agreed that it would on the whole be better for the moment to withhold information from Italy about the letter when sounding them about their views on a peace with Austria. I regretted the decision, but as the letter was sent to the French President and it had been communicated to me under conditions of strict secrecy, I felt I had no right to go beyond urging the French to persuade Prince Sixte to permit us to deal frankly with Sonnino. This he could not see his way to allow.

A conference of the French and British Premiers with Baron Sonnino was arranged for April 19th, at St. Jean de Maurienne. Prince Sixte, who had intended to visit England, decided to wait and meet me on my way through Paris. This meeting took place on Wednesday, April 18th, 1917, immediately on my arrival in Paris. We had an extended discussion about the possibility of a separate peace with Austria, and I stressed the point that it would be essential to come to an agreement with Italy about the terms of any settlement it was proposed to make. I urged the Prince to allow us to state the position fully to the Italian Premier and Foreign Minister. I told him that he could safely trust the secret to both Sonnino and Boselli, the Italian Premier, but he was unwilling to increase the burden of personal responsibility which he was carrying by this extension of the circle to which the peace move was known, and I gave him my promise to respect his wishes. He told me that Ribot proposed to raise the matter with the Italians at the conference by referring to recent statements of Count Czernin about Austria's wish for peace, which had been quoted in Italian newspapers. I suggested that it would be even better to base the discussion upon Count Mensdorff's manœuvres in Switzerland, where I had information that he was giving out a good deal of peace talk, and the Prince warmly supported this idea.

On leaving me, the Prince wrote the following letter to William Martin, the official at the Quai d'Orsay who had arranged the interview:

"Paris,
18th April, 1917.

"Monsieur le Ministre,

"I am most deeply indebted to you for having overcome all difficulties and brought about a meeting between Mr. Lloyd George and myself. The interview went off perfectly, and must be of great value. Mr. Lloyd George expressed a great anxiety to see me again next Friday, on his way home. I asked him to apply to you to let me know at what hour I should call upon him. You see, I am still reckoning upon your unfailing good nature and upon your friendship for myself both for this, and also to arrange for me interviews with M. Ribot before and after my interview with Mr. Lloyd George.

"Believe me, Monsieur le Ministre, yours most gratefully and affectionately,

SIXTE DE BOURBON."

Next day M. Ribot and I met the Italian Premier and Foreign Minister at St. Jean de Maurienne. The Alpine snows had not yet melted in the valley. The conference took place in a railway carriage, drawn up beside the station. The chief subjects for discussion, forming the ostensible object of the conference, were Italy's aspirations in Asia Minor, and the question of Greece. When these had been dealt with, we proceeded to talk about the prospects of an early peace with Austria, basing this upon the rumours which had reached us from various sources that the Dual Monarchy was contemplating some move of this nature. The minute taken of our discussion notes that there was some conversation on the subject of the recent indications of Austria's desire for a separate peace with the Allies. I pointed out that the British Admiralty had absolutely no doubt that from a naval point of view the elimination of Austria would be a very decided advantage to the Allies. Provided that Austria made a separate peace with all the Allies, and not with Russia only, the British military authorities were also agreed that the military advantages to the Allies would be very considerable. I pointed out, however, that the conclusion of a separate peace between Austria and Russia would probably not be advantageous from a military point of view, but that it was Italy mainly that would be affected, since large Austrian forces would then become available for concentration against Italy. This was far more probable than that Austrian troops would be employed on the Western Front.

Baron Sonnino did not like the idea of any separate peace with Austria. He conceived that the Central Powers were endeavouring to entangle the Allies in peace negotiations. It would, he said, be very difficult to induce public opinion in Italy to carry on the War if peace were once made with Austria, and he did not respond at all to my suggestion that if Austria were eliminated Italy could then employ her strength in the realisation of her *desiderata* in Turkey. On the whole, therefore, Baron Sonnino thought it would be advisable for the Allies not to listen to any suggestions for a separate peace, all of which, he believed, were aimed at dividing them one from the other, and endeavouring to represent first one of the Allies and then another as standing in the way of peace.

Sonnino was mainly responsible for bringing Italy into the War on the side of the Allies. We therefore attached great importance to his views. We saw no prospect of inducing Austria to part with the territory for the redemption of which Italy had entered the War and borne such heavy losses. The Emperor Karl was reluctant to make any concession to Italy. Baron Sonnino's natural resistance in those circumstances was for the time fatal to any further progress with the negotiations.

Eventually the following formula was adopted on M. Ribot's initiative:

> Mr. Lloyd George, M. Ribot and Baron Sonnino had a discussion about the approaches which Austria might be inclined to make to one or more of the Allied Powers with a view to securing a separate peace.
>
> They reached an agreement that it would not be opportune to enter on a conversation which, in present circumstances, would be particularly dangerous and would risk weakening the close unity that exists between the Allies and is more than ever necessary.

Would M. Ribot and I have succeeded any better had we revealed to Baron Sonnino the whole of the facts? I doubt it. The reading of the Emperor's letter, in which Italy was not even mentioned, would have exasperated him. He was a hot-tempered man and once irritated he was not easily soothed. A few hours in a snow-laden valley would not have chilled his anger. Apart from that, Austria was not in the least ready to make concessions which the most reasonable Italian statesman would have accepted.

Bülow induced Austria to offer certain territorial concessions to buy Italy's neutrality before she came into the War. Sonnino had persuaded his colleagues to reject these offers and to fight for more. He could not have accepted the same terms after the heavy casualties which Italy had incurred.

The fact was that Baron Sonnino had vast ambitions for Italy, which he hoped to see realised as a result of the combined effort of all the Allies. He knew that Britain and France would fight to the end against Germany, and that America was now committed to support them in the conflict. A peace with Austria at this stage must necessarily be a compromise, out of which Italy would not have secured much. Sonnino was convinced of the ultimate victory of the Allies. He was therefore loth to contemplate a separate peace with Austria unless he could be assured that it would secure to Italy all the gains she might hope to receive through complete victory — the Trentino, Trieste, Dalmatia, and all the islands in the Adriatic. A peace that did not secure these, he assured us, would result in a revolution in Italy. Baron Sonnino declared that Italy had been actuated in entering the War by her passion to reclaim the *terra irredenta,* and that she could not possibly make peace terms with Austria in which these war aims were not realised. He declared that no Government could remain in office a day in Italy which proposed a peace without attaining these objectives. The people would sweep it away, would rise in revolution, banish their King and set up a republic on the basis of a fight to a finish. Satisfactory terms could not be obtained at this stage when the Central Powers were still winning great victories. Britain and France could not honourably throw over an ally which had come into action on our side at a critical stage in the War. That is why we concluded that nothing more could be done with the Emperor's letter.

We discovered subsequently that the Italian General Headquarters had sent an emissary, a week before our meeting at St. Jean de Maurienne, to offer to the German and Austrian Ministers in Switzerland a peace with Italy on the sole condition of the cession of the Trentino — neither Dalmatia, nor Trieste, nor even Gorizia being demanded. And although the offer was unknown to Sonnino, it was definitely stated by the Emperor Karl in a communication sent through his envoy to Prince Sixte, that Giolitti and Tittoni approved it and that the offer came from the King of Italy.

This attempt to make a secret peace with Austria was inspired by Cadorna's fear that the Italian Army had grown war-weary, and that the Italian people, who had never been as enthusiastic as their allies about the War, were on the brink of a revolution. A few months later, part of his apprehensions were justified by the collapse at Caporetto. But at St. Jean de Maurienne we knew nothing of the doubts felt in the highest military circles in Italy as to the morale of some of the troops. The unyielding spirit of Sonnino had no misgivings and the Italian peace seekers had not deemed it prudent to take him into their confidence.

On the following day, April 20th, 1917, I met Prince Sixte again in Paris on my way back from the Conference. I told him of the difficulties we had experienced with Italy, made the greater by our inability to tell Sonnino that we really had a definite offer to consider. "We have utilised the statements of Count Mensdorff and such information as we could get through other channels," I told him, "but it has not been easy."

I told the Prince that my impression was that Sonnino would insist on the Trentino, Dalmatia and the coastal islands of the Adriatic as his minimum demands for peace with Austria. Trieste might be a subject for negotiation, but unless something substantial on these lines were offered to Italy, she would hold out against peace, and as we were bound to Italy by our Alliance we could not make peace without her.

The Prince replied that there was little prospect of Austria making such concessions to Italy unless she very desperately wished for peace, and that Italy's war achievements to date could hardly be said to warrant Austria conceding to her the spoils of victory. I pointed out to him that we were now in the position, with America's backing, of being able to carry on indefinitely till we won a victory that would enable us to dictate terms, and if Austria refused to make an offer now that would placate Italy, she might have to pay more dearly still at a later stage. I said that I still hoped that these considerations would weigh with the Emperor.

On April 22nd, M. Jules Cambon saw the Prince. The latter gives the following summary of the interview:

"M. Jules Cambon told me that he had been instructed to give me the French Government's reply to the Emperor's letter. He first of all assured me that the secret had been kept from Italy by M. Ribot and Mr. Lloyd George alike. The latter, he said, was particularly careful in this respect. In view of the importance of transmitting the reply accurately, I asked him if I might take it down, and he dictated to me, as follows:

'No overtures of peace from Austria can be considered without an equal consideration of the views of the Italian Government. Now, the proposals which have been submitted to us totally ignore the claims of Italy, while we have ascertained from the conversations which took place at Saint Jean de Maurienne that the Italian Government is not disposed to abandon any of the conditions upon which it came into the War. This being so, there is no good in our carrying on negotiations which can only end in a deadlock. If, at a given moment and in altered circumstances, the Austrian Government were to consider that fresh efforts might well be made to secure a separate peace, Austria must then take into account the aspirations of Italy, which cover Trieste as well as the Trentino. We have greatly appreciated the feeling of sympathy for France and her allies which the Emperor has shown.' "

Prince Sixte wrote at once to the Emperor, sending him this reply of the French Government, and urging him to keep open the degree of understanding he had reached with France and England as a basis for a further advance towards peace. This letter he took to Switzerland and delivered to Karl's emissary, Count Erdödy, giving him at the same time a verbal account of the course the discussions had taken.

On May 4th, 1917, the Count rejoined Prince Sixte in

Neuchâtel, bringing him letters from the Emperor and Empress, urging him to visit them again at Vienna, as there were points about which they were not yet clear. He also brought a verbal message from Karl, stating categorically that he was prepared to negotiate a separate peace with the Entente, provided that he would not thereby be required to join in attacking Germany.

As regards the prospects of peace, the message informed Prince Sixte that Austria had already received five peace offers, mainly from Russia. But they included the one from Italy, three weeks before, in which nothing was demanded beyond the Italian-speaking portion of the Tyrol. That offer the Emperor had refused, as he did not want to be engaged in two separate negotiations at once. "Consequently Italy is now looking to gain further advantages by way of England, which is impossible. The Emperor is quite well able to defeat Italy, but why kill another hundred thousand men? Far better to make peace."

The Prince decided to accept the invitation to visit Vienna. Meantime he sent back to Paris the officer who had accompanied him as his travelling companion, entrusting to him an account of the verbal message he had received through Count Erdödy. This was passed over on May 9th to Poincaré and Ribot, and the latter wrote to me on May 12th, sending me a copy of the statement. M. Ribot's letter was as follows:

"Paris,
12th May, 1917.

"Dear Mr. Lloyd George,

"I am anxious that you should not be left in ignorance of any of the conversations which may take place between the people you know of, in regard to the intentions that Austria-Hungary might have of making a separate peace.

"In this connection, I am sending you a note summarising the declarations made three days ago, to a very reliable person. You will observe what is said in this note about the steps which Italy has taken with a view to making terms. It seems most unlikely that any request of this order could have been made, without at least the tacit authorisation of some responsible person. However that may be, the document which I am sending you is not without interest for the indications that it gives as to the state of mind of the Emperor, and of the resolve already formed to relinquish the Trentino to Italy.

Believe me,
A. RIBOT."

To this covering letter was attached a document dated May 9th, 1917, containing the message brought to Prince Sixte verbally by Count Erdödy. It ran:

Prince S. having written on 24th April to his brother-in-law that the English and French Governments could not make peace without Italy, and having intimated to him that, in the view of Mr. Lloyd George, the essential requirements of this Power would be the Italian-speaking Trentino and the Dalmatian Islands,[1] the Emperor replied to him that there was something in his letter which was not clear. A letter from the Empress indicated that this lack of clarity arose in regard to the attitude of Italy.

In the course of a conversation which took place on 4th May, Count E. explained that, as a matter of fact, peace had already been proposed five times to Austria since 1915, chiefly by Russia. As for Italy, she had done the same three weeks ago, asking for nothing but the Trentino. The Emperor had refused to respond to these overtures, so as not to duplicate the negotiations being carried on by Prince S. From the Italian requirements enunciated by Mr. Lloyd George, the Emperor concluded that Italy was trying to obtain through the mediation of her allies even more than she was asking directly.

Besides, these demands had no warrant in ethnography. The Dalmatian Islands did not contain Italians. Their inhabitants

[1] I had certainly urged the concession of Trieste as well.

would kill the Italians who came there. Even in the Trentino, a plebiscite made under a neutral and impartial administration would turn against Italy. In any event, the Emperor would not allow such a procedure, which would create a precedent for other nationalities.

The hypothesis of a rectification of the frontier on the Isonzo, which has been brought into consideration in the course of this conversation, is not ruled out *a priori,* but it was declared that the cession of Gorizia, through which the railway line runs to Trieste, was impossible.

While he could assuredly defeat the Italians, the Emperor prefers to avoid new hecatombs; so he wishes to continue negotiations in order to attain peace. He agrees to make a separate peace with the Entente, but he does not wish to be compelled for the time being to perform an act of positive hostility against Germany, such as it would be to attack her the moment that peace was concluded. He does not think that for her part, Germany will attack him. If she does so, he thinks he is capable of holding his own.

At the present time he warns the Entente that, out of eighty divisions, Germany has just moved forty-one from the Eastern Front to take them to the Western Front. He adds that the Russian soldiers — and even the officers — are constantly coming into the Austrian lines to ask whether peace has been made, and that they only shoot when there are Generals present. The Austrians are being careful not to take the initiative in hostilities. It is not the same on the German Front, where they continue to use their machine guns on the Russians.

During the final negotiations, an armistice would have to be concluded which would leave the troops in their present positions. Count E. thinks that as soon as this armistice has been concluded, the workers in the German factories would go on strike and would cease to manufacture munitions. [There were serious troubles in Germany on May 1st. In Austria, care had been taken to announce the arrival of provisions coming from Roumania, and food was satisfactorily distributed as May 1st was approaching; and this averted all trouble on that date.]

The Emperor thinks that a peace with Austria would bring about one with Bulgaria and Turkey. He considers that we should avoid the inclusion of these Powers in the negotiations so as to avoid wasting time.

Peace made, Austria would be able to let the wheat of Russia come through for France and England; in return, it would feel itself obliged to let the quantities — which are in fact definitely fixed — of wheat sown by the German Army in Roumania and Turkey pass through, as it would have compunctions about depriving Germany of this corn, which is her property.

The associating of Austrian and German troops is being progressively diminished. Prince S. strongly urged the Emperor to make Count Czernin hold his tongue.

Austrian sympathy goes out to France, with whom she would like in the future to maintain close associations. In this connection, although Prince S. had suggested to him that, to save his face, the Emperor might hand over the Trentino to Italy by way of the mediation of France and England, and not directly, the Emperor is of opinion that a direct handing over would be better, as it would avoid rousing Austrian opinion against us.

As M. Ribot had pointed out in his covering letter, there were two features of special interest in this Note. The first was the information about Italy's secret approach to Austria to secure peace terms — of which we had no previous knowledge; certainly Sonnino could not have been aware of it when he met us at St. Jean de Maurienne. The other was the fact that the Emperor was evidently ready to consider seriously the cession of the Trentino to Italy in order to make a separate peace with us.

While this news was on its way to us, Prince Sixte was in Vienna, where he stayed from the 5th to the 11th of May, 1917, seeing his brother-in-law and discussing peace prospects with him. Though himself only interested in the desires of France, the Prince urged on the Emperor that it would be wise for him to concede what was necessary to Italy in order to secure an early peace, for if America were to take part in the final peace settlement, she would probably want to partition the monarchy.

The Emperor expressed agreement with this view, and said that Austria wished after the War to ally herself with France, and through France, with England and possibly America, to assure alike her own independence and the peace of the world. As matters stood, the Italian difficulty seemed alone to block the way. He told the Prince again about the Italian approach at Berne to the ambassadors of the Central Powers. The envoy was an Italian Colonel, whose identity was known, and who was not in any sense a private adventurer.

On May 9th, 1917, the Emperor handed to the Prince a second letter for the Allies, expressing the wish to keep the negotiations open. It was accompanied by a note in German by Count Czernin, setting out the points which had been made clear in the conversations between Sixte and Karl. Armed with these documents, the Prince returned on May 12th to Neuchâtel, where he parted from Count Erdödy, the Emperor's envoy, after getting from him the following further statement by Karl about the Italian offer:

Neuchâtel,
12th May, 1917.

The Emperor states that the Italian demand for peace was made in the following way: —

A special delegate came from the Italian General Headquarters to Berne, about a week before the interview at St. Jean de Maurienne. He went first to the German Minister and then to the Austrian. Their demand was addressed first to Germany, and offered peace on the sole condition that Austria should cede the Trentino; Gorizia and Monfalcone remaining Austrian so that the railway communication with Trieste need not come within range of Italian guns. Only Aquilea was to become Italian.

The offer was inspired by the general attitude of the Italian Army, now weary of the War, and by fear of a revolution. *Sonnino knows nothing of this move. It is certain, however, that it has been made with the approval* of a strong group of politicians (*e.g.*, Giolitti and Tittoni) *and that it comes from the King of Italy.*

Germany was asked to put pressure upon Austria to make her accept these terms.

Count Erdödy also amplified the documentary material carried by the Prince with further verbal statements about the arrangements that would be involved in the separate peace; discussing matters such as exchange of prisoners, the food situation, relations with America and the situation on the Russian Front. Germany would be unable to feed her people once Austria-Hungary abandoned her. She would have insufficient corn and fats. "What Germany principally lacked was fats, grease for cooking, and grease for her machinery. A dinner without grease was in Germany a contradiction in terms." "In Germany there had been very serious outbreaks, due to hunger. The general feeling was that the workers there ought to force the Government's hand to make peace, supposing Austria were to do so. . . . The ill feeling between Germany and Austria was increasing, on account of the Austrians being better fed than the Germans."

As regards the cession of the Trentino, the Emperor could only do this in return for some sort of immediate compensation. He could not postpone that in the hope of getting Silesia from Germany, and in any case could not bargain for compensation at the expense of his ally's territory. One of the African colonies of Italy, or concessions in Greece, might be considered.

The Prince reached Paris again on May 16th, but it was not until the 20th that he succeeded in getting an interview with the President and M. Ribot. They had a lengthy but unsatisfactory discussion. M. Ribot found himself unable to see anything except the difficulties in the way of doing something definite. The offer of the Emperor to reinstate Serbia he found inadequate without definite mention of Cattaro and Durazzo. Nothing had yet been settled about Roumania. Moreover, there was the Polish question. As to Italy, it was impossible to ask her to be content with less than had been promised her when she came into the War. The Italian peace offer to the Central Powers doubtless proceeded from the Giolitti Party and from General Porro, the Deputy Chief of the Italian General Staff, but he could not believe that the King and Cadorna were privy to it. Anyhow, they could do nothing till they had invited the King of Italy to pay a visit to the French Front, and had a talk with him about the whole matter.

Prince Sixte said he must now visit England and call on me, as I had asked him to let me know the result of his interview and talk it over with him. Sixte noted that "from 31st March to 22nd April the French Premier's attitude was, in the words of a privileged spectator of these negotiations, that of a man who will successively 'hesitate, procrastinate, suspect, withdraw, and then stand still.' "

When the Prince asked what reply he was to send to the Emperor, Ribot explained that this could not be settled out of hand, as it would take some time to arrange the King of Italy's visit to the French Front, and therefore the matter was not pressing. There was "plenty of time." Unfortunately, the Emperor had presented the opportunity to the French: the initiative was therefore in their hands, and they grasped the lever with a jealous clutch which resented any other hand. When I showed some impatience at delays and doubts in seizing this opportunity to detach Austria and thus bring the Central Alliance tumbling to the ground, I was accused of being "apt to be quick in action" or according to Jules Cambon, "an impetuous Celt."

I wrote to M. Ribot on May 14th, acknowledging his letter and the document containing the information which had reached Paris on May 9th from Count Erdödy. In my reply I said:

The letter, of which you have been good enough to send me a copy, seems to me to be a document of grave importance, and having regard to the critical situation in Russia it would, in my judgment, be a very serious responsibility for you and myself if we failed to make further enquiry as to the possibilities which this letter opens up of dividing the Central Powers. Under the circumstances, I think it highly desirable that you and your informant and myself should have an early conference as to the best method of investigating further the suggestions made in the letter of which you sent me a copy.

M. Ribot did not at this stage adopt my suggestion of a meeting to confer about the developments of the matter, but after seeing Prince Sixte he wrote me on the 20th of May, 1917, advising me that the Prince was about to visit me. His letter ran:

"Dear Mr. Lloyd George,

"Prince S. should arrive in London to-morrow. He will lay before you an autograph letter which you will read with interest. We have repeated to the Prince that it was impossible for us to do anything without Italy. I hold to the opinion that the step which is spoken of in the letter cannot have been authorised by the King. It seems to me absolutely necessary to get to the bottom of the matter. The simplest way would be to speak of it to the King himself, and for this purpose, to invite him to come to France to pay a visit to our Army and to the British Army, which would enable us, without raising suspicion, to arrange an interview with him, with H.M. the King of Great Britain, and the President of the Republic. You could accompany His Britannic Majesty in the same way as I should accompany M. Poincaré. We could see if it is possible to open up a conversation with some chance of coming to terms. You will not disguise from yourself the fact that an understanding will be very difficult. We cannot, in fact, sacrifice Serbia, nor above all, Roumania, which only came into the War at our request. We must in any case act with the greatest prudence, and I think that, until further notice, confidences which have been entrusted to us, and which it was our duty to accept, ought to remain between those persons alone who have up to the present had knowledge of them.

"Believe me, dear Mr. Lloyd George, etc.,

A. Ribot."

Prince Sixte arrived in London in the evening of May 22nd, and on the following day he came to see me at Downing Street, bringing the autograph letter with him.

This second letter from the Emperor Karl was in the following terms:

"9th May, 1917.

"My dear Sixte,

"I note with satisfaction that France and England share my views upon what I believe to be the essential basis of a European peace. At the same time they express their opposition to any peace in which Italy does not participate. As it happens, Italy has just proposed to me to make peace with the Monarchy, renouncing all the inadmissible claims which she has up to this date advanced for the annexation of the Slavonic States of the Adriatic. She has limited her claim to that portion of the Tyrol where the language is Italian. I have for my part postponed the examination of this matter until I hear from you what answer France and England will make to my offer of peace. Count Erdödy will tell you my view and that of my Chancellor on the various points involved.

"The good understanding which the Monarchy has reached with France and England on a number of essential points will enable us, we are convinced, to overcome the remaining difficulties which stand in the way of the conclusion of an honourable peace.

"I thank you for the help you are at present giving me in this task of peace-making, which I have undertaken in the common interest of our countries. As you told me when you went away, this War laid upon you the duty of remaining faithful to your name and to the historic past of your House, first by attending to the wounded on the battlefield, and afterwards yourself fighting for France. I fully understand your motives, and although we were separated by events for which I have no personal responsibility whatever, my affection for you is unaltered. I trust that with your consent it may be possible to express my own personal views to France and England without employing any other interpreter than yourself.

"I beg you to be assured once again of my most warm and fraternal affection.

CHARLES."

The note written by Count Czernin, which was attached to the Emperor's letter, was in the following terms:

(1) A one-sided cession of territory on the part of Austria-Hungary is out of the question; in the event of a compensation by counter-cession the idea could be discussed, provided that account is taken of the fact that the ground heroically defended and watered with the blood of our soldiers has for us an incomparably higher value than any new territory.

(2) What are the guarantees which are offered us that in a Peace Conference the integrity of the Monarchy (subject to the rectifications of frontier already agreed on) will be preserved?

(3) A definite answer can only be given after the foregoing two points have been replied to, *since Austria-Hungary cannot before this enter into discussions with her allies.*

(4) In any event, Austria-Hungary is prepared to go on with the discussions, and in future as in the past is ready to work for an *honourable* peace, and therewith also to prepare the way for general World Peace.

I studied both these documents with great interest, and got from them not too favourable an impression of the prospects of carrying through a peace negotiation with Austria.

Czernin was clearly opposed to any concessions to Italy and he also contemplated not a separate peace talk with Austria but a negotiation in which all Austria's allies were to be consulted. That would have been fatal. As far as Austria herself was concerned, the main difficulty, of course, was still Italy. Sixte doubted whether Austria would consider one of the African colonies of Italy a sufficient compensation for the surrender of the Trentino. He gave me all the further details he could about the alleged Italian offer to Austria. It was clearly a story about the truth of which it would be hard to get verification unless the quarters in Italy responsible for the move saw fit to own up to their action.

I told the Prince that if any progress were to be made, we should have to arrange discussions among persons capable of making responsible decisions. Something might be done if a meeting could be arranged between Czernin, Ribot and myself. I did not want a meeting of diplomats who had no authority to commit their respective countries.

I made an arrangement for the King to receive Prince Sixte and myself that afternoon at three o'clock.

After the visit to the Palace I arranged with Sixte that I would communicate forthwith with M. Ribot, and on hearing from him would be better able to give the Prince an answer to take back to the Emperor Karl.

I wrote at once the following letter to the French Premier:

"10 Downing Street,
Whitehall, S.W.1.
23rd May, 1917.

"Dear M. Ribot,

"I saw to-day your informant and took him to the King. The latter concurs in your suggestion that a meeting should be arranged in France between the two Kings and President Poincaré, with their representative Ministers. Will you kindly take the necessary steps to invite the Kings of England and Italy to visit the French Front at an early date?

"In inviting the King of Italy, it might be intimated that President Poincaré was anxious to have an immediate discussion on the Russian situation, as to which he had received special information. I fear that unless the King of Italy is told that there is some special object in an early meeting he will postpone it for some weeks, when the opportunity which now offers may have passed away. We want if possible to concentrate our efforts on crushing the German military power. No other power counts. May I ask for your views on these suggestions? The special messenger will await a reply.

"A thousand congratulations on your powerful speech in the Chamber. It has created a great impression on this side.

Yours etc.,
D. LLOYD GEORGE."

M. Ribot's reply to this letter, written on the 24th of May, was as follows:

"Dear Mr. Lloyd George,

"In accordance with your advice I am about to telegraph to M. Barrère for him to invite the King of Italy to pay a visit to France as early as possible under the conditions that you suggest.

"It is of the greatest urgency that we should hold a conversation. I have asked M. Paul Cambon whether I can come for the week-end if you will be in London on Sunday and Monday next. I can hardly spare more than these two days, and, at a pinch, of the daytime of Tuesday.

"If I am not held up by vital affairs, it is my intention to set out for London on Saturday, with the Minister for War, M. Painlevé.

"It would be best for us to come to a really sound agreement about the question of Salonika and that of Greece. We shall also have to talk about Russia and Asia Minor.

"I am very touched by what you have said about my speech.

I am pleased to see that Lord Robert Cecil spoke yesterday in the same sense in the House of Commons.

"I will expect a telegram either from you direct or from M. Paul Cambon, so that I can make my arrangements.

Very affectionately yours,

A. RIBOT."

The Anglo-French Conference for which M. Ribot asked in this letter was duly held in London on Monday, May 28th, running on to Tuesday morning. Greece was the principal topic of discussion, and the Stockholm Conference and problems of tonnage were also reviewed. But of course the Prince Sixte correspondence could not be brought into conference, as it was still a matter of the strictest secrecy.

Meantime Prince Sixte, after parting from me, had paid a visit to Paul Cambon and had then retired to the Isle of Wight to be at hand for further developments. His account of his interview with Cambon reveals the immense suspicion which that diplomat felt for Italy, and makes it easy to understand why these negotiations were not pressed through with much fervour by French statesmen. Cambon was quite clear that the Italians would prove a rock upon which the hopes of a separate peace with Austria would founder. He was no less clear that this would on balance be a good thing. For if once Italy got enough out of Austria to be willing to sign a peace with her, he was confident that she would forthwith drop her alliance with the Entente, and render them no further help in the War. She would on the contrary seize the opportunity while other countries were exhausting themselves in the conflict, to expand industrially and commercially, and advance her own interests at the expense of France.

Cambon was of opinion that peace between Austria and Italy would benefit those two Powers only and not France, and that the shock sustained by Germany would not balance the loss of Italy's support.

Cambon was a man of remarkable perspicacity and judgment, but where strong prejudices intervene the shrewdest man is often no better than the fool. To hold that the possible defection of Italy would not be compensated tenfold if the millions of Austrian troops were withdrawn from the ranks of our enemies; if Turkey and Bulgaria were cut off from Germany and forced to make terms; if the Austrian submarines were withdrawn from the Mediterranean, and submarine bases were closed; if our Armies in Salonika, Egypt, Palestine and Mesopotamia could be reduced to garrisons; if the corn of Russia and the Danube could be brought to France and if on the other hand, the food, petroleum and other supplies of the Dual Monarchy and Roumania were withheld from Germany; if Prussian militarism, deserted as it would be by its allies, and opposed by the most powerful nations in the world, were forced into a position of foredoomed defeat — to ignore all these advantages which must follow from a separate peace with Austria, and be prepared to forego them all, rather than let Italy have a chance of becoming stronger economically and industrially — appears an unbalanced attitude of mind. Yet this seems to have been the quite serious view taken by Cambon. To some extent he influenced Ribot. He damped his ardours with suspicions and clogged his activity with doubts.

The Cambons — Jules and Paul — were exceptionally able diplomats. They were intensely patriotic. France was their faith — their shrine — their worship — their deity. The first commandment of the true French patriot is: "Thou shalt have no other gods but France." It is a type or quality of patriotism which springs more naturally from the soil of France than that of any other land. Are Englishmen also not patriots? Yes, they are, but with them patriotism is a duty, with Frenchmen it is a fanaticism. Great leaders of men prove their gift of leadership by the appeals they address to those who under their command are called upon to fight against odds. Nelson's call to the English sailors was to respond to England's expectation that they should do their duty. Napoleon's appeal was to the glories of France. It was a love of country planted and raised during the torrid summer of the great Revolution, when the integrity and independence of France were threatened by all the monarchs of Europe, and matured whilst the French legions under Napoleon were tramping through the streets of every capital (except one) where these monarchs reigned. They were beaten in the end by a combined Europe. But national greatness does not depend as much on victory, as on the grandeur of the struggle put up by a people. No other country possesses the experiences of France, and one has always to remember, in dealing with French statesmen, that this great era of their national glory is at the roots of their policy. In negotiating with them it is a complex which interferes seriously with any attempt to secure a reasonable accommodation which takes the interests of other nations into account. It is always obtruding itself at inconvenient moments.

Cleverly, and with every appearance of helping them along, the Sixte *pourparlers* were manœuvred into futility. The subtle and expert Cambon brain directed the stately steps of the unsuspecting Ribot hither and thither — anywhere so long as they did not lead on the direct road to a peace with Austria which would make Italy bigger, stronger, more triumphant, whilst France was still wrestling in her own mud with her deadly adversary — her strength flowing steadily out of her torn veins. No patriotic Frenchman could bear that thought without a pang of jealousy. That explains the attitude of Jules Cambon, the rumbling protests about "secret diplomacy" in the French Chamber, and the French journals. It accounts also for the faltering M. Ribot.

The British Government were helpless. We were entirely in the hands of France. The offer had been made to her, and the confidential intermediary, Prince Sixte, was a Frenchman; although he was devoted to the Empress Zita, he was mainly concerned with what he felt to be French interests. M. Paul Cambon's assurance to him that he would really be doing France no service if he carried the negotiations through successfully must have cooled his zeal and checked his activities. A French Royalist Prince could not face an insinuation that he had bargained away the interests of France to serve an enemy relative.

In the matter of the invitation to the King of Italy we were again in the hands of the French. Whatever the terms of the invitation sent, they were not effective in persuading Sonnino to come to France with his monarch. On May 30th, Prince Sixte returned to London, eager to complete his mission by securing our answer to the Emperor's letter, and then get back to his guns on the Belgian Front. But no reply had as yet come to hand. I persuaded him to stay on a few days longer until the Italian reply had been received. A first answer turned up a few hours later, but it was of an evasive nature. Baron Sonnino said that he saw no need for a meeting of the Allies at present. I thereupon sent off a letter to him by special courier, emphasising the fact that the proposed meeting was of real importance.

No answer to this had arrived by June 5th, when Prince Sixte called on me for a final interview before returning to the Continent. But in the meantime, on June 3rd the Italian Government had proclaimed a protectorate over Albania. This action may have been inspired by the comparative failure of the offensive which Cadorna had launched on the Isonzo on the 12th of May. A measure of advance had been achieved, but had been brought to a standstill without coming anywhere within striking distance of the road to Trieste. Failing to get near that city, the Italians had consoled themselves by announcing the annexation of Albania. It was not a step calculated to simplify the problem of negotiations with Austria.

When Prince Sixte called on me for the last time on June 5th, I told him how fully I shared his annoyance at the delays which the Italians were making.

The Prince asked me to let him have some answer even if the Italians would not meet us. I assured him that we should do our best to insist on an answer from Sonnino and from his Sovereign. "The chance of peace with Austria is too important for us to let it slip. For the moment, we can only say that these negotiations with Italy make the whole thing long and difficult, but that, once they are settled, things will move faster."

On reaching Paris, the Prince had an interview with M. William Martin, of the French Foreign Office, who told him that Baron Sonnino had no intention of meeting the English and French Ministers. Sixte asked for some message that he could convey to Karl as the answer of the French to his letter. But for some time longer he heard nothing. On June 20th he was told that in M. Ribot's opinion, "Nothing can be done for the present; we can do nothing without Italy." On June 23rd, M. Jules Cambon had a long interview with the Prince, and explained the situation to him as it appeared to the French Foreign Office. They were having a good deal of trouble with Italy, because both France and Italy were making large demands with respect to Asia Minor, "on the principle of ask the more to get the less." In Greece the French and Italians were also pursuing conflicting policies. Sonnino was refusing to meet the other Allied Premiers in a discussion. M. Cambon said that I was taking up energetically the idea of negotiations with Austria, whereas the French were not too eager to press these forward rapidly. But the Allied Premiers would be meeting in mid-July for a conference. The French President shared Cambon's view that Italy could not be allowed to get the Trentino until France had secured possession of Alsace-Lorraine — an attitude which really made it impossible for the prospective terms of a separate peace with Austria to be executed until Germany was defeated. In view of this conversation, Prince Sixte returned to his regiment and abandoned his efforts at peace-making.

Meantime in France, where, throughout the War, it seemed all but impossible to keep a secret, some kind of rumour appears to have leaked out about these negotiations. In a debate in the Chamber on June 5th, charges about "secret diplomacy" were levelled at the Premier, M. Ribot, who repudiated them with virtuous indignation. "Secret diplomacy has been mentioned: there can be no secret diplomacy! The fullest publicity should be and shall be given here!" The denial may not have been more than diplomatically truthful, but the attack doubtless scared Ribot away from any attempts to press further with negotiations.

The Italians did not come into conference until July 25th, when an Inter-Allied Conference was held in Paris. By this time M. Ribot felt it too late to challenge Cadorna about the alleged Italian peace approach to Austria. But he took the course of showing Sonnino all the correspondence. If he felt entitled thus for reasons of overriding public interest to break his solemn promise to Prince Sixte, it surely ought to have been done in April. I never urged it. In April I entreated Prince Sixte to release the French Government from its bond, but when he firmly declined, I felt we were bound to keep faith at all costs. This revelation did not penetrate Baron Sonnino's resistance. By this time the question of negotiating a separate peace with Austria had resolved itself into a struggle between Giolitti and Sonnino for the soul of the King, and the Italian Foreign Minister resented our interference in a matter of domestic controversy. The correspondence was not of course discussed in open conference, but at the session in the afternoon of July 26th I pointed out the possibilities of action to drive Austria out of the War.

Thus the negotiations opened up through Prince Sixte fell to the ground. Even after waiting for two months, I was unable to give any answer beyond the fact that as yet nothing had been settled with Italy. France, which was in responsible charge of the negotiations, was at heart unwilling to press them forward. Jealous in any case of Italian expansion, she was particularly averse to helping her neighbour to enjoy possession of her irredentist territories while still uncertain whether she herself would be able to secure her lost provinces. These considerations appear to have outweighed with the French politicians the immense military advantages to be secured by eliminating Austria from the conflict.

There was also an element of distrust which has always disturbed the relations between allies in every combination that ever existed. If Italy were satisfied, France was convinced she would render no further help in the War. When one bears in mind that our hopes of success in these negotiations were based on the assumption that Austria would betray Germany, we had no right to complain of the cynical suspicions of France.

Baron Sonnino might perhaps have pleaded in 1919 that his obduracy was justified by the terms of peace which Italy enforced as a result of her victory. They were territorially and strategically more advantageous than any she could have hoped to secure by any settlement that was possible in 1917.

It was not until October 12th that M. Ribot made any statement which could be regarded as his reply to these peace overtures from Austria. On that date he made a speech in the French Chamber, in the course of which he said:

> "A little time since, it was Austria who declared herself ready to make peace with us, and to satisfy our desires; but she deliberately left Italy out of account, knowing that, were we now to listen to those counsels of deceit, Italy would soon recover her independence and would become the enemy of a France that had forgotten and betrayed her. We did not consent to this!"

This may perhaps be regarded as the final negative answer of France, six months overdue, to the Emperor Karl's appeal for peace.

"Counsels of deceit" is not a phrase altogether fair to the young Emperor's efforts for peace. He sincerely yearned for peace and so did his French Consort. There is almost a poignancy in his letters to his brother-in-law. He was horrified by the environment in which he mounted his throne. He shuddered at the prospect for himself and his family. In a little over twelve months he was an exile from his native land. A few years later I visited a modest villa at Madeira which was lent to the ex-Emperor Karl by a kindly islander. There he had died in poverty. He was too poor to pay for a doctor to save his life and he was buried at the expense of the same charitable merchant who had provided him with a refuge. In reading through my papers, I could see how the shadows of this tragedy had darkened the fateful effort of poor Karl to escape from impending doom.

CHAPTER VIII

THE VATICAN AND KUHLMANN PEACE MOVES

War horrors breed a desire for peace — Scale of British losses — Lord Lansdowne's courage — Labour unrest in belligerent countries — Jane Addams and the Austrian Premier — Disillusionment in Germany — Effect of food shortage — Aims of the German peace note — New situation in the summer of 1917. — Bethmann-Hollweg dismissed — The Reichstag resolution — Unwillingness to surrender Belgium — New Chancellor's speech — Ludendorff demands a peace of victory — My Queen's Hall reply to Michaelis — Mr. MacDonald's peace resolution — Mr. Asquith challenges Michaelis — Bonar Law refuses a patched-up peace — Labour opposes MacDonald's resolution — Vatican peace note — British reception unfavourable — Attitude of Allies — Cabinet decides to see German reply before answering the Pope — German invincibility confirmed — President Wilson's reply to the Pope — German reply ignores Belgium — The point put to Germany through the Vatican — The Kaiser's memorandum — Ludendorff sets out the military demands — Austro-Hungarian peace terms — Ludendorff's view endorsed by Michaelis — Hindenburg's support for Ludendorff policy — Von Kuhlmann tries his hand — A message through the Spanish Foreign Office — Villalobar's despatches — Mr. Balfour's memorandum on peace feelers — Mr. Bonar Law's letter — French also approached by Von Lancken — Briand eager to enter discussion with Germany — My examination of military outlook — Haig obsessed with Passchendaele — Haig opposed to inconclusive peace — Allies invited to agree in a joint reply to Germany — Kuhlmann's "No, never" speech — Alsace-Lorraine not to be restored — Kuhlmann dare not offer to restore Belgium — Peace move only approved by German Headquarters as a war manœuvre — No German disarmament.

HAVING regard to the accumulating horrors of the War, it would have been surprising had there been no growing desire for peace. Figures of casualties were everywhere sternly repressed. But after the Somme, concealment of their vastness was no longer possible. The blue uniforms of the wounded and the black vestments of the mourners were visible everywhere.

Britain, up to the Battle of the Somme, had not lost men on the same scale as the rest of the belligerents. But by the end of 1916 her losses were greater than those she had sustained in the aggregate in all her wars put together since the Wars of the Roses, and had cost more than all the wars she had ever waged.

In spite of optimistic dispatches from the battle areas, we were making no headway on any front. On at least two fronts the enemy were advancing. Our reputed victories seemed to end in nothing but a shuddering accumulation of debts and deaths. The end of the year 1916, therefore, witnessed the first manifestations of a desire that the anguish of nations mangling each other in savage combat should be terminated for the sake of our common humanity. The sentiment was by no means confined to those who had opposed the War from the start. In fact, the call for peace would have been louder and more general had it not been that pacifism was discredited in the eyes of the general public by its association with men and women whose views on other subjects were regarded as violent and subversive. There was also the natural fear that any peace move might, and undoubtedly would, have the effect of encouraging the enemy or weakening the morale of our own people. Every stir towards peace in enemy countries was quoted and headlined in Allied countries as a proof that we were winning, and that our foes knew it and were clamouring for a cessation of the fight. That is why men and women who thought the time had come for making peace hesitated to say so in public. Lord Lansdowne displayed great courage and a high sense of public duty when he wrote and circulated amongst his colleagues in the Cabinet, at the end of 1916, his memorandum calling for negotiations. I did not accept his view of the situation. In August, 1914, he was in favour of waging war on Germany if she attacked France, whether Belgium were invaded or not. I resisted that policy up to the very hour when Belgium was threatened. But once having started the fight, I felt we must see it right through, until the German military machine was smashed. Nevertheless, my respect for Lord Lansdowne's character and patriotism was enhanced by his willingness to face misconstruction and unpopularity by promoting negotiations for peace at a time when the enemy was not only unbeaten, but to all appearances, taking the battlefield as a whole, was winning.

The decision come to by the Asquith Cabinet in November, 1916, that peace overtures were undesirable until the German military power was broken, has already been recorded by me in my second volume. The war weariness which first began to show itself in all the belligerent countries in 1916 grew rapidly in 1917.

In all the belligerent countries there was labour unrest, due largely to the growing scarcity and price of food. This restlessness was accentuated by the fact of the Russian Revolution and the spectacle of the growing power of Labour in that great country. Many of the workers' leaders everywhere saw in that upheaval a more hopeful prospect for the emancipation of their class and the amelioration of its conditions than in a military victory. The revolutionary slogan of "No Annexations or Indemnities" was finding an echo in other countries. The German Socialists were perceptibly influenced by its appeal and it had a definite response also in this country. The feeling here found expression in the multiplication of peace demonstrations held openly without interruption or resentment in all parts of the country, and attended by earnest and enthusiastic crowds. It was also apparent in the increasing labour troubles which interfered seriously with the production of war material. It never seemed to affect the soldiers and I received no reports and heard no rumours of pacifist talk in the trenches, behind the lines, or in our ships. The men who had to bear the hardships and face the dangers of war were not clamouring for peace — they were not even talking about it. There was a sullen determination not to give in until their side won. But in France and Italy, and most of all in Russia, the soldiers were discussing peace, and Governments were nervous as to the dependence that could be placed on their fighting value if they were too highly tested. Generals doubted whether their men could any longer be depended upon to face the slaughter of great offensives. General Pétain had no doubts on the subject, and for that reason he avoided attacks on a great scale. General Cadorna tried his hand at peace overtures with Austria, assigning as his reason the apprehensions he felt as to the influence of insidious peace propaganda on his troops. The Russian Generals constantly put off projected and promised offensives because they could not trust their troops to advance into the fire.

As to enemy countries, one heard as early as 1915 that Austria was tired, and that some of her leaders were becoming frightened of the ultimate effect on the Monarchy of the unexpected prolongation of the War. In 1916, Jane Addams, the famous American leader of women's movements, called upon me at Number 11, Downing Street, on her return from a Continental tour. She had visited Germany, Austria and France and wished to tell me all about it and at the same time influence me in the direction of peace. In Vienna she had had an interview with the Austrian Premier. Having explained to him that she had come there to find out whether it was not possible to bring this horrible war to a peaceful end, she said: "I have no doubt you are saying to yourself at this moment, this American woman is quite mad." He replied: "Mad? Do you see that door?" At this she thought he was terminating the interview brusquely, but he went on, "Every hour of the day and far into the night men come through that door and say to me: 'We want more men for the trenches — we want more guns — more ammunition, more money.' Mad, indeed? You are the only sensible person that has passed through that door for a long time." The Austrians were not happy about the war they had provoked. A sense of impending catastrophe was chilling the air of Vienna.

As to Germany, there was no sense of fear, but rather of disillusionment. Her wonderful army was everywhere winning resounding triumphs, but the final triumph seemed no nearer. Victories did not seem to bring victory. The German military chiefs were gambling on the tables of death for world supremacy. From time to time they made wonderful coups, but so far the only real winner was the grim croupier. And now came the U-boat triumph with sinkings of British, Allied and Neutral ships that ran into millions of tons. But England did not slacken her efforts or lower her arrogant flag by an inch. Ammunition was flung more lavishly than ever on the German lines in France and Flanders. Unless Hindenburg won this year, the Americans would arrive next year. There was not much time to lose. And the food situation was growing steadily worse. There were strikes in the workshops, the Socialists were agitating for peace overtures, and now the Centre had joined them in bringing pressure to bear upon the Government. The German soldier stood in his battered trenches as firmly as ever, and was willing to give to his faltering allies an example of the way to fight battles from Beersheba to the Carpathians. In fact, at this stage of the War, the German and the British troops alone on the whole battlefield remained quite unshaken by horror propaganda. It is fair, however, to say that neither army had endured the same losses as the French and, moreover, they were better supported in the matter of guns and ammunition than the Italians. But if the German in the battle lines were still resolute, at home in the Fatherland there were misgivings. The German people were beginning to crave for an honourable and not necessarily a triumphant end to their sacrifices. Food, and especially the fat foods that bring contentment, because they give warmth and comfort, were scarce and becoming scarcer. The rich lands of Russian and Roumania had been scraped clean and it would take another year to dig out their inherent fertility. All Germans were prepared to fight to the last for the integrity and independence of the Fatherland, but most of them viewed with growing reluctance the idea of continuing the colossal sacrifices being made for world dominance. Annexation had ceased to appeal to those whose sons and husbands and brothers were facing death to achieve conquest. They certainly were not prepared to make that sacrifice to avenge further the death of an Austrian Prince, for whom even his own people had no special affection. They thought that the millions of dead (foes and friends) were an adequate oblation on the tomb of this undistinguished personage.

The German Peace Note of December, 1916, was prompted partly by a desire to propitiate this sentiment and partly with the purpose of demonstrating to hesitating allies and uneasy neutrals, especially to the most powerful of all the neutrals, the United States of America, that the prolongation of the War was due to the spirit of rapacity and revenge which animated Allied statesmanship. There was also the knowledge that the wish for peace was spreading amongst all circles in England. The Lansdowne move was known in Germany. German statesmen were anxious to take advantage of this gesture to weaken Britain's will. Their Peace Note was so arrogant in its tone that it had the opposite effect in both England and America from that which it was intended to produce. The proverbial clumsiness of German diplomacy once more defeated its purpose. To be quite frank, Allied statesmen were in no mood for peace conferences. France was very much exhilarated by the prospect of the new model offensive which was at last going to rupture the German line. The British Army was stronger in numbers and equipment than it had ever been. It had fought one great battle and had shown that the half-trained levies of Britain could hold their own with any soldier in the field. The imminence of the Russian Revolution was not foreseen at that date. When it came, America was in the field. For a long job it was a good swop.

The French defeat in May, ending in a certain collapse in the temper of the French Army, coupled with the crash of Russia, created a new situation. The Peace Party in Germany thought this was a propitious moment for renewing the overtures bungled away in the winter. They were supposed to have secured a measure of sympathy, if not actual encouragement, from Chancellor Bethmann-Hollweg. This amiable bureaucrat was not a man of war by proclivity or proficiency. He was therefore an object of distrust and almost detestation to the fighting admirals and generals of Germany. They knew he had assented to the War with reluctance and that he waged it without enthusiasm. When he surrendered to militarist dictation, he did so in such tactless words as showed that he was not thinking so much of weakening the Army abroad, but of propitiating his enemies at home. When they found him, as they thought, intriguing with Socialists and Catholics to stop the war on terms which flung away their conquests, just as they imagined they were winning out on land and sea, they were infuriated, and they succeeded in persuading the intimidated Kaiser to get rid of this troublesome minister who had no love for dominion gained through slaughter. He was succeeded by Michaelis, an intelligent — but not overintelligent — official of the Wilhelmstrasse. He knew why he was given the Chancellorship. He was there to obey the orders of the real

Masters of Germany. He was not to quarrel openly with the timorous defeatists of the Reichstag. He was authorised to delude them by a show of pacific disposition. On the other hand, he was to make clear that the time and terms of peace were for him to declare and not for them. On July 19th, 1917, the Reichstag passed the following resolution:

> As on 4th August, 1914, so on the threshold of the fourth year of the War, the German people are inspired by the words contained in the speech from the Throne "We are not led by desire for conquests." Germany has taken up arms for Liberty and Independence, and for the integrity of her territory. The Reichstag desires a peace of conciliation and a lasting reconciliation of all peoples.
>
> Enforced territorial aggrandisement with political, economic and financial control, cannot be reconciled with that programme. The Reichstag also rejects all plans about economic isolation and the enmity of peoples after the War. The freedom of the seas must be made sure. Only an economic peace can pave the way for friendly coöperation among the peoples. We will also strongly encourage the creation of international law organisations.
>
> Germany will fight until the Allies stop threatening her and her allies with conquests.

The motion was opposed fiercely by the Junker Party, but carried in spite of their resistance by 214 votes to 116. The resolution itself expressed in general words the desire of the German Parliament for peace. As to the terms it was vague. There was no definite and clear declaration that all the occupied territory in the West, the East and the South-east would be restored without condition or reservation. Neither Belgium nor Poland were alluded to by name. Inferentially they were included in the phrase about "No forcible acquisition of territory." But there was nothing said about adjustments of frontier or conditions to be imposed on them in the interests of military security or economic coöperation. Many — perhaps most — of the Deputies meant honestly to give back the occupied territories wholly and unreservedly. Some of them certainly did not. Here is an extract from one of the speeches delivered in the debate by a Deputy, explaining the meaning of the resolution:

"The War must end in some tangible result. The Imperial Chancellor has now shown us the tangible result in the East. For the West he has spoken with greater caution. Belgium, an *avulsum imperii,* must not remain England's bulwark. The necessary result of that is that she must be in our power from the political, military and economic point of view. (Hear, hear.) But this would not touch the political organisation of the country. The really final terms of peace might settle that. We pursue — and I repeat this after the Imperial Chancellor — no war of conquest. But we must adjust our frontiers in accordance with our own interests."

More ominous than these omissions was the speech delivered the same day by Chancellor Michaelis. He said:

"Germany did not wish for war and did not strive for expansion of her power by violence. Therefore she will not prosecute the War a single day longer after an honourable peace is obtainable, merely to make conquests by violence. What we wish is, first, to conclude peace as those would who have successfully carried through their purpose. . . . A nation of not even 70,000,000, which, side by side with its loyal allies, had held its place, weapon in hand, before the frontiers of its country against the manifold superiority of masses of nations, has proved itself unconquerable. To me our aims are clear from this situation.

"First of all, the territory of the Fatherland is inviolable. With an enemy who demands parts of our Empire, we cannot parley. If we make peace we must, in the first line, make sure that the frontiers of the German Empire are made secure for all time.

"We must, by means of an understanding and give and take,

guarantee the conditions of existence of the German Empire upon the Continent and Overseas. . . . The Government feels that if our enemies abandon their lust for conquest and their aims of subjugation, and wish to enter into negotiations, we shall listen honestly, and ready for peace, to what they have to say to us. Until then we must hold out calmly, patiently, and courageously."

He ended his speech with these significant words:

"The Constitutional rights of the Imperial Administration to conduct our policy must not be narrowed. I am not willing to permit the conduct of affairs to be taken from my hands."

It was not merely that he added a blur to the vagueness of the Reichstag about Belgium, but he ended up with a stern warning to that timorous assembly to mind their own business.

On the same day the German Chief of Staff, General von Ludendorff, said:

"In starting the submarine war the supreme Army Command was guided by the desire to hit the enemy's war industry, especially his production of ammunition. Through the submarine war our armies in the West have experienced great relief, and the enemy supply of ammunition has decreased. The U-boats have accomplished this task. The coöperation of the Navy and Army has proved to be perfect. The Supreme Army Command expects from the U-boat war that it will interfere with England's readiness for war by lessening her tonnage. The fulfilment of this expectation will also come, and with it in spite of America, the end of the World War and *a peace such as is desired by the Supreme Army Command.*"

Two days later, on July 21st, speaking at a Belgian demonstration at the Queen's Hall, I dwelt on the Michaelis speech. The Reichstag had no executive authority and had no means, short of revolution or the refusal of supplies to the Armies in the field, by which they could impose their will on the executive. It was therefore the Chancellor's speech that mattered at this stage. Parliament did not control the Administration as it does here. The Chancellor was the man I would have to deal with and not the President of the Reichstag or Herr Scheidemann. I intended the speech as an invitation to the German Chancellor to clear up obscurities in his declaration to the Reichstag. I said:

"There is a new Chancellor. The Junker has thrown the old Chancellor into the waste paper basket with his scrap of paper, and they are lying there side by side. You will not have to wait long before Junkerdom will follow. What hope is there in his speech of peace — I mean an honourable peace, which is the only possible peace? It is a dexterous speech. A facing-all-ways speech. There are phrases for those who earnestly desire peace — many. But there are phrases which the military authorities of Germany will understand — phrases about making the frontiers of Germany secure. That is the phrase which annexed Alsace-Lorraine; that is the phrase which has drenched Europe with blood from 1914 onward; that is the phrase which, if they dare, will annex Belgium; and that is the phrase which will once more precipitate Europe into a welter of blood within a generation unless it is wiped out of the statesmanship of Europe. But there are phrases for men of democratic mind in that speech — many. He means to call up men out of the Reichstag to coöperate with the Government; they are even to get office. But there were phrases to satisfy the Junkers. There was to be no parting with Imperialistic rights. Ah! They will call men from the Reichstag to office, but they will be not Ministers, but clerks. It is the speech of a man waiting on the military situation, and let the Allies — Russia, Britain, France, Italy, all of them — bear that in mind. It is a speech that can be made better by improving the military situation. If the Germans win in the West, if they destroy the Russian Army in the East, if their friends the Turks drive Britain out of Mesopotamia, if the U-boats sink more merchant ships, then all that speech, believe me, means annexation all round and military autocracy more firmly established than ever. But, on the other hand, should the German Army be driven back in the West, be beaten in the East, and should their friends the Turks fail in Baghdad, and the submarines be a failure on the High Seas, that speech is all right. We must all help to make that a good speech. There are possibilities in it of excellence. Let us help Dr. Michaelis; let us give assistance to the new Chancellor to make his first speech a real success. But, for the moment, it means that the military party have won.

"I want to repeat in another form a statement which I made before. What manner of Government they choose to rule over them is entirely the business of the German people themselves; but what manner of Government we can trust to make peace with is our business. Democracy is in itself a guarantee of peace, and if you cannot get it in Germany then we must secure other guarantees as a substitute. The German Chancellor's speech shows, in my judgment, that those who are in charge of affairs in Germany have, for the moment, elected for war."

As to Belgium I said:

"The determination of the Allies is this, that Belgium must be restored as a free and an independent people. Belgium must be a people and not a Protectorate. We must not have a Belgian scabbard for the Prussian sword. The sceptre must be Belgian, the sword must be Belgian, the scabbard must be Belgian, the soul must be Belgian."

How accurately I had gauged the real meaning of the Michaelis speech will be apparent when I come to relate the decision of the German Imperial War Council held a few weeks later at Berlin.

On July 26th there was a debate in the House of Commons on an amendment to the Consolidated Fund Bill moved by Mr. Ramsay MacDonald. In the course of his speech Mr. MacDonald called upon the Government "in conjunction with the Allies to restate their peace terms accordingly."

He referred to the Reichstag resolution and said that it was:

" . . . one of the difficulties whenever peace comes, whether after military victory or in any other event, that this Government and the Allies will have to face — the difficulty of not being able to deal directly with the representatives of the German people or with the German people themselves. . . ."

He put forward a demand that the Government should "promote in every way the consultation of Allied peoples."

He was seconded by Mr. Trevelyan who declared in the course of his speech:

"To my mind the primary test of good faith to us in England — without which we shall all regard peace as impossible — is a clear understanding that Germany shall evacuate and restore Belgium and France without attaching economic or strategic considerations to it."

In the course of the same debate Mr. Asquith said:

"I am, I confess, like the Chancellor of the Exchequer (Mr. Bonar Law), unable to attach any very definite significance to the array of more or less ambiguous generalities of which this Peace resolution consists. . . . Peace . . . is subject to one all important condition; that it is a peace which does not defeat the purposes with which the free nations of the world have entered upon and have continued the War, and that it does not turn to waste the immeasurable losses and suffering which they have shared and are sharing in common. . . .

"I want to put a very plain and specific question with regard to that. Is Germany prepared not only to evacuate Belgium, not only to make full reparation for the colossal mischief and damage which has accompanied her devastating occupation of the country and her practical enslavement, so far as she could carry it out, of large portions of the population; is she prepared not only to do that — this is a very plain question which admits of a very simple answer — but to restore to Belgium, not the pretence of liberty, but a complete, an unfettered and an absolute independence. I should like to know the German Chancellor's answer to that question — not the answer of the Reichstag. I ask him now as far as I may. . . .

"Meantime, we should not be helping the advent of peace if we were to give the impression that there is any halting in our determination or any doubt of our ability to carry on, if need be, the burden which we took up with a clear conscience for great ends, and which we can only in honour lay down when we feel sure that those ends are going to be achieved."

Mr. Wardle, the Labour Member for Stockport, in his speech on the same Motion, associated himself "freely" with what Mr. Asquith had said.

I myself was in France at the time of this debate in the House of Commons and was therefore unable to take part in it, but Mr. Bonar Law in replying said:

"Here we had for at least 20 years a great military Power, controlled ultimately by one man, which hung as a shadow over the world as a vast thunder cloud which might burst at any moment. I say we are fighting for peace in the time to come. If a patched-up peace comes now with that German military machine still unbroken, still in the hands of the same people who directed it for the 20 years before the War, have we any security? I think we have the reverse. Have we any security that the same danger which has ruined this generation will not ruin our children when this war is over?"

And in referring to the resolution itself he said:

"There is one curious feature to be noticed in the terms of this amendment. The honourable gentleman (Mr. Ramsay MacDonald) gave us a full translation of that resolution, but in the amendment based on the resolution there was one curious omission. The resolution contains these words. 'One of the conditions is freedom of the seas.' That does not appear in the amendment. What does that mean? My Right Honourable friend, the late Prime Minister, explained the circumstances in which this resolution was passed. It came as the result of a crisis. Attempts were made to get something which would settle that crisis, and do not let this House mistake for a moment that these words, to which no importance is attached by those who move the amendment, were one of the features which enabled a large section of the Reichstag to vote for this resolution. What do the Germans mean by freedom of the seas? It has only one meaning. It does not arise in time of peace; it arises in time of war, and this is the meaning of it, and it can have no other meaning — that in war a nation with naval power is not to use that power, but a nation with military power is to be subject to no restrictions."

Mr. Snowden, in the course of his speech, said that Mr. Asquith had:

". . . endorsed the suggestion that each nation and each people should be given the right to decide the Sovereignty and the Government under which they would live. If we accept that, that settles the question of Alsace-Lorraine."

In the course of the debate, one of the Labour Members read out a resolution adopted by the Labour Party on the question of peace terms.

"The invasion of Belgium and France by the Germany Army threatens the very existence of independent nationalities and strikes a blow at all faith in treaties. In these circumstances a victory for German Imperialism would be to defeat and destroy democracy and liberty in Europe. The Socialists of Great Britain, France and Russia do not pursue the political and economical crushing of Germany. They are not at war with the peoples of Germany, but only with the Governments of those countries that are oppressed.

"They demand that Belgium shall be liberated and compensated.

"They desire that the question of Poland shall be settled in accordance with the wishes of the Polish people, either in the sense of autonomy in the midst of another State or in that of complete independence, and they wish that throughout all Europe, from Alsace-Lorraine to the Balkans, those populations that have been annexed by force shall receive the right freely to dispose of themselves."

This will account for the paucity of MacDonald's following in the division, for there certainly was nothing in the Reichstag resolution that would give any hope that the Labour terms would be conceded by the German Government.

Only nineteen Members voted for Mr. MacDonald's Amendment. Three Labour Members out of the total thirty-seven Labour strength in the House of Commons followed Mr. MacDonald and Mr. Snowden into the lobby. The rest were Liberals, who mustered sixteen out of the total two hundred and sixty of the Party in the House. The remainder followed Mr. Asquith and myself into the Government lobby. The result of the division fairly reflected the attitude of the general public in our country towards the Michaelis declaration and the Reichstag resolution.

A division in the House of Commons does not always give a faithful indication of the state of opinion outside. But in this case it is safe to say that had there been a general election immediately after that division, not one of the Minority Members would have been returned.

There was a desire for peace, but a very few believed that the German authorities meant a real peace of the kind we could honourably accept. The British people, as well as their leaders, suspected a trap. It may be said they had been misled by propaganda. Let those who still think so suspend judgment until they read the official account of what was going on behind the scenes in Germany at that date.

The next serious Peace Move came from the Vatican. On August 16th, the belligerent Governments received a Note from the Vatican, in which, after a striking exordium dwelling on the increasing horrors of this war, the Pope asks:

Shall, then, the civilized world be nought but a field of death? And shall Europe, so glorious and flourishing, rush, as though driven by universal madness, towards the abyss, and lend her hand to her own suicide?

Disclaiming any special political aim, and heeding neither the suggestions nor the interests of either of the belligerents, and stating that he is impelled solely by the feeling of his supreme duty as the common father of the people, he suggests terms of peace:

. . . in order no longer to confine ourselves to general terms, such as were counselled by circumstances in the past, we desire now to come down to more concrete and practical proposals, and to invite the Governments of the belligerent peoples to agree upon the following points, which seem as though they ought to be the bases of a just and lasting peace, leaving to their charge the completion and the more precise definition of those points.

First, the fundamental point should be that the moral force of right should replace the material force of arms; hence a just agreement between all for the simultaneous and reciprocal diminution of armaments, according to rules and guarantees to be established, to the extent necessary and sufficient for the maintenance of public order in each State; then in the place of armies, the establishment of arbitration with its exalted pacifying function, on lines to be concerted and with sanctions to be settled against any State that should refuse either to submit international questions to arbitration or to accept its awards.

The supremacy of right once established, let every obstacle be removed from the channels of communication between peoples, by ensuring, under rules likewise to be laid down, the true freedom and common enjoyment of the seas. This would, on the one hand, remove manifold causes of conflict, and would open, on the other, fresh sources of prosperity and progress to all.

As to the reparation of damage and to the costs of war, we see no way to solve the question, save by laying down as a general principle, complete and reciprocal condonation, which would, moreover, be justified by the immense benefits that would accrue from disarmaments; all the more, since the continuations of such carnage solely for economic reasons would be incomprehensible. If, in certain cases, there exist, nevertheless, special reasons, let them be weighed with justice and equity.

But these pacific agreements, with the immense advantages they entail, are impossible without the reciprocal restitution of territories now occupied. Consequently on the part of Germany there must be the complete evacuation of Belgium, with a guarantee of her full political, military and economic independence towards all Powers whatsoever; likewise the evacuation of French territory. On the part of the other belligerent parties, there must be a similar restitution of the German colonies.

As regards territorial questions like those at issue between Italy and Austria, and between Germany and France, there is reason to hope that in consideration of the immense advantages of a lasting peace with disarmament, the parties in conflict will examine them in a conciliatory spirit, taking account, in the measure of what is just and possible, as we have before said, of the aspirations of the people and, as occasion may offer, coördinating particular interests with the general weal of the great human society.

The same spirit of equity and justice must reign in the study of the other territorial and political questions, notably those relating to Armenia, the Balkan States, and to the territories forming part of the ancient Kingdom of Poland, to which, in particular, its noble historical traditions and the sufferings endured, especially during the present war, ought justly to assure the sympathies of the nations.

Such are the principal bases upon which we believe the future reorganisation of the peoples should be founded.

BENEDICTUS XVI.

As the Holy See had no diplomatic relations with either France, Italy or the United States of America, we were asked by Cardinal Gasparri to be so good as to forward the appeal to the President of the French Republic, the King of Italy, and the President of the American Republic.

The reception of the Note in the British Press was respectful but unfriendly. Although the Pope had preserved a judicious reticence, the Vatican, as a whole, was supposed to be more favourably inclined to the Central Powers than to the Allies. The *Times* unequivocally denounced the Note and said "it must be rejected." It was "pro-German and anti-Ally." The "scheme was permeated with German ideas."

These criticisms represented the general attitude of the Allies towards the Pope's appeal. When the Cabinet met to consider what reply should be given to the message, Mr. Balfour indicated to the War Cabinet the attitude of our Allies on the subject so far as it was at present known, which was as follows:

FRANCE. — M. Ribot considered that it would suffice to reply by a receipt in the ordinary form. If the British Government considered a more formal answer necessary the two Governments must meet. On the other hand a personal letter from M. Albert Thomas to the Prime Minister was read which indicated that, in his opinion, the Allies ought to give a collective reply.

ITALY. — Baron Sonnino was not disposed to send any answer, and expressed the opinion that the experience of the previous collective answer to the President of the United States was not very encouraging.

Russia. — The Minister for Foreign Affairs considered the Pope's appeal as purely pro-German, and had ordered Russian representatives abroad to propose that the Allies should make some suitable joint answer.

United States of America. — Information had been received from a private but reliable source to the effect that President Wilson was doubtful if he would reply at all, but that if he did, his answer would probably take the form of an appreciation of the humanitarian consideration which had animated the Pope's appeal, but would point out the following objections:

(1) That there is no ground for the belief that the Pope's proposals would meet the views of any belligerent, and for this reason they did not form a good basis for negotiation.

(2) That they practically advocate the *status quo* before the War.

(3) That the entire disregard of International Law by the enemy makes it impossible to rely on any undertakings that he might give, and that Germany is morally bankrupt. President Wilson, however, was understood to hold the view that the door to negotiation should not be entirely closed.

Mr. Balfour drew attention to the fact that the British Government had already acknowledged the receipt of the Pope's Note, and in doing so had stated that his proposals had been received with the most sincere appreciation of their lofty and benevolent intentions, and that they would be studied by His Majesty's Government with the closest and most serious attention.

The Cabinet finally decided after having thoroughly examined the whole situation that the Secretary of State for Foreign Affairs should convey an intimation to the Vatican in the sense that, in reply to President Wilson's Peace Note, the Allies had formulated their war aims, but the Central Powers had not, and that on the present occasion we did not propose to send any detailed answer until we had received the reply of the Central Powers.

Those who directed the affairs of the nations knew in their hearts that unless the issue was fought out to a finish, any peace attained at that hour must be in the nature of a truce — a slightly more lasting Peace of Amiens, with war to be renewed on the first pretext when the nations had rested and reëquipped. Germany would have guarded against a repetition of the mistakes which had prevented her plans coming off at the start and were now standing in the way of her complete triumph. In 1914 she did not anticipate a protracted war and was therefore not prepared for it. She would have seen to it that next time her stores of copper and rubber were adequate. When war broke out, her granaries had no war reserves. In spite of that fact, she had committed the rashness of selling corn to Holland. She had no stock of fertilisers and her soil was now therefore impoverished without hope of renewal. She had underestimated the expenditure of ammunition in war under modern conditions. She had therefore no adequate supply of certain essentials. Necessary food ingredients, especially fats, were exhausted, and comforts like coffee were no longer available. All this she could provide against during a long truce, and it need not be very long.

"Never again" for her military leaders did not mean no more war, but not another war under such improvident conditions. France and Italy also had their military "Never agains." Both had committed errors of judgment and were guilty of equally disastrous omissions which delayed victory and nearly brought them irreparable defeat.

Had France foreseen the march through Belgium which

turned her flank, she would have fortified her frontiers from Switzerland to the sea. That she could put right during a short cessation of hostilities. Russia could have improved her transport and increased the size and equipment of her arsenals. Nothing would have been settled by the peace except the invincibility of the German Army. The legend of the "invincible army" would have been completely established by the failure of the colossal Allied offensives of the Western Front and the overwhelming Russian and Roumanian defeats on other frontiers. Alsace-Lorraine would still have remained a source of irritation. As to the naval front, Germany would never enter into war again with a second-rate fleet that would not enable her to protect her commerce and assure her food supplies and her supply of war material. Almost more important, there would be time to repair the cardinal mistake made in underestimating the dread possibilities of the submarine, especially of the larger type. There would be swarms ready to launch under the waters by next time.

The temper of the ruling elements in the belligerent countries was not yet tuned or turned towards peace. A patched-up peace would have effected no change in the Governments that constituted the Central Powers. It would have established the power of military autocracy more firmly than ever.

This is the real meaning of President's Wilson's reply to the Pope's message, and the explanation of his reluctance to respond at this stage to its appeal. Most pacifist of rulers, the President thought the cause of permanent peace would be damaged by any settlement which would be acceptable to the military rulers of Germany. They must first of all be overthrown and not only their authority, but their prestige be destroyed. The Allied Governments, in 1917, came to exactly the same conclusion as their predecessors had reached in 1916, on the question of entering into peace *pourparlers* with Germany. No real peace was possible until the military strength of Germany was broken. That accounts for the reluctance shown by the Allies to give a favourable response either to the Reichstag resolution, the Papal Note or the Kuhlmann overtures.

As the Allies had already stated their peace terms, it was thought desirable to leave to President Wilson the task of replying categorically to the Papal Note. The President was definitely of the opinion that the time had not yet arrived for peace negotiations, and that any peace attainable under present conditions would only mean a renewal of the conflict later on. As the blame for rejecting peace overtures has been attributed to the British Government, it is worth while reproducing President Wilson's reply in full:

Every heart that has not been blinded and hardened by this terrible war must be touched by this moving appeal of His Holiness the Pope, must feel the dignity and force of the humane and generous motives which prompted it, and must fervently wish that we might take the path of peace he so persuasively points out. But it would be folly to take it if it does not in fact lead to the goal he proposes. Our response must be based upon the stern facts and upon nothing else; it is not a mere cessation of arms he desires; it is a stable and enduring peace. This agony must not be gone through with again, and it must be a matter of very sober judgment what will ensure us against it.

His Holiness in substance proposes that we return to the *status quo ante bellum,* and that then there can be a general condonation, disarmament, and a concert of nations based upon an acceptance of the principle of arbitration; that by a similar concert freedom of the seas be established; and that the territorial claims of France and Italy, the perplexing problems of the Balkan States, and the restitution of Poland be left to such conciliatory adjustments as may be possible in the new temper of such a peace, due regard being paid to the aspirations of the peoples whose political fortunes and affiliations will be involved.

It is manifest that no part of this programme can be successfully carried out unless the restitution of the *status quo ante* furnishes a firm and satisfactory basis for it. The object of this war is to deliver the free peoples of the world from the menace and the actual power of a vast military establishment controlled by an irresponsible Government which, having secretly planned to dominate the world, proceeded to carry the plan out without regard either to the sacred obligations of treaty or the long-established practices and long-cherished principles of international action and honour; which chose its own time for the war; delivered its blow fiercely and suddenly; stopped at no barrier either of law or of mercy; swept a whole continent within the tide of blood, not the blood of soldiers only, but the blood of innocent women and children also, and of the helpless poor; and now stands balked, but not defeated, the enemy of four-fifths of the world. This power is not the German people. It is the ruthless master of the German people. It is no business of ours how that great people came under its control or submitted to its temporary zest, to the domination of its purpose; but it is our business to see to it that the history of the rest of the world is no longer left to its handling.

To deal with such a power by way of peace upon the plan proposed by His Holiness the Pope would, so far as we can see, involve a recuperation of the strength and renewal of the policy; would make it necessary to create a permanent hostile combination of the nations against the German people, who are its instruments; would result in abandoning the new-born Russia to the intrigue, the manifold subtle interference, and the certain counter-revolution, which would be attempted by all the malign influences to which the German Government has of late accustomed the world. Can peace be based upon a restitution of its power or upon any word of honour it could pledge in a treaty of settlement and accommodation?

Responsible statesmen must now everywhere see, if they never saw before, that no peace can rest securely upon political or economic restrictions meant to benefit some nations and cripple or embarrass others, upon vindictive action of any sort, or any kind of revenge or deliberate injury. The American people have suffered intolerable wrongs at the hands of the Imperial German Government, but they desire no reprisal upon the German people, who have themselves suffered all things in this war which they did not choose. They believe that peace should rest upon the rights of peoples, not the rights of governments, the rights of peoples great and small, weak or powerful, their equal right to freedom and security and self-government, and to a participation upon fair terms in the economic opportunities of the world, the German peoples of course, included, if they will accept equality and not seek domination.

The test, therefore, of every plan of peace is this: Is it based upon the faith of all the peoples involved, or merely upon the word of an ambitious and intriguing Government on the one hand and of a group of free peoples on the other? This is a test which goes to the root of the matter, and it is the test which must be applied.

The purposes of the United States in this war are known to the whole world — to every people to whom the truth has been permitted to come. They do not need to be stated again. We seek no material advantages of any kind. We believe that the intolerable wrongs done in this war by the furious and brutal power of the Imperial German Government ought to be repaired, but not at the expense of the sovereignty of any people — rather in vindication of the sovereignty both of those that are weak and of those that are strong. Punitive damages, the dismemberment of empires, the establishment of selfish and exclusive economic leagues, we deem inexpedient, and in the end worse than futile, no proper basis for a peace of any kind, least of all for an enduring peace. That must be based upon justice and fairness and the common rights of mankind.

We cannot take the word of the present rulers of Germany as a guarantee of anything that is to endure, unless explicitly supported by such conclusive evidence of the will and purpose of the German people themselves as the other peoples of the world would be justified in accepting. Without such guarantees, treaties of settlement, agreements for disarmament, covenants to set up arbitration in the place of force, territorial adjustments, reconstitutions of small nations, if made with the German Government, no man, no nation, could now depend on. We must await some new evidence of the purposes of the great peoples of the Central Empires. God grant it may be given soon, and in a way to restore the confidence of all peoples everywhere in the faith of the nations and the possibility of a covenanted peace.

ROBERT LANSING,
Secretary of State of the
United States of America.

This reply put a definite termination to the Vatican efforts for peace. The "scrap of paper" had shattered confidence in German Imperialism. President Wilson, like the Asquith Government, came to the conclusion that its overthrow was a condition precedent to a durable peace.

The German reply to the Papal Note was not given until the 21st of September. In spite of the Pope's explicit declaration that the complete restoration of Belgian independence was a *sine qua non,* the German answer contained no reference to Belgium. That reply caused profound disappointment even amongst the Germanophiles of the Continent. It was said that the Giolittians in Italy were "almost angry" while the clerical papers did not hesitate to manifest their disappointment or discouragement. In Vatican circles the sterility of the reply was attributed to the fact that the answer of the Central Empires had been completely reconstructed since the taking of Riga. (The German army leaders by this date were so confident that they could finally repel the British attack on Flanders that they organised an advance in Russia which ended in the capture of the important port of Riga.) We know now what took place in official circles in Germany between the date of the Reichstag resolution and their reply to the Papal Note. The facts have been revealed by the ex-Chancellor, Dr. Michaelis, and by General Ludendorff. Our Ambassador to the Papal See seems to have talked to Cardinal Gasparri as to the importance of securing a definite declaration from the German Government as to its intentions with regard to the complete independence of Belgium, and the compensation to be made to her for the damage done by the War. The French Government associated themselves with this communication, which was passed on to Chancellor Michaelis by the Papal Nuncio at Munich. On the strength of this message, the Chancellor seems to have arranged a Crown Council with the Kaiser and the Chiefs of the Army and Navy on the 11th of September. After a good deal of discussion, in which the Army Chiefs put forward extreme demands, the result of the conference was summarised in the following form, written and signed by the Kaiser in his own hand:

> The annexation of Belgium would be a mistake. Belgium can be restored. The Flemish coast is certainly very important and Zeebrugge cannot be allowed to fall into English hands. But the Belgium coast by itself cannot be kept. There must be a close economic association of Belgium with Germany. Belgium herself has the greatest interest in that.[1]

As there was considerable ambiguity in this short note, General Ludendorff three days later sent a memorandum to the Chancellor setting forth at considerable length his views on the peace terms which ought to be insisted upon. He summarises his demands in the following memorandum. He indicates in a footnote that the terms he sets out here were adopted. The memorandum has special importance because the Army Headquarters exercised much greater influence and authority on the general policy of their Government in Germany than in any other belligerent country. When the British Imperial War Cabinet discussed the terms of peace,

[1] "The General Staff and Its Problems", General Ludendorff, Vol. II, p. 489.

they did not call the Army or Navy chiefs into consultation. Nor did the French Government. But in Germany the position was entirely different. The German Chancellor and his colleagues would not dare to formulate conditions of peace without first of all submitting them to Hindenburg and Ludendorff and obtaining their approval. The reason is obvious. Neither the French nor the British Generals could flourish in the face of their respective governments such a dazzling array of crashing victories as those which the German Generals could compile. They marched into any conference with Ministers through an Arc de Triomphe as crowded with the names of battles they won as that which Napoleon erected for himself. Incidentally, the memorandum has also its historical value from the point of view not only of understanding what were the German ideas of the appropriate peace terms, but also as a revelation of the view of the Army chiefs as to the military position:

At the conferences in Berlin our position and that of our enemies has been under discussion. I regard it as my duty to return once more to this subject and set down in writing the line of reasoning I adopted. I have extended it here with regard to Longwy and Briey, agriculture and maritime trade.

Judging by the reports of the departmental representatives, our home situation is difficult in respect of fodder and coal; in the latter case, unfortunately, omissions in earlier months are partly responsible. Our financial system is extremely strained. Thanks to the Reichstag majority, our domestic situation has become very unsatisfactory. The labour, and therefore the recruiting questions have become even more difficult. Yet I think that these internal difficulties may be overcome by the firm control of the present Government. It is quite possible.

As I will now explain in greater detail, Austria-Hungary is firmly bound to us for the next few months. Even Bulgaria will be more conciliatory when the French have won local successes west of Lake Ochrida. We are always sure of the Turks. I need say nothing more to show that our military position is secure and that the U-boat campaign is producing its effects.

On the other hand, the position of the Entente is considerably worse.

Russia is tending even more obviously towards internal dissolution. She thus progressively falls out as an effective enemy. Her internal conditions must undoubtedly produce a food and fuel crisis in the winter. This situation will react on Roumania. Affairs in the East have taken a turn which is very favourable for us. The other Entente Powers can no longer fully rely on Russia and Roumania. Our alliance has nothing similar to show.

Italy is apparently reckoning on a victory in the twelfth Isonzo battle. It will be denied her. The internal situation will then tend to precipitate a crisis. The coal shortage must be very great.

It is not to be believed that the new ministry in France will be permanently more bellicose than its predecessor. We may anticipate the contrary. France, too, is faced with a coal crisis.

All recent reports from England agree that the U-boat campaign is effective, the food situation is serious, and the English Government has to contend with great social difficulties. The pressure for peace is becoming stronger. I need go no further into this matter. If England took really serious steps, it would be a sign that she no longer believed she could win. It is no long step from that to the conviction that she might lose.

Since Russia's downfall, America has become the hope of the Entente. Although she is not to be underestimated, she must not be overestimated. At the moment England seems to be afraid that the leadership of the Entente will pass to America.

We need not stop to discuss what are her relations with Italy and her other allies, but it is certain that there is great friction between the members of the Entente.

So far the year 1917 has not brought the Entente great military successes. England has only won Mesopotamia. The great victories on land and at sea (U-boats) have been on our side.

I draw the following conclusions: —

Our military situation is more favourable than that of the Entente. Our alliance is firmer. Our internal difficulties are less than those of the Entente.

Yet, notwithstanding all this, I am of opinion that it is desirable that we should try to get a peace before the winter sets in, so long as it brings us those essentials which we need to secure our economic position hereafter and gives us an economic and military position which allows us to face another war of defence without anxiety.

The sources of our economic and military powers of resistance are to be found — apart from the Army and Navy — in our agriculture, our mineral wealth and our highly-developed industry.

Without Roumania and other occupied areas, we should have been in a critical position with regard to food. Even with Roumania it has been serious enough. It would become still more acute, if, as we must anticipate later, we had to feed Belgium. At the moment we are quite unable to do so. *We must, therefore, have an increase of territory. That territory can only be found in Courland and Lithuania, which offer good agricultural opportunities.* In view of the attitude of Poland and for military reasons, we must fix the frontier of Lithuania to the south of Grodno *and somewhat enlarge East and West Prussia. Only thus shall we protect Prussia. Moreover, from a military point of view, the frontier is too unfavourable at various points in the provinces of Posen.*

Whether we shall attract the other Baltic provinces through Courland must be left to subsequent political developments.

I will only touch upon the question as to the favourable influence an improvement in the food situation would have on our relations with the neutral States. *Corn and potatoes are power, just like coal and iron.*

Our mineral wealth and our industries are located as unfavourably as possible — on the frontiers of the Empire. The Government and the Reichstag realised the difficult situation of the Upper Silesian coal basin even before the War and increased and strengthened the fortresses there. That by itself is not enough.

We must protect Upper Silesia by annexing further areas also. This would be facilitated by liquidating the enemy-owned mines there and transferring them into German possession.

In the west we have the two great centres of the Lorraine-Luxemburg ore fields with the Saar Basin and the lower Rhenish-Westphalian industrial area, which tends to extend more and more along the Belgian and Dutch frontiers. These areas have not been in danger during the War, owing to the fact that we got the start of the Entente in our strategic deployment. Besides, the importance of the industrial areas was certainly not fully realised at the beginning of the War. But there is no doubt now — and we must take the fact into account — that our enemies will do everything they can to injure us in these areas. If they should succeed, we should not be in a position to conduct a war of defence. We should also be in a hopeless position economically. There is no need to discuss the consequences to our domestic situation.

The unconditional protection of these two areas is a matter of life and death for us. *We must get everything we possibly can and which our position justifies. If we do not do so, our position will always be a subject of the greatest anxiety to us, and it would be better to go on fighting and not even think of peace.* We must be quite clear that what we fail to get will have to be made good in peace by heavy military expenditure (aerial defences, the maintenance of an aerial force, a formidable system of frontier defences), so far as it can be made good.

The Lorraine iron basin demands a protective belt on the west. The wider it is, the easier will it be to secure that protection. If we kept the frontiers we had before the War, it would mean that every political excitement would affect the mines and the great body of labour employed there. As soon as hostilities began, the works would be paralysed and exposed to destruction. Moreover, there are mines in the strips of territory we should aim at securing. The annexation of this area would also enable us to be more economical with our own ore. As the German production of ore is unfortunately somewhat limited, this point is not immaterial. But first and foremost the areas we must secure will give us a guarantee that the mines now in German possession will work even in war, if they have direct military protection.

It is obvious that the region will still be exposed to great danger from artillery and aviators and will make strong defensive measures necessary, as we cannot advance our frontiers there to the Meuse.

All the more essential is it that the lower Rhenish-Westphalanian area should be made inviolable. What the Flemish coast is to England, from the point of view of air attacks on that country, the line of the Meuse at Liège is for the industrial area, though in an even higher degree. *We must control the region on both sides of the Meuse and south as far as St. Vith. Hitherto, the only method of securing this aim has seemed to me the incorporation of the area in the German Empire. I must leave the question whether there is any other method to others. I have not yet succeeded in finding one.*

The possession of the Meuse line by itself is not enough to give the industrial area the security it requires. *We must keep an Anglo-Franco-Belgian army even further away. That can only be secured by binding Belgium so closely to us economically that she will seek political union also.* The economic association will not be realised without strong military pressure — a considerable period of occupation — and without our possessing Liège. *The neutrality of Belgium is a phantom on which no practical reliance can be placed.*

We should only be absolutely safe, especially if the Dover-Calais tunnel scheme materialised, if we were in military occupation of the whole of Belgium and held the coast of Flanders. In spite of all England's difficulties, that cannot at the moment be achieved.

The question is whether we ought to continue the War until we reach that goal. In my opinion it is our duty to do so, if England retains any territory in France (Calais). If she does not do so, the occupation of the Flemish coast would be no reason for us to continue the War through the winter.

We must look for other methods of producing those effects on England at which we aimed with our occupation of the Flemish coast. I consider that this is possible if Belgium is closely associated with the German Empire economically, divided into Walloon and Flemish areas, takes over her own defence against France and England in course of time, and has her own army and navy after the period of occupation comes to an end.

The association of Belgium with Germany will have as a result that Holland, if she pursues her obvious interests, will be attracted to us, especially if her colonial possessions are guaranteed by a Japan which is allied to us. In that way we shall reach another part of the coast of the continent which faces England, and realise the aim for which the navy is even now striving, justly recognising its importance. *We shall have a position with regard to England which will enable us to keep our trade going in the next war. That is the third great object which we must always keep in mind.*

To this aspect of affairs belong, besides Russia, *points d'appui overseas in South America, a colonial empire in Africa and naval stations in or outside the colonial empire.* At the very moment when we are abandoning the Flemish coast, the navy has a special claim by way of compensation to *points d'appui* — the Imperial Chancellor has himself said so — *which will enable it in the next war to keep the way to the world seas open to Germany and thereby secure her imports from abroad.* The greater our failure to achieve this aim, the larger must be the stocks of raw material which we shall have to accumulate, getting no return, in Germany.

I need only mention that a favourable commercial treaty with a Denmark closely associated with us would increase our maritime strength and freedom of trade enormously.

LUDENDORFF.[1]

14th September, 1917.

The footnote gives an idea of the conditions of peace which would be imposed at this date by Austria-Hungary:

[1] "The General Staff and Its Problems", by General Ludendorff, pp. 491–498.

(1) Integrity of the Monarchy.

(2) Slight improvements in the frontier against Russia.

(3) Strategic rectifications of frontier against Roumania (Iron Gate, and eventually the Bistrica valley).

(4) Restoration of the Kingdom of Serbia, though it must surrender the areas promised to Bulgaria, the Albanian portions to Albania, the Matschwa from Belgrade. With a view to satisfying Bulgaria, Baron Burian will eventually concede still more territory to that country. The rest of restored Serbia shall be joined in a close economic association with Austria.

(5) Restoration of the Kingdom of Montenegro, which will surrender certain areas to Austria-Hungary and Albania.

(6) Independence of Albania under Austro-Hungarian protectorate.

(7) Strategic rectifications of frontier against Italy. (Certain barren and mountainous districts.)

These arrogant documents were written by Ludendorff at a time when Sir Douglas Haig was assuring us that the German Army was crumbling under his terrible onset in Flanders.

The Army policy in Germany was definitely expansionist in the West as well as the East. It may be said that this memorandum simply represented the extravagant demands put forward by the military, but the military were definitely on top and the fact must not be overlooked that the Germans were in actual occupation of the territories they contemplated annexing and of a good deal more. A letter written by Michaelis the day after the conference shows that in so far as Belgium is concerned, there was no substantial difference between him and General Headquarters. As to annexations on the Eastern frontier, soldier and civilian were in complete accord. Such difficulties as existed had reference to expansion on the Western Front. This is what Michaelis wrote on September 12th to the Army Chiefs:

After the conclusion of yesterday's conference under His Majesty's Presidency, I felt myself compelled to give you and General Ludendorff my thanks for having supported me in so far-sighted a manner, and by no means from the purely military standpoint alone, in keeping our war aims within bounds in expectation of soon entering into negotiations, either in the autumn or spring.

I take it that the demands of Main Headquarters, demands on which you think there should be no weakening, mean that you both claim Liège and a protective belt for the safety of our western industrial area; that you both hope that as a result of the close economic association of Belgium with Germany, a situation will arise which, on purely egotistical economic grounds, will make it impossible for her to have military differences with us, so that when everything has been done in Belgium which can be demanded by us for the purpose of safeguarding the economic bond — and of course that will take several years from the time of the first negotiations — military safeguards can be allowed to lapse. Liège and so forth would therefore be demanded as a security for a limited period only.

I now want to make Your Excellency an urgent request that when the expected visitors reach headquarters, especially the visitors who belong to the annexationist school (for instance, I myself had to recommend Count Westarp to take a trip to Austria!) and who, knowing little about events among our allies, are thus inclined to regard a peace on the principles indicated with regard to Belgium as a bad one, you will inform them of your views so that extreme ambitions may be checked. We must show them what the enemy's intentions were with regard to us and what we have actually obtained — instead of destruction and dismemberment, intact frontiers in the West and a certain prospect of using the raw material in the occupied areas; commercial and transport facilities by rail and water; preferential treatment in the port of Antwerp; an influence over the Germanophile Flemish population; our neighbors themselves to bear the cost of the damage we have inflicted upon them; the destruction of English influence on the coast of Flanders and northern

France, and the demand for the return of our colonies as an object of compromise!

The next part up to the end was not read by the Minister-President Bauer in his speech of July 28th, 1919. The result was that the sense of the answer was completely distorted.

In addition, there is the fact that we gain enormously in power and influence in the East in political, economic and military matters.

Does this look like a "starvation" or "renunciation" peace? Who would dare to make another attack upon Germany, who has maintained herself victoriously on hostile soil three and four years against an immense superiority of numbers, and has only just given incomparable proof of her might in the furthest East?

No, our die-hards must possess their souls in peace! If we can bring peace to our poor, tormented people and the world on the lines set forth above, we should do so and not fight even a month longer for the sake of some naval station, however valuable. Please help in the work of enlightenment!

I maintain that if the whole of my letter had been read out, the representatives of the Government would not have succeeded, even for a moment, in obtaining a certain measure of success with some of their electors in reproaching me for having irresponsibly rejected an "offer of peace."

MICHAELIS.

On September 15th, Field Marshal von Hindenburg wrote a letter to the Chancellor which indicates clearly that the military had by no means modified the views they had expressed at the Crown Council:

In accordance with your Excellency's wish I will help in enlightening leading men on our intentions with regard to Belgium, intentions on which agreement has been reached among the authorities in anticipation of peace being reached this year. I do not conceal from myself that in the navy and many patriotic circles the evacuation of the Belgian coast will be regarded as a heavy blow, which will only become tolerable when the compensations materialise which Your Excellency also conceded to the navy. In agreement with General Ludendorff I think that the compensation should take the form of *points d' appui* within and without our colonial empire. I must add two points. *The economic union of Belgium with Germany will not be realised without pressure upon that country, even after the conclusion of peace.* An occupation of several years will serve the purpose, and in any case this would be necessary on military grounds while England and America are evacuating France. The *German holding of Liège must continue after the occupation, even it it lasts several years.* Its main purpose is the direct military protection of the lower Rhenish-Westphalian industrial areas. It is only when we are in occupation of Liège, and are and remain undisputed masters of the situation, that we can take the necessary military and administrative measures. *I am therefore bound to think that we could not leave Liège within any period that is ascertained or could be fixed in the treaty.*

VON HINDENBURG.

Anyone who after perusing this correspondence is still of opinion that a Peace Conference at this stage of the War would have led to any practical results must be a person in whom rooted partisanship completely strangles all judgment. It is evident that no German plenipotentiary would be allowed at such a conference to append his signature to a document restoring the independence of Belgium unconditionally.

But German statesmanship was still anxious to entice the Allies into a Peace Conference at a moment so favourable to the Central Powers. It continued to pursue what was known as the Peace Strategy. The Allied offensive on the Eastern and Southeastern Front had completely collapsed, and the French Army had retired for its rest cure after the failure of its offensive in the West. But America was arming, and Britain, in spite of Ludendorff's statement to the contrary, was beginning to grapple in earnest and effectively with the submarine menace. This might very well be Germany's best chance of securing an advantageous settlement. Her wisest leaders fully realised the position and were not prepared to throw away the chance. Von Bethmann-Hollweg, Michaelis, the Pope and the Emperor Karl having failed, the German Foreign Minister, Von Kuhlmann, tried his hand. He was the ablest diplomat who had yet appeared on the scene. He was well and favourably known in England. He had been a counsellor of the German Embassy in London for years before the War and it was known that his influence with the German Foreign Office was greater than that of the Ambassadors whom he served. Those who came into contact with him believed that he was anxious for good relations between his country and ours. The outside public were, however, suspicious of him. They ascribed a certain sinister wiliness to him and thought he was engaged in a game of hoodwinking trustful Ministers and journalists. But of his ability as a diplomatist there can be no doubt. He had recently been appointed German Foreign Minister. He was not deluded by the confidence displayed by the General Staff as to the ultimate result of the War. He knew Britain well, her stubborn will, her confidence in her invincibility, her inexhaustible resources. He also knew America with her gigantic reserves of men, money and material. He therefore knew that this was the last chance for making a profitable settlement which would present itself to Germany. Had he been complete master of the situation in Germany, no one could tell what might have ensued. But he was not. He had the unstable Kaiser, the weak Michaelis, the stubborn and arrogant Great Headquarters of the Army, and the Prussian aristocracy to overcome before he could put through any settlement which had the slightest chance of acceptance by the Allies. He nevertheless made an attempt.

On the 18th of September, our Ambassador in Spain was told by the Spanish Foreign Minister that he had heard:

". . . from one of his own diplomatic representatives that the Government of Germany were desirous of making a communication to Britain in regard to a peace settlement. He assured us that Spain had no desire to intervene or take any part in the matter, but he could see no objection to passing on the news to me. He asked whether His Majesty's Government would care to receive this suggestion from Germany, or would refuse all discussion of it? I told him that I could not say anything, but would send word to you and tell him what you replied. But I pointed out that the possibility of discussion depended on what the German proposals were, and that they would have to be very different from those so far made in the German Press. The Minister could tell me that the message came from a very exalted personage, but would give no further particulars."

At the time we were not told who "the exalted personage" was or how the communication came to the ears of the Spanish Minister. Since then we have ascertained that the source of the Minister's information was Villalobar, the Spanish representative at Brussels. Later on I had the opportunity of reading the actual dispatches which passed between Brussels and Madrid, and as they tell the full story — a story which is full of dramatic as well as historical interest — it had better be given in the original words:

BRUSSELS TO MADRID, 9th September, 1917.

I think that I have told you that the German Foreign Minister Kuhlmann was my colleague for a long time in London, when he was Counsellor to the German Embassy and I held a similar post in that of His Majesty. We are united by bonds of friendship, loyalty, and sympathy, and on my congratulating him on his well-deserved promotion, he replied in terms of the most affectionate character. To-day Lancken has received a secret cipher telegram from him, stating that he greatly desires to speak to me, and that as he wants an extremely secret interview which could not take place either in Brussels or in Berlin, he would like me to travel to some other place in Belgium or to come to

Cologne, where, as soon as I arrive in Germany, he promises to observe my most strict incognito while waiting for me. He says nothing further, but I suppose he wants to make some communication referring to peace which might be of interest to the [King?] and his Government. He begs me to leave here on Monday 10th, and to send him a reply if I accept his proposal. As this compromises nobody and it might be advisable to accept, I am making arrangements for the journey, advising Your Excellency immediately, both because it is my duty to do so, and because you may have some special communication to make to me before I travel. I need scarcely add that whatever its subject may be, I shall immediately telegraph to Your Excellency the substance of my conversation with Kuhlmann.

The following reply was sent by the Spanish Foreign Office:

MADRID TO BRUSSELS, 10th September, 1917.

I consider that the journey and interview proposed in the telegram received to-day are not in accordance with the interests of the public service, and I ask you to abstain from carrying out the project.

BRUSSELS TO MADRID, 14th September, 1917.

Your reply to my telegram of the 8th did not reach this Legation till Wednesday evening a few hours before my return from Cologne; I went there on Monday, as I advised you, as I had not received any reply from you previous to my departure.

The interview which was absolutely private, and secret, and without any importance if Your Excellency regards it as inopportune, consisted in the following:

The German Foreign Minister Kuhlmann told me that he proposed a reply to the Note of the Vatican in a moderate, courteous, and somewhat evasive manner, because, together with the official Note, Rome had communicated to him privately an official message from England, and had disclosed a telegram which Salis, the Prime Minister, had received from London asking, as was reasonable, what answer Germany proposed to make with regard to Belgium. Wherefore maintaining that it was to Germany's interests to speak firstly and principally with England, and, if possible to initiate conversations in this way before entering into negotiations, he proposed while sending an official reply to the official Note of the Vatican to state concerning the second Note that he had already initiated conversations (through another channel) and that he would reply later. For this reason he begged me to forward some indication of this through the British Minister at The Hague, and if the affair promised well, to make a pretext of giving details concerning the provisioning of Belgium and to go to London to speak of his projects regarding Belgium, which he told me would be in conformity with the aspirations of Great Britain. He repeated he desired to initiate preliminary peace conversations, in the first instance, with Great Britain if that were possible. He indicated that he asked this of *me,* because he knows me well, since I am communicating with him on other affairs of a general nature, and being aware of my friendship for England and my services to the Allies.

I replied that I was visiting him without the knowledge of Your Excellency or of the King and his Government, obeying the dictates of pure friendship and previous comradeship, and that I could not do anything without the knowledge of my superiors, that however much I might desire to see my Sovereign the arbiter of the coming peace, I could not personally take part in negotiations of any kind without the orders of my superiors, even though Belgian affairs are in question and I have been discussing with him other matters of a general character relative to the Service without instructions.

He replied that he quite understood my position, and that since the favour which he asked of me was a partly private one, reducing itself to discovering whether on a basis which must be agreeable to England, the latter were willing, before entering upon official negotiations, to hold a conversation which would compromise nobody and to discovering this in an absolutely confidential and secret manner, he would assist me to avoid any embarrassment, and he went so far as to tell me that if the conversation which he desired me to initiate in Holland and in England should not prove successful, I could deny all intervention on the part of my Government in order not to compromise it, while according to my judgment and pleasure, I could make it appear that I had intervened, naturally with your permission, where I saw that certain results were to be obtained. He told me that, assuming that what he knew from Rome was official, and taking into consideration the extent to which he was prepared to go to meet England, he thought the negotiations might proceed, and that in the case he strongly desired that the Spanish Government should not be excluded from the peace negotiations, if peace, as he hoped, were to result from the step taken by Rome. I replied that I would disclose my interview with him to you, adding that I knew nothing about his projects regarding peace negotiations, nor about the intentions of the Spanish Government on these points, but that I would give him an answer as to whether I could interest myself in the affair or not; I repeated that I was not authorised to take part in this interview, to which I had consented only out of personal friendship.

My personal impression is, and naturally this is included in the absolute secrecy to which I am bound by the confidence which he showed me in the rest of his conversation, *that Germany appears inclined to propose a peace which would meet the greater part of the Allies' desires, and especially those of England regarding the independence of Belgium and other matters which are of interest to Great Britain.* I regret that I did not receive your telegram before, since naturally I should have refused the interview to which I consented, as I took the non-arrival of your expected telegram for consent. In view of Your Excellency's reply, I shall refuse, or withdraw from the affair. Kuhlmann agreed that if Your Excellency authorised me to make private representations he would either give me further details through Baron Lancken or would come himself to some point in Belgium other than Brussels, in order to see me; he begged me to answer with all urgency since if he could not reply by means of me to the official indications alluded to, he would do it through another agency (which he indicated to me was not far removed from

Holland). I shall be much grieved if the proceeding in any way inconveniences Your Excellency, but I have long been disposed to sacrifice my personal position, which Your Excellency may dispose of in any way that is most advantageous to the service of the King and his Government. I earnestly beg you to transmit such orders as Your Excellency may consider appropriate.

I feel that before receiving your telegram I had no reason to avoid the interview, which in any case would have been futile, since Kuhlmann could equally well have come to Brussels and have visited me, and I could not have shut the door of the Legation in his face.

What he asked of me does not appear to compromise or trouble anyone; because one may say so and withdraw without danger and without result.

Provided that the fact of the official English communication is certain, there may be an opportunity for the intervention of His Majesty, which in that case would be opportune.

Please give me fresh instructions and believe that I much regret not receiving the previous instructions in time, if the conversation I have reported proves in any way inconvenient to Your Excellency.

BRUSSELS TO MADRID, 18th September, 1917.

Baron Lancken has just returned from Berlin, to which place he was urgently summoned, and has asked me very confidentially, on the instructions of the German Foreign Minister, whether I have received any reply to my telegrams. I replied that I was expecting an answer and he added that they desired that I should at least obtain permission to "sound" my English colleague at The Hague, for in view of the close relations which I maintain with him in connection with the Relief of Belgium, no particular significance would be attached to a conversation between him and myself on this subject. He also gave me a private hint that if an absolutely private and secret conversation could be brought about between a German and an English diplomatist, without in any way implying peace negotiations, they were confident of being able to settle the matter, and for this reason desired to know without delay if I could take this step. *In that case they will disclose all the aspirations of Germany, and the concessions which she is willing to make,* without thereby implying any negotiation; otherwise they will act through another channel.

They count in any case on our absolute discretion, which I promised, although I would promise nothing further without previous orders from you. Baron Lancken also told me that he intended to go to The Hague before long, and added confidentially that he would afterwards go to Switzerland, where he was to see someone from Paris.

I am reporting all I know, because I consider it fitting that Your Excellency should be informed, although in absolute secrecy, of what appears to be the nucleus of an effort to secure a settlement, and if this effort comes to nothing, my silence will not in any way prejudice the interests of the Service. But I omit all personal comments as long as I cannot count on the complete approval and further order of Your Excellency.

BRUSSELS TO MADRID, 19th September, 1917.
Personal and Very Private.

I have just received your telegram. You are perfectly right in regard to the difficulty of your telegram arriving before my departure for Cologne, but, having no more time than that at my disposal, I thought it my duty, while informing you in any case, not to delay my journey and I still think that the text of my telegram indicated this; I relied further in any event on the confidence with which you have always been good enough to honour me and on the assurance that whatever might happen it was my duty to be careful not to compromise either Your Excellency or the Spanish Government, while considering it on the other hand my duty not to lose any opportunity likely to further the royal service.

I believe that I have in no respect compromised the Government, since, if you disapprove of the proposal made I can sacrifice my standing with my interlocutor in the manner which you may direct.

Referring to the latter part of your telegram and amplifying my telegram, I believe it wiser to gain time on the pretext of a delay in the telegrams than to speak of the necessity of thinking over the matter carefully, lest, in so delicate a matter, undue suspicions arise that we are consulting in other quarters; since I regard it of the highest importance that he should not doubt our good faith in view of the absolute confidence which my interlocutor has shown me.

The step which I am requested to take in The Hague at least, *should, I think, be granted,* since even in the event of non-acceptance it may be regarded as a favour to the other side if the approaches are made with the skill and tact which should not in any case be neglected.

I feel it my duty to inform you that in my opinion the desire and need for peace on the German side are so great that we must remember that the matter will be taken up through another channel if we withdraw, an opportunity being thereby lost of advancing the interest of the King and our country.

I do not know whether Spain has been approached from other quarters or whether promises with regard to an intervention in favour of peace have been made by the other side, for which reason only Your Excellency's superior judgment can discern how far it is more expedient to take advantage of an offer from one or the other side or to bring together two such offers.

If I could have had a conversation with you I believe the difficulty could have been cleared up. At one time I thought of asking permission to travel to Spain, but the material lack of time, since I believe that events are moving fast, the secrecy of the negotiations and the need to avoid comments on my movements remove all possibility of such a conversation.

I await orders, trusting that Your Excellency will not forget my loyalty to the King and my zeal in your service.

MADRID TO BRUSSELS, 19th September, 1917.

In reply to your telegram, I have to inform you that the matter is occupying my attention, and I hope to be able shortly to forward my instructions.

Although neither I nor any member of the Cabinet saw any of these telegrams that led up to the Spanish Government's communiqué, they felt that the communication itself was a matter of sufficient consequence to call for the most careful examination. Mr. Balfour's view of the matter was expressed in the memorandum he submitted to me on September 20th, which ran as follows:

Secret.

PEACE NEGOTIATIONS

From the Foreign Office point of view we have now reached the most critical and difficult stages of the War. When hostilities began, diplomatic relations between the belligerents were, of course, completely severed; when hostilities are over, the regular machinery of diplomacy will, of course, be reëstablished. But we are now in the middle stage, when fighting has lost none of its violence, when all the natural channels of diplomacy are still choked, but when, nevertheless, some, at least, of the belligerents are endeavouring to start informal conversations about terms of peace.

From Austria, Bulgaria, and Turkey, hesitating and inconclusive advances have thus been made to us and, I believe, to France also. But there is this significant difference between the case of Austria and the cases of Bulgaria and Turkey — in the case of Austria, the advances have come from the highest quarters in the established Government — in the cases of Bulgaria and Turkey, on the other hand, the advances have been made on behalf of rebels, or would-be rebels, against the Powers that be.

Now would-be rebels are dangerous guides. They are apt to take too rosy a view of their powers and prospects. They have the sanguine enthusiasm of the gambler, and though they sometimes make a fortune they more commonly lose one. This consideration would naturally induce us to take the Austrian proposals more seriously than those of her two Eastern allies. But, on the other hand, all the indications appear to show that Austria is so tightly bound to Germany, that, *as things are at present,* she could do no more for the cause of peace than press moderation upon her arrogant partner. Whatever change in her attitude the coming winter and spring may produce, it seems more than doubtful whether *at the present moment* anything will induce Austria to break away from Germany.

The last to enter the diplomatic field is Germany.

A private telegram just received from Sir A. Hardinge, which I have circulated to the Cabinet, shows beyond question that the German Foreign Office is desirous of entering into conversations with the British Government; *probably* with a view of arriving at some basis of discussion as regards the terms of peace, *possibly* with the amiable purpose of sowing dissensions among the Entente Powers. Speaking generally, therefore, the situation is this:

Representatives of the Opposition in Turkey and in Bulgaria have informed us that their respective countries are weary of the War, and that under certain conditions the Governments that are keeping them in the War could be overthrown. Austria, or, at least, the Austrian Court, desires peace, but will not act without Germany. Germany has expressed her desire for a noncommittal talk about terms of peace.

Clearly the last of these overtures is the most important. It is, moreover, the only one which has reached us through the orthodox channel of a neutral Foreign Office, and we must without delay consider what line we propose to adopt with regard to it.

I venture to lay down, if only for purposes of discussion, the following propositions:

(1) We cannot ignore Kuhlmann's proposal. To do so would greatly help the pan-German forces at Berlin. It would also, I think, weaken the Government in Britain. It would tend to unite Germany in favour of the War and to disunite public opinion at home, which is quite ready vigorously to support the War, if war be necessary, but would shrink from anything which looked like an unreasonable determination to fight for fighting's sake.

(2) What we do must be done with the full knowledge of our Allies. I have little doubt that Kuhlmann would greatly prefer that the conversations with the British Government which he

desires should be kept secret, and he would desire this whatever be his motives in initiating this new policy. If his object is to make mischief between the Allied Powers, his best course is evidently to carry on negotiations secretly until they have reached a stage which lends itself to misrepresentation, and then to betray them. If, on the other hand, as I am inclined to believe, he is genuinely anxious to find a basis for settlement, this end might well seem to him easier of attainment if he begins his diplomatic conversations with a dialogue rather than with a general debate.

It must be remembered that one of the most serious perils incident to all peace negotiations of the kind proposed is that they give a Power like Germany unique opportunities of sowing dissensions among its opponents. We need not fear, indeed, that any of the Allied Governments will prove willingly faithless: but, with the exception of Britain and America, they each have to deal with a public opinion which is moved in the main by national considerations. If, therefore, either France or Italy (for example) were offered *now* all, or more than all, that a successful war could ultimately give them, it might be exceedingly difficult for any Government to induce them to go on fighting for interests that were not their own.

I do not see any method of effectually parrying this danger. But our best chance is perfect frankness, and it seems therefore clear that we should do nothing without fully informing France, Italy, America, Russia and Japan. It is quite possible that if, and when, we communicate our intention to the Germans, they may drop the whole matter. This does not, however, alter my opinion that we should lay ourselves dangerously open to misconception if we indulged in even the most noncommittal conversations behind the backs of our friends.

I suggest, therefore, that the Cabinet should authorise me to call together the Allied Ambassadors and tell them that a neutral Power had informed us that Germany was desirous of entering into conversations with us on the subject of terms of peace, and that in our opinion it would be wise to listen to any proposals that she might have to make; it being clearly understood that we should at once communicate them to our Allies without in any way committing ourselves until the Allies had had an opportunity of fully considering them.

If this course be adopted in principle, we should have further to consider whether the sort of communication I have suggested should be made also to the smaller Powers, now very numerous, who have joined in the War on our side. I am, on the whole, against this course. Needful secrecy will be difficult enough in any case; but if all the States, European, Asiatic, and South American, who have committed acts of war on Germany, are to be taken into our confidence, the proposal might as well, indeed much better, be proclaimed at Charing Cross. At all events a proclamation at Charing Cross would accurately represent the facts.

However this may be, I cannot believe the Germans would ever consent to this degree of publicity. I doubt whether they will consent even to our communicating their proposals to the great Powers of the Entente; but this we must risk. Indeed, if I am to speak my whole mind, I am by no means sure that a refusal on their part to proceed further in the matter — and on such a ground — would not, *at the moment,* be the best thing that could happen to us.

A. J. BALFOUR.

Foreign Office,
20th September, 1917.

At the time this document was received I was taking a short holiday down in Wales, and it was forwarded to me there. I also received at the same time the following letter from Mr. Bonar Law:

"11, Downing Street,
Whitehall, S.W.
21st September, 1917.

"My dear L.G.,

"I think we can hardly take any action till we know (perhaps you do now) what happened with Painlevé's negotiations with Austria, and in any case I do not feel sure that it might not be right, with the approval of Painlevé, to invite the Germans to indicate what they mean without consulting all the other Allies. I feel sure, however, that this is too important to be dealt with at all or even considered by the Cabinet till you have considered it.

"Possibly you may think it worth while to send a message to Painlevé urging him to be here on Monday.

"I am sorry to urge you to shorten your holiday, which no one ever needed more, but I do think that it is almost necessary that you should be back in time to consider this on Monday. I wonder what you think of the attack yesterday. It looks to me better than I expected. Haig's report is, so Robertson told us, that our casualties are slight, but I do not know what that means.

"I have to take a new departure about Exchequer Bonds and wish your approval before doing it. The change will have to be announced to the Bankers on Wednesday.

Yours sincerely,
A. Bonar Law."

I immediately returned to London and the situation was discussed at a meeting of the Cabinet. By that time Mr. Balfour had ascertained that the Germans had also approached the French through their intermediary, Von Lancken. With regard to him and his proposals, Mr. Balfour reported that this individual had been First Secretary to the German Embassy in Paris before the War, and had subsequently been sent to Belgium, where he was supposed to have played a somewhat sinister part in the Nurse Cavell affair. Under orders from Von Kuhlmann, Von Lancken had made approaches to M. Briand through a lady who was half-French and half-German and personally acquainted with M. Briand. This lady was asked to tell M. Briand that Germany was willing to make peace. M. Briand had quite properly communicated the information to M. Painlevé, who had forwarded it to Mr. Balfour through M. Cambon, the French Ambassador. The suggested terms were so favourable to the

British and French as to arouse suspicion that their object must be sinister. They included the following terms:

Cession of Alsace-Lorraine by Germany.
Restoration of Serbia.
Territorial concessions to Italy.
Colonial concessions to Great Britain.
Restoration of Belgium.

The significant feature, however, was that neither Russia nor Roumania were referred to. M. Cambon, so Mr. Balfour informed us, had expressed the apprehension that, if once it became known in France that the cession of Alsace-Lorraine was included in the offer, it would be very difficult to keep France in the War.

If Russia and Roumania thought that we were discussing a peace on these lines they would probably themselves make a separate peace at once.

Beyond the above, no details had been given and the available information was absolutely vague. Moreover, this approach to the French was of an entirely informal character.

The approach to us, Mr. Balfour continued, was through a formal channel, having been sent by the British Ambassador at Madrid, who had himself received it from the Spanish Government, who had received it from Germany through official channels, it was said from a most exalted quarter. Mr. Balfour was quite confident that it constituted a genuine approach.

A discussion ensued as to the answer to be given to the Spanish Government. It was decided that I should go over to France immediately to see the French Premier, M. Painlevé, before coming to any final conclusion. The following day I met M. Painlevé at Boulogne.

According to a note taken at the time, I ascertained from the conversation with M. Painlevé that the German peace

BARON VON KUHLMANN

approach to France was serious. The suggestion was that M. Briand should meet in Switzerland either an ex-Chancellor, the present Chancellor, or some more exalted person. M. Painlevé had said that M. Briand had fluctuated somewhat in his reports of what terms the Germans were prepared to offer. At one moment he had said that they were willing to give up everything that the Allies desired in the West — *e.g.*, Belgium and Alsace-Lorraine. Afterwards he had said that they were willing to *discuss* Alsace-Lorraine. One of the most serious considerations was that M. Briand was in favour of entering into this negotiation. M. Painlevé and M. Ribot, however, were both opposed to it. What M. Painlevé seemed to fear was not that the approach was not bona fide, but that it *was* bona fide. He evidently doubted whether France would continue fighting if it were known that the Germans had offered both nine tenths of Alsace-Lorraine and the whole of Belgium. French Ministers took the same general view about the desirability or otherwise of peace *pourparlers* with Germany as we did — that it was undesirable to enter into any negotiations until the German military power was broken.

My views as to the policy we ought to adopt depended on the military prospects. There were obvious and multiplying indications that Russia could no longer be depended upon for effective military assistance. It looked as if she meant to go out of the War. I was anxious to have military opinion as to the effect of this defection, if it occurred before America was ready to take her place. Robertson, whom I consulted, was of the opinion that, if Russia collapsed, the chances of our achieving a military victory were gone. I decided to obtain the views of General Foch and Sir Douglas Haig. Foch, whom I met at Boulogne, did not accept Robertson's estimate of the position. I proceeded from Boulogne to our General Headquarters in France to place the matter before Sir Douglas Haig. He agreed with Foch's opinion. It detracted somewhat from the value of his opinion that he based it largely on the joyous arithmetic of the optimistic Charteris, which demonstrated beyond question that there were not many untattered German divisions left on the Western Front after our attack, which had taken place in Flanders the day I arrived at G.H.Q. and that some of this miserable remnant was of inferior quality. Sir Douglas Haig promised to give me in writing his considered views as to the military position which would be created in the event of the complete elimination of Russia from the War.

When the promised document arrived, it seemed to me to be more concerned with convincing the Cabinet of the importance of prosecuting the Passchendaele offensive and of guaranteeing to the Commander-in-Chief an unfailing supply of men to fill up casualties than it was with the problem which I submitted to him. He repeatedly expressed the most complete confidence that if we fulfilled his requirements as to men, the Germans could be defeated whether Russia went out of the War or not.

A few extracts from this inebriated document will be given in the Passchendaele chapter. It breathes the fumes of a confidence stimulated by the constant draughts of carefully distilled reports placed on the table of the Commander-in-Chief. One must bear in mind Ludendorff's survey of the military situation which I have already given. Neither Haig nor Ludendorff were consciously bragging. They both sincerely believed that their appreciations were well founded in irrefragable facts: such is the intoxication produced by the unlimited power whose slightest expression carries death or mutilation to myriads.

Holding as he did this view of the military situation, Haig deprecated the alternative of "accepting an unsatisfactory peace" instead of maintaining our offensive:

It would mean not only the almost certain renewal of the War hereafter at a time of Germany's choosing, but the entire loss of the faith and respect of our Overseas Dominions, America, and our other allies, and indeed of the entire world, East and West. More, it would entail a loss of self-respect from which Great Britain could never recover. The effect on the 2,000,000 men in France, who have done so much and suffered so much, and who are so confident in their power to win, would be calamitous and immediate.

It would be better for the future of our race to fail in next year's offensive than to accept the enemy's terms now when after more than three years of splendid effort we have brought the German resistance so near the breaking point.

But I see no reason to apprehend failure. Everything goes to show that the power of endurance of Germany and her allies is so severely strained that the mere fact of our ability and evident determination to maintain the struggle to the end may suffice to turn the scale at any moment.

Even if they hold out till next year, and if our success in the field then is of a limited nature, our enemies cannot possibly face a further prolongation of the War, with the full development of America's strength, which will then be developing, to be reckoned with.

The confidence of Foch in the certainty of victory next year was based on opinions formed in a calmer atmosphere than that of a great battle which had already lasted three months. It was for that reason more reliable and impressive. It confirmed the conviction I had already formed, that now the submarine peril was being mastered, a complete Allied triumph was assured, notwithstanding the defection of Russia. When the Cabinet discussions on the Kuhlmann proposals were resumed, the part I took was influenced by the fact that my conclusions as to the military prospects had been fortified by the highest military opinion.

It was decided to empower the Foreign Secretary to summon a meeting of the Ambassadors of France, America and Japan with the Chargés d'Affaires of Italy and Russia and to submit for their consideration the following reply to the German Government:

"His Majesty's Government would be prepared to receive any communication that the German Government may desire to make to them relating to peace, and to discuss it with their Allies."

This meeting was held on the 8th of October.

The Allied representatives were in complete agreement with the views expressed in this telegram. It is significant of the French view that M. Cambon added:

". . . that, in his opinion, it would be impossible to continue the War with vigour, or even to continue it at all, if the Powers once reached the stage of discussing terms round a table. It followed that, before this stage of 'round-table discussions' was reached, we must be fully assured that the main objects of the Allied efforts had already been secured."

No reply was given by the German Government to this telegram, but the day after it was dispatched to Madrid and probably before it was received in Berlin, the famous "No, never" speech was delivered by Von Kuhlmann, which showed that M. Briand had been completely misled by his informant as to the German attitude on Alsace-Lorraine:

". . . I think it proper to give a clear and firm statement of our attitude, since curiously enough there still seem to be misconceptions in this respect among our enemies, and even among one or other of our neutral friends.

"There is but one answer to the question, 'Can Germany in any form make any concessions with regard to Alsace-Lorraine?' The answer is: 'No, never!'

"So long as a single German can hold a gun, the integrity of the territory handed down to us as a glorious inheritance by our forefathers *can never be the object of any negotiations or con-*

cessions. I am sure that, whether on the Right or on the Left, you will stand for that with equal resoluteness and equal self-sacrifice.

"I am not one of those who think that a candid statement of such a fact might be detrimental to the rise of a clear and sincere will for peace. On the contrary, I think such a will can only prosper and be fruitful on the ground of absolute clearness. Therefore, I think it necessary to state emphatically with all possible conciseness and clearness, as against all other questions which have of late so markedly come to the fore in public discussion, and which have taken up so much space, that what we are fighting for and will fight for to the last drop of our blood, is not fantastic conquests, but, before all, the integrity of German soil."

Von Kuhlmann stated that "absolute clearness" was essential to the will for peace. But we could not help observing that whereas he left no doubt as to the decision of the Imperial Government of Germany on the question of Alsace-Lorraine, he refrained from making any statement about its intentions on the question of Belgium. This speech was regarded as a slamming of the door by Germany, but not before a glimpse had been given as to the designs of the men who mattered there. They disclaimed conquest, but all the same, they meant to extend the area of their dominion — economically, diplomatically and militarily. As far as considerable territories were concerned, they avowed the intention to annex.

I believe Kuhlmann was genuinely desirous of restoring Belgium. He secured from the Crown Council a Minute which seemed to sanction that policy. He knew that restoration of Belgium was Britain's chief war aim. Both the British Premier and ex-Premier had categorically asked the German Government whether they were prepared to clear out of Belgium entirely and restore her independence in its full integrity. They were told by the Papal Nuncio that this was the matter to which the British attached the greatest importance. But no assurance was forthcoming to the Pope or to the Allies. Why? Kuhlmann knew that the moment he gave a categorical and unambiguous answer satisfactory to the Allies, Junkerdom would be in arms, and "the place he knew would know him no more." He wished first of all to lure the Allies into a talk round the table and to play them one against the other. This would foster suspicion and perhaps dissension amongst the Allies, especially if Russia were included, as she must be, in the conclave. If the conference failed, it would be known in Allied Countries that the Germans had "in principle" agreed to abandon Belgium. Thus Allied morale would be sapped. As a war aim, the manœuvre might have been considered by some to be legitimate and would no doubt have been effective. Kuhlmann may have been genuinely anxious for peace, and I think he was, for he realised his country's peril better than the Generals. But the latter, I am convinced, only consented for tactical reasons to this peace feeler, which they never ceased to regard as risky. They viewed it with a greater measure of apprehension than they did the Flanders offensive.

In reading Ludendorff's war books, one can see that Army Headquarters tolerated these overtures merely as a diplomatic offensive to divide and weaken the enemy. In fact, it was known as the "peace offensive." No Government in Germany was strong enough to defy these heroes of a hundred victories.

With such men in authority, could the Allies have made peace in 1917? Yes, of a kind. So they could have in 1916.

Would Belgium have been restored? Perhaps — probably, on terms. Amongst those terms would certainly have been the surrender of Liège and the Congo, with the imposition of economic and military conditions in what was left of

Belgium, and an addition to German territory in the Baltic. Poland might have been granted autonomy under the protection of Germany, after a further slice of its territory had been cut out of the Russian provinces. Alsace-Lorraine would have remained German. The Briey iron mines of France would have come under German control. Germany would have had her colonies restored to her. What would have happened to Italy? She might have been given a few slices of Italia Irredenta on the condition that Austria had a liberal equivalent in Russia and Roumania. German military prowess would have been higher than ever. The terror inspired by her redoubtable army would have been deeper. Would Germany have scrapped that powerful army in the interests of world peace and security? Has France dismantled her huge armaments? The man who thinks that Hindenburg and Ludendorff would have agreed to such a proposal then is fit only for a private nursing home. Having through years of sacrifice achieved a greater Germany, they would not have thrown away the formidable military organisation that had won it for the Fatherland. If they or one of them were sincere in their acceptance of the theory of a conspiracy to destroy that Fatherland, would they break up the machine that had held all the conspirators at bay for three years and inflicted terrible punishment on them all on land and sea?

Turkey would have been persuaded to concede a spurious autonomy to the Arabs — as delusive as Abdul Hamid's "reforms" for Armenians. Bulgaria would have been rewarded for her services by chunks of Serbian and Roumanian territory. A suitable present would also have been found for Constantine. He had earned it and would not have been forgotten. What a peace as a result of cruel sacrifice! Too horrible to think of!

CHAPTER IX

THE CAMPAIGN OF THE MUD: PASSCHENDAELE

1. How the Plans Were Laid

Heroism and stupidity of Passchendaele, Verdun and Somme — Flair more valuable than military training — Transport preparations in December, 1916 — Responsibility for delays — Admiralty's part in urging campaign — Politicians not responsible — Robertson's letter to Joffre — Reasons for letter — No decision by War Committee — Mr. Asquith's draft letter — Plumer's plan covered only Messines attack — G.H.Q. sets out its plan — Cabinet kept in ignorance — Conditions laid down by G.H.Q. as essential — Robertson's attitude — No report to Cabinet before preparations — Russia's collapse.

And now we come to the battle which, with those of the Somme and Verdun, will always rank as the most gigantic, tenacious, grim, futile and bloody fight ever waged in the history of war. Each of these battles lasted for months. None of them attained the object for which they were fought. In each case it was obvious early in the struggle to every one who watched its course — except to those who were responsible for the strategic plan that wrought the grisly tragedy — that the goal would not be reached. Taken together they were responsible for the slaughter or mutilation of between two and three million of brave men. The tale of these battles constitutes a trilogy illustrating the unquenchable heroism that will never accept defeat and the inexhaustible vanity that will never admit a mistake. It is the story of the million who would rather die than own themselves cowards — even to themselves — and also of the two or three individuals who would rather the million perish than that they as leaders should own — even to themselves — that they were blunderers. Hence the immortal renown and the ghastly notoriety of the Verdun, Somme and Passchendaele battlefields; the fame won by sustained valour unrivalled in the annals of war; the notoriety attained by a narrow and stubborn egotism, unsurpassed amongst the records of disaster wrought by human complacency.

Falkenhayn, Joffre, and Haig were trained soldiers who had worked hard to master their profession. But there is no profession where experience and training count less in comparison with judgment and flair. The intervals between great wars are fortunately so considerable, and in this age of restless invention the change in mechanism and therefore in methods is also so considerable and so rapid, that imagination, resource, initiative and flexibility are more essential to success in the vocation of the soldier than in any other.

The battle of the Flanders mud, better and more bitterly known as the Battle of Passchendaele, had been put into Sir Douglas Haig's tenacious brain as early as 1916. If it failed it was not for lack of the most elaborate and prolonged preparations. In July, 1917, he told the War Cabinet that he had been preparing for it the whole year. Meanwhile he was impatient of any other plan. The Chantilly [1] proposals provided something for him to go on with, whilst he was completing his preparations for the real campaign of the year. The Nivelle "break-through" was a crude and inconvenient rival to the Flanders operation. The capture of the Messines Ridge, a perfect attack in its way, was just a useful little preliminary to the real campaign, an *aperitif* provided by General Plumer to stimulate the public appetite for the great carousal of victory which was being provided for us by G.H.Q.

The Commander-in-Chief had caught fire with this idea in 1916. G.H.Q. had been burning with it ever since and was now red-hot. Even the drenching rains of August and September could not put it out. Fire in peat can be quenched by

[1] The Chantilly Conference of Generals was held on November 15, 1916.

continuous heavy rains, but not if the smouldering stack is completely under cover.

The sector of the enemy's front which it was intended to attack, and the objective which it was sought to attain, had been chosen by our military and naval advisers in the late autumn of 1916. It was to be an operation for clearing the coast of Flanders, as a minimum objective. There was also the prospect of a break-through which might end in "rolling" the Germans out of Belgium. Attrition was an afterthought of beaten Generals to explain away their defeat, and perhaps to extract some residue of credit out of a bad scheme badly handled.

Sir Eric Geddes received orders about December, 1916, to develop the transport arrangements by road and rail between all the ports on the Northeast coast and our Flanders Front with a view to carrying great numbers of troops and vast quantities of material into that area. When he complained, in January, that he was short of fifty thousand tons a week of material to carry out his orders, it was assumed by the War Cabinet that the urgency of his need for all that immense consignment of steel rails and road material was because he was being pressed by the Commander-in-Chief to perfect the arrangements for the spring offensive so as to enable the British Army to strike at the time indicated in the plan. It was discovered afterwards that most of the supply was required to make and improve roads and rails to bring up troops, ammunition, equipment and supplies for the Flanders attack in the late summer. He was given all the material and facilities he asked for. Never has there been a single battle staged with such tremendous and prolonged preparations. If therefore it failed, that failure is not attributable to any neglect to supply the High Command with all that was needful in the way of men, guns, tanks and ammunition to make and to sustain their attack, or to any lack of facilities for carrying these into the sphere of action. The despised civilians did all that could be expected from the wit, work and the devotion of man to make the plans of the military leaders a success — politicians, manufacturers, shippers, engineers, and most of all the humble civilians who were called up after a few months' training to face the most terrible artillery and machine guns in the world in order to carry out impossible orders issued by Generals who had no idea what the execution of their commands actually meant.

If there were delays, the High Command were alone responsible for them. The Commander-in-Chief could have broken off the Arras attack at any time after the French had abandoned serious pressure on their front. That was in May. If therefore he did not commence his Flanders assault until practically August, it was not because he was delayed by any obligation to the French to persist in the Nivelle offensive. That had been virtually suspended three months before the first Passchendaele attack.

It is difficult and confusing to trace the origin of this adventure. The apologists of the High Command have been known to ascribe the blame in the first place to the Admiralty, who were making urgent appeals to the Government to capture the Flemish coast in order to destroy the submarine nests located at so short a distance from vital sea routes. It is suggested that Ministers succumbed to naval insistence, and, according to Sir William Robertson, informed him that "there was no measure to which the War Committee attached greater importance than the expulsion of the enemy from the Belgian coast and that arrangements should be made to include a plan of that nature in the operation of the following year."

The legend that politicians were responsible for constraining the High Command into the Passchendaele attack was revived in the late autumn, when it had become clear to the men engaged in actual operations that they were being called upon to undertake an impossible task. Brigadier General Baker-Carr, who was associated at that time with the tanks in the battle area, in his interesting and revealing book, says:

> To anyone familiar with the terrain in Flanders it was almost inconceivable that this part of the line should have been selected. If a careful search had been made from the English Channel to Switzerland, no more unsuitable spot could have been discovered. . . .
>
> We were told, of course, that policy rather than strategy had dictated it *and that the C.-in-C. had been compelled, against his better judgment, to accede to the desires of our civilian rulers*. . . .
>
> Policy must usually dominate strategy, but on occasions circumstances will arise that render political desiderata impossible of attainment.
>
> If there had ever been the most remote chance of achieving our ultimate purpose, viz. the capture of the ports used as submarine bases, no sacrifice would have been too great. But this remote chance never existed, even at the very commencement. . . .[1]

By the time this statement was made to General Baker-Carr, G.H.Q. were becoming anxious to pass the responsibility for the whole of this insane enterprise on to other heads, either the politicians who constituted the Government in London, or the French, who were supposed to be urging it as a means of sparing their army. Both British Ministers and French Generals were strongly opposed to the undertaking, and conveyed their misgivings to the British Command.

I have carefully examined all the available documents in order to track down the originator or originators of this muddy and muddle-headed venture. The minutes and the

[1] "From Chauffeur to Brigadier", by Brigadier General Baker-Carr, Chapter XIV, p. 226 *et seq.*

memoranda which I shall quote later on will show clearly that I resisted to the very last the whole project before it was ever commenced, and confidently predicted its failure, giving reasons for my prediction. After its failure was beyond reasonable doubt, I did my best to persuade the Generals to break it off. The only question therefore as far as my individual responsibility is concerned, is whether the initiation of this reckless enterprise can be laid at the door of the Asquith Government — of which I was a member. The Ostend scheme had been repeatedly discussed as a desirability or possibility, but always turned down by British and French as an impracticability. At the Chantilly Conference of Generals in November, 1916, which settled the outlines of the Allied campaign for 1917, nothing was said about a great Flanders offensive. Nor was it mentioned at the Paris Conference which ensued. But a fortnight later Sir William Robertson wrote the following letter to Marshal Joffre:

"1st December, 1916.

"My dear General,

"My Government has been viewing with some anxiety the increase of German naval activity on the coast of Belgium, which clearly has for its object the interruption of communications between Great Britain and France. It is undoubtedly the case that the German Navy is learning by experience, and that, owing to the facilities for raiding the Channel which the possession of Ostend and Zeebrugge affords the enemy, it is becoming increasingly difficult to ensure uninterrupted traffic.

"The British Admiralty consider that we must be prepared for still greater activity and enterprise in this direction on the part of the Germans next year, and that if the enemy is left in possession of Ostend and Zeebrugge the threat to our communications may then be very serious. It is obvious that the maintenance of sea communication between Great Britain and France is vital to the successful conduct of the War on the Western Front, and in these circumstances my Government desire that the occupation of Ostend and Zeebrugge should form one of the objectives of the campaign next year.

"I am accordingly instructing Sir Douglas Haig to place himself in communication with you *with a view to this operation being given a place in the general plans of operations for next year,* and to the necessary preparations being made to carry it out.

W. ROBERTSON."

Son Excellence
M. le Maréchal Joffre"

Why was Sir William Robertson in such a hurry to include this attack "in the general plans of operations for next year?" It had not been agreed to by the Cabinet. It had not even been thought out by the Staff at that date. Sir William Robertson saw that there were political changes pending. There was every prospect that men who were not strict communicants of the great Western Church — Mr. Bonar Law and I — might take command of affairs. The Government must therefore be committed in advance by a document which would have the validity of an Inter-Allied Military Convention. He was therefore in a hurry to incorporate the Flemish campaign in the Chantilly Pact.

In the minutes of the proceedings of the War Committee, there is no record which would indicate that the question was ever even raised during the months of November or December. As it is not included in any of the minutes of that Committee, the letter must have been the result of some informal conversations between the Prime Minister and Sir John Jellicoe, and afterwards between Ministers. We were at the time very preoccupied with the submarine menace and the Admiralty despaired of coping with it by any naval methods. They were therefore anxious for a military advance along the Flemish coast which would capture harbours used as submarine bases, mostly for the smaller craft.

We decided to ask the military experts to consider the possibility of such an enterprise *and report to us*. That report never reached the Cabinet.

There is a draft letter addressed to the C.I.G.S. prepared for Mr. Asquith's signature by his direction. There is a personal note at the top of the draft which states that:

> It was prepared by direction of the Prime Minister for him to send to the C.I.G.S. as the result of a discussion, between the Cabinet Ministers forming the War Committee, on Monday afternoon, 20th November. Before it was sent, however, Sir William Robertson stated that the matter was to be discussed between General Sir Douglas Haig, the First Sea Lord and C.I.G.S. on Thursday afternoon, 23rd November. Consequently the Prime Minister decided not to send the letter. The draft, however, was sent to C.I.G.S. on 22nd November, for his information in connection with the forthcoming conference.

However, if the letter had been dispatched it contains no "instructions" for a military offensive in Flanders. Here is the unfinished and unsigned draft.

> 10, Downing Street,
> 21st November, 1916.
>
> After you had left the War Committee yesterday a very important discussion took place on the question of the submarine menace, and more particularly in regard to the protection of the routes through the Narrow Seas to France and Holland. The War Committee were absolutely unanimous on the very great desirability, if it is practicable, of some military action designed either to occupy Ostend and Zeebrugge, or at least to render those ports useless as bases for destroyers and submarines. There was no difference of opinion on the War Committee that the submarine constitutes by far the most dangerous menace to the Allies at the present and there appears no reason to doubt that the arrangements of the Admiralty for dealing with these craft would be immensely facilitated if the enemy could be deprived of these bases.

The strain on the Admiralty in the protection of the essential routes in and about the Channel is at present very great, and locks up large numbers of craft that would otherwise be used to deal with the submarine in other waters. The provision of convoy for transports alone requires a great number of destroyers and the recent decision of the Army Council to bring home 7,000 men a day on leave has added materially to this burden. The provision of escort for the ships bringing food from Holland makes another serious drain on the resources of the Admiralty, and at present they are unable to provide more than one convoy a week for this highly important service. . . .

There is no operation of war to which the War Committee would attach greater importance than the successful occupation, or at least the deprivation to the enemy, of Ostend, and especially Zeebrugge.

I desire therefore that the General Staff and the Higher Command in France, in consultation with the Admiralty as necessary, *shall give the matter their closest attention and that you will report to me personally at an early date what action you consider feasible.*

Mr. Asquith left office on the 7th of December, and if a report was ever presented to him, nothing seems to have been decided by him. There was no further discussion on the subject in the Asquith War Committee, nor did the War Cabinet consider the project until June, 1917.

A plan of operations for a limited offensive in Flanders was submitted to Sir Douglas Haig by General Plumer, who was then commanding the Second Army. This dealt exclusively with a projected attack on the Messines-Wytschaete Ridge — an old notion of General Plumer's. He planned it as an isolated operation to capture high ground to the east of Ypres, primarily in order to relieve the pressure on that fated town and salient. When the more ambitious project of an attack to capture the Passchendaele Ridge, Roulers and Thourout with a view to a converging attack on Ostend in order to clear the Belgian coast was suggested to him, he deprecated the proposal. He thought the ground unsuitable for such an attack and that it would be a prolonged and very costly operation. Headquarters tried to reassure him by suggesting that it afforded the chance of a surprise break-through.

The first document issued by G.H.Q. on the idea of a great Flanders offensive is very significant. I wish it had envisaged not merely the first, but also the final reaction of Headquarters upon the venture. It is signed by General Kiggell, the Chief of the General Staff in France.

"G.H.Q.,
6th January, 1917.

"*Second Army.*

"With reference to your G.352, dated the 12th December, 1916, giving your plan for offensive operations north of the river Lys, the Commander-in-Chief desires me to draw your attention to the following points with a view to re-casting the plan.

"1. The operations north of the river Lys will not take place until after the subsidiary British attacks elsewhere and main French offensive operations have been carried out. It is therefore to be anticipated that the enemy will have been severely handled and his reserves drawn away from your front before the attacks north of the Lys are launched.

"*Under these circumstances it is essential that the plan should be based on rapid action and entail the breaking through of the enemy's defences on a wide front without any delay.*

"2. *The plan, as submitted by you, indicates a sustained and deliberate offensive such as has been carried out recently on the* Somme *Front. In these circumstances the enemy will have time to bring up fresh reinforcements and construct new lines of defence.*

"3. The object of these operations is to inflict a decisive defeat on the enemy and to free the Belgian coast.

"The immediate intention is to break through the enemy defensive systems on the approximate front HOOGE-STEENSTRAATE with the object of securing the line ROULERS-THOUROUT and, by advancing in the northeasterly direction, to threaten the coast defences in rear.

"The Belgians and French will coöperate by attacking from DIXMUDE and NIEUPORT respectively.

"4. The operations naturally divide themselves into two sectors and will be organised under two separate Army commands:

"(*a*) The attack on the MESSINE-WYTSCHAETE RIDGE and ZANDVOORDE, with the object of forming the defensive flank for the decisive attack, will be carried out by the Southern Army.

"(*b*) The decisive attack, from the approximate front HOOGE-STEENSTRAATE with objective ROULERS and THOUROUT, will be executed by the Northern Army. *It is essential that this attack should be carried out with the least possible delay.* The Belgians will coöperate by attacking from DIXMUDE in the direction of CLERCKEN and ZARREN.

"5. Will you please submit your plans by the 31st January, giving your recommendations as to how these operations should be carried out.

"The scheme should include:

"(*a*) Your recommendations as to the point of junction between, and the areas allotted to, the two attacking armies.

"(*b*) Your estimated requirements in divisions, guns, and tanks, assuming that a total of ten Corps Headquarters will be allotted for the operations.

"(*c*) Any further railway construction you may consider necessary.

L. E. KIGGELL, Lieut.-General,
Chief of the General Staff."

On the 15th of January, G.H.Q. sent the following note to the Second Army:

Method of Execution of Attacks and Timings:

The very great superiority in numbers, and it is hoped, in quality, of troops which we may reasonably anticipate, provides what must be the underlying idea of the operations, i.e., *to break through the enemy's trench system and get to open fighting with the least possible delay so as to defeat the troops immediately available before they can be reinforced.* The depth of the enemy's trench system is not so great as to preclude the hope of doing this were observation of the rear lines available. This lack of observation is undoubtedly the great obstacle to the achievement of a rapid break-through, and the *most effective way of overcoming it is the employment of as large a number of tanks as is found possible as a result of the reconnaissance now being carried out.*

These documents were never shown to me or to any of my colleagues. The promised report on the project never materialised until the summer, although we had been committed by the incorporation of the project, without our knowledge, in the Chantilly plan of campaign for 1917.

It is very important to observe that at that date G.H.Q. in France laid down several essential conditions and criteria of success. (1) That there must be not only great but "very great" superiority in numbers and perhaps quality on our side; (2) That before the operation began the enemy should be drawn away from the British Front before the attacks north of the Lys were launched; (3) That it must be in the nature of a surprise to the enemy, that he shall not receive such notification of the impending attack as would enable him to bring up his reserves before the British Army could break through his lines of defence; (4) That it must be a clean break-through and not a grinding operation like that of the Somme; (5) That it was dependent on the employment of a large number of tanks as a means of overcoming difficulties. These were regarded by the High Command in January as conditions precedent to success.

When the attack was made later on, none of these conditions were possible or even contemplated. By July the whole character of the operation had been changed, and all the conditions which, in January, Sir Douglas Haig had stipulated as being essential to success, had been eliminated. Unfortunately, before these changes took place, "the plan" had been set up and enshrined at G.H.Q., and it became an impiety to doubt its infallibility.

Sir William Robertson always took the line that the Asquith Government had given him definite instructions to undertake a campaign for clearing the Flanders coast. It was his way of casting the responsibility for whatever happened on to the shoulders of others — preferably the politicians. That was one of the politician's utilities. He could find men, munitions and money for the Generals and take the blame for the way they were misspent.

It had been stipulated by the War Committee in 1916 that the military experts should report to them after they had concluded their examination of the idea of an operation to clear the Flemish coast. Such "instructions" as were given by the Asquith Government were orders to report. The fact that such a report was never submitted before June, 1917, may be due to the final plans not having been settled before that date. That, however, did not prevent preparations on the most tremendous scale being made from December onwards. They were revised and re-revised. Not one of the various plans or proposals was brought to the notice of the War Committee until June, 1917.

But even if it were conceivable (and it certainly is not) that my predecessor had, without any decisive consultation with his colleagues, without giving them a hint of what he was doing, without any examination of the military possibilities, and not only without a plan, but without any preliminary survey of the ground by experts, given random instructions to the Chief of the Staff to undertake a vast campaign on the most unsuitable ground, circumstances had changed so completely since then that it was imperative that there should be a reconsideration of this rash enterprise. By the summer all the conditions of success laid down by the General Staff had disappeared. There were two outstanding events which had substantially modified the military position and made a great offensive by the Allies on the West a less feasible operation. The Russian Revolution and the grave trouble in the French Army had effected a complete metamorphosis in the possibilities of a great offensive against the Germans. The military power of our great Ally in the East was disintegrating. Russia could no longer be depended upon for effective attack. We were getting less assured day by day of her reliability and of her capacity for resistance, let alone attack. The Russian Revolution was saturated with pacifism. Its inspiration and most popular slogan was "Peace." The Russian peasants and workers passionately desired the fighting to be brought to an end. They were not particularly concerned about terms. They had endured enough sacrifice at the behest of incompetent authority. They did not mean to put up with it any longer. The pacifist spirit had permeated the trenches and it was a matter of considerable doubt whether the Russian troops could be relied upon to do any more serious and sustained fighting until the Revolution had settled down. Whether Russia would even then prosecute the War with increased vigour or patch up a separate peace, no one could foretell. The Germans knew the situation on that front better than anyone, for there were interchanges of civility between soldiers on both sides. But men who are under the influence of the revolutionary temper are uncertain in their action; one day friendly, the next day they may be ferocious. The Germans could not therefore feel quite certain that these fever-stricken warriors now resting quietly in the opposing trenches might not be seized with a sudden delirium, and if they did, whether they would turn on their old officers or fling themselves madly on their old foes. Consequently, until peace was concluded, the German High Command could not abandon their defences or attentuate their line beyond the margin of possibilities. But they were safe in permitting a considerable diminution in their full establishment on that front and in reducing the quality of their troops to a certain extent. Thus they could and did transfer some of the best and freshest to the Western Front and substitute for them divisions exhausted in great battles in the West without filling them up to full strength. Their best fighting material and their reserves were thus available for the West. The uncertainties of the Russian situation were so great that it would be the height of imprudence to commit the British Army to a sustained offensive on the assumption that Russia could be relied upon effectively to hold up the Germans on the Eastern Front.

The Cabinet Committee on War Policy, which was engaged in a careful examination of the military position, drew the deduction from their review of the Russian situation that:

(*a*) It would not be prudent to base our plans on any increase in the Russian military effort this year;

(*b*) The possibility could not be dismissed that Russia might refuse to continue the War through the coming winter, either because the Government insisted on making a separate peace, or because the soldiers refused to remain in the trenches.

A more disturbing element was the state of the French Army.

2. The Condition of the French Army and Consequent Change in French Strategy

French offensive slackens — French Army morale cracking — Disturbing rumours — General Pétain's reassurance — Mutiny kept secret — G.H.Q. incredulous of French difficulties — Haig misrepresents French attitude — Painlevé's evidence of change of plans — French inferiority in heavy guns — Decision of Foch and Pétain — Clemenceau says, "Wait for Americans" — Evidence of Sir H. Wilson and Charteris — Pétain's loyalty to Haig — Foch condemns Flanders plan — What Wilson suppressed — Wilson's visit to Haig; effective blarney.

A fortnight after the Nivelle attack there was a perceptible slackening in the French offensive. This enabled the Germans to strengthen their forces opposite the British Army, which was pressing its attacks with an incessant and as we know now, with an insensate fury. The limit of possible victory had already been reached and neglected weeks ago. If the French for any reason had decided to ease off, they ought to have informed their Allies of their intention and of the cause. Their excuse is the confusion of counsel as between Chantilly and Paris, which followed the great disappointment. At Sir Douglas Haig's pressing request, I went over to Paris with him and Sir William Robertson to urge the French to keep up the attack on their section whilst we were, in accordance with the French plan, pressing the enemy on our sector. I met the French Ministers and General Pétain, who had virtually succeeded Nivelle as the head of the French Army. They offered no explanation of the sudden abatement of French effort. To all our appeals that the combined offensive should be continued, we received a favourable response from the Ministers. But Pétain was strangely reserved. When the committee adjourned he came to me in the corridor and in a half-chaffing tone he said, "I suppose you think I can't fight." I replied, "No, General, with your record I could not make that mistake, but I am certain that for some reason or other you won't fight." He did not answer, but passed it off with a good-humoured smile. My reply shows the impression that interview left on my mind.

As to the state of the French Army, the terrible strain it had undergone for three years — a continual stress of horror which was beyond human endurance — at last broke the discipline of the finest army ever sent to the battlefield by one of the most fearless and valiant races the world has ever seen. No race in Europe has engaged in more incessant fighting. Amongst the peoples of the earth none is more patriotic. Therefore no ordinary shock or infirmity of spirit would account for the sudden defection of French troops. For the first time for over three years there was a muffled crack in the indomitable front presented by Frenchmen to their redoubtable foe. It was not the snap of pusillanimity, but of resentment. They were filled with righteous indignation at the way in which they had been mishandled by their leaders. They had been sent to face death when, owing to a variety of unexpected events, every counsel of prudence ought to have restrained their commanders from giving the order.

It is true that they had lost more heavily and gained less in territory and captures of guns and prisoners in carrying out Joffre's hopeless offensives, but this time there were circumstances which differentiated their failure from all other attempts. It came at the end of a series of fatuous attacks of exactly the same kind, all repelled and all ending in appalling slaughter of devoted men. Survivors and substitutes had been assured over and over again by their Generals that this plan differed essentially from that which had been pursued and had ended in such futile massacres at Artois, Champagne, and the Somme. The same inducement was tendered to Lord Milner and myself by M. Briand at the Rome Conference, when he urged us to accept the Nivelle offensive. M. Briand assured us that General Nivelle reported that the German forces had, to a considerable extent, been used up, and that they were not nearly so thick on the ground as they used to be. He pointed out that there was considerable difference between the character of the enemy's troops now and in the early part of the War. Formerly, all the enemy troops consisted of *troupes de choc,* but now only a portion of the enemy's forces could be regarded as such. Hence, in most parts of the line we should find rather mediocre troops opposed to us. Besides, the new offensive would be entirely different in method from those hitherto attempted. That was the solemn warranty of Nivelle and his Staff and we were all anxious to believe it. The soldiers who had to take the personal risks accepted the assurance in all confidence and it gave them renewed courage.

But as soon as the troops went over the top they found that they had to pass through exactly the same experiences as those to which they had been subjected in the discredited offensives of the past few years — machine guns playing upon their crumbling ranks from positions which had not been touched by their artillery — a few kilometres of captured wilderness littered with dead and wounded comrades — a break-through as remote as ever — the enemy still entrenched behind a line of impregnable earthworks. That had happened before under Joffre. They were promised faithfully that it would never occur again — and here it had happened. Added to this is the fact that the actual losses, great as they were, were at first grossly exaggerated by apprehensive rumours, and that the arrangements for the wounded had been badly bungled. After the repulse the troops were at first just sullen and discontented, but there was no actual outbreak of insubordination. Gradually the disquieting facts as to the conditions under which the offensive was launched percolated down to the trenches. It became known that there had been serious dissensions amongst the Generals before the attack; that some of the more experienced amongst them opposed the attack altogether, and predicted that in the circumstances success was impossible. It also became known that the plans had either by misadventure or treachery fallen into the hands of the enemy in time for him to readjust his dispositions for defence and that the High Command were fully cognisant of that fact, but that, nevertheless, they persisted in carrying out an operation, the details of which were fully in the possession of their foes — and that without changing the tactics in any particular. The troops felt they had been fooled and sold and their comrades butchered. There was a wrangle of generals which passed down through their staffs to the fighting soldiers in the trenches. When politicians joined in the excited disputations and the rival strategies of these generals became a political issue, the poor infantry, who were the designated victims of blundering generalship, felt that as they were immediately concerned they also had a right to take sides and to protest in their own way. Camps were placarded with notices declaring the intention of the soldiers to refuse to go back again to the trenches, whilst their fellows were earning fifteen to twenty francs a day, working in safety in the factories. A battalion ordered to the front refused to proceed and dispersed into a wood. Soldiers coming home on leave sang the *Internationale* in the trains and demanded peace. Mutinies occurred in sixteen different Army Corps, the mutineers alleging that they had been sacrificed by treacherous or inefficient generals. A force of fifteen thousand Russians, which had been sent to France to fight on the Western Front, openly revolted and had to be bombarded by artillery fire into surrender. A number of young infantrymen marched through the streets of a French town, "baa-ing" like sheep to indicate that they were being driven like lambs to the slaughter. The ominous symptoms which preceded the Russian Revolution, and later on the German, appeared in the French Army in 1917. The French Government dealt promptly and prudently with a situation which, tactlessly handled, might have ended in a complete collapse of the French resistance. General Nivelle was dismissed and General Pétain, who was known to the troops to have opposed the peccant offensive, was made Commander-in-Chief. The measures he adopted to still the mutiny and to restore discipline to the French Army were a triumph of wise leadership. He took the soldiers into his confidence, talked to them, assured them there would be no more "great offensives" of the Somme and the Chemin des Dames types, and appealed to their patriotism to defend the integrity and security of the land they loved. He promised them relaxations in the matter of leave and improvements in their conditions behind the lines. These promises he took immediate steps to redeem. He also administered final punishment to some of the leaders of the mutiny, but those upon whom sentence of death was actually carried out were comparatively few. By such means discipline was restored. The French Army, as it proved later on, was as capable as ever of defending French soil against attack by the enemy, but it was quite evident to any observer that it could not be depended upon to attempt any attacks on the German entrenchments on a grand scale — certainly not for some months to come. The French Army and the French nation, having suffered so severely owing to the swaggering garrulity of its High Command and of the host of soldiers and civilians who were given its indiscriminate confidence, now imposed a reticence and a secretiveness which effectively succeeded in withholding these disquieting incidents for some time, not only from their foes but also from their friends. For days after the outbreak, nothing was known outside the French military zone as to what had happened. Information on the subject was then imparted to our G.H.Q. The Germans never discovered the fact for weeks. Had they done so, they would certainly have taken steps to profit by the disaffection in the French lines in order to crumple up their most formidable military foe. When the news ultimately reached German Headquarters, great counterattacks were launched upon the entrenchments captured by the French, but by that time French discipline, and to a large extent French morale, had been sufficiently restored for defensive purposes, and the attacks were repulsed with heavy losses.

The British Army was represented at French Headquarters by Sir Henry Wilson. British Ministers had no direct communication with him. Such news as he gathered was carefully filtered at the War Office ere it reached the Cabinet. We only saw such intelligence from the French side as was good for us to read. Our Ambassador was ill, so we were not kept fully posted through the Foreign Office. When I met Pétain in May, he told me nothing of his trouble with the troops. Neither did French Ministers convey any hint of anxieties about the state of the Army. French and British Generals had a professional loyalty to each other which prevented them from giving any information to the politicians of either country which the soldiers of that country were anxious to keep from their ears. We heard echoes of the chatter that filled the *estaminets* of France, but we were told not to listen to that pernicious gossip.

British Headquarters at home and in France carefully kept to themselves the information conveyed to them, and it did not reach the ears of British Ministers for some time after the Commander-in-Chief and Sir William Robertson had been acquainted with the facts. Even then the full extent of the mutiny was not known. And British G.H.Q. discredited the confidential information officially given to them by French G.H.Q., as it was accompanied by an intimation that the French Army could not be depended upon to undertake any further great offensive operations until 1918. Our Generals affected to be convinced that the French were exaggerating the depth and dimensions of the trouble in order to pass the rest of the fighting on to the British Army until the Americans came in, or in order to induce the British Army to take up more of the line. This was an unfair and somewhat discreditable imputation against honourable men. Foch and Pétain were both men of staunch integrity, upright and straightforward in all their dealings. They were both opposed to the Flanders offensive on its merits and said so before it began. They never approved of it. All that Ministers knew, apart from rumours, was that there had been trouble in the French Army. How much was known by Sir Douglas Haig and Sir William Robertson? They certainly knew that General Pétain, the Commander-in-Chief of the French Army, and General Foch, who was the chief military adviser of the French Government, after full consideration of all the factors of the situation, had completely changed the views held at Chantilly as to the Allied strategy on the Western Front during the year 1917, and that they were now in favour of waiting for the Americans, meanwhile confining Allied activities on the Western Front to limited offensives. But Sir Douglas Haig gave the impression to the War Committee that the French Generals still approved of the launching of a great campaign on the Flemish coast, which certainly could not be characterised as a limited offensive. That implication was not even approximately accurate, and our military advisers knew it. On that point the evidence is overwhelming.

What was the new plan which the French High Command had irrevocably decided upon with the full approval of their Government? It is set forth by M. Painlevé, who was then Minister of War, in his revealing book, "*Comment j'ai nommé Foch et Pétain.*" He glosses over the troubles in the French Army: patriotic Frenchmen ever since the mutinies have done their best to suppress the record of this weakness to which the intrepid spirit of French youth temporarily succumbed. There is no need for their reticence. The reputation of the Army that held Verdun against the overwhelming artillery of the Teuton, and for eight months, shell hole by shell hole, fought to retain every metre of the charred plateau in French hands, is too well established to be shaken by an outbreak due to just exasperation at the bungling use made of their valour by rash leadership. The fact remains that the dominant element in the change of policy was that the nerve of the troops was completely rattled, and that they could not be trusted for some months to carry out any military plan which would involve a sustained attack upon the German entrenchments in France.

M. Painlevé attributes the transformation in the strategic ideas of the French High Command to three facts: the unreliability of Russia, with the imminent prospect of a complete collapse on that front, and the promise of the Americans to have a million men in the fighting line in France by the summer of 1918. As he puts it, "Russian power was waning from day to day and America was not yet with us." The third reason was the need for improving the equipment of the French Army before launching another extensive attack on the German fortresses. This last explanation of the change in the French military view as to the conditions of a successful offensive has a special interest now that we are considering the essentials of disarmament. It had a personal interest for me, as I was largely responsible for the artillery policy adopted by the British Army. I concentrated on heavy cannon of the howitzer type. The French took a different line.

A belated examination of the comparative strength of the rival armies on the Western Front revealed to the French the fact that in numbers the Allied troops had only a slight superiority, whereas in guns of heavy calibre, in bombing aeroplanes and in poison gas the enemy had a definite superiority.

Until the Battle of the Chemin des Dames enforced the warning of Verdun, the French were devoting far too much of their manufacturing strength to the output of ammunition, especially of the lighter kind, and too little to the manufacture of heavy guns. A curious vanity impelled them to build up pyramids of excessive ammunition, the sight and record of which gave great pleasure to parliamentary committees, which love to feast on statistics. M. Albert Thomas, who knew his committee men well, gorged them with prodigious figures of output. He made them multi-millionaires with field-gun ammunition, but the priesthood of the *soixante-quinze* would not give him the opportunity, of which he was the man to make the best use, to manufacture in sufficient numbers the heavy guns and howitzers which, whilst they would have the effect of reducing the number of the output, would have raised the French artillery to an equality in power with the Germans. The fact of German superiority in this respect had been either unknown to both the British and French High Commands or carefully withheld by them from their respective Governments. Why should they have done so? Was it that the Army leaders had not yet fully comprehended the extent to which this was a war of machinery? Or was it because men with a plan, in their eagerness to try it, are apt to overlook facts that do not fit in with its execution, and these men knew that a revelation of Allied inferiority in equipment on the Western Front would have led to a postponement of their offensive?

Joffre, during the Battle of the Somme, had his attention called to the French weakness in howitzers, and his visit to me at Cavan's Headquarters in September, 1916, was prompted by a desire to secure fifty of our six-inch howitzers for use on the French Front. But they were utterly inadequate to make up the deficiency.

It had been assumed that the disparity discovered during the Battle of Verdun between the German and French heavy calibres had since been made up. The enquiries instituted after the Chemin des Dames revealed the disquieting fact that the German heavy artillery was still superior. That had something to do with damping down the eagerness for attack, which constituted the main impulse of French strategical teaching. Both Pétain and Foch were now, according to M. Painlevé, "in view of the state of their divisions, denouncing the dangerous folly of a great general offensive, a few months after that of April 16th", and M. Painlevé adds significantly that France "should be grateful to her two great commanders who, by their resolute patience, saved their armies from the fate which befell those of Ludendorff in 1918."

According to M. Painlevé's testimony, Generals Foch and Pétain had decided, after a careful review of all the salient facts of the military position in the early summer of 1917, upon the following policy. I quote his words:

The million American soldiers promised us, guaranteed our definite superiority of effectives for 1st July, 1918.

Four great manufacturing programmes were to guarantee us for the same date a definite superiority in munitions:

1. The output of fighting aeroplanes, followed by a programme for bombing aeroplanes, would make us masters of the air;

2. The output of heavy artillery, which would double our numbers of heavy guns;

3. An order for 2,500 small tanks (followed by a supplementary order for 500): it was the clear vision of Pétain which was responsible for ordering these in spite of the advice of many staff officers;

4. An enormous order for poison gas and smoke shells. The latter were to form a cloud in front of the tanks. As for the poison gas shells, the Germans had, at the Battle of Verdun, shown us the formidable and lasting effect of "yperite" shells, which rendered the artillery preparations and counter-bombardments much more effective. . . .

These programmes were inspired by the painful lessons of 16th April; the necessity for the mastery of the air, for the means to destroy underground trenches and pill boxes, for protection against machine guns by tanks, for rapid preparations in case of surprise, etc. . . .

This outline of what he calls the "long-dated" military policy was to be supplemented by an economic policy which would involve the pooling of cereals amongst the Allies, the rationing of France in minerals and a "hermetical blockade" of the enemy. Attention was to be diverted to the enemy front in the Balkans as "an essential element of victory." General Pétain had in May suggested a combined offensive in Italy as an alternative to persisting with the Nivelle scheme. This idea was not pressed for reasons which I deal with later on. The Pétain-Foch policy was placed before the military mission of the Senate whose President was M. Clemenceau. After its examination had been concluded by that body, M. Clemenceau summed up the views of the Commission by saying: "Very well. We must hold on for a year. In a year there will be a million Americans in France and we can advance." Clemenceau was opposed throughout to the Flanders offensive. But he did not interfere, as our Generals were so intent on the enterprise. Thus the French dropped the policy of the great offensive and substituted the strategy of what Henry Wilson whimsically called "squatting and pulling faces at the Boche", until the Americans arrived.

Sir Henry Wilson was the liaison officer between French Headquarters and ours. A report prepared by him was laid before the War Policy Committee by the C.I.G.S. Sir Henry Wilson admits in his diary that the Pétain and Foch plan had been imparted to him and also the Pétain and Foch view as to the projected offensive in Flanders. There is no reference to this important information in the report he prepared for the War Policy Committee after consultation with Sir Douglas Haig. According to Sir Henry Wilson's diary, General Foch was definitely opposed to the Haig strategy in Flanders. Brigadier General Charteris, Haig's biographer, who was at the time the chief of Haig's Intelligence Staff, says that Pétain believed that all prospect of breaking through on the Western Front should be abandoned for the year and "that the British as well as the French Armies should confine their fighting to small operations with limited objectives."[1] This information was withheld from the Cabinet.

All Charteris' extravagant reports as to German losses, German morale, broken German divisions, German shortage of ammunition, and generally, as to the gradual fading away of the German might, were passed on to the Cabinet, but we were never put in possession of this expression of Pétain's opinion. The fact that the French Commander gave his approval to the Flanders attack was communicated to the War Cabinet, but the essential fact that Pétain and Foch disapproved of that attack, of which G.H.Q. were cognisant, was withheld.

Pétain had made it quite clear to Wilson as the liaison officer between British and French Headquarters that he disapproved of Haig's Flanders campaign. Here are extracts from Wilson's diary on this point:

11th May: "Went to see Pétain. . . . He is opposed to Haig's plans of attack. . . . He is opposed to big attacks, and favours small fronts and great depths."

On May 19th, Pétain repeated to Wilson his objections to the Haig project:

"He told me that, in his opinion, Haig's attack towards Ostend was certain to fail, and that his effort to disengage Ostend and Zeebrugge was a hopeless one."

Pétain promised Wilson to make his position and his plans absolutely clear to Haig when he met him. He seems to have

[1] "Field Marshal Earl Haig", by Brigadier General Charteris, p. 269.

redeemed this promise immediately and thereby caused great offence to the British Commander-in-Chief.

In spite of his conviction that the Flanders attack was a mistake, Pétain nevertheless, when Haig persisted in his scheme, gave both his approval and loyal support to the utmost which was compatible with his own duty to the shaken Army he was coaxing back to strength. He agreed to take over a small portion of the British line and to coöperate with two minor attacks at Verdun and Chemin des Dames, and ultimately he was able to give directions for a small French force under General Anthoine to coöperate with the British in Flanders itself. The Pétain limited offensives were highly successful. They took the Germans by surprise and achieved their objectives. They were not of the ruptural type. They were local in their character and were intended to be local in their results; the Germans assessed them at their true purpose and did not shift any great reserves to the attacked quarter for a counter-offensive. With these exceptions, the fighting on the Western Front for the remainder of 1917 resolved itself into a desperate duel between the British and Germans, in which almost every effective German division on the Western Front was successfully engaged by the British. Nevertheless the German Front was never broken and the British attack failed to achieve even its first objective line.

As to Foch, he was even more emphatic in his objection to the Flanders offensive. Writing in his diary on May 17th, Wilson says that "Foch was also anxious to know whether our Admiralty insisted upon Ostend and Zeebrugge being taken."

General Callwell, Sir Henry Wilson's biographer, commenting on this entry in Wilson's diary, says:

This was a point that Wilson appreciated, for he was beginning to doubt whether, in view of the likelihood that the

Germans would bring strong forces across from the Eastern Front consequent on the rapid deterioration in Russian belligerent potentialities that was setting in, Haig's plan for recovering the Belgian littoral would prove feasible.

When Haig, in spite of the doubts expressed by French Generals as to the wisdom of his venture, insisted upon launching his great campaign, Foch, according to Wilson:

"*. . . wanted to know who it was who wanted Haig to go on 'a duck's march through the inundations to Ostend and Zeebrugge.' He thinks the whole thing futile, fantastic and dangerous, and I confess I agree,* and always have. . . . So Foch is entirely opposed to this enterprise, Jellicoe notwithstanding."

Early in June, the British Army in France was given a practical lesson in the difficulty which Pétain would experience in affording them any effective aid in a great offensive policy. It had been agreed between the British and French Commanders that when Plumer was about to launch his attack on the Messines Ridge, the French should, in order to divert German attention and reserves, make an attack on some part of their front. This operation was to come off on June 10th. On June 2nd, General Debeney had a conference with Sir Douglas Haig at which the latter was informed that the attack by the French must be cancelled because the morale of the troops was such that it could not be carried out.

Wilson, in the comment he makes on this cancellation, in his diary on June 4th, says:

> This endorses and underlines all that I have been saying for the last month or more, and I think, and hope, that it will finally dispose of Haig's idea of taking Ostend and Zeebrugge.[1]

Why was it that things which Wilson, as liaison officer, had been saying for the last month or more to his military

[1] "Field Marshal Sir Henry Wilson", by Major General Sir C. E. Callwell, K.C.B., Vol. I, p. 359.

superiors, were never passed on to the Cabinet? And why was it that it was all omitted in a report, prepared by him after consultation with Haig, which aimed at inducing the Cabinet to accept a plan which Wilson thought, in agreement with Foch, was "futile, fantastic and dangerous?"

How the grave character of the mutinies in the French Army was deliberately minimised will be demonstrated by an extract from General Wilson's report to us.

> The condition of the Army is still good, wonderfully good considering all that it has gone through, but there are signs of unrest here and there which, *though not yet serious,* makes me anxious for a long future. . . .

Nothing is said in the Wilson report of the mutinies and seditious demonstrations. Were they not serious? We only heard from independent sources vague rumours of what had happened amongst the troops, and of Pétain's promise to the troops that there would be no more Champagne, Somme or Chemin des Dames offensives.

General Wilson further states in this report that:

> The Committee have received information of a serious case of disaffection in one regiment of the French Army, though General Pétain is understood to be satisfied that he has the trouble in hand. The most disturbing symptom, however, of the weakening of the French Army is that General Pétain was reluctantly compelled to relinquish the offensive operation he agreed to undertake in concert with the British attack on the Messines Ridge. . . .

These paragraphs would not give us any idea of the dimensions and character of the outbreaks, *e.g.,* how the mutinies were spread over 16 Army Corps. Wilson does say:

> . . . nobody who knows the French Army of to-day — that is, the younger men in it, those who do the most of the fighting, will say it is as fine an instrument now as it was last autumn.

He suggests, however, that the real weakness is not so much in the Army as behind the lines:

> The collapse of Russia has hit France very hard. For years and years before this war France built all her hopes on Russia, lent her vast sums of money to prepare herself for the War, and, therefore, the fall of Russia has come as a much greater shock to the French, than it has to us. . . .
>
> France is tired; the country is being governed by a set of men which does not contain, in my opinion, a single man of outstanding ability, of broad, farseeing and statesmanlike views nor of personal character and prestige which might be claimed as a national asset.
>
> The countrywomen of France — the real mainstay of the country — are tired. They dread more heavy losses, they are frightened of greater taxation, they can no longer work their little farms and their little businesses as they could during the first three years of the War, partly because they are tired and disheartened, and partly because labour gets less and less available, and money more and more scarce. . . .
>
> In short, France is beginning to die away. I believe, if we and America know how to handle her, she will still go through the War to a victorious end, and in brighter times she will still be capable of feats of arms which at this moment are quite out of her power to achieve. Without being at all desperate, the condition of France is serious, and she merits, and must receive, the utmost sympathy and the greatest possible assistance. . . .[1]

Wilson used this information, not in order to impress upon the Committee the futility of the Flanders campaign without active French support, but in order to persuade them that it was necessary for us to win striking military successes in order to keep France in the War. But he never hints at the conclusion he had come to that these successes were not to be won in the direction or on the lines planned by Haig, and he carefully suppresses his information as to the convic-

[1] Report to C.I.G.S., dated July 6th, 1917.

tion of the French military leaders that the Haig plan was doomed to fail. In fact, the document was clearly prepared in concert with the British Staff to influence the War Committee to go forward with the plan of G.H.Q. for a great campaign in the North without regard to the change in essential conditions. It was subtly contrived to tell us enough to justify a strong offensive by the British Army without revealing any of the facts that might lead us to turn down the Flanders scheme.

How came it that this eminent soldier, who was specially charged with the duty of acquiring all intelligence as to French movements, opinions and conditions which had a bearing on the conduct of the War by Britain, should have deemed it compatible with his highly responsible position to withhold from the Government on the eve of an important decision by them, vital information that had actually been imparted to him as the liaison officer of the British Army? The story of the preparation of the memorandum which he submitted to the War Committee is told by his own biographer.

On his way to England, Wilson was invited to stay at G.H.Q. at Blondecques, Haig's headquarters. Before he went there he "felt misgivings" and "was somewhat troubled as to the possible issue of the contest." Haig, however, seems to have soothed his anxious spirit. Wilson says:

"He was most nice to me, begged me to do something with my 'great brains', and said that there was always a bed and a welcome at his headquarters for me."

Wilson then hinted that he was on the lookout for employment. Haig answered that:

"He knew it well, that he trusted me absolutely, and that I had been invaluable to him and so on. So we parted."

This was from Haig who, as all knew, distrusted Wilson through and through.

Having by these means dispelled Wilson's doubts, Haig proceeded to explain to Wilson that the War Cabinet was opposed to the plans of G.H.Q. for the Flanders offensives, and he urged him to give these plans his support when he was called before the War Cabinet on arrival in London.

The biographer says that Wilson came back to England after the interview feeling that a special responsibility had been imposed upon him in connection with the contemplated offensive on a great scale to be undertaken by the British Expeditionary Forces. The memorandum he wrote for the Cabinet as the result of this wangling visit to G.H.Q. shows that he discharged that responsibility by toning down some facts and entirely suppressing others which, starkly revealed, might have frightened the War Committee into vetoing an attack which he himself was convinced would fail.

Thus, although the French view was communicated to our military chiefs, it was not passed on to the Cabinet.

3. Discussions with the Government on the Policy of the Flanders Offensive

Messines Ridge offensive — Plumer's careful preparations — A clean victory — Cabinet War Policy Committee discuss Passchendaele — Haig's outline of the plan — The scheme summarised — Sceptics in the Cabinet — Sir Douglas Haig's argument — Jellicoe supports the plan — My appeal for reconsideration — Arguments against the plan — Alternatives — Robertson's reply — Danger of German offensive in the West — Opposed to Italian suggestion — Haig's statement: no heavy losses anticipated — Main principles of strategy — Divided opinions in the War Committee — Difficulty of overruling expert military advice.

In May, Sir Douglas Haig undertook a limited offensive with a view to capturing the Messines Ridge. That he called the First Phase in his campaign. The greater operation was only intended to take place "several weeks later and would not be carried out unless the situation were sufficiently favourable for it when the time came."

The Messines attack was left to General Plumer. He prepared the plan with his usual care, thoroughness and caution. The idea, as I have already mentioned, was originally his. The whole ground had been thoroughly observed, surveyed and registered under the direction of General Harington, one of the outstanding Staff Officers of the War. It is not too much to say that had he been at G.H.Q., Passchendaele would never have become one of the blackest horrors of history. One special feature of the Messines attack was the elaborate undermining of the German advanced positions. For months companies of men had been burrowing under the German advanced positions. Nothing was left to chance. Plumer believed not only in the possibility of making an effective attack on the Messines Ridge, but in the advantage which would be gained by the garrison of the Ypres salient through securing possession of the high ground on the right from which the German artillery poured their deadly missiles on our trenches and communications, every part of which was under their observation. But Plumer wished to treat it as an isolated operation and not as part of a general offensive in Flanders. To this last he was opposed, although the War Committee were not informed of his doubts. For reasons which the event revealed, he did not believe in the feasibility of an attack on a great scale in that area and at that time. Although later on he carried out the particular operation that was entrusted to him in the attack on the Passchendaele-Staden Ridge with skill and success, he was never convinced of the wisdom of this particular campaign. In fact, the more he saw of the ground, the more rooted became his aversion to the whole plan. When I met him in Paris in November, on his way to take command of the British Army in Italy, he told me that he was delighted to get away from that "terrible mud." He put the Messines attack in a totally different category. The position was one which had an important tactical value for the British Army in that area. It was a life-saving operation, for the Ypres salient was a deathtrap. Moreover, the Ridge could be captured entirely in the course of a single attack, and the success could be rendered very much less costly because the element of surprise would be introduced through the springing of the mines under the German trenches.

The Messines attack was a clean victory, in the sense that it was a victory without any qualification or reserve. The objectives — the real objectives — were attained up to the last entrenched ruin and concrete machine-gun emplacement. The casualties were comparatively light. The operation was conducted with great dexterity and precision, and much credit is due to General Plumer and his Staff for the way the attack was planned and carried out.

Soon after the Messines victory, the Commander-in-Chief and the Chief of the Staff for the first time placed the whole of their plans for an extended offensive before the War Cabinet. A Committee of the Cabinet had been appointed on June 8th, 1917, to consider War Policy on all fronts — sea and land. It consisted of Lord Curzon, Lord Milner and General Smuts, with myself as Prime Minister in the Chair. Up to that date, the Flanders project had never been submitted to the examination of the Government by the Chief of the Imperial General Staff or the Commander-in-Chief. It was understood that G.H.Q. had such a project in contemplation, but, to use the Commander-in-Chief's words, it would not be undertaken "unless the situation was sufficiently favourable for it when the time came."

On June 19th, a meeting of the Committee was held to discuss the matter. Sir Douglas Haig was brought over to explain his plans. Sir William Robertson also attended as the Chief of the Imperial General Staff.

It is recorded that the Committee examined a raised map which Sir Douglas Haig had brought with him, and the Field Marshal explained his plans in full detail.

I take the outline of his plans from a document prepared by him and sent to all his Army Commanders. In order to enable the reader to follow the various stages of the contemplated offensive, I have attached a map based on Sir Douglas Haig's orders. This is the projected campaign as sketched out by Headquarters:

1. The general situation at present is favourable to the attainment of considerable results in the offensive operations we are about to undertake.

Russia has resumed active operations apparently with excellent results and on a considerable scale. The effect on the Russian people of the successes gained is reported to be such as may lead to the development and maintenance of still greater efforts.

Before this Russian attack the endurance of the Central Powers and their allies was based on three main factors: hope that Russia would make peace, or at least remain inactive; confidence in the power of the German Armies to hold their "impregnable" positions; and belief in England being starved into submission by the submarine campaign before the Armies of the United States could take the field in strength.

We know that German faith in the submarine campaign must soon be abandoned entirely. Confidence in the invincibility of the German Armies had already been so severely shaken that it cannot survive many fresh defeats. And hope of Russian inaction has now been dispelled.

Coming at a moment when the heavy attacks the enemy has been making on the French Front have failed to achieve success, and when he is looking forward with grave anxiety to a resumption of the British offensive and to the possibility of renewed attacks by our French and Italian Allies, this sudden resumption of a dangerous offensive on the Eastern Front is a very heavy blow to him.

We were justified in hoping for success with the possibility of great results from our next offensive before we had this convincing evidence of Russia's intention and ability to fulfil her whole duty to her allies. We are still more justified in this hope now, and our plans must be laid to exploit to the full the possibilities of the situation.

With this object the following instructions are issued in confirmation and amplification of those already given to Army Commanders:

2. The Fifth Army assisted on its right by the Second Army and coöperating on its left with the French and Belgians, is *first to secure the* PASSCHENDAELE-STADEN *Ridge.*

To drive the enemy off that Ridge from STIRLING CASTLE *in the south to* DIXMUDE[1] in the north is likely to entail very hard fighting lasting perhaps for weeks; but as a result of this we may hope that our subsequent progress will be more rapid.

3. Subject to modifications necessitated by developments in the situation, *the next effort* of the Fifth Army, with the French and the Belgians — *after gaining the Ridge mentioned* above — will be directed northeastwards to gain *the line* (*approximately*) THOUROUT-COUCKELAERE.

4. *Simultaneously* with this advance to the THOUROUT-COUCKELAERE line the Fourth Army, acting in combination with naval forces, will attack the enemy about NIEUPORT and on the coast to the east of there.

5. The Fourth Army and the forces attacking the line THOUROUT-COUCKELAERE will *afterwards* operate to join hands on *the general line* THOUROUT-OSTEND and *to push on towards* BRUGES.

6. Operations eastward, and towards LICHTERVELDE, from the PASSCHENDAELE-STADEN Ridge will be required to cover the right flank of the advance on THOUROUT; and *possession of the high ground between* THOUROUT *and* ROULERS will be of importance subsequently to cover the *flank of the advance on* BRUGES.

7. *In the operations subsequent to the capture of the* PASSCHENDAELE-STADEN *Ridge opportunities for the employment of cavalry in masses are likely to offer.*

8. The Second Army will cover and coöperate with the right

[1] Please follow the names on map (page 360).

flank of the Fifth Army as already ordered and will be prepared to take over gradually the defence of the main Ridge from the Fifth Army, possibly as far as PASSCHENDAELE or even to a further point.

The Commander of *the Second Army* will also be prepared with plans *to develop an advance* towards the line WARNETON-MENIN, or to push forward on the right of the Fifth Army *to the line* COURTRAI-ROULERS (throwing out a flank guard along the line of the LYS), if circumstances should render such movements desirable as the situation develops.

9. *As far as can be foreseen at present the main operations after the capture of the* STIRLING CASTLE-PASSCHENDAELE-DIXMUDE *Ridge, will be those directed towards* OSTEND *and* BRUGES.

In these circumstances our resources, to the utmost possible limit, will be concentrated on these operations; and, provided the degree of success gained is sufficient to justify it, we must be prepared to reduce the garrison of the remainder of our line to mere outposts with a few centrally placed reserves.

The Commanders of the Armies south of the river LYS will accordingly be prepared with plans to release as large forces as possible to ensure the success of the main operations. Those plans should be so designed as to admit of the gradual withdrawal of forces to the north as the situation develops.

Meanwhile as much activity as possible will continue to be displayed along our defensive front, in order to wear down and deceive the enemy, thus preventing any transfer of his forces from that front.

10. The above outline of possibilities is issued to enable Army Commanders to foresee and prepare for what may be required of them. The progress of events may demand modifications or alterations of plan from time to time and — especially in view of the comparatively short period of fine weather which we can count on — our progress before winter sets in may fall short of what would otherwise have been within our power this year.

The general situation is such, however, that the degree of success gained and the results of it may exceed general expecta-

tions, and we must be prepared for the possibility of great developments and ready to take full advantage of them.

11. *The extent of the success gained will depend* much on the concentration and continuity of effort at the right time and place, and the necessary concentration must be attained by a bold reduction of force at other points, and by ensuring that to the utmost extent possible every fit man takes his place in the ranks. Army Commanders will satisfy themselves that, during the coming offensive, no man fit to be in the ranks is employed elsewhere without most urgent and necessary reason.

12. The drafts available to replace casualties are limited in number and in the great struggle before us it is essential that, without in the least degree relaxing the strength and continuity of our efforts, we shall conserve the energy of our officers and men so that we may outstay the enemy. For this the utmost use must be made of all means of offence and defence at our disposal. All ground gained must be held, by rifle and bayonet alone if no assistance is obtainable from other arms. In the attack, more especially in the earlier attacks, each step must be thoroughly prepared and organised. Every advance must be carried out steadily — but none the less vigorously — with thorough combination and mutual support between the troops employed. The tendency of isolated bodies of troops to dash forward beyond the reach of support must be held in check. This tendency, springing from the finest motives, is of the greatest value if controlled and used for adequate objects, whereas if uncontrolled and misapplied it leads to the loss of many of the most gallant officers and men without the gain of compensating advantages.

Conducting our operations on these principles, as has been done with such success on so many previous occasions during the past twelve months, *we may look forward with confidence to still greater successes in the near future.*

It will be seen that it was not a campaign for the capture of the village of Passchendaele. That in itself would only have added to the difficulties of the British Army by substituting a new and narrower salient than that which had cost us so dearly at Ypres. It was not a scheme even for capturing the whole of the Passchendaele Ridge, from Messines to Dixmude. That was only the "first objective." After that there would be opportunities for the employment of "cavalry in masses." We should then swoop onward to the capture of Roulers and Thourout and the ridge or ridges between them, which would have brought the British Army within sight of the North Sea. On the right we were to push onward as far as Courtrai. Then there was to be a converging movement from Thourout and Nieuport, right along the coast for the capture of Ostend. But this was not the final objective, for when Ostend was captured, our victorious armies were to take Bruges on their way to even greater things. There is more than a hint that the success gained might exceed general expectations, and that we must be prepared for the possibility of even greater developments.

The reference to "masses of calvary" contemplated a beaten foe in full and disordered retreat. Where would that retreat end?

When Sir Douglas Haig explained his projects to the civilians, he spread on a table or desk a large map and made a dramatic use of both his hands to demonstrate how he proposed to sweep up the enemy — first the right hand brushing along the surface irresistibly, and then came the left, his outer finger ultimately touching the German frontier with the nail across. He must have been in this mood when he indited this tremendous order of battle to generals who between them commanded a million and a half of troops, the flower of the Empire's youth.

The War Policy Committee were then taken up into the aerial tower built during the past six months or more by the industry and imagination of G.H.Q. to view this thrilling prospect. It is not surprising that some of us were so captivated by the splendour of the landscape opened out to our vision that their critical faculties were overwhelmed. Mr. Bonar Law, Lord Milner and I still remained sceptical.

It must not be forgotten, in judging the perpetrators of this ambitious but ill-advised venture, that all the facts that mattered were in the possession of G.H.Q. before they ever completed their scheme. Now we realise what a foolhardy project it was, when all the known facts are taken into account — that is, known at the time to G.H.Q. But the most vital were withheld from the War Cabinet.

I have in my possession notes taken of the discussions which ensued, and a full Minute of the statement which I made at the end of our consultations.[1] I have also a copy of a written memorandum which I submitted in the course of the discussion to Sir William Robertson and Sir Douglas Haig for their consideration, and copies of their replies. The Commander-in-Chief based his argument in favour of the enterprise on the following considerations:

He led us to believe that it was not an isolated operation where the whole brunt of the attack on the German lines in the West would be left to the British Army. He opened the proceedings by stating that both the French and the Belgians were in agreement with the project and promised effective coöperation. When it was urged that the condition of the French Army would make it improbable that they would undertake an offensive on such a scale as would prevent the Germans from taking fresh divisions from the French Front to ours, he replied that Pétain had assured him that his offensive would be of a character to avoid that possibility. As to Pétain's "agreement" with the plan, he never informed the Committee that both Pétain and Foch were opposed to the idea and that they would have preferred that Haig should

[1] I hope the verbatim Minute of the discussion will one day be published.

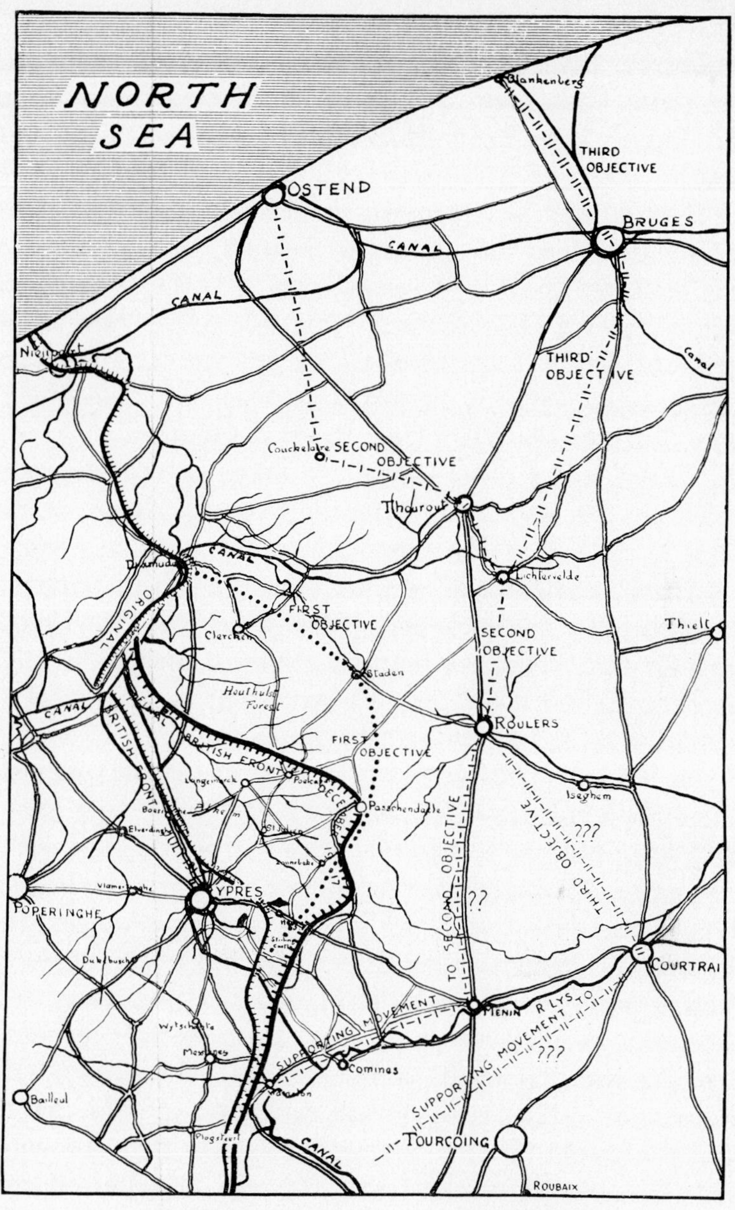

Original British Front Line, July, 1917 . . .	
First Objective, Passchendaele-Staden Ridge .	
Second Objective, Roulers-Thourout-Couckelaire-Ostend .	-I-I-I-I-I-I-I-I-I
Third Objective, Bruges	-II-II-II-II-II-II-II-
Suggested supporting movements of 2nd Army:	
To Second Objective	??
To Third Objective	???
Limit of actual advance, December, 1917 . . .	

take over part of the French line and keep the Germans busy by attacks here and there on a limited front.

He laid great stress on the "exhaustion" of the German Army and its loss of morale.

He reviewed the German position in detail. He said that they had only thirteen "fresh" and thirty-five "used" divisions in reserve. Their communications were inferior to ours. Their morale had greatly deteriorated. In confirmation of this he read the following extract from a report:

"Morale: The following are the impressions of a member of the American Relief Committee, who left Belgium at the beginning of May: —

> "The morale of the German troops is bad; they realise that they are beaten, but live in the hopes that something will turn up to save them from disaster.
>
> "There has lately been noticeable deterioration in the uniform and equipment of the German troops; the latter no longer present a smart appearance.
>
> "The rations of the troops not in the fighting line have been reduced, and there are many complaints.
>
> "Rolling stock is much worn out.
>
> "The morale of the civilian population in Belgium is excellent."

In further confirmation of his estimate as to the poverty of the German morale, Haig stated that at Messines the Germans had known we were about to attack, and had made every preparation for defence, but were completely defeated.

When it was pointed out to him that on the whole Western Front the Germans had, according to War Office information, a superiority in artillery, especially in the heavier calibres, which were the most important factors in such a struggle, Sir Douglas Haig alleged that the Germans were now short of ammunition, and that their guns were very inaccurate. Sir William Robertson came to his support by stating that he thought the estimates of the Intelligence Department of the War Office as to the German artillery were exaggerated. When the War Committee expressed apprehension as to the probability of so great an operation causing heavy casualties, which owing to the difficulties we were experiencing with man power would be difficult to replace, the Commander-in-Chief thought there was no ground for our fears. He called attention to the slightness of the losses we had sustained in capturing Messines and the Vimy Ridge, and how in the latter case we had penetrated far into the German line in the course of a single day with comparatively small losses. In that attack, one division, according to him, had pierced the German Front to a depth of five miles. If this attack were equally successful, that would enable us to reach a portion of the Passchendaele Ridge which constituted the first offensive in the course of a single day without any serious casualties.

As to man power, and supplies of ammunition and guns, Sir William Robertson anticipated no difficulty. As for men, he hoped to have one hundred and fifty thousand to send out, with which to supply the twenty or thirty thousand wanted to complete the establishment of the Army in France, and *replace the casualties suffered in the attack.* He would also send out the 67th Division. He considered the position to be sufficiently favourable to justify undertaking the operations in the manner proposed by the Commander-in-Chief.

As to the results he expected from this venture, the Commander-in-Chief made it quite clear to the Committee that he anticipated not merely that he would capture the Passchendaele Ridge, but that the operation would result in our securing the Flemish Coast.

Admiral Jellicoe was called in to bear his testimony to the grave need of achieving this aim before the winter, and he stated categorically that unless that were done, the position would become impossible, and that unless we cleared the Germans out of Zeebrugge this year, we could not go on with the War next year through lack of shipping. This startling and reckless declaration I challenged indignantly, but the First Sea Lord adhered to it.

I concluded our discussion at this meeting of the Committee by appealing to General Robertson and Sir Douglas Haig to realise our difficulties in regard to man power.

"We were now reduced to scraping men up from munition works, mines, and agriculture, and from among those formerly rejected on medical grounds. Popular agitation was growing stronger against those measures. We were most anxious to support Sir Douglas, particularly in view of his brilliant successes at Vimy and Messines, but I did not want our army to be drawn into a military enterprise before it was ready for it, for it would involve serious trouble at home in regard to men, which would not be worth while on behalf of a failure. At the moment we were bearing the whole burden of the War, for America was not yet able to play its part, and I would prefer to reserve our strength until next year. While I quite understood Sir Douglas Haig's point of view, the Committee must consider whether it would not be better to hold our hand until the French Army had been resuscitated by the intervention of America."

After the first day's discussion, I thought it desirable to set down in writing my objections to the operation, so as to afford Sir William Robertson and Sir Douglas Haig an opportunity for considering them carefully before we resumed our talk. The first part of my statement was an endeavour to summarise some of the arguments which had been advanced in support of the proposed offensive and which I have already stated. I then gave my arguments against the plan:

Arguments Against the Plan

1. A great attack which fails in its objective whilst entailing heavy casualties must necessarily discourage the British Army and thus lower the splendid morale which it now exhibits, and

might very well have disastrous effects upon public opinion in Britain and France.

2. The Cabinet must regard themselves as trustees for the fine fellows who constitute our army. They are willing to face any dangers, and they do so without complaint, but they trust to the leaders of the nation to see that their lives are not needlessly thrown away, and that they are not sacrificed on mere gambles which are resorted to merely because those who are directing the War can think of nothing better to do with the men under their command.

3. It is therefore imperative that before we embark upon a gigantic attack which must necessarily entail the loss of scores of thousands of valuable lives, and produce that sense of discouragement which might very well rush nations into premature peace, that we should feel a fair confidence that such an attack has a reasonable chance of succeeding. A mere gamble would be both a folly and a crime.

4. *What are the chances of success?* Our superiority on the Western Front, even assuming the French put in the whole of their strength, amounts to 15 per cent. in men. In guns there is an equality. In ammunition each army has an adequate supply for the purposes for which it needs ammunition. We have a sufficiency of ammunition for offensive purposes. There is every reason to believe that the Germans have an adequate supply for defensive purposes. In leadership, in discipline, in quality of troops, taking the armies through and through from Nieuport to Mulhausen, there is something like equality. But in reserves — and this is vital — the Germans are this year superior to the Allies. The Russian Front is not likely to absorb any of their reserves, so that practically the whole of these are available for the West. The French have practically no reserves: their reserves are not adequate even to supply the wastage on a non-fighting basis. The A.G.'s paper reveals only too clearly what our position is in respect of reserves. The C.I.G.S. in a speech the other day said the nation was prepared to do anything as long as it was clearly told what was expected of it. Unfortunately that is only partially true. The nation was told that we wanted the young men out of

the munition yards. Our efforts provoked a strike which lost us hundreds of guns and aeroplanes and did not in the end give us the men. Supposing we make a similar attempt to get men out of the mines, — who is prepared to guarantee that there will be no strike amongst the miners? No one in his senses would suggest we should take any more able-bodied men from agriculture and the shipbuilding yards, until the submarine menace has been completely overcome. Of that there is no immediate prospect. The reëxamination of the medical rejects has provoked a violent campaign throughout the land, which has materially assisted the pacifist propaganda. That the A.G. admits. Can anyone point to any reservoir of men available for army recruiting, the enforced enlistment of whom would not excite the same unrest, disaffection and labour troubles which have baffled all our other efforts to raise men for the British Army?

5. Even our superiority of 15 per cent. is based on the assumption that the French will count as much in this attack man for man as either the Germans or ourselves. In the face of repeated warnings which we have received from well-informed and competent observers, it would be madness on our part to proceed on such an assumption. Our two military representatives with the French Army have deemed it to be their painful duty to intimate in the most explicit terms that we cannot this year rely upon the French Army to take its full part in such an enterprise as we contemplate. For the moment, its fighting spirit is impaired — it is full of distrust, suspicion and discouragement. I fear we do not always sufficiently appreciate the terrible character of the sacrifices already made by the French nation. Two millions of their young men have already been put out of action either through death, disease, mutilation or internment.[1] No country in this War has sustained anything like the losses which have been borne so heroically by the French people. They were looking forward to this year as the year of their liberation; they had been told that the Russians had been reëquipped, that the

[1] This is the figure arrived at after deducting out of the total casualties the wounded who have returned to the ranks.

The Naval Attaché confirms these reports in an alarming letter to the First Lord.

British Army had enormously increased its strength in men, guns and ammunition, that the Italians had also improved their army; and they were anticipating a great converging movement which would overwhelm the resistance of the Central Powers and bring the War to a victorious issue. The collapse of Russia has been to them a bitter disappointment. The failure of their offensive has intensified this disappointment, and for the moment the French Army and nation are suffering from a natural wave of dejection. The marvel is that under such repeated discouragements as have attended their efforts during the last three years, this depression has been so long deferred. Even the bravest waver under these conditions. It has been clear for some time that their leaders are rootedly opposed to undertaking operations on a great scale this year. Even if we persuade them at a conference, the instinct of the French Army will re-assert itself, and the further we go from the Conference, the less will be the disposition to carry out its resolution. That is exactly what happened after the last Paris Conference. The agreement was as satisfactory as any arrived at, at any conference during the War. The execution completely failed. We cannot drag an unwilling army with doubting leaders and a disheartened nation into the most gigantic battle ever waged.

It is therefore proposed that we should rush into the greatest battle of the War, against an enemy almost equal in number, quite equal in equipment, still the greatest army in Europe in everything that constitutes an efficient fighting force, with larger reserves than our own, to make up the deficiency during this year, holding formidable defensive positions which he has taken three years to strengthen and to perfect; and we are to launch this attack with doubtful support from our most powerful and important ally — a support so hesitating that the Germans might be able to afford practically to deal with it without concentrating behind the attacked front any great masses of men and guns. They could then afford to convert their present slight inferiority of men and guns opposite the British Army into an actual superiority.

I know too well that those who are anxious to plunge into

this fight might persuade themselves that the promises of the French sufficiently meet the exigencies of the case. In their hearts they must know that this cannot be so. Even if the French Army pulls its full weight, the Allies can only command a bare superiority on the Western Front. If it pulls less than its full weight we shall be attacking the strongest army in the world, entrenched in the most formidable positions with an actual inferiority of numbers. *I do not pretend to know anything about the rules of strategy, but curious indeed must be the military conscience which could justify an attack under such conditions.*

6. Although a great success might cheer up the French people and inspire them to greater deeds, a failure might very well be disastrous in its effect on French opinion. We have been warned by General Wilson that even a repetition of the Messines Ridge will not be regarded in France as a substantial success, and that it will produce no beneficent effect on the French mind. I ask whether the C.I.G.S. anticipates that anything better than Vimy and Messines can ensue as the result of this attack. *Brilliant preliminary successes followed by weeks of desperate and sanguinary struggles, leading to nothing except perhaps the driving of the enemy back a few barren miles — beyond that nothing to show except a ghastly casualty list.* I earnestly entreat our military advisers as well as the Cabinet to think again before they finally commit the British Army to an attack, the failure of which may very well weary the Allied nations into accepting any plausible peace that might be offered them by an equally weary foe.

Since our last review of the situation, when the Commander-in-Chief was present, we have had a good deal of authoritative fresh evidence as to the condition of the French Army. We should be guilty of a serious dereliction of duty if we did not give due weight to the very grave reports presented by General Wilson, Colonel Spears and the Naval Attaché and *to the important information we have received as to the report made to the French Ambassador by M. Abel Ferry.* Their reports have more than confirmed the apprehensions we had formed and we should not be justified in risking scores of thousands of British lives on the assumption that we could disregard the solemn admonitions involved in these documents.

Alternatives

The fundamental error of the Allied strategy up to the present has been the refusal of their war direction to recognise the fact that the European battlefield is one and indivisible. A corollary to this error has been the concentration of the strongest armies on the attacking of the strongest fronts, whilst the weakest fronts have been left to the less well-equipped armies. We have thus allowed the Balkans to be captured by the Central Powers, who had at any rate the intelligence to realise the strategic importance of that area. Austria and Turkey, which might by well-directed blows have been overthrown in 1915 or 1916, have been regarded by France and England as mere "side shows" having no bearing upon the general result of the campaign. This narrow and unimaginative conception of our military strategy will, I predict, always be pointed to as the reason why the Allies, in spite of their overwhelming preponderance, have been so successfully held at bay by an enemy considerably inferior in numbers. The question is whether it is too late even now to retrieve the consequence of this mistake. I believe another opportunity is presenting itself to the Allies, and the same prejudices and narrowness of outlook are conspiring to repeat our blunders. Austria and Turkey are still the weakest fronts, but we still insist on ignoring that fact, and wasting our strength on endeavouring to break through the strongest and best-fortified, the most skilfully and powerfully held front in the whole battlefield. If either Turkey or Austria were overthrown it would be the beginning of the disintegration and consequent destruction of the Central Powers. If Austria were defeated it would lead to a separate peace with that Empire. Turkey and Bulgaria would be isolated, and being left without supplies or support from the Central Powers could much more easily be overthrown. The Russian Army could then concentrate against Germany alone; a million men would be withdrawn from the Austrian frontier and thrown on to the German Front. The

French, the Russians, and ourselves could by next year spare nearly a million men from the attack on Turkey and the Balkans, and the Italians could in the first instance spare men for an attack on Turkey, where they have great hopes, and afterwards to assist their Allies in France.

A separate peace with Austria would have this additional advantage, which is not altogether to be despised. The feeling between Austria and Germany which has long ago ceased to be cordial, would be so aggravated that Germany would not dare to leave her Austrian frontier entirely unprotected. Thus with an additional million Russians thrown on to her Eastern frontier, and an additional million French, British and Italians, with perhaps half a million Americans on her Western frontier, a portion of her troops detached to watch her Southern frontier, the breaking-up of the German power would only be a matter of a few months at the outside. We could thus achieve the only peace which is ever likely to be a permanent one in Europe by the imposition upon Germany of terms which would completely cripple her offensive power.

But two questions must first of all be answered. Is it feasible by any military plan to bring about the defeat of Austria during the coming autumn? And in the second place, if Austria were defeated, would she then make a separate peace with the Allies?

I firmly believe that it is within the compass of the Allied resources, if properly directed, to inflict a heavy blow and possibly even a decisive defeat upon Austria this year. What is the Austrian position? It is from the military point of view an exceptionally weak one. Out of her population of 50,000,000 nearly 30,000,000 are racially and politically antagonistic to the war aims of the Empire. Three fifths of the population belong to races the majority of whom are in alliance with us — Slavs, Roumanians, Poles, Italians. A case which would have been analogous to that of the Austrian Empire would have been that of this country if we were at war with the United States of America, with three fifths of our population Irish, the United States placing in the forefront of its war objectives the emancipation of the Irish race from English control. From a military point of view the Austrian plight is a singularly perilous one. How dangerous it is may very well be inferred from the ease with which whole Austrian battalions on the Eastern Front have surrendered. There is the case the other day of the Austrian regiment that marched into the Russian lines with its bands playing and its banner flying. It is clear that the Austrian troops are not putting up a serious resistance against the Russian advance. Economically the food position is grave. The Hungarian harvest this year is but 40 per cent. of the normal. In finance the situation is so serious that the actual figures of the Austrian budget were withheld from Parliament. As to man power the reports indicate that there are no reserves behind the lines. No wonder that the information received from Spain which on Austrian matters is first hand, indicates a pleased surprise on the part of the Austrian military authorities that the Allies have not yet taken advantage of these circumstances to press a vigorous offensive against the Austrians. The famous Erzberger Speech in the Reichstag is believed to have had reference to the grave condition of Austria, and the suppression of all Austrian news in the *Frankfürter Zeitung* is also attributed to the same cause. The repeated and urgent peace advances made by Austria during the present year, many of them emanating directly from authoritative quarters, prove that those who have the direction of affairs in Austria are nervous and alarmed as to the prospect. All the information received points in one direction — that Austria is on the point of a collapse, and that it needs but powerful and vigorous pressure to precipitate her downfall.

As to whether Austria would in the event of a great military defeat make a separate peace with the Allies, all the indications point in the direction; in fact, as I have already stated, actual overtures in that direction have already been made. No peace could be possible without satisfying the legitimate claims of Italy and no Italian statesman would be allowed to make peace without securing both the Trentino and Trieste. The Trentino, Austria would, I understand, be prepared even now to surrender. Trieste she cannot give up unless the Italians actually conquer it. But if Trieste were captured, then it would be easier for Austria to concede it.

Can Trieste be captured? The Italian lines are now eight miles away from that city. We are promised that by a vigorous offensive we can drive the German Army with its well-equipped, well-led and homogeneous force, a distance of between twenty and thirty miles and capture Zeebrugge and Ostend. Surely then, there ought to be a chance of driving the more demoralised, more heterogeneous, less well-supported Austrian Army a distance of eight miles. In the north we have practically no superiority of men in attacking the Germans. The Italians have a superiority of between fifty and one hundred per cent. over the Austrians. What they lack is guns and ammunition; these we can supply. It may be said that if the Austrian position is in peril, the Germans will realise just as certainly as we do the disastrous consequences which might ensue to the Alliance, and would therefore throw in masses of men and guns to support the Austrians. My answer to that is threefold:

1. By skilful measures of concealment we could bring our additional guns up to the Italian Front without the knowledge of the Austrians. There are forty of our howitzers already in position. It is proposed, I understand, to double the number. Ammunition could be piled up behind these in quantities adequate to the supply of three hundred howitzers. The Austrians ought not to discover the arrival there of the additional howitzers until the bombardment begins, and it would take even Germans a few weeks to bring up fresh divisions to the Isonzo. Meanwhile the Hermada ought to be captured, and that would place Trieste at the mercy of the Italians.

2. If the Germans move troops from the Western Front or the Eastern Front to the Isonzo, that would be the time to attack their lines in France, and even if we sent another three hundred guns to the Italian Front we should still have twice as many heavy guns left and at least three times as much ammunition as we had at the commencement of the Somme offensive.

3. What does it matter whether we fight Germans in the north of France or in Italy? The only difference would be that if

we fought them in France we should be doing it at the expense of our own troops, whereas in Italy we can use the enormous reserves of the Italians. And this leads me to the next point.

4. France has no reserves. I have already pointed out what the A.G. says about the unsatisfactory condition of our recruiting. But Italy has masses of well-trained men behind the lines. The Italian casualties have been comparatively slight, and the Allies have not up to the present used Italian man power to the best advantage. Is it not now the turn of the Italians to take their share of heavy fighting? If the Germans really divert their troops to Italy — and that is the assumption of those who oppose this Italian project — then the French Army will get the rest it stands sadly in need of, and our Army, instead of exhausting its limited reserves, will have time to accumulate.

This Italian scheme has the additional advantage that it requires no ships. The moral impression throughout Italy would be incalculable. The enthusiasm with which our small contingent of heavy guns was received is the best possible proof of that. They have already increased enormously Britain's hold on the Italian mind, and if we sent a few hundred guns with large stores of ammunition, and these enabled the Italian Army to cleave a way through to Trieste, Britain would win a place in the heart of Italy from which she could never be driven. The Italians are eager to carry out this plan; they are willing to risk their men, and the plan proposed by General Cadorna has had the full support of General Foch, probably the ablest strategist in the French Army. If the plan failed in achieving its full object, what is the worst that can happen? That the Italian Army after making an advance of a few miles would be brought to a standstill. It would have sustained heavy casualties. But even then it would have weakened the Austrian Army; it would have occupied large forces of Austrians and Germans, and to that extent it would have helped the Russians with that further offensive which they propose making in September.

When we met at noon of the following day to resume our discussion, both Sir William Robertson and Sir Douglas

Haig read out statements which they had prepared in reply to mine. According to their statement, before the Somme offensive the Germans had had a superiority of nearly 600 guns of 5.9-inch calibre and above, whereas at the present time the Allies had a superiority of 7. On the other hand, the strength of the German Army had increased by nearly 160,000 men since that battle.

Sir William Robertson said that, personally, he was sceptical of Austria making a separate peace, as her whole future depended upon her relations with Germany, to whose wheels she was tied in a variety of ways, economic, industrial, political, etc. Assuming, however, that she would make a separate peace if fairly heavily punished, he was doubtful whether she could be so punished. *The artillery could not be got there and got ready for battle in less than six weeks.* The passage of this number of guns through Italy *could not be concealed* and the enemy might be expected to have the best part of a month for counter-preparations.[1] And the Germans, as soon as they discovered what we were up to, would be there before us, as they enjoyed the advantage of an interior position, which enabled them to move their troops more quickly than we could move ours.[2]

The Allied offensive on the Western Front had prevented the Germans from undertaking any offensive operations in Italy. If Germany were relieved from serious pressure on the Western Front, she would be in much the same position for attacking Italy as she was last March, but plus the advantage she might get from the weakening of the Russians, and therefore if she decided to reinforce the Italian Front to the extent regarded as possible by Cadorna, not only

[1] Our military representative at the Italian Front, General Delmé-Radcliffe, was of opinion that guns and ammunition could be transferred to the Italian Front without attracting the attention of the enemy.

[2] The Germans repeatedly moved troops from front to front without our discovering it.

could he not defeat Austria but he himself would need support.

So much for the prospect of Austria being defeated. As regards our position, if the seventy-five batteries were sent *we must necessarily pass to the defensive for all practical purposes,* and be prepared to suffer losses similar to those suffered by the Germans while on the defensive this summer.[1] *Also we must abandon all hope of making either our air or sea situation more secure* so far as the Belgian coast was concerned, *and, in fact, the Germans might conquer us by an attempt to take Dunkirk,* and if they succeeded the situation would become even worse than it was now. He "did not say that they would succeed, as this would depend to some extent upon the reinforcements that Germany might be able to bring over from the Russian Front and upon the power of her artillery. *This power has not been great recently,* and as the number of heavy guns she has on the Western Front are approximately equal to the Allies, her failure must be due to other reasons — for instance, the declining morale, inferiority in the air, inefficient employment of the guns, or want of ammunition. He did not pretend to say which; it might be a combination of all." In a striking but sinister sentence he said that: *"We should follow the principle of the gambler who has the heaviest purse and force our adversary's hand and make him go on spending until he is a pauper."*

Germany would bring over heavy reinforcements if Russia continued to do nothing or if she dropped out of the War altogether. The best chance we had of keeping her in the field was to continue our activity, for if we stopped being aggressive she might think that we admitted our failures. Further, the Russians were themselves supposed to be pre-

[1] This is on the assumption that Germans attack us on the Western Front, *i.e.,* do not send any divisions to Italy.

paring for an offensive early next month, and had asked us to keep up our pressure.

The conclusion he had arrived at, taking the broadest possible view of the general situation, was that our chances of obtaining good results were certainly no greater in Italy than they were in the North, while the risks involved were much greater in the former place than in the latter. *He deprecated as strongly as anyone our incurring heavy casualties without a corresponding return,* BUT THE PLAN AS OUTLINED BY THE FIELD MARSHAL SHOULD SECURE US AGAINST THIS MISTAKE. *He had shown, and he understood the War Cabinet agreed, that we must continue to be aggressive somewhere on our front, and we ought, of course, to do this in the most promising direction.* The plan provided for this and would enable us to derive a real advantage till the enemy showed signs of weakening, *while at the same time it permitted of our easing off if the situation so demands.* Doubtful situations, such as the present one, had always arisen in war, *and great mistakes had been made by endeavouring to find a fresh way round as soon as the strain began to be felt. We should be on our guard against this mistake.*[1]

He was therefore in favour of continuing our present plan on the chance of getting a success in the North, not only because of the military situation but also because of the necessity of trying to improve the air and sea situation, and he was consequently averse to diverting any of our resources to Italy. We should, however, do all we could to provide Italy with means for increasing her ammunition supply as she has already had far more guns than she could keep employed, and in this connection he would remind the War Cabinet that there was no reason why Italy should remain inactive throughout the winter, as operations

[1] What about the Peninsular War and the march through Georgia, one attacking Napoleon on a vulnerable flank, and the other turning the flank of the Confederacy in the American Civil War?

could continue on the Isonzo up to the end of January.

Asked whether, by the last paragraph, Sir William Robertson meant that we could, if we wished, help the Italians at some later date, he replied that we could consider it.

Sir Douglas Haig said that his views had been asked as to the expediency of delaying our main attack as planned by him until 1918, in order that the British Army might still be strong in that year. He himself knew the situation at the present moment, but could not forecast the future. *He considered the present moment favourable. He was fully in agreement with the Committee that we ought not to push attacks that had not a reasonable chance of success, but that we ought to proceed step by step. He himself had no intention of entering into a tremendous offensive involving heavy losses. His plan was aggressive without committing us too far.*[1]

Sir Douglas Haig then read his statement "on the strategical situation with special reference to the comparative advantages of an offensive in Northern Belgium as against an offensive from Italy against Austria."

I give the following extracts from the Memorandum.[2]

The railway capacity of Northern Belgium is sufficient for the maintenance of some forty German divisions north of the River Lys and possibly even more.

But given our present superiority in the air, we could almost certainly cause such serious interruptions and consequent disorganisation in the railway working (by bombing important junctions) as to upset all calculations.

In any case the limiting factor may be taken as the number of German divisions available rather than as a question of railway capacity.

On the 17th June, Germany had *156 divisions on the Western*

[1] This undertaking, coupled by a similar promise already given by Sir William Robertson, had a considerable influence on the Committee.

[2] The full text of Sir William Robertson's and Sir Douglas Haig's Memoranda are given in Appendices Nos. I and II.

Front. Of these, 25 were in the Army entrusted with the defence of Northern Belgium, leaving 131 for the defence of the remainder of the German line. . . .

Of the 131 divisions available for defence on the long front (roughly, 400 miles) from the Lys to Switzerland, only 43 were fresh. . . .

German divisions have a low establishment and no less than 17 Landwehr divisions of comparatively poor quality are included in the figures given.

One division in line to about two miles of front on which attack is expected is as much as we need expect to be employed against us; and, allowing for the flooded area, fourteen or fifteen divisions may be taken as the largest force that will be placed in line between the Lys and the sea. The reserves at first available behind that front are unlikely — for the reasons given above — to exceed ten divisions, and there may be two or three divisions in addition placed on the coast itself.

If fresh divisions can be brought from Russia we may confidently expect them to be centrally placed, at some distance back, until the situation is clear; or they may be used to relieve exhausted divisions at special points, the latter being drawn into central reserves.

At present Germany's reduction of her forces on the Russian Front is practically limited to exchanging fresh troops there for tired ones from the West. *But the number of her good divisions in the East is limited and, moreover, it is estimated that her transport facilities will only suffice to move ten divisions a month from the East.*

For all these reasons we are justified in calculating that the Allies will have a considerable superiority in infantry on the front of attack — probably not less than two to one. And our capacity for exchanging tired divisions for fresh ones along our defensive line will not be less than that of the Germans.

In guns and ammunition, judging by experience and information from captured orders, etc., our superiority will be even greater; while, in the air we may regard our superiority as still more assured. The last mentioned factor is of immense importance from the points of view of artillery efficiency, information, damage behind the enemy's lines, and general morale.

As regards the alternative to an attack in Belgium, namely, attacking Austria from Italy, the arguments against this are overwhelmingly stronger than those in favour of it.

Then comes a paragraph which is a most compendious exposition of the policy I had been pressing upon the Allies ever since December, 1914.

It has always been accepted as the most effective form of war to attack and destroy the enemy's strongest forces as soon as possible IF THERE IS A REASONABLE PROSPECT OF SUCCESS. *If there is not a reasonable prospect of success the next best course is to weaken the enemy by holding his main forces and attacking his weaker ones, if that be possible. The possibility depends however, firstly, on being able to hold his main forces, and secondly, on being able to defeat his weaker ones.*

If we were to detach largely to Italy it is probable that we could still hold the Germans on the Western Front, *but it is not certain* and it would depend much on the French.

It is at best very uncertain that we could defeat Austria. . . .

A decision to transfer troops to Italy would mean abandonment of our offensive in Belgium. A consequent gain of time to Germany; very dangerous disappointment in France and, to some extent, in Russia; small prospects of success against Austria supported in probability by German troops; a possibility of reverses on the Western Front; and a possibility of still more serious reverses on the Italian Front.

Against all this we have a reasonable chance of success in Belgium which may have greater results than even a bigger success against Austria, and which at least may be expected to open the way for greater results subsequently.

It is *not impossible that Germany aims at inducing us to detach from the Western Front — that is a very usual form of war, often employed with telling effect.* But whether she is deliberately trying to induce us or not there seems no doubt that our wisest and soundest course is to continue to wear down the German forces on the Western Front, as we are undoubtedly able to do.

Lord Curzon asked whether when Sir Douglas Haig spoke of having a reasonable chance of success he merely meant that he expected to capture his first objective.[1]

Sir Douglas Haig replied that he referred to the complete operation which he had explained to the Committee on the previous day.

I said I had no doubt whatsoever about the desirability *of carrying out Sir Douglas Haig's plan if it was reasonably likely to succeed and was practicable.*

General Smuts said that he had had a long talk with the First Sea Lord in order to ascertain what importance he attached to the proposed operations. *Admiral Jellicoe had replied that, in his paper, he had, if anything, understated the case.* He himself had not up till then been aware of the extent to which the Germans could use the bases on the Belgian coast.

The First Sea Lord, Admiral Jellicoe, entered at this point and in reply to Lord Curzon, who asked him to develop the case he had made in the two papers circulated to the Committee, said that two points were in his mind. The first was that immense difficulties would be caused to the Navy if by the winter the Germans were not excluded from the Belgian coast. He could not develop the reasons for this better than he had already done in the papers circulated. *The position would become almost impossible if the Germans realised the use they could make of these facts.*

The second point, he felt, was that if we did not clear the Germans out of Zeebrugge before this winter we should have great difficulty in ever getting them out of it. The reason he gave for this was that *he felt it to be improbable*

[1] That included the capture of Ostend and Zeebrugge.

that we could go on with the War next year for lack of shipping.

I said that the most serious point in *Admiral Jellicoe's remarks was the statement that we could not continue the War next year for lack of shipping.* This statement, made in such a quarter, must be tested. If it was accurate, then we should have far more important decisions to consider than our plans of operations for this year, namely, the best method of making tracks for peace.

I said that I would not have taken up this question unless I had supposed that the *First Sea Lord had gone in detail into the whole question before he made so serious a statement.* It would probably be necessary for the Committee to see the First Sea Lord and the Shipping Controller together on the subject. I then asked the First Sea Lord as to whether the Admiralty were making any progress in the organisation of an offensive section of the Operations Division.

The Committee then adjourned until the following day. During the afternoon the members of the War Committee had a full discussion amongst themselves as to the reply the Government should give to the military chiefs. There was a marked divergence of opinion. General Smuts was strongly of the view that the Generals had made out their case for at least having a good try. Personally, he thought the chances were highly favourable. Lord Curzon inclined in the same direction — but not quite so definitely. Lord Milner, Mr. Bonar Law and I thought the project a mistake, when Britain, with practically the only unshaken army, was holding the pass until the Americans arrived; that it had none of the elements of success, that it would be very costly and that it therefore ought to be discouraged. Mr. Bonar Law did not, however, think we were entitled to overrule the military and naval authorities on a question of strategy. Lord

Milner and I also hesitated to go that length, especially in view of the fact that the Chief Military Adviser of the Cabinet supported the Commander-in-Chief, and that on the question of accepting the responsibility of vetoing the operation we would have no support in the Cabinet. I had seen Lord Balfour and talked the matter over with him. He was impressed by General Smuts' support of the plan and was also in favour of having a try. It was therefore decided that I should once more sum up the misgivings which most of us felt and leave the responsibility for decision to Sir William Robertson and Sir Douglas Haig, on the understanding that if the progress they made with the operation did not realise the expectations they had formed, it should be called off and effective help be rendered to the Italians to press their offensive.

4. Continuation of Deliberations: Misrepresentations to the Government

French attitude towards suggested offensive — How we were misled — Unsuitable character of the ground — "Ridiculous maps" — Generals doubt wisdom of project — Decision not to veto the plan — My final appeal to Haig and Robertson — Robertson's change of view — Grave danger if unsuccessful — Our lack of adequate superiority — Lesson of previous offensives — Chances against success — Strategical alternatives — Possibilities against Austria — Dangers of Russian defection — Italians need guns and ammunition — Robertson reasserts faith in Flanders campaign — My most painful regret.

It must be remembered that we were not placed in full possession of facts which would have justified our taking a stronger line. In the course of the discussions that took place between the War Policy Committee of the Cabinet and the Commander-in-Chief and the Chief of the Imperial Staff and the conversations before and after the formal meetings, Ministers were misled on several critical points:

First of all we were misled as to the French attitude towards the offensive. This was vital, for without their active and wholehearted coöperation the attack could not hope to succeed. When the Germans were almost equal in numbers and superior in artillery to the combined forces of the British and French, an offensive by one of them alone was doomed to failure. On this point the following facts were concealed:

1. Ministers were told confidentially that the offensive was urged upon us in the first instance by the French as the only means of saving France from collapse, just as pressmen were subsequently informed in confidence that its continuation was attributable to French entreaties that we should keep on fighting. We were not informed that, so far from urging us on, the leading French Generals had done their best to dissuade us, and had stated emphatically that they condemned the project and thought it a foolish venture, which must fail. They also made it clear that the greatest service we could render to them would be to take over more of their line. They had conveyed these opinions to Sir Douglas Haig and Sir William Robertson. These eminent Generals, in stating their case for the scheme, had concealed these important facts from the Government.

2. The salient facts as to the condition of the French Army and the extent of the demoralisation in its ranks were also withheld or minimised. We were not told that the French plan was to wait for the Americans and meanwhile to increase their equipment, husband the Allied resources and only engage in limited operations not involving heavy casualties, but perhaps also to help the Italians in their offensive. Headquarters having determined in their own minds that the French were inventing or exaggerating their mutinies to shirk responsibility for action, they felt it would be undesirable to confuse and distract our innocent minds by repeating to us such canards.

3. We were not informed that the new Commander-in-Chief of the French Army, and some of his leading generals, favoured a combined attack on the Italian Front. Had we

known that there was such high authority for this strategical move, the Government might have taken a different view of this alternative to Passchendaele. As to the possibilities of such an offensive, we were misled. We were told positively by Sir Douglas Haig that it was already too late to make the necessary preparations for affording the Italians the assistance they would need to start an offensive on that front. But the Germans made their preparations in September to assist the Austrians to stage the offensive which late in October inflicted the heaviest disaster ever sustained by the Italian Army. And the Allies were able in November in a very short time to throw two hundred thousand troops and a considerable number of guns into Italy to prevent that disaster from developing into utter collapse.

But even if the French situation had been favourable, there was the question to be considered of the wisdom of undertaking a great offensive before the Americans arrived and the further question of choosing this particular sector for the attack. On these two issues let us first consider the question of the desirability of the British Army this year putting its whole strength into the extensive attack on the German entrenchments in the West, seeing that the Russians were practically out of action, the French were discouraged, and the Americans were not ready.

In order to persuade us that the time was opportune we were told by the Commander-in-Chief that we should have a superiority of two to one in infantry — it was untrue; that the enemy had no effective reserves — that was not in accordance with the facts; that the German morale was so broken that they would not put up anything like the resistance which they had hitherto offered — that was misleading; that they had inaccurate guns and inadequate ammunition we found otherwise. He minimised the German reserve of man power and informed the Cabinet that "if the fighting was kept up at its present intensity for six months, Germany would be at the end of her available man power." The fighting for the next six months was very much more intense than any hitherto witnessed, and at the end of it Germany was certainly not at the end of her man power.

Let us next consider the ground selected for these operations. We knew nothing of its specially unsuitable character for operations which involved a heavy bombardment. This turned out to be one of the foremost elements in the failure of the plan. The chosen battlefield was a reclaimed swamp which was only prevented from returning to its original condition of a soggy morass by an elaborate system of drainage, constantly kept in order by the most careful and constant scouring and repairing of ditches and waterways on the part of the cultivators. Any bombardment of this ground was bound to block and destroy every conduit, with the result that the whole area would be converted once more into an impassable quagmire.

Even if the weather conditions had remained favourable, the whole terrain was traversed by a number of little becks which would swell into pools as soon as the culverts were smashed, the banks broken and the channels choked. Such ground was hopeless for tanks, whose effective activities were an essential part of the original plan of a surprise attack. You might as well try to take tanks across the Slough of Despond.

The special conditions which render this tract of country more liable to flooding than the ordinary Flemish land were brought to the notice of G.H.Q. by the Tank Corps some weeks before the battle began. As soon as the Tank Corps were informed that they were expected to operate in that area they instituted inquiries as to the character of the ground. They soon ascertained the fact of its reclamation

THE BATTLEFIELD OF PASSCHENDAELE, 1917

and of the elaborate system of drainage which alone prevented its reverting to a morass. They knew that under these conditions such a long bombardment as always preceded the infantry advance in all their great offensives would render the ground utterly unsuitable for tank operations. The result of this investigation was sent to Headquarters, but no notice was taken of it. Some time later, the Tank Corps Staff prepared maps to show how a bombardment which obliterated the drainage would inevitably lead to a series of pools, and they located the exact spots where the waters would gather. The only reply vouchsafed to this effort to save the Army from disaster was a peremptory order that they were to "Send no more of these ridiculous maps." Maps must conform to plans and not plans to maps. Facts that interfered with plans were impertinences.

The Chief of Sir Douglas Haig's Intelligence Staff stated that the Commander-in-Chief was himself

". . . anxious about the weather conditions that were to be anticipated. Careful investigations of the records of more than 80 years showed that in Flanders the weather broke early each August with the regularity of the Indian monsoon: once the autumn rains set in, difficulties would be greatly enhanced."[1]

The War Committee were not made acquainted with this "careful investigation" of the records and what they portended in the way of "enhanced difficulties", and it will be found that in the whole discussions with the War Committee, not a word was said about the meteorological drawbacks and the peculiar conditions which rendered the terrain of the struggle specially disadvantageous for a sustained attack.

But the most reprehensible suppression of essential information was the withholding from the Government of the

[1] "Field Marshal Earl Haig," by Brigadier General Charteris, D.S.O., p. *272*. In his diary, he further adds, "I do not think we can hope for more than a fortnight, or at the best, three weeks of really fine weather."

fact that all the generals called into consultation by Sir Douglas Haig has serious misgivings about the whole project and had expressed their doubts to him. The knowledge of that fact would naturally have carried great weight with all the members of the War Committee, and as most of them already entertained serious apprehensions, it would have been decisive. No hint was given to us of the fact that the generals who were in command of the armies which were chosen to carry out the projected offensives shared our hesitation. We know now that the officer who advised the principal attacking army on all artillery questions deprecated the plan on the ground that there would be no elbow room for the artillery to operate. His opinion was passed on to G.H.Q. Of this we knew nothing.

We were invited to discuss Sir Douglas Haig's plan not merely without full knowledge of the essential elements, but with a definite suggestion that the decisive facts in this and other respects were quite contrary to what they were in reality.

I do not propose to discuss at this stage the boundaries of the legitimate functions and responsibilities of military experts and Governments respectively for strategy. I will content myself now with the statement that if soldiers, for reasons of their own, wish to commit Governments to a military operation, perfect candour and a complete revelation of all facts and considerations within the knowledge of either soldiers or statesmen which are relevant to sound decision, are not only an obligation of honour they owe to each other, but a duty they owe to the country whose interests are committed to their charge. A prospectus issued with a view to inducing the public to invest their capital in an enterprise must reveal all material facts. The Government were the trustees of the public and were asked to invest in this wild military speculation not only hundreds of millions of public money, but the lives of hundreds of thousands of brave men whom they had called to the ranks. More than that, they were invited to risk the fate of Britain on what Sir William Robertson later on called "a gamble", where the truth that mattered was wilfully and skilfully kept from their cognisance. That is a serious charge, and I should certainly not have felt justified in making it, unless there were contemporary records which bear out my indictment. If the whole truth, as it was known at the time to the military staffs, had been exposed before the members of the War Committee, the Flanders offensive would have been turned down.

As it was, we had to judge upon a basis of essential facts suppressed, distorted and misrepresented. I am therefore not in the least surprised that some of my colleagues came to the conclusion that upon the case as represented to them, the Flanders offensive had a reasonable chance of achieving considerable success, and that it was at any rate worth trying. The Committee attached great weight to the undertaking given them by both Sir William Robertson and Sir Douglas Haig that the attack would be abandoned as soon as it became evident that it was not likely to succeed in its purpose. Even on the facts known to us, I was opposed to the enterprise, and so were the majority of the members of the War Committee, but, for the reasons which I have indicated, they did not think they were justified in accepting the responsibility of imposing a peremptory veto without a test being made of the possibilities of such an attack. I was authorised to make a statement on these lines which would fairly represent our general attitude.

This I did on June 21st. I made a final effort to persuade Haig and Robertson to abandon this foolhardy enterprise. I felt they were plunging into a perilous hazard when the conditions demanded unusual circumspection and preparation of men and equipment for the coming year's final attack on the citadel of the Central Powers. Our officers and men needed training. A few months ago most of them were civilians. And even those who had been at the front for a much longer period had not been afforded leisure and opportunity for learning and teaching the lessons of a war waged by methods of which veterans had no previous experience. The following is a summary of my speech to the War Cabinet Committee:

I had devoted many hours of anxious consideration to the plans put forward by Field Marshal Sir Douglas Haig, and supported by the Chief of the Imperial General Staff, and on the previous evening I had discussed the question very fully with my colleagues. I felt that at this stage it would be desirable to make Sir Douglas Haig and Sir William Robertson acquainted with the conclusions which I had reached, and I expressed the hope that they would give careful thought and full weight to the considerations which I was going to place for them. My view was that the responsibility for advising in regard to military operations must remain with the military advisers. Speaking for myself, and I had little doubt that my colleagues agreed with me in this, I considered it would be too great a responsibility for the War Policy Committee to take the strategy of the War out of the hands of the military. This made it more important that the military advisers of the Government should carefully weigh my misgivings as the head of the Government in regard to the advice they had tendered. If, after hearing my views, and after taking time to consider them, they still adhered to their previous opinion, then, subject to the condition they had themselves suggested as to breaking off the attack if it did not work out in accordance with expectation, we would not interfere and prevent the attempt.

I entreated Sir Douglas Haig and Sir William Robertson

to remember that a most momentous decision had now to be taken and that a wrong step might bring disaster to the cause of the Allies.

The first point which I raised was that I felt somewhat disturbed at the recent change of attitude on the part of the Chief of the Imperial General Staff. I reminded the Committee that at the Paris Conference of the 4th and 5th of May, I had discussed the question with Sir William Robertson and the latter had himself felt some misgivings in regard to aggressive operations unless the French were able to coöperate with a strong offensive. My own doubts at that time had been due to the collapse in Russia and the consequent ineffectiveness of the Russian Army and the opposition of Generals Alexeieff and Pétain. General Robertson however had expressed the view that if the French would undertake really serious offensive operations, by which he meant some such operations as our own, calculated to hold a fair proportion of the German reserves on the French Front, then he was prepared to agree to an offensive.

Now General Pétain had found himself obliged, for reasons which were really beyond his control, and for which he could not be blamed, to go back on his undertaking. In consequence, there had been no big French offensive operation in concert with the attack on the Messines Ridge. Hence, it appeared to me that Sir William Robertson had made a very serious change in his advice in agreeing to Sir Douglas Haig's plan, which involved the commitment of forty-two divisions in an attempt to fight right through to a depth of twenty miles, while the French contented themselves with relatively minor operations further to the south.

I then turned to an examination of the prospects of success. I pointed out that failure would be very serious business. All the world would recognise, if Sir Douglas Haig only succeeded in reaching his first objective, that our operations had failed to realise their full scope. I felt that we were not in a position to play with the disintegrating forces that were operating in all belligerent countries on both sides, but more especially on the side of the Allies, owing to the hopeless position of Russia. Every one would know that we were aiming at a much greater prize than Sir Douglas Haig's first objective and that the real object of our operations was to clear the Belgian coast. Only that morning I had noticed an extract from the *Frankfürter Zeitung*, which showed that our intentions were already realised in Germany. In reckoning up our chances of success I pointed out that we must advance fifteen miles before we could really begin the first operation for freeing the Belgian coast. What reason, I asked, was there to believe that we could first drive the enemy back fifteen miles and then capture a place ten miles away? For a success on this scale one of the following conditions was essential:

1. An overwhelming force of men and guns;
2. That the enemy should be attacked so strongly elsewhere that his reserves would be drawn off;
3. That the enemy's morale should be so broken that he could no longer put up a fight.

None of the above conditions obtained at that time.

The numerical superiority of the Allies on the Western Front, including 25,200 Portuguese, 18,000 Russians, who were forming committees and talking revolution, and 131,000 Belgians, did not exceed 15 per cent. More than this, however: the French did not, in their present temper, count as available for any offensive enterprise on a great scale. They were a little out of hand and wanted rest, so that the French Government had been obliged to grant them extended leave. In comparing the value of the French and German soldier, it had to be remembered that the French soldiers represented one out of six of the population, whereas the Germans only included one out of eleven, which must make a difference in quality. The French Army included all kinds of material in the line that were on the ration strength but did not constitute soldiers.

I myself did not pose as an expert in strategy but, nevertheless, I understood that an overwhelming superiority in men and material was agreed by all strategists as essential to success in an offensive, particularly under modern conditions. I agreed that we might very likely make a success of a first attack, but assaults on the German lines were like hitting India-rubber.

I reminded the Committee that during nearly three years of war I had never known an offensive to be undertaken without sure predictions of success. Similar reasons to those given now had always been adduced as to why we should do better than last time, and I had always been told that by applying the lessons of the past we should succeed. This experience had not unnaturally made me feel sceptical. On this occasion I was more especially sceptical, owing to the lack of numerical superiority, to which I had already alluded. I pointed out that in heavy guns we were barely equal to the enemy. It was true that we were told we had a good deal more ammunition than the Germans, but I asked whether the Germans had not ample supplies of ammunition for the defensive. According to my experience in the present war, something like a superiority of five shells to one was required for the offensive as compared with the defensive. To try and break the enemy's army with no material superiority in men or guns, with no adequate support from the French, with Russia broken, with the Germans able to exchange fresh divisions brought from the Eastern Front for the divisions already shattered on the Western Front — (a point which appeared to me to have been lost sight of in those calculations) — why should we succeed? I asked why we should anticipate a greater measure of success on this occasion than in the Battle of the Somme, where we had only succeeded in making a dent of five or six miles? Yet our military advisers were just as sanguine then as they were now.

I said I was told that the experience of Arras and Messines rendered success more likely. I agreed that these operations had both been very brilliant. In both, however, there had been an element of surprise. I reminded the Committee, however, that in the case of the Battle of Arras, the main attack was to have been delivered by the French further to the south, and consequently the bulk of the German reserves had been accumulated in front of General Nivelle's main attack. In my view all that the Battle of Arras demonstrated was that with surprise you could obtain an advance of five or six miles. It provided, however, no illustration or proof of what you could do when the Germans were concentrating their main reserves behind their lines, as they would to meet the attack now contemplated. In regard to the Battle of the Messines Ridge, I pointed out that the mines had provided an element of surprise.

The chances, however, were against a success. The cost in human life would be very heavy, and failure would react widely at home and abroad, while the Army would be seriously weakened. For these reasons I urged the Chief of the Imperial General Staff and the Field Marshal to pay me the compliment of considering the above case and of giving me an answer, not that day, but after they had taken a few days to think over it.

Concluding this part of my statement, I said that none of my colleagues, whether they were in favour of or opposed to the adoption of Sir Douglas Haig's plan, were sanguine of success.

I then said: The question will be asked: Does this rejection of Sir Douglas Haig's plan mean that we are to do no more fighting on the Western Front? The answer was in the negative. It was not the Committee's business to suggest alternatives, but that of the military advisers. Nevertheless, I would like to ask our military advisers to consider two alternatives.

The first of these was to adopt what might be called the Pétain tactics, namely, a punch here and there and a process of wearing down the enemy by that means. We had plenty of ammunition and could punish the enemy heavily. Having in view the privations of the Germans, the prospect of a big reinforcement from America and of a regeneration of the Russian Army, the enemy, feeling that time was against him, might be considerably damaged and discouraged by such a course.

The second alternative was to undertake an operation which was, in the first place military, and, in the second place, diplomatic, with the object of detaching Austria from Germany, namely, an attack on the Austrian Front.

I felt that the fatal error which had been committed in the present War had been continually to attack where the enemy was strongest. Surely, it was a mistake to deliberately aim our spear against the thickest part of the enemy's armour. If we had made efforts earlier in the War to knock out Austria, we should be in a far better position now. I felt, however, that we had another chance of effecting this. There was not the smallest doubt that Austria was anxious to be out of the War. This was not a matter of conjecture, but of absolute knowledge. Austria, however, was not willing now to pay the price demanded by the Allies, although if another heavy blow were struck against her she might be brought to accept our terms. I pointed out the difficult internal situation of Austria, with about half her population disaffected. I compared it to the position that this country would occupy if Wales, Scotland, and either the South or the East of England had a hostile population, whilst only a patriotic and bellicose core remained in the centre. The account that had reached us of the sessions of the Austrian Chamber showed us that the nation was sulky. This appeared to offer a special opportunity for a military and diplomatic success. The prize was far the biggest in sight. If Austria could be forced out of the War, Bulgaria and Turkey would automatically have to go out. No more ammunition could reach Bulgaria and Turkey and both would have to make terms. Next year the whole of the forces now locked up in Salonika, Mesopotamia, and Egypt would be set free for operations on the Western Front. Moreover, Italy would then be bound to support us, for I did not contemplate coöperation with Italy without a bargain that if Austria was reduced to terms, Italy should support us in our attacks against Germany. How then was this result to be accomplished? I then pointed out that the Italians had enormous resources of men, but an insufficiency of guns. The Austrians were unaccustomed to any bombardment on the scale experienced on the Western Front and probably the first time that they were exposed to it they would succumb. Taking into consideration the great Italian preponderance of men, the addition of heavy guns that they lacked should give them a chance of success.

If success was achieved on the Italian Front, I believed that victory in the War was assured. A separate peace with Austria would then be practicable, and having eliminated Austria from the War, Germany would be at our mercy.

I then called attention to the peril we should be in if Russia went out of the War leaving Austria still fighting. It might even endanger the prospect of ultimate victory.

(Sir Douglas Haig, being asked by me at this stage whether he had any hope of victory this year, at once replied that in his view he would have a very good chance of victory this year. Only to-day he had received information that the German companies were from 50 to 70 strong as compared with an original establishment of 250, that a regiment (German 163rd) refused to attack on the 18th June, that a proportion of men of the 1919 class were already in the companies at the front, etc.)

I welcomed Sir Douglas Haig's sanguine views, but did not personally attach great importance to this sort of information.

Continuing the main thread of my argument, I stated that I was very seriously alarmed about the Russian situation. Our aim therefore should be to get Austria out. General Delmé-Radcliffe[1] had expressed the view that if we sent men and guns to the aid of the Italians, we could secure secrecy as to their movements, and had suggested various expedients for doing so. If the Germans came to the assistance of the Austrians, then you would be fighting them with Italian aid. Up to now, our losses, and those of the French, had been very heavy, but this was not the case with the Italians. It would be the first time that the Italian resources of man power had been properly utilised to pull their weight in the War. The French and ourselves had no substantial numerical superiority over the Germans, and it would be very advisable for the Allies at last to make use of the great Italian superiority in men.

Lord Curzon remarked that the Italians themselves had entirely failed to make proper use of their great numerical superiority over the Austrians. I pointed out that this was due to the fact that the Italians never had any superiority in gunfire until their last attack, and on that occasion they had been short of ammunition and had been compelled to break off their attack for this reason. We, however, had the ammunition as well as the guns. I asked the Chief of the Imperial General Staff to take a day or two to think these

[1] Our liaison officer with the Italian Army.

matters over and begged him carefully to weigh the points which I had put. Personally, I said, even if my colleagues agreed, I would not be willing to impose my strategical views on my military advisers, but I had felt that I would not be doing my duty if I concealed my great misgivings about the advice they had given. If, after full reflection, they advised against the suggestions I had propounded I would, nevertheless, support them. I felt, however, that we were at the parting of the ways. *I believed that one course would lead to victory and the other course to a hopeless and costly struggle bringing us no nearer victory.*

Sir W. Robertson said that the first note he had made had been to ask to have time to prepare his reply. He and Field Marshal Sir Douglas Haig both fully appreciated the great responsibility which lay on me. He agreed that this might be the greatest decision in the War, and he wished to say that neither he nor Sir Douglas Haig resented any of my criticisms or suggestions. He would do his best to answer the questions, but he pointed out to the Committee that an officer of forty-one years' soldiering is bound to base his views partly on military experience and instinct and knowledge of the service, and similar considerations which it was difficult to formulate briefly in writing.

After the conclusion of the meeting I instructed the Secretary to ask Sir William Robertson and Sir Douglas Haig to consider the desirability of examining the Italian proposition on the spot in consultation with General Cadorna.

It is, of course, a matter of history that our military advisers, in face of this appeal from me, still decided to adhere to their view as to the feasibility of the Flanders offensive. Could I have gone behind these exalted Commanders and conducted independent investigations on the spot into the facts and conditions? It is a momentous question and should we ever have the misfortune in future to be landed in another war, that problem will arise once more. I deal with it later on when I come to discuss the issue of whether the Government ought not to have peremptorily ordered a breaking off of the battle. I had no expert military counsel which I could weigh against theirs. I was not aware at the time that the French generals and some of our own generals thought the attack was a mistake. As I was not aware then that Pétain and Micheler had urged the alternative of an offensive on the Italian Front, I could quote no military opinion in favour of my thesis. Profound though my own apprehensions of failure were, I was a layman and in matters of military strategy I did not possess the knowledge and training that would justify me in overriding soldiers of such standing and experience. Accordingly, the soldiers had their way. And it is one of the bitter ironies of war that I, who have been ruthlessly assailed in books, in the Press and in speeches for "interfering with the soldiers" should carry with me as my most painful regret the memory that on this issue I did *not* justify that charge.

5. The Four Months' Battle for a Fraction of the Objective

Instructions to Fifth Army — Strategic blunder of G.H.Q. — Initial success of July 31st — August rains — Flanders mud — Heroic endurance of British troops — Gough urges abandonment of offensive — Short objectives adopted — Haig's groundless optimism — Effect on German Army.

The operations were entrusted to the Fifth Army under the command of Sir Hubert Gough. The directions given to him by the Commander-in-Chief were to capture "the Passchendaele-Staden Ridge and the railway Roulers-Thourout." The object was stated to be to "facilitate a landing between the Yser River and Ostend and in combination with a force so landed, to gain possession of the Belgian coast. These directions end with an extraordinary sentence. "*It is open to you* . . . to visit the area of the operations." Having regard to subsequent developments, this permit to view the ground has a sinister import.

The first attack was prefaced by a prolonged and teriffic bombardment which thoroughly churned up the soggy ground. A downpour of rain did not improve matters. On the left, the first two lines were reached, but not the "green line" which was the ultimate objective of the first day's attack. On the right, little progress was made and the casualties were undoubtedly heavy. The failure on the right was serious. It meant that the further we drove the Germans on the left, the more we should be creating a dangerous salient commanded by artillery planted on the heights to the right. It is to Gough's credit that he pointed this out when the plan was first disclosed to him and that he urged that the Second Army should attack these heights simultaneously with his effort to capture Pilkem. His suggestion was not adopted. The consequence was exactly what he foresaw. The further he advanced, the more did he bring his men under German guns placed on the hills to the right of Passchendaele. Consequently, the losses were very heavy and the difficulties of a further advance were enormously increased by a continuous bombardment from heavy guns which, being on the high ground, had perfect observation of every move down in the swamps. After suffering heavily for several weeks from this obvious disadvantage — that is, obvious to those who were taking part in the fighting, but not to G.H.Q. — the Second Army were ordered, in September, to attack on the right, and they gradually cleared the enemy from these particular heights.

But the reports sent from G.H.Q. on the 1st of July revealed no ground for dejection. In fact, the enemy had been driven back at least a mile on a considerable part of the front, and some battalions had penetrated the enemy line to a depth of two miles. It was at least a greater success than our first attack on the Somme. It was not a repetition of the Vimy Ridge achievement, such as Sir Douglas Haig anticipated in his statement to the War Committee, but the High Command were entitled to claim that two more such battles might enable them to attain at least a portion of the Passchendaele-Clerken Ridge, which constituted the first objective of the campaign. According to their view the capture of the remainder of that crescent of high ground would enable them to dominate the plains on the other side, and to sweep onward with greater ease with the help of "masses of cavalry", to the important railway junction of Roulers. But alas! The next battles were a failure. Practically no progress was made in the costly assaults of August. They were not admitted as such, but nevertheless they were undoubtedly defeats by every test that stamps a battle as a victory or a repulse. The August failures were put down to the wet weather. As if it had never rained before in that dripping climate! There is a well-known legend of the sun standing still to enable a battle to be won in the Vale of Ajalon, but there is no legendary precedent which would justify our modern Joshuas in expecting that it would dispel the clouds over the lowlands of Flanders. Here is the rainfall in that country during the years of the War up to and including 1917:

	July	*August*	*September*	*Total*
1914	124 mm.	40 mm.	75 mm.	239 mm.
1915	74 mm.	107 mm.	65 mm.	246 mm.
1916	98 mm.	71 mm.	78 mm.	247 mm.
1917	104 mm.	106 mm.	16 mm.	226 mm.

These figures show what a reckless gamble it was to risk the life of the British Army on the chance of a rainless autumn on the Flemish coast.[1] But even if the rain had been below instead of above the average, as it actually turned out to be, the destruction of the drains would have sufficed to make the ground unfit for military operations. The drenching rains simply helped the broken drains to convert a reclaimed marsh into an impassable quagmire.

Here is a description of the battlefields by a competent observer:

"After our preliminary bombardment, which lasted for 16 days with ever-growing intensity, and the German retaliation thereto, the whole surface of the ground consisted of nothing but a series of overlapping shell craters, half-full of yellow, slimy water. *Through falling into these ponds hundreds upon hundreds of unwounded men, while advancing to the attack, lost their lives by drowning.*[2] The mere act of walking over this tortured swamp, unencumbered by the 60 pounds weight which the soldier carries in action, was one that entailed considerable effort, though one was able to move at one's own pace and choose the easiest routes. The original roads had almost ceased to exist, and, in order to enable wheel traffic to move at all, even in the area behind the line, it was necessary to lay down corduroy tracks which were constantly destroyed by shell fire. Furthermore, at this period, the Germans had established a definite superiority in the air and these tracks and the 'duckboard' walks were daily machine-gunned by low-flying aeroplanes. Every yard of ground had been carefully 'registered' by the enemy's guns, and a peculiarly effective form of gas shell, containing 'mustard gas' had been evolved. . . ."[3]

Having talked freely to certain officers at Headquarters about the state of the ground, this observer was hauled over the coals by an important member of the Staff for his in-

[1] Charteris notes in his diary on 4th August: "If it were not that all the records in previous years had given us fair warning, it would seem as if Providence had declared against us."

[2] My italics.

[3] "From Chauffeur to Brigadier", by Brigadier General Baker-Carr. Chapter XIV.

TROOPS MOVING OVER PASSCHENDAELE BATTLEFIELD BY MEANS OF A DUCKBOARD, 1917

discreet candour, and the following conversation which he records will give an idea not merely of the attitude of G.H.Q. towards disagreeable facts, but of their complete ignorance of what was going on.

"You asked me how things really were and I told you frankly."
"But what you say is impossible."
"It isn't. Nobody has any idea of the conditions up there."
"But they can't be as bad as you make out."
"Have you been there yourself?"
"No."
"Has anybody in Operations Branch been there?"
"No."

The officer adds:

"I am absolutely convinced that the department responsible for the staging of the Ypres offensive had not the remotest conception of the state of affairs existing and accordingly formulated their plans on a hopelessly incorrect basis. . . ."[1]

This officer was associated with the tanks. Their assistance had been regarded by G.H.Q. as one of the essentials of success. The ground was utterly unsuited to their movement.

General Baker-Carr's account is confirmed by a statement published by Captain Liddell Hart in his book, "A History of the World War."

Perhaps the most damning comment on the plan which plunged the British Army in this bath of mud and blood is contained in an incidental revelation of the remorse of one who was largely responsible for it. This highly placed officer from General Headquarters was on his first visit to the battle front — at the end of the four months' battle. Growing increasingly uneasy as the car approached the swamplike edges of the battle area, he eventually burst into tears, crying, "Good God, did we really send men to fight in that?" To which his companion replied that

[1] "From Chauffeur to Brigadier", by Brigadier General Baker-Carr. Chapter XIV.

the ground was far worse ahead. If the exclamation was a credit to his heart, it revealed on what a foundation of delusion and inexcusable ignorance his indomitable "offensiveness" had been based.[1]

I could quote written testimony from hundreds of reliable witnesses which would amply corroborate these statements. It is unnecessary to do so, for Sir Douglas Haig himself gives a vivid confirmation in his final dispatch:

> The low-lying clayey soil, torn by shells and sodden with rain, turned to a succession of vast muddy pools. The valleys of the choked and overflowing streams were speedily transformed into long stretches of bog, impassable except for a few well-defined tracks, which became marks for the enemy's artillery. . . . To leave these tracks was to risk death by drowning, and in the course of the subsequent fighting both men and pack animals were lost in this way. In these conditions operations of any magnitude became impossible. . . .

It is true that this was written in December, 1917. But the Staff Officer who was responsible for this passage only visited the ground after the whole fight was over.

Artillery became bogged, tanks stuck in the mire, unwounded men by the hundreds and wounded men by the thousands sank beyond recovery into the filth. It is a comment upon the intelligence with which the whole plan had been conceived and prepared that after the ridge had been reached it was an essential part of the plan that masses of cavalry were intended to thunder across this impassable bog to complete the rout of a fleeing enemy. For months, hundreds of thousands of British troops fought through this slough. They sheltered and they slept in mudholes. When they squelched along, they were shot down into the slush; if

[1] "A History of the World War", by Liddell Hart.

General Charteris, in his published diary, records that on 9th August: "The front area now baffles description . . . it is just a sea of mud, churned up by shell-fire."

wounded, they were drowned in the slime: but the survivors still crept and dragged onward for four months from shell hole to shell hole, with their rifles and machine guns choked with Flemish ooze, advancing about a mile a month. It was a tragedy of heroic endurance enacted in mud, and the British Press rang with praises of the ruthless courage, untiring calm and undaunted tenacity — of the Commander-in-Chief! It was not the fault of the newspapers. The truth was carefully eliminated from official *communiqués* and Press dispatches from the front. There was a relentless and clever censorship exercised.

The Commander of the attacking Army, General Gough, has himself given a faithful account of the conditions under which his Army was called upon to fight. He thought it so hopeless that in the middle of August he advised Sir Douglas Haig to discontinue.

"The state of the ground was by this time frightful. The labour of bringing up supplies and ammunition, of moving or firing the guns, which had often sunk up to their axles, was a fearful strain on the officers and men, even during the daily task of maintaining the battle front. When it came to the advance of infantry for an attack across the water-logged shell holes, movement was so slow and so fatiguing that only the shortest advances could be contemplated. *In consequence I informed the Commander-in-Chief that tactical success was not possible, or would be too costly, under such conditions, and advised that the attack should now be abandoned. I had many talks with Haig during these days and repeated this opinion frequently, but he told me that the attack must be continued.*"[1]

Gough endeavours to excuse Haig's stubbornness by stating that he had valid reasons for continuing these desperate enterprises, as for instance, the condition of the

[1] "The Fifth Army", by General Sir H. Gough, p. 205.
At this very date Haig reported to the Government that: "The time is fast approaching when the enemy will be unable to maintain her armies."

French Army and the need for engaging the Germans so that they should not deliver a knock-out blow to the Russians. Haig also urged the possibilities of the Germans turning on the Italians. It never occurred to him that the same results might have been better achieved by attacking the enemy on more favourable ground. The Cambrai operation later on revealed alternative possibilities of a more hopeful character, even on his own front. Gough, having received his orders to go on, made another general attack on the 22nd of August, but he reduced his objectives to those within a short distance from his line. He assigns as his reason for this restricted operation that:

> "It was impossible for the men to go forward over any long distance: my object was to spare the troops to the utmost possible degree, while at the same time complying with my orders from G.H.Q. to the effect that the battle must be continued."

It must seem incredible to those who have no experience of the tyrannical repression imposed on honest men by professional etiquette, that Gough's entreaty to the Commander-in-Chief that he should break off the attack was never reported to the War Cabinet. Whether Sir William Robertson was told of it, I am not in a position to say. I do not know the limits and bounds of military reticence in these matters. Does it end with the forbidding of communication to civilians, or does it extend to those who are inside the Services, although they may be in a position where knowledge of the true situation is essential to the faithful discharge of their functions. Sir William Robertson ought to have been told, and if he was informed, then he was in duty and honour bound to pass on so important a fact to the Government. He and Sir Douglas Haig had given a promise to the Cabinet that they would break off the attacks as soon as it became clear that victory was unattainable. At that time I was pressing Robertson to redeem that promise on exactly the same grounds as were being urged by the general in command of the attacking Army. I failed to persuade him that the time had arrived to call off this offensive, but in discussing the matter he certainly never informed me that the general who was in command of the operations agreed with me. Did he know? If he did not, then it is only right that those who were in his confidence at that date should say so. Haig knew.

Gough, having received his orders from G.H.Q., continued to press on after it had become quite obvious that the object of the campaign was unattainable. He does not seem to have withheld his opinion on that point from the Commander-in-Chief, but he states that:

"On the 28th (September) Haig held a conference, at which he expressed somewhat optimistic views, and gave the opinion that our repeated blows were using up the enemy's reserves and that we might soon be able to push on with no definite and limited objectives as heretofore. *He thought that it might be possible that tanks and even cavalry could get forward.* . . . From a tactical outlook his hopeful opinion was not justified when one considered the ground, the weariness of our own men, and the stout hearts which, in spite of all, were still beating under the German tunics.

"A letter from Plumer to G.H.Q. two days later threw some cold water on these hopes. . . ."

Here indeed was a Commander-in-Chief who had completely lost his balance. General Gough need not wait until he reached the ridge before throwing in "masses of cavalry." The time had already arrived for the great charge which was to ride down the beaten foe with irresistible fury and scatter them along the plains of Belgium as the Prussian squadrons had chased the flying rabble of Napoleon's broken army after the route of Waterloo.

I shall be interested, when Sir Douglas Haig's Memoirs

appear, to find whether that important letter from General Plumer throwing cold water on these frenzied expectations will be included amongst the documents. It was not communicated to the Government. Did Robertson know of its existence? Haig knew.

I know now that all the generals engaged in this battle were opposed to its continuance and were convinced that its objectives were unattainable. Sir Douglas Haig alone retained his faith in the merits and ultimate triumph of his project. In his opinion, the generals on the spot were too readily discouraged by reports pouring in as to the difficulties of the terrain. He also had his reports which dwelt on the more cheerful material that came in from the front. It is true that they came from men that had never seen the battlefield. Their admirable poise was not upset by contemplation of its gruesome realities. There were two courses open to Sir Douglas Haig. One was to go to the Cabinet and admit that the campaign was a complete failure based on an absurd miscalculation of essential facts. He would have to own up that the criticism directed against the scheme by the Prime Minister had been justified by the event. The other course was to persevere stubbornly with his attacks, knowing that at the worst he would gain some ground, with a chance that one day the enemy morale might break and that opportunity would then come for exploiting a defeat. He gambled on the latter chance rather than face the dread alternative of a confession of failure to the politicians who had deposed Lord French for a less stupendous error of judgment at Loos.

I was trying at this date to persuade Robertson and Haig that the conditions had arisen which made it imperative that they should carry out their undertaking to the Cabinet to break off the attack whenever it became clear that it could not succeed. Had they told me that all the generals responsible for the actual fighting were of that opinion, the Cabinet would have issued a peremptory order. Its members were not prepared to do so in the absence of any authentic military support for so unprecedented a proceeding. Haig's and Robertson's only answer to my plea was the exceptionally wet August. When the weather improved, the ground would solidify and progress would be easier. The weather did improve in September, but the ground got gradually worse, if that were possible, and General Gough says that, after fighting through the driest September for many years:

". . . the state of the ground has been frightful since the 1st of August, but now it was getting absolutely impossible. *Men of the strongest physique could hardly move forward at all and became easy victims to the enemy's snipers. Stumbling forward as best as they could,* their rifles also became so caked and clogged with mud as to be useless."

This was the terrain over which Haig ordered that tanks should be driven and cavalry were to charge, without any limit to their objective. Infantry could barely "stumble forward" but horsemen could gallop along! Gough's summing-up of the battlefield is very vivid. Here is a sentence:

"Many pens have tried to describe the ghastly expanse of mud which covered this water-logged country, but few have been able to paint a picture sufficiently intense."

During the exceptionally dry spell in September some successes of a limited character were scored, fractions of a mile captured each time with a few prisoners. There is no doubt that up to about the middle of September the incessant and severe fighting, together with the terrific bombardment, and the reckless disregard of casualties incurred by the attacking troops in an advance, were making an impression on the German Army. Never had there been such a deluge of explosives. It poured for forty days and forty nights, without a moment's cease. It is computed that during this time we fired over twenty-five million shells. Never had there been a more persistent indifference to losses in men and officers. Our men advanced against the most terrible machine-gun fire ever directed against troops in any series of battles, and they fell by the thousands in every attack. But divisions were sent on time after time to face the same slaughter in their ranks, and they always did their intrepid best to obey the fatuous orders. When divisions were exhausted or decimated, there were plenty of others to take their places. Ludendorff admits in his book that owing to defective tactical arrangements it was for him till well into September a period of great anxiety, and that at some points his troops were no longer displaying the firmness which he had hoped for. He then changed his defensive tactics, and afterwards he soon came to the conclusion that the position was completely re-established and that he was safe. But we still went on hammering, making some apparent, but no real progress except in the dispatches from the front. These rang out peal after peal of swelling triumph.

6. The Tactics of Deception

Dope for British public — Casualties miscalculated — Explaining away the facts — Difficulty of interference; lesson of French mutiny — Problem of dismissing Haig — Attitude of Charteris; bright reports for Haig — His predictions of success — Subservience of Fleet Street — Specimen report from the *Times* — Sir Philip Gibbs' admission — Attack ends in fiasco — Change of policy and its failure — G.H.Q. ignorant of battlefield — Duty of generals to know the ground — Haig's courage — Paper strategy — British and German officer casualties — German reserves for Riga and Caporetto.

While the ghastliness I have inadequately summarised was proceeding, and brave men were being sacrificed to the stubborn infatuation of the High Command, the public at home, official and unofficial, were all dosed day by day with tendentious statements about victories won, and progress made towards more assured and even greater triumphs.

Enemy depression became as deep and his morale as quaky as the bogs of Passchendaele. We were assured that the German peace manœuvres were the indications and expedients of despair. In her fear of the approaching crash, Germany was appealing now to the Socialists, then to Von Kuhlmann, and again to the Pope, to sue for peace in a hurry. The reports passed on to the Ministers were, as we all realised when it was too late, grossly misleading. Victories were much overstated. Virtual defeats were represented as victories, however limited their scope. Our casualties were understated. Enemy losses became pyramidal. That was the way the military authorities presented the situation to Ministers — that was their active propaganda in the Press. All disconcerting and discouraging facts were suppressed in the reports received from the front by the War Cabinet — every bright feather of success was waved and flourished in our faces. Early in October we were officially informed that the British casualties up to the 5th of October were 148,470, whilst the German casualties were 255,000. We know now that the British casualties were already almost twice the number then given to the Cabinet, and that the total German casualties opposite the whole of the British Front for the last five months of the year only aggregated 270,701.

Every disquieting fact was explained away without any difficulty. If anyone pointed out that the prisoners captured were few, and those mostly wounded, there was a ready and complete explanation given by the C.I.G.S. It was stated that on account of the nature of the ground, the Germans had no dugouts as they had at Vimy, so they were pounded to death on the surface by our terrible bombardment before our troops had the opportunity of catching them alive. The enormous (estimated) German casualties were referred to as a proof of this. If we expressed doubts about the number of guns captured in comparison with Arras, then we were told that the Germans planted their artillery on the ridge, well behind the pillboxes. We would get these guns right enough when the ridge fell into our hands.

The statements about German morale were sometimes grotesque in the gullibility they displayed. The C.I.G.S. came in one day with the statement that "fires had been observed in the Lille area; that the Germans were burning some villages to the north of that town; that this might be preliminary to a withdrawal in that region, where their present line was dominated by the Messines Ridge."

Another day came another cock-and-bull story about indications that the Germans were making arrangements to withdraw from another part of the line, which Sir William Robertson regarded as a "proof that they were preparing for emergencies." The German Armies were visibly cracking under the hammer blows of Haig. We must keep on. To faint or to falter now would be to throw away the chance of finally destroying the foe, when we were daily tightening our grasp on that chance.

It may be said that we must have been a very simple lot to have been taken in by all this selected trash. Politicians are liable to be attacked from every flank — simultaneously. They are suspicious, subtle, crafty and designing, and at the same time they are gullible, simple and foolish. In this case we were not taken in, but our means of ascertaining the facts were blocked by the complete coöperation that existed between the War Office and G.H.Q. We were dependent as to the number of casualties on both sides on reports picked and winnowed by G.H.Q., who were bent on making a case for continuing the offensive. These reports were sent on, not to us, but to the C.I.G.S., whose view was that Haig must be supported at all costs and that (whatever he might say privately to his intimates) the Western Front must not be discredited in the hearing of its detractors. Could we then have gone behind these potentates and in the middle of the battle conducted an inquisition into the methods of the High Command, encouraging officers and men to tell us what they thought of their superiors? We had before our eyes the example of the semi-public intervention of the French in the case of the Nivelle offensive. Some of the most distinguished generals in the French Army were opposed to that offensive. Some of the ablest generals in our own Army were doubtful of the wisdom of initiating and pursuing this offensive. But there was a vital difference in the two cases. The dissentient French generals communicated their doubts frankly to the Government. Our generals imparted their views to the Commander-in-Chief, but never whispered one hint of their hesitation to any politician. One of them afterwards informed me that had I asked him the question at the time, he would have placed loyalty to his Commander first. The Nivelle precedent had its drawbacks. It stopped that attack, but came dangerously near to fomenting general mutiny in the French Army. The result was almost fatal to the cohesion and confidence of the French Army. It put it out of effective action for months. We could not risk a repetition of that experiment at this time. The British Army was then the one Allied Army in the field which could be absolutely relied upon for any enterprise, however hazardous and arduous it might be. We could not take any chances with it. It is said that I ought to have taken the risks and stopped the carnage. Let me confess that there were, and still are, moments when I am of the same opinion. But let those who are inclined to condemn me and the War Cabinet for not taking the hazard, weigh carefully and fairly the conditions at that time.

Passchendaele could not have been stopped without dismissing Sir Douglas Haig. Sir William Robertson would have resigned. Had both disappeared without any preliminary fuss which would have rattled the Army, there would have been a sense of relief amongst all the fighting men from one end of the line to the other. But I could not have done it without the assent of the Cabinet. I sounded the Members of the Cabinet individually on the subject and I also spoke to some of the Dominion representatives. They — or most of them — were under the spell of the synthetic victories distilled at G.H.Q.

Nowhere was there a more ecstatic belief in these imaginary victories than at the château and village where the Field Marshal and his Staff were quartered.

I visited General Headquarters some time about the end of September. I found there an atmosphere of unmistakable exaltation. It was not put on. Haig was not an actor. He was radiant. He was quiet, there was no swagger. That was never one of his weaknesses, but he had the satisfied and confident demeanour of a leader who was marching his army step by step surely and irresistibly, overcoming all obstacles, including good advice from Gough and Plumer and the Prime Minister, forward to the penultimate triumph of the War. This time it was purely his own. The politicians had tried to thwart his purpose. His own commanders had timidly tried to deflect him from his great achievement. He magnanimously forgave us all. He received me hospitably and pleasantly, without any of the humiliations of Canossa. The French could claim no share in this victory, which was breaking the might of the great army of Germany and leaving it a nervous wreck to be finally disposed of in 1918. Something must be left for the Americans, otherwise they would be disappointed.

General Charteris, who was an embodiment of the Military Intelligence which he directed, glowed with victory. For him the news was all good. If there were any elements that might have caused doubt in more discriminating minds, at least General Charteris had not discerned them. And if he had, he was proof against their maleficent influence. He could not help his hopeful reports. His computations were not mathematical, but temperamental. From the mass of information that came into his office he chose his facts and figures by attraction and not reflection. He could only be caught by a bright fly. That he swallowed up to the gut.

It naturally pleased Haig to have carefully chosen and nicely cooked little titbits of "intelligence" about broken German divisions, heavy German casualties, and diminishing German morale served up to him every day and all day. He beamed satisfaction and confidence. His great plan was prospering. The whole atmosphere of this secluded little community reeked of that sycophantic optimism which is the curse of autocratic power in every form. At Chantilly, the same kind of thing blunted the native shrewdness of Joffre and turned the head of Nivelle. It blinded the Czar to the approach of the menacing icebergs that were converging towards his golden barque and ultimately crushed it like matchwood.

When the time came to review Passchendaele, Sir William Robertson attached most of the blame to these reports.

As for General Kiggell, the Chief of Staff, he had the air of a silent craftsman, whose plans, designed and worked out by his art in the seclusion of his workshop, were turning out well and proceeding inexorably without a hitch to the destined end.

During this visit, Sir Douglas and his Staff dwelt repeatedly on the visible deterioration in the physique and smartness of the German soldiers, judged by the specimens captured in recent victories. I expressed a desire to see them. The proposition was received without any enthusiasm. Would I not prefer to see the Vimy Ridge where I could get a view of the German positions? I preferred to see the last batch of German prisoners. I saw the last "cage", and I thought the men were a weedy lot. They were deplorably inferior to the manly samples I had seen in earlier stages of the War. It was some years after the War that I ascertained on authority which is unimpeachable, that on that occasion G.H.Q. rang up Fifth Army and stated that the Prime Minister was coming down and would go to Corps Headquarters to see German prisoners. Instructions were given to inform the Corps — I forget which one it was — of this, and to tell them to see that able-bodied prisoners were removed from the Corps cages.

Whether that message was passed on to the appropriate quarters, I have no direct evidence. But this I do know, that the prisoners I saw did not comprise any "able-bodied specimens." I feel certain that the Commander-in-Chief had no part in this disreputable endeavour to deceive the Chief Minister of the Crown. But it was all in keeping with the effort made to create an impression that although the Belgian coast was not as yet much nearer, those who stood between us and that objective did not possess the requisite quality to bar the way much longer against our tremendous onslaughts.

This is the visit to which I have already alluded in the chapter on the Kuhlmann peace overtures, and which I paid in order to ascertain the views of the Commander-in-Chief on the situation. A few quotations from this estimate will give an idea of the attitude of exaggerated optimism with which he viewed his achievements in the battle which was then in progress.

At the present moment there are 147 German divisions on this front, of which 135 have been driven from their positions or withdrawn, broken by their losses since the 1st April, 1917 — many of them twice and some three times. No less than 77 of these divisions have been thus overcome — several more than once — during this period by the British Armies. I quote this as a proof of what our armies are capable of.

Our offensive in front of Ypres continues to make good progress. The enemy is undoubtedly considerably shaken and the ground we have already gained gives us considerable advantages and renders us less dependent on weather in following up our success further. Our troops are elated and confident; those on the enemy's side cannot but be depressed and we have good evidence of it.

In the circumstances it is beyond question that our offensive must be pursued as long as possible. I have every hope of being able to continue it for several weeks still and of gaining results which will add very greatly to the enemy's losses in men and morale, and place us in a far better position to resume an offensive in the spring.

Amongst other advantages, we shall end this year's campaign with practically all the observation points originally held by the enemy in our possession — a very important consideration.

The considerable wastage imposed on the enemy by a continued offensive may be expected to leave at the end of the year but a small balance, if any, of the 500,000 men in the reserves he now has available, and he is likely to commence the new year with only some 500,000 to 600,000 reserves at his disposal, including the whole of the 1920 class, which, judging by experience of the 1918 class, will be of low fighting value. At the normal rate of wastage, therefore, since the 1921 class will not be fit to take the field next year, the enemy's man power will be running out next May or June at the latest. This is a factor of first-rate importance, and no alleviation of this respect would be gained by a return of prisoners from Russia if the latter should make peace, since this would be far more than counterbalanced by the loss of the great numbers of Russian prisoners now available for labour in Germany.

Then came the usual stuff from the Charteris stillroom about the inferior quality and the shattered condition of the German divisions:

Nineteen of the German divisions now on this front are of poor quality, only fit for the defensive on quiet fronts; 135 of the remainder have already suffered heavy defeats this year and that number will be increased in the next few weeks. Of the 179 German divisions, therefore, the value of at least 154 (135 + 19) must be written down considerably.

The German forces are being replaced now in large proportion by quite inferior material and the proportion of such material in the German ranks will increase rapidly in the future, while, by May or June, the German reserves will be exhausted.

If anyone wants to understand the conditions under which we were called upon to judge appropriate action, let him examine the back numbers of any of the journals of that date.

There was an elaborate and sustained effort to create an atmosphere of impending victory on an eventful scale. The reports from the Front, official and unofficial, became rosier and ruddier. G.H.Q. could not capture the Passchendaele Ridge, but it was determined to storm Fleet Street, and here strategy and tactics were superb. The press correspondents at the front were completely enveloped and important publicists and newspaper proprietors in this country were overwhelmed. Lord Northcliffe had, ever since 1916, been the mere kettledrum of Sir Douglas Haig, and the mouth organ of Sir William Robertson.

The *Times* reports were therefore ecstatic.

In September there was a fierce battle in which we advanced about one thousand yards into the enemy's defence zone on a limited front. We took about three thousand prisoners, but there is nothing to show that we captured any guns. Our losses were heavy. The report of the *Times* special correspondent is strikingly headed:

GERMAN DEFENCE BROKEN

In his dispatch he says that:

. . . in this battle we have broken the elaborate scheme of

defence which was the last blossom and ultimate triumph of German strategists. This is, from the strategic point of view, the most signal triumph of this attack. It is not merely that it is ground of the first importance that we have taken, or the number of German regiments we have shattered, *but we have broken, and broken at a single blow,* in the course of some three or four hours, the German system of defence.

All that happened was that we had with heavy casualties pushed back the enemy less than two thirds of a mile on a narrow front. The ridge, which was the first objective of the battle, was after weeks of sanguinary fighting, still in the possession of the Germans, and most of it remained in their possession when the Commander-in-Chief finally called off the fight. We had therefore to win another "shattering victory", pushing the enemy back another kilometre, picking up another three thousand of his wounded in the recovered ground. We again utilised this captured post as a starting point in the first week in October for still another smashing triumph a few hundred yards ahead.

This last battle, which produced no tactical, let alone strategical, results of any importance, was hailed in the *Times* as "the most important British victory of the year." It adds:

"In short, the particular task which Sir Douglas Haig set his armies, has been very nearly accomplished."

We had captured two or three kilometres of the ridge which Sir Douglas Haig had informed us was the first objective in his big drive.

As a matter of fact, the whole of the ten weeks' ghastly struggle had not given him, up to and including this last fight, one sixth of his first objective.

The *Times* has two leading articles on successive days on the Broodseinde victory, as it was called. Who remembers the name now? (Try it on one of your friends.) In each of these leading articles the *Times* waxes lyrical over the result.

It assures its readers that "our object is already secured." The British public were congratulated on the fact that at last we were in sight of Bruges. They were not told that this city was fifteen miles off, nor were they reminded that the Germans had been in sight of Ypres, only two miles off, for over three years. It extols the way in which Sir Douglas Haig was winning back what was lost in the First Battle of Ypres: ". . . with a tenacity and a calm, unhurried persistence which compel the admiration of the world. . . .

"With each successive stride the arrangements grow more exact, the results more certain, the losses lighter."

But the *Times* correspondent did not constitute the whole of the orchestra. There were other minor players.

Sir Philip Gibbs throws some light upon the difficulties of a war correspondent in the introduction to a reprint from his despatches at the front. As it appeared at a time when he was still a war correspondent, it is phrased with considerable restraint.

"There is no criticism in this book, no judgment of actions of men, no detailed summing up of success or failure. That is not within my liberty or duty as a correspondent with the Armies in the Field."

All the same, his sense of duty to the public who were looking to him for a truthful account of what their sons and brothers and husbands were passing through in the battlefield did not prevent his suppressing every check or repulse, and exaggerating with unbridled extravagance every trifling advance purchased at a terrible cost (the latter also suppressed). Here are some of the phrases from a description by him of a battle that drove the enemy back for three quarters of a mile on a limited front, with a capture of three thousand prisoners, a large number of whom, according to him, were purely wounded men left on the battlefield, and just a few guns. His jubilant report describes this as:

". . . a smashing blow, the most smashing defeat we have inflicted on the enemy, a complete victory. . . ."

Referring to the enemy he adds:

"We have him beat. One of the greatest victories we have had in the War."

He even gave the impression that the succession of victories won in Flanders might shortly lead to the attainment of a victorious peace. Here is a choice example of the kind of ecstatic reporting to which we were subjected:

> One of the prisoners, a professor . . . thinks "it will not be long before Germany makes a great bid for peace by offering to give up Belgium. By mid-winter she will yield Alsace-Lorraine; Russia will remain as before the War; except for an autonomous Poland; Italy will have what she has captured; and Germany will get back some of her colonies."[1]

Whether he himself talked to this accommodating don or whether the information was supplied to him as a titbit by the "Intelligence" Department, is not clear. All we know now is that as a result of this "smashing defeat of the enemy" nothing happened except the capture of a ruined village, and preparations for more victories of the same sort, all of them announced in turn as "triumphs of unparalleled magnitude." Whilst this triumphal crawl through the mud was proceeding, Ludendorff was sending divisions to Russia to capture Riga and to the Italian Front to help Austria.

The fighting went on until the first week in December. When it was finally concluded, the attack had completely failed in all the purposes for which it was originally designed. We had not cleared the Flemish coast. We had not broken through the enemy's defences into open country. The cavalry charge had not come off. Not a single cavalry horse had wetted his hooves in the slush. If the reader will

[1] "From Bapaume to Passchendaele, 1917", by Sir Philip Gibbs, p. 320.

refer back to the plan of attack, he will understand better how this dreadfulness had ended in an utter fiasco. He will see marked on that map the stages by which we were to reach our final objective. The Passchendaele-Staden Ridge was only the first stage. At its utmost limit it was only five miles from where we started. The last objective was twenty-five miles distant. The ridge which constituted the first stage in our advance was eighteen miles in length. After over four months' terrible fighting, resulting in casualties which reached nearly four hundred thousand and an enormous expenditure of ammunition — the greatest blaze of high explosives ever yet fired on any battlefield — we had only captured five miles of the ridge, that is about a fourth of our first line of projected advance. To achieve our full aim, we had several more lines to attack and get through. During the whole battle we recovered less ground, we took fewer prisoners, we captured fewer guns (about one fourth) than we did in the despised Nivelle offensive, and that with nearly three times the casualties we sustained in that operation, which was always alluded to by the Staff as a "failure."

When it was realised some time in September that a break-through was impracticable and that the clearing of the Flemish coast this year was out of the question, G.H.Q. substituted the policy of "wearing down the enemy" as the primary purpose of their strategy. How did that thrive? We lost four hundred thousand men in our direct and subsidiary attacks. The enemy did not lose on the whole British Front during that period a quarter of a million men. Our losses were nearly five to every three of the Germans. In their Verdun offensive, the Germans had the excuse that they were slaying five Frenchmen for every three they lost. We could not claim that measure of justification for our persistence in the Passchendaele folly. The balance of attrition, which was already heavily in favour of the enemy, was, by this offensive, tipped still more definitely in his favour. The French and the British between them had sustained casualties since the War began which aggregated over five millions. Against this, the enemy loss in fighting us was three millions. I learn that an elaborate effort is being made to gerrymander the casualty returns — both British and German — so as to present a more favourable balance sheet for this adventure. Such a proceeding is dishonest, whether it be historical or commercial, and whatever the nature and whoever the person that inspires it. The fact that it conforms to the spirit of dispatches that announced a series of glorious victories when the sum total was a wretched disaster is no more a justification for the historian than it would be for an auditor who put forward as a plea for cooking the accounts the fact that he was doing so in order to preserve the continuity of the directors' reports. That is not an unknown practice where the public have to be misled as to the extent of the deficit. The losses must be cut down, the gains overstated so as to show a profit on the concern.

So much for the bovine and brutal game of attrition on the Western Front. On the Eastern Front, it was ending in millions of Russians and hundreds of thousands of Roumanians quitting the battlefield.

It was all a terrible miscalculation. Those who were responsible for planning and persisting in the plan when it had failed, were not men of imagination. All that quality was concentrated in the information bureau. The planning department were conspicuously devoid of it. In the absence of this rare gift there ought to have been a meticulous examination of the ground and a careful and honest survey of the enemy's resources in men and munitions. Unfortunately, the General Officer who prepared the plans for attack after attack across kilometres of untraversable quagmire, and the general who had control of what was by a strange irony called

"Intelligence", and whose business it was to sift all the information that came in, and to prepare the reports upon which plans were based, never themselves got near enough to the battlefield to see what it was like. They worked on the basis of optimistic reports in the shelter of a remote château, out of sight of the mud and far from the sound of the deadly clatter of the machine guns. Where draft plans had been submitted, received and approved, the fatal ink which in a few days would be converted into blood, set forth orders and instructions which were not smudged by a drop of the devastating rain that drowned the wounded warriors who fell in a vain attempt to realise these paper dreams. If General Headquarters received any reports as to the conditions under which the men were asked to attack, those reports were never passed on to the War Council. Were they presented to the Commander-in-Chief? Gough told him something of the realities. But Haig was not a man to encourage discouraging reports.

A great deal of the catastrophe is due to the change effected by modern methods of warfare in the opportunities and therefore in the personal risks and responsibilities of commanders. At Waterloo, Napoleon and Wellington could see the whole battlefield with their eyes, and with the help of field glasses almost every hump and hollow. Even then Napoleon overlooked the sunken road.

But in modern warfare, the more important the general, the less he feels it to be his duty to see for himself what the battlefield is like. Wellington's generals were on the field amongst their troops. No general in this War — and these remarks apply to every Army in the field on both sides — was expected to visit No Man's Land until the battleground had been made safe for "brass hats" by the retreat of the enemy to an invisible distance. Some of them courted danger to inspire their troops and to view the ground for themselves, and in doing so, several fell. But the rule was that generals no longer led but sent their troops into action. This transformation may have been inevitable, owing to the magnitude and the character of the operations and also owing to the increased power and range of the weapons used. But the increase in the danger factor cannot be pleaded in defence of so revolutionary a change. Admirals share risks with their sailors in a sea fight. The departure from time-honoured ideas as to the duty of personal observation is due either to an exaggerated estimate of the importance of the individual general, or to an underestimate of the qualities of the officers available to take the places of superiors in rank who have fallen. The price paid in this War for immunity to generals was prodigious. No one suggests that it is the duty of generals to lead their men up to the barbed wire, through the mud, whilst machine guns are playing upon them. But, had men high up in military rank, ordering or continuing an offensive, been obliged by the exigencies of duty to view for themselves something of the character of the terrain of attack and the nature of the operation they were ordering their officers and men to undertake, the fatuous assaults of the Somme, Monchy, Bullecourt, the Chemin des Dames and Passchendaele would never have occurred; or at any rate one such experience would have been enough.

It is not for me to express an opinion as to whether the change which has taken place in the duties and dangers of generals is justified. This comment, however, I am entitled to make. If generals are no longer under any necessity to join their men in an attack or even to go within the zone of fire, it is more incumbent upon them than ever to exercise the greatest care in ascertaining the kind of task they call upon their officers and men to carry through. Apart from good generalship, the obligations of comradeship and of common decency demand it. The men who persisted in the Passchendaele assaults could not have known the conditions under which their orders had to be executed. It is an insult to their intelligence, let alone their humanity, to believe otherwise. I have quoted reputable evidence to prove that some of them had no idea of the actual state of the ground which they commanded tanks and troops to cross. Gough knew and passed his knowledge on to Haig. It seems to have made no impression on the latter's obsessed mind. His apologists quote his obduracy as a proof of the sublime courage that disdained obstacles and dangers. The fact that they were obstacles and dangers which had to be faced only by others and not himself would not, I feel sure, weigh with him. Had he been a humble officer he would have faced them without quaking. No one ever cast a doubt on his personal courage. But it demanded a much higher courage to own up that he had been guilty of a grave error of judgment — that the operation he had planned was an impossible one — that, in fact, he had been wrong and the subordinate generals and interfering politicians had been right.

Thus G.H.Q. never witnessed, not even through a telescope, the attacks it ordained, except on carefully prepared charts where the advancing battalions were represented by the pencil which marched with ease across swamps and marked lines of triumphant progress without the loss of a single point. As for the mud, it never incommoded the movements of this irresistible pencil.

No wonder that nothing daunted a staff working under such conditions. They could afford to be the very incarnation of ruthlessness and vicarious heroism: the gods of war, not on the battlefield, but in their temple.

I was privileged, whilst this horrible battle was proceeding, to have a talk with one of Haig's most prominent military advisers, who afterwards owned that he had no idea of the conditions under which the battle was fought. I entreated

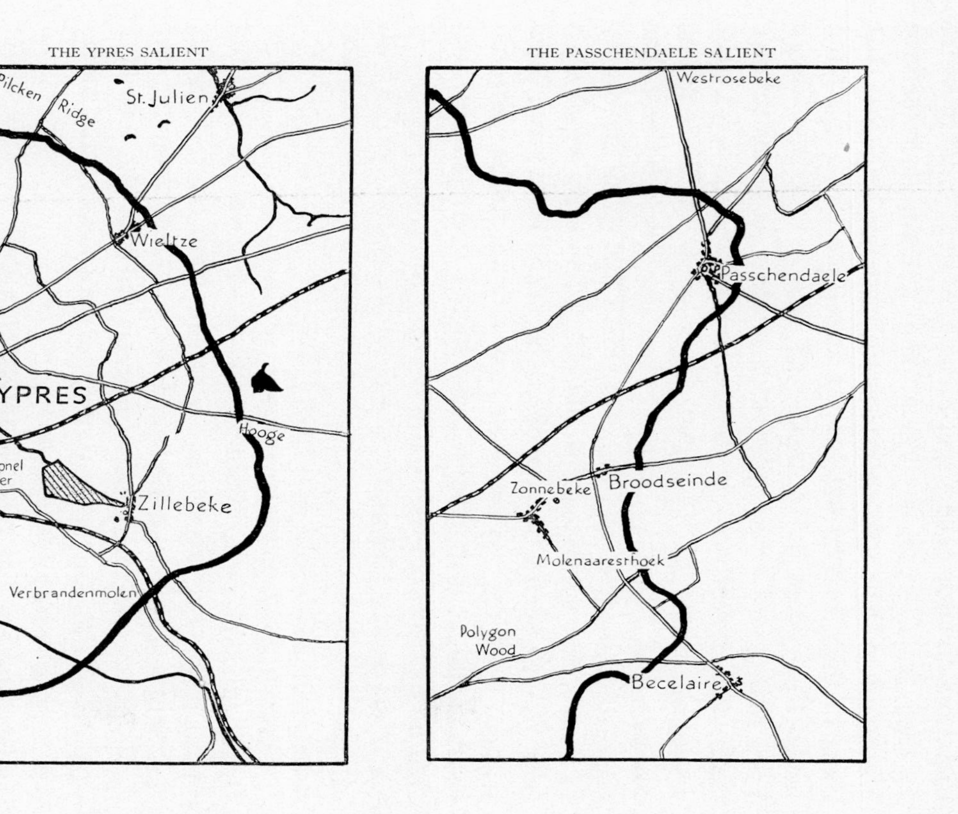
THE YPRES SALIENT
Pilcken
Ridge
St. Julien
Wieltze
YPRES
Hooge
Shrapnel
Corner
Zillebeke
Verbrandenmolen
St. Eloi
THE PASSCHENDAELE SALIENT
Westrosebeke
Passchendaele
Zonnebeke
Broodseinde
Molenaaresthoek
Polygon
Wood
Becelaire

him once more to reconsider the prospects of this venture in the light of what had actually happened. But he also was imbued with the relentlessness of his Chief. He treated me as a stupid civilian who knew nothing of war. When I alluded to the terrible casualties, he reminded me in Hotspur strain that you could not expect to make war without death and wounds. When I pointed to the wet season which had soaked the ground and made it unfit for the passage of tanks, artillery or men, he said: Battles could not be stopped like tennis matches for a shower. Here again was Mars, but, I thought, Mars under an umbrella.

As to the effect upon the enemy's morale, no doubt they suffered heavy losses in this protracted struggle. It is contended by the apologists of Passchendaele that they lost heavily in officers. As a matter of fact, their casualties in officers were not comparable to ours. We lost a total of seventeen thousand — seven officers to every two of theirs. The loss to them was a serious one. Much more serious was the loss in officers and N.C.O.'s for us, for the Germans had a much larger proportion of men with a long army training to draw upon for making up this deficiency than we had. As to the casualties amongst the N.C.O.'s, officers know well how much they depend upon the experience and shrewdness of their chevroned assistants. The loss in N.C.O.'s was irreplaceable. The best answer to the claim put forward that the enemy had been shattered either in spirit or in reserves, is that when the attack was at its hottest and we were boasting that the German reserves had been almost exhausted, Ludendorff detached some divisions for an attack on Riga; and when we were exultant over the winning of what we regarded as a decisive victory at Broodseinde, his response to our pæans was to send five German divisions to Austria to start a crashing offensive against the Italians. And when we thought that their last reserves had been sent away to save

Austria, the Germans found fourteen divisions on the Western Front to smash up our offensive at Cambrai. It means that at the moment that we were claiming that we had succeeded in breaking through the German defence system, the German High Command were confident that our whole offensive was an assured failure, and they acted on that assumption.

7. Consequences of Passchendaele

Scanty achievement of the offensive — G.H.Q's. remarkable admission — Passchendaele nearly fatal to Allies — Growing extravagance of war — Waste of man power — Protecting the Staff Officers — Lost opportunities against Turkey — Report of the Versailles Council — Responsibility for Caporetto — And for the German break-through in March, 1918 — One of the greatest disasters of the War.

No soldier of any intelligence now defends this senseless campaign; certainly not one who is not implicated by some share of responsibility for it.

As I have already pointed out in the previous section, not even the first objective of the campaign had been attained. The fight came to be known as the "Battle of Passchendaele", but the capture of this village gave us only one fourth of the first ridge which the Army had to occupy as a starting point. It left the Army with a narrower salient than the deadly salient of Ypres, which had already cost us so much. The enemy still surrounded it on three sides, and at some points their lines were nearer to ours than they had been to Ypres before the battle began. Soon after the termination of the campaign, Headquarters realised that at an expense of four hundred thousand men, they had only forced the British Army into a more dangerous position than it was in before the battle commenced. On December 13th, G.H.Q. issued one of the most remarkable documents which ever emanated from a victorious staff. It constitutes such a comment upon the great triumph that I quote textually from it:

. . . the following special instructions are issued as a guide to the manner of dealing with the Flesquières and Passchendaele salients.

These salients are unsuitable to fight a decisive battle in. It is, however, desirable to retain possession of them if they are not attacked in great force; and in the event of attack in great force to use them to wear out and break up the enemy's advancing troops as much as possible before these can reach our battle zone of defence which will be sited approximately as a chord across the base of each salient.

In accordance with this policy the salients will be held firmly until the battle zone of defence behind each has been prepared. The defences of the salients will then be organised into advanced or "outpost" zones, and as these defences become more complete, so the garrisons can be reduced to what is required for the purpose in view.

I need hardly say that this document was withheld from the War Cabinet. And no wonder, for it constitutes a written admission by G.H.Q. that the only strategical or tactical result it achieved by the terrible fighting which very nearly broke the British Army, was the establishment of salients which were "unsuitable to fight a decisive battle in" and which could not be retained if they were "attacked in great force." And the advice is given that they should follow the tactics pursued by the German Army of organising their defence in such a way as to make the enemy pay for all the ground he recovered. As a matter of fact, when the anticipated attack came, in April of the following year, the enemy recovered the whole of the precious ground, after a few hours' fighting and with comparatively slight losses.

The Passchendaele fiasco imperilled the chances of final victory. Had it not been for the effect of the blockade on the morale of the German people, the disappointment caused by the failure of the submarine campaign, combined with the arrival of the American troops in France in swelling numbers, the failure of the Flanders offensive in 1917 might well have been fatal to Allied prospects in 1918. It weighed down the balance of man power still further to the side of the Central Powers. The desertion of Russia and the defeat of Roumania had already created an adverse balance. The gigantic casualties of Passchendaele pressed down appreciably the Allied end of the grisly scales. Our military leaders had acquired the habit of prodigality in their expenditure of life.

One of the unavoidable evils of war is that it tends to become an orgy of increasing extravagance. Gladstone, who tried to run the Crimean War economically, thereby provided an excuse for military negligence which created one of the worst military scandals in history. Sir Michael Hicks Beach's initial frugality prolonged the Boer War. In this war, the skimping policy of the Indian Government ended in conditions in Mesopotamia which exceeded the horrors of Scutari. It is difficult in war to hold the balance even between parsimony and profusion. By the third year of this War everyone concerned was thinking in millions. The small army of just over a hundred thousand was to-day contemptible in size to British Generals. We had already called over five million men to the colours. Shells which numbered thousands in 1914 were fired by the million in a single battle in 1917. The first attack on the Passchendaele slope used up about five million shells, but the supply flowed in at the rate of millions a month. We were all shocked by the casualty list of Neuve Chapelle in the spring of 1915. Compared with the offensives that followed, the Neuve Chapelle losses were insignificant. But these casualties, which had already run into millions, had all been replaced. The British Army that entered upon the Flanders campaign was larger than that which had started the Somme fight, although meanwhile its losses had considerably exceeded the million.

Wellington's reply to those who wished him to undertake risky enterprises was "This is England's only army." With difficulty, the Government had been able to spare him thirty thousand men. But in this war the generals knew that every able-bodied young man up to and including men who had reached the prime of life could be called up for national service. They grudged every man who was kept at home for essential national work. They were always nagging about it. They lavished the lives placed at their disposal in foolish frontal attacks on impregnable lines, in spite of the lessons of every war since modern weapons were perfected. They then sent home requisitions for more units to bring their depleted battalions up to strength, out of the inexhaustible resources of Britain in man power. If these orders were not immediately complied with, there came querulous complaints and petulant suggestions that victory was impossible unless gaps were filled up. Most of these gaps in our manhood were rent by clumsy and unintelligent craftsmanship at the top. The wastage of all material was appalling. Whilst hundreds of thousands were being destroyed in the insane egotism of Passchendaele, every message or memorandum from Haig was full of these insistences on the importance of sending him more men to replace those he had sent to die in the mud. If Britain said, "Where are my lost legions?" then anyone who asked such a question on her behalf was betraying the Army and attacking our soldiers. The word "soldiers" always had exclusive reference in the War Office Press to those whose tasks were discharged on the safe side of the front line; to those who never set foot on the stricken field until the poor "units" which had to be replaced had already made it safe for inspection. To prevent that misrepresentation which is always ready to misapprehend, let me repeat here what I am saying elsewhere — that from what I know of the brass-hatted soldiers, I have no doubt that had it been part of their duty to march at the head of their men, and share their perils, they would have done so without faltering. I am not seeking to establish any distinction or discrimination between the soldiers who fought and those who did not. My sole complaint is that those who arrogated to themselves the task of what they called "defending the soldiers against the politicians" always confined their defence to the latter class of soldier. I cannot recall a single article in which they sought to protect the former against the strategy which condemned them to a useless carnage in the execution of ill-conceived projects.

The effect on the morale of the Army was perceptible. Buchan's "History of the War", a book which throughout has taken a favourable view of our High Command, says about the effect of this particular battle that:

> For almost the first time in the campaign there was a sense of discouragement abroad on our front. Men felt that they were being sacrificed blindly; that every fight was a soldier's fight, and that such sledge-hammer tactics were too crude to meet the problem. For a moment there was a real ebb of confidence in British leadership. That such a feeling should exist among journalists and politicians matters nothing, but it matters much if it is found among troops in the field.[1]

Mr. Buchan wrote this whilst he was in uniform, but even for a Staff officer, this contempt for journalists and politicians is a little cheap and gratuitous. The morale of the public behind the lines is essential to victory in a protracted struggle. In sustaining its spirit through discouragement the despised pressman or politician has his uses. The politicians had, moreover, the responsibility for organising the resources of the country. But although they matter, Mr. Buchan would be right in saying that the loss of morale amongst the fighting troops matters most.

[1] "A History of the Great War", by John Buchan, Vol. III, p. 592.

According to this "History", the brunt of the criticism was directed against General Gough:

> His old reputation had become a little dimmed, and among his soldiers he had acquired the name of a general who tried his troops too high, and used them blindly as battering rams against the stoutest part of the wall. The criticism was not wholly just, but it was widely made.[1]

How unfair that criticism was we know now, for he protested as far back as August against proceeding with the battle. His objections were overridden and he was peremptorily ordered by his Commander-in-Chief to continue the hopeless struggle.

Expression was given to the feeling amongst the rank and file in a remarkable book called "Four Years on the Western Front", by a Rifleman. He took part in the battle, and the division in which he was a humble unit was almost completely destroyed without achieving much. He says:

> Something like a feeling of indignation came over us, that whole divisions should be squandered as though we had an unlimited reserve of men, and human life counted for nothing. One attack after another had produced disappointment, heavy losses, limited gains.[2]

There can be no doubt that when the battle came to an end, the fighting spirit of the troops that had passed through this prolonged horror was at its lowest. It was a calamity unforeseen by G.H.Q. that their frayed nerve was to be put to another test before they had been given time to recover. It was this Army under the same General that was doomed to bear the brunt of Ludendorff's great coup on the Oise in March, 1918. No soldiers in that condition could have sustained such an onslaught. It is no reflection on their valour to

[1] "A History of the Great War", by John Buchan, Vol. IV, p. 189.
[2] "Four Years on the Western Front", p. 273.

say that they broke. So much for the claim of the apologists of Passchendaele that German morale alone had been impaired. As if British troops were not also flesh, blood and nerves!

Another of the incalculable consequences was that it completely slammed every other door of opportunity for the Allies — but alas! not for the Central Powers. There can be no doubt that Turkey could have been knocked out and forced to make peace, had the Allies sent a couple of the cavalry divisions (which proved to be worse than useless on the Somme, at Passchendaele and at Cambrai) and a few more heavy guns and ammunition to Palestine. As General Allenby proved, the resolute façade the Turks presented to the Allies on the lines of Gaza-Beersheba had nothing behind it. It was part of the War Office game to pretend that the Turks had formidable forces with ample reserves and that if they were attacked seriously the Germans would rush to their succour and beat us off. They may have believed it, but if so, either their information was defective, or they were easily taken in. In either event, it was a failure of intelligence. There was a paper prepared in December by the Military Council at Versailles and signed by Generals Weygand, Cadorna, and Henry Wilson exposing the whole crumbling bogey of Turkish prowess which had so long frightened our timid military leadership in Egypt — but not in Mesopotamia. Here is the report:

> There remains the Turkish theatre. To inflict such a crushing series of defeats upon the Turkish Armies as would lead to the final collapse of Turkey and her elimination from the War would not only have the most far-reaching results upon the general military situation, but might also, if not too long deferred, be in time to enable the Allies to get into direct touch with, and give effective help to, such elements of resistance to German domination as may still exist in Roumania and Southern Russia. Even

a lesser measure of success such as would definitely liberate the Arab regions of the Ottoman Empire from the Turkish yoke and compel the Germans to divert considerable forces to the East in order to save Turkey from destruction, would, both from the point of view of the military situation and from that of eventual peace negotiations, greatly strengthen the Allied position, and be worth any effort that can be made compatible with the security of our defence in the Western theatres.

The present condition of Turkey is one of almost complete material and moral exhaustion. The Turkish forces have progressively dwindled, till they now amount to 250,000 men at the utmost, *and will dwindle even more rapidly if seriously attacked, owing to the entire lack of reserves.* Such as they are, these forces are dispersed, and are necessarily dispersed over enormous areas. The communications between the different fronts are so defective that any transfers of troops can only be carried out extremely slowly and with heavy wastage through sickness and desertion. The main railway communication with Constantinople and the Central Powers is itself of very limited capacity, and vulnerable to air attacks. Reinforcement of troops or munitions from Germany could only be accumulated very gradually, and the sending of them would involve a heavy strain on the enemy's transport resources.

Sir William Robertson expressed himself as being in complete agreement with the conclusions drawn from known facts by the Versailles Council. By the date of their report, Allenby's advance had exposed the hollowness of the Turkish menace. For that reason the General Staff at the War Office could no longer sustain their convenient assumption of Turkish strength. The information upon which they were based had come mainly from the Intelligence Department of our own War Office, and must have been known to the Staff. But to communicate such information to the War Cabinet before the Allenby victories meant that they might be tempted to deflect an extra division and a few guns from the attack on Passchendaele, and perhaps — most disastrous of all — send to Palestine some of the invaluable squadrons of cavalry that might at any moment be urgently needed to charge into the flying rout of the demoralised German Army in Flanders. The fact remains, that but for the distraction of Passchendaele, Turkey might have been forced to make peace, and the Black Sea might have been opened to Russia and Roumania. Bulgaria would not have held out much longer, for it was known that her peasants, who were never enamoured of the War, were getting thoroughly tired of squatting on their perch in the Balkans, whilst their fields and their harvests were being neglected.

The Flanders campaign was directly responsible for the Italian disaster. As I have already pointed out, General Pétain was agreeable, after the Chemin des Dames affair, to sending assistance in men and artillery to Italy to enable General Cadorna to undertake a real attack on the Austrian position. Had Haig taken the same view, we would have been saved the disasters of Caporetto and Passchendaele, both of which tipped the balance of man power and prestige so heavily in favour of the Central Powers. The inadequate state of the defences of Gough's Army in front of Amiens in March, 1918, was entirely attributable to Passchendaele. The French Government and Army had been pressing hard for an extension of the British Front ever since May. The Army Commission of the Senate had gone into the matter in great detail and had reported strongly in favour of bringing pressure to bear on the British Government to take up more line in France. It has been represented that Haig's persistence in the Flanders campaign was due to Pétain's entreaties. Pétain was opposed to it from beginning to end: but he was exceedingly anxious that we should occupy more front line. It would materially have assisted him in his very difficult task of reorganising and strengthening the French Army. There was an overwhelming case in favour of the request. France was very much more exhausted than we were. She had called up fifteen per cent. of her population, whereas we had only recruited ten per cent. of ours, and her casualties were heavier by at least a million, for she had borne the brunt of the fighting during the first two years of the War, whilst we were building up our Army. Sir William Robertson never denied that there was a good case, and he would have been quite willing to meet the French demand, but Haig said he needed every available man for the Flemish campaign. He succeeded in postponing the decision until the campaign was well over. When, at last, he agreed with Pétain as to the limits of the extension, it was February before the change could be effected. When Gough took over the line up to the Oise, he found the defences were very unsatisfactory, but his troops were tired out by their unparalleled experiences and were in no condition to start digging. This was known to the Germans. The advantage they took of it will be told in another volume.

Passchendaele was indeed one of the greatest disasters of the War, and I never think of it without feeling grateful for the combination of seamanship and luck which enabled us to survive and repair its unutterable folly. There is no better illustration of its calamitous effect than the episode of Cambrai.

CHAPTER X

THE BATTLE OF CAMBRAI

Tank Corps seeks a favourable battlefield — General Fuller plans a "theatrical blow" — Objection of G.H.Q. — Brilliant opening success — Lack of reserves causes defeat — Success of German counterattack — Secrecy about defeat —Cabinet indignant at lack of news — An inquiry ordered — Changed tone of *Times* — The Inquiry burked — Fighting troops blamed — Staff Officers' excessive modesty — Lack of tactical training.

When the Tank Corps officers perceived how completely their predictions as to the effect of a heavy bombardment on a drained morass had been realised, they came to the conclusion that as far as their machinery was concerned, it could render no effective help under such conditions. They were equally convinced that victory was unattainable by any other arm on such a battlefield. They therefore set about making a study of the whole of the British Front with a view to formulating a plan for attacking the enemy on a sector where tanks had a fair chance of showing what they could accomplish. The tanks had failed to achieve much on the Somme because in spite of the protest of all those who knew anything about that ingenious contrivance, Sir Douglas Haig insisted on throwing a few specimen machines into the fight without waiting until a sufficient number had been manufactured to enable him to hurl a resistless mass of them against the enemy lines. It was part of the "Tanker" dream to effect with a large number of machines a surprise attack for which the enemy were not prepared. The Tank leaders asked for a fair opportunity to demonstrate the value of their invention. They were given the swamps of Passchendaele. When General Gough appreciated that it was ground over which even infantry could do no more than crawl, it is not surprising that the Staff of the Tank Corps were convinced that their heavy cavalry could not make progress across such sodden ground. Early in August, therefore, their Chief General Staff Officer, Colonel (now General) Fuller, drew up an alternative project. In his preface to the plan he said:

> From a tank point of view the Third Battle of Ypres may be considered dead. To go on using tanks in the present conditions will not only lead to good machines and better personnel being thrown away, but also to a loss of morale in the infantry and tank crews, through constant failure. From an infantry point of view, the Third Battle of Ypres may be considered comatose. It can only be continued at colossal loss and little gain.

He proposed that "in order to restore British prestige", what he called "a theatrical blow" should be struck at Germany before the winter. He suggested that preparations should be made for an attack in the direction of St. Quentin. As this would involve a combined British and French operation, it was thought better that the operation should take place on the British Front, and Cambrai was substituted for St. Quentin. General Byng, to whom the idea was submitted, was favourably inclined, but G.H.Q. objected strongly on the ground that the Romans laid down the military doctrine that you could not win a decisive battle in two places at the same time, and that the Commander-in-Chief could not spare the necessary troops for the Tank project, as he must concentrate every available man in the Ypres sector. But as the failure of the mud offensive at last oozed even into the minds of its projectors, they became more inclined to consider the idea of an independent Tank attack further south. But even then they could not be induced to let go their Passchendaele offensive altogether. They were stuck in the mud and could not get out of it without getting through it to the ridge. They had to improve their positions or run the risk of being driven out of all the fine swamp they had made and annexed at such cost. So when the Cambrai attack was undertaken, it had to be launched without any reserves. Not an extra battalion could be spared from the suction of the mire.

The first onset of the tanks, on the 20th of November, was a brilliant success. Within a few hours the Hindenburg line was broken by these inexorable machines, and a penetration effected in the enemy lines as deep as that which had been achieved after months of terrible fighting and colossal losses on the Somme and at Passchendaele. It is generally acknowledged now that the advance was badly muddled by General Byng and that he could, even with the resources at his command, have made a much better job of it. But what converted victory into a defeat was the total lack of reserves. When it was essential that there should be fresh troops available to support and exploit the attack, there was not a single platoon in reserve. They were all floundering in the Flemish slough. The Germans, having been allowed by a magnanimous enemy plenty of time to recover from their surprise, prepared a counterattack, and fully a week later they launched their onslaught after deliberate and careful preparation. The German Army whose divisions, we were assured, had all been used up by the great offensive, was able to muster fourteen divisions to overwhelm our scattered and tired troops. Five of these divisions had been transferred from the Flanders battle area, and nine from other portions of the Western Front. These they could spare in addition to the six divisions that had already gone to Italy and the five divisions that had captured Riga. How could they have raked up three separate striking forces of twenty-five effective divisions, in the aggregate, after a battle of fourteen weeks' duration, which we were assured had shattered their Army in the West and destroyed their reserves?

When the counterattack came, there was nothing behind to give any help to our outnumbered and exhausted divisions. The Germans not only recaptured most of the ground we had gained, but at one point penetrated to a distance of fifteen hundred yards behind our original line. All that was left to us of our conquest was the indefensible salient of Flesquières. A resounding victory was converted into a disastrous rout. For this, Passchendaele was directly responsible. Had our Army not entered upon that fatal campaign, the Battle of Cambrai in 1917 might have been one of the decisive battles of the War. It was the only complete surprise the British Army had contrived to inflict upon the Germans. Their strongest defences had been broken through. For the first time we had reached the open country behind their lines. Had there been adequate reserves to throw in, Cambrai would have been captured, the German defence system would have been dislocated, a new retirement would have been imposed on the enemy, and the time and strength he devoted to prepare his March offensive against our lines would have to be spent in reorganising his own defences. One fourth of the men flung away so profligately at Passchendaele would have sufficed to win this signal victory, and to exploit it.

When the first news of our great triumph reached London, the War Office ordered that all the church bells of the metropolis should be set a-ringing. A few days after the chimes had ceased to thrill the hearts of Londoners, the counterattack came, and our troops were driven back pell-mell — such of them as escaped capture. The Staff who were responsible for the joy bells were ashamed to publish the news of the reverse. Even the War Cabinet was kept in the dark. Messages came from Headquarters, sent at a time when the enemy had actually penetrated inside our original defences, about the "hostile attacks" on this front having been completely repulsed; how ten of these attacks "had been broken up by our rifle or machine-gun fire or crushed by our artillery." But that skill in manipulating news to convey a false impression which had served Headquarters so well in the Flanders attack failed completely at Cambrai. One reason was that we actually lost ground. Some days after the defeat had occurred the real news percolated through. General Maxse, who was a member of the Court of Inquiry subsequently appointed, blamed the wounded for disseminating alarming news. According to him they were always doing it. It was a very reprehensible practice and deserved censure. News from the front should be confined to official dispatches written by men who never saw the fighting, and whose calm was therefore in no danger of being irritated or upset by wounds.

The Cabinet, several days after the disaster, recorded its dissatisfaction that the fact of so complete a reverse having been sustained "if this were correct", had not been reported to the War Cabinet, and it was urged that if we had inflicted a corresponding reverse upon the enemy, the news of our success would have been communicated in a few hours.

We were also anxious to have an explanation why such a surprise should have been inflicted on our forces, if our aerial support was as complete as it had been alleged to be, and if our defensive arrangements were properly organised.

The only reply that could be offered by the Secretary of State for War was that the Field Marshal Commanding-in-Chief was probably himself "ignorant of the causes of this reverse." This was about a week after our defeat.

The confusion that existed was given as an explanation of the paucity of news, and the Chief of the Staff compared the chaos with what had happened during the retreat from Mons, when, although he himself was present, he was quite unable to obtain information. He did not inform Ministers that the attack had been ordered without any reserves, nor did Sir Douglas Haig in his reports deem it necessary to in-

GAINS AND LOSSES AT CAMBRAI.

Original Line of 19th November, 1917:

Line of Furthest Advance:

Final Front Line, 7th December, 1917:

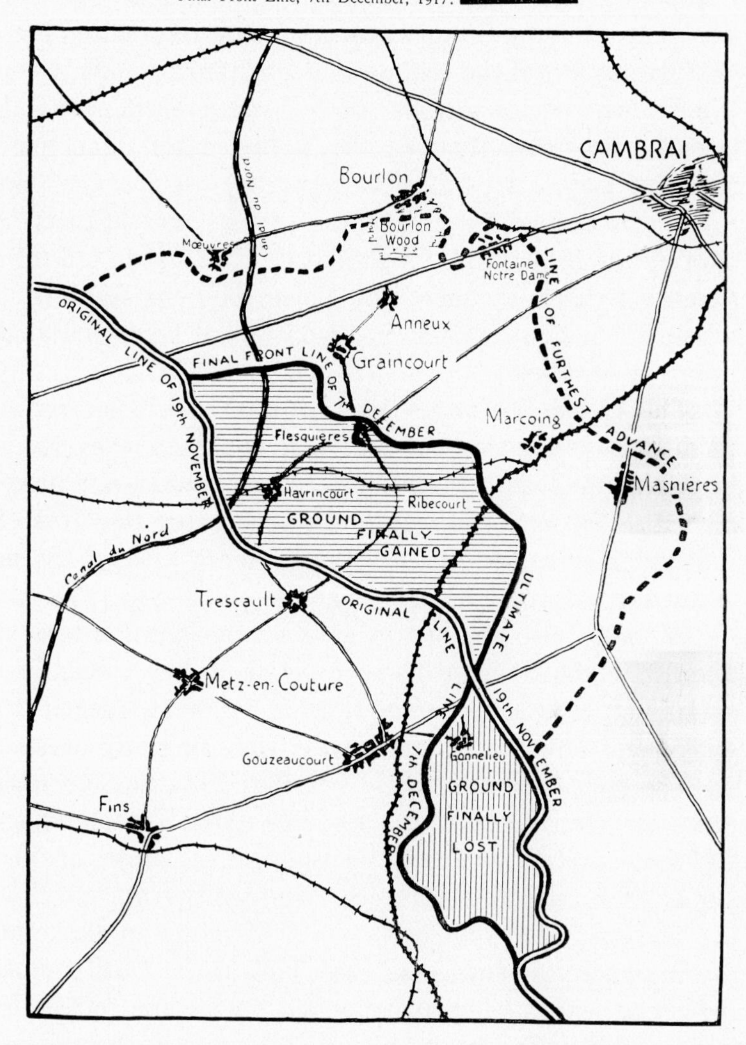

form the Government of that important factor in our repulse. The Cabinet also called attention to the "discrepancy between the nature of the German success and the reports which had been consistently received from official sources in regard to their weakness and the deterioration of their morale."

The Cabinet ordered that there should be a thorough inquiry into the circumstances which had been responsible for the reverse. The news of the disaster produced a disconcerting effect on public opinion, which had been stimulated to such a sense of exhilaration by gulping the heady wines which had fermented in the inexhaustible vats of the Intelligence Department at G.H.Q.

The *Times,* which had hitherto been amongst the most inebriated of all our journals with the Haigean triumphs, was steadied by this shock and wrote a caustic article about the "reversal of fortune on our own front, of which the truth is slowly leaking through the correspondents' tales of heroism."

It says that "we can no longer rest satisfied with the fatuous estimates, *e.g.*, of German losses in men and morale, which have inspired too many of the published messages from France."

It exculpates Sir Douglas Haig from any blame for the disaster, except in so far as this was attributable to his choice of subordinates and his inveterate devotion to those who had served him too long. It does not allude to the vain efforts made by these subordinates to persuade him to give up the wasteful attack on the Passchendaele Ridge, which was directly responsible for the Cambrai fiasco. Perhaps Lord Northcliffe had not been informed about these attempts. The *Times* continued:

"The merest breath of criticism on any military operation is far too often dismissed as an 'intrigue' against the Commander-in-Chief."

It demands "prompt, searching and complete" inquiry.

This indeed represented a complete change from the ecstatic eulogies of Brookseinde, but it came too late to save us from the much greater catastrophe of Passchendaele. An inquiry was set up, but it turned out to be an utter sham. General Byng, who was responsible for the battle arrangements, was never called. But inadequate as was the investigation, it reveals something of the causes of the defeat. Without making any specific reference to the absence of reserves, of the insufficiency of the equipment for making and sustaining the attack, it suppresses facts, but gives glimpses which expose the blunders and shortcomings of the operation.

As to the three divisions that were overrun with practically no resistance, it was reported that they were "weak in numbers." It was stated that:

> . . . they did not retreat or run away. They were surprised to such an extent that only two men got back out of the left battalion of the 55th Division, and less than 100 men got back from most of the battalions engaged in the three divisions.

These battalions had gone into action at only half their strength.

German aeroplanes:

> . . . flew at altitudes which have been described by witnesses as being lower than 100 feet, firing their machine-guns into our infantry both in the front trenches and in rearward positions. The moral effect of these was very great, and no doubt tended to facilitate the enemy's success.

Not only were there no British aeroplanes, but even the Court of Inquiry considered there was a "paucity of guns", and that this "facilitated the assembly of the enemy and the assault upon our front lines."

Where were our aeroplanes? Probably hovering over the swamps of Passchendaele. Where were our guns? Digging fresh shell holes in the same marsh to impede our own advance.

But the High Command who prepared the plans, knowing that they had not sufficient troops, guns and aeroplanes to carry them out, were exonerated from blame.

The main part of the blame was cast upon the officers and men who had fought so well and so successfully, who were not apprised of the great preparations made by the Germans for a counterattack, and who, when that overwhelming attack materialised, were left to meet it without any supports.

There was one member of the Court of Inquiry who excelled himself on this occasion. His wrath is directed, not at the great Generals who were really responsible, but at the lower ranks who too readily believed the rumours of disaster. The public at home were misinformed "not merely by the newspapers and Members of Parliament, but also through the medium of 400,000 officers and men who proceeded backwards and forwards on leave."

He is specially angry with the wounded:

"The most prolific propagators of baseless stories are the wounded. Moreover, they get home before the telegrams, and rapidly spread the foolish notion that if they had been in charge of the conduct of the operations, things would have been very different."

One of his remedies for this calamity is that the senior local commander on the spot should tell his own story to the public as soon as possible after the event. And here is a specially rich quotation from his diatribe against the garrulity of the wounded:

"Unless we adopt some such method of conveying the truth, the longer the War continues and men's minds are unsettled, the more will the public at home be at the mercy of false notions, which are detrimental to the efficiency of the Army as a whole, and to the morale of the nation."

His anxiety for instituting some new method of "conveying the truth" has a peculiar irony, having regard to the glowing reports of victory issued from Headquarters about the fighting in Flanders. The same observation applies to his suggestion that:

"Something must be done at G.H.Q. by appointing a soldier to help the newspaper correspondents to understand the telegrams which come in during the course of an important battle. These correspondents might perhaps then avoid filling the columns of their newspapers with a torrent of rubbish."

In alluding to the public opinion that the Battle of Cambrai had ended in a "German success instead of a British victory", he says:

"I cannot help thinking that *we soldiers* with our extreme reticence and horror of all forms of publicity, may be somewhat to blame for this result."

Clearly, "we soldiers" does not include those who are wounded in the battle, neither does it comprise the four hundred thousand officers and men who had survived Passchendaele and Cambrai and gone home on a short leave. There is neither reticence nor truth to be found in them.

There is one part of his report however which has an historical and also a military value, but it conveys an indirect and probably unintentional condemnation of the Flanders campaign. In attributing the defeat at Cambrai to the ignorance displayed by officers and men of the elements of defensive tactics, he attributes their deficiencies in this respect to the fact that there was no opportunity afforded them of training. Its importance is enhanced by the fact that General Maxse was probably at the time the highest authority in the British Army on the subject of training soldiers. He gives an illustration from his knowledge:

> The writer of this note is acquainted with one corps which during the past twelve months happened to have 30 divisions in it. Of these 30 divisions two were splendidly trained, a dozen were trying to train and the remainder had little, if any, definite system of training at all. They had, instead, a dozen excellent reasons for explaining why they remained untrained. The corps commander concerned had no opportunity to insist upon improved methods of training, because the divisions were not in his corps for a sufficient time for him to get to know them or report upon them. All he gathered from one year's experience was a rough idea that about half the divisions were untrained and the other half were semi-trained.

The reason was obvious. The exigencies of these repeated offensives did not give any commander the necessary opportunity for giving the requisite training to men under his command. Every division in its turn was thrown into the trenches. When it came back behind the lines it was exhausted, depleted, having probably lost its most experienced officers and N.C.O.'s. Out of the sixty-four British divisions in France, fifty-seven were thrown into the Flanders fight. What chance was there for any commander to train his men?

The report was a complete justification of General Pétain's policy of limited offensives and preparations for the campaign of 1918. But what a condemnation of the strategy of the fatuous campaign of the Flanders coast!

CHAPTER XI

THE CABINET'S DILEMMA

Impossible to publish true accounts — G.H.Q. entertains the journalists — Could Haig have been dismissed? — No better General in sight — Robertson's qualities — His excuse for continuing the fight — The man-power argument — The gag of Army discipline — Probable reaction of public opinion at home — Effect on the Allies — Political complications.

As it became clear to my mind in August that the Flanders attack would fail without achieving any of the purposes for which it had been commenced, I made repeated efforts to stop the carnage. Gough had come to the same conclusion and without my knowledge was doing his best to secure a discontinuance of an operation of which he, better than anyone, realised the futility. The glowing accounts of shattering victories in September and October, which were inspired by Headquarters, were greedily swallowed by a public thirsting for encouragement in their sacrifice. Ministers could not launch a publicity campaign to disillusion them. Public opinion in most of the Allied countries was disintegrating behind the lines. Russia was going out of the War, tired and torn. France was dejected, disappointed and inclined to be disaffected. Italy wanted an end of it, so long as it could find a decent way to get out. America was not yet in. She was in no hurry. Britain was still fighting with all her grim wont. In these circumstances one could not afford to tell her plainly that her vaunted successes were costly shams. Herein G.H.Q. had the politicians at disadvantage and they made the fullest use of their vantage ground. An order from Downing Street to stop a fight which the British public were told was gradually but surely reducing all the renowned legions of the enemy to a broken and demoralised rabble of beaten and dispirited men, would not be tolerated.

When the offensive was in danger of an official mandate to stop it, newspaper proprietors, editors and publicists of all kinds were invited to the front — assuming that G.H.Q. could be included in that dangerous zone — to see for themselves how well things were going. They were brought there, not to witness the real struggle, but at a safe distance to enjoy the sensation of doing so, whilst partaking of the hospitality of the famous soldiers who planned the attacks. The battle-field was only seen by them in maps, shining and solid, where achieved advances were displayed without being defaced or pulped by the gruesome sludge or disfigured by a mass of red dots representing casualties. They returned to England suitably impressed with the resistless advance of the great offensive. They saw for themselves on the spot that Ostend was not far — on the map. And Bruges was already actually visible to our victorious Army. Why stop when we were already in sight of complete victory?

What action ought I to have taken to ensure that the military mistakes which had exhausted the man power and almost destroyed the morale of the Alliance should not be repeated in 1918? There were several courses open. The most obvious was to dismiss our Chief Military adviser, who had failed us so badly, and the Commander-in-Chief who had proved himself as a strategist to be unequal to the gigantic task committed to his charge. Let me deal first with the case of Sir Douglas Haig. It is easy now to say: "You ought to have sacked him." There is no man to-day, military or civilian, who does not deplore the Flanders offensive of 1917 — not merely as a good idea badly bungled, but as a rash and ill-conceived venture impossible of execution under circumstances which must have been known or ought to have been known to those who planned it. At that date the campaign had its worshippers everywhere — except amongst those who fought through it. It was extolled in the Press and on the platforms, and a peremptory dismissal of the victor would have been regarded as if Wellington had been recalled after Badajoz. But apart from that, I had to ask and answer another question. Who could be put in his place? It is a sad reflection that not one amongst the visible military leaders would have been any better. There were amongst them plenty of good soldiers who knew their profession and possessed intelligence up to a point. But Haig was all that and probably better within those limits than any others within sight. He was a good Corps Commander. But to command a group of great armies comprising two million men on a battle front of over one hundred miles was a position that demanded not ordinary capacity but intellect of an exceptionally high order. Haig's best friends will not claim for him that he was a man of that quality. He was a painstaking professional soldier with a sound intelligence of secondary quality. He had the courage and stubbornness of his race and also a large measure of their business capacity. In the Peninsular War he would have won renown as a general — under Wellington. In this war he would have done well as Commander of an Army Corps or an Army where the strategy was determined by a bigger man. He did well in the concluding stages of the 1918 campaign — under Foch's supreme direction. But he did not possess the necessary breadth of vision or imagination to plan a great campaign against some of the ablest generals in the War. I never met any man in a high position who seemed to me so utterly devoid of imagination.

Haig had a gift of careful scrutiny of detail and gave his attention to the minutest point. That was an invaluable gift. Those things which were visible through ordinary professional glasses he could see more clearly than most soldiers; but when intuition and genius were necessary for vision, he did not possess the requisite intellectual equipment. But which of them did? Had we removed Haig, we might have set up in his place a man who had not his mastery of the profession, with no other and greater gifts to make up for that deficiency. When I was considering the problem I sent General Smuts and Sir Maurice Hankey around the front to report to the War Cabinet on the condition of affairs generally, and I confidentially asked them to look and see for themselves whether amongst the generals they met, there was one whom they considered might with advantage attain and fill the first place. They came back with a very disappointing report as to the result of their investigations. Since the War I have been told by men whose judgment I value that the only soldier thrown up by the War on the British side who possessed the necessary qualities for the position was a Dominion General. Competent professional soldiers whom I have consulted have all agreed that this man might and probably would have risen to the height of the great occasion. But I knew nothing of this at the time. No report ever reached me either as War Secretary or Prime Minister, which attributed any special merit to this distinguished soldier. The fact that he was a civilian soldier when the War broke out may have had something to do with the tardiness in recognising his exceptional abilities and achievements.

There were eminent generals in the British Army who had shown conspicuous gifts in their spheres of leadership, but none of them was fitted to lead an army five times as large as Napoleon ever had under his command, in a military undertaking which would have tested even his genius to its utmost.

With regard to Sir William Robertson, he was not a

strategist nor did he arrogate to himself the rôle of a planner of campaigns. I never believed that he had the mind for it. He was a good administrator. For the rest, he accepted Haig's strategy and subordinated everything to it. The part he chose to play was that of providing Haig with the necessary men and material to enable him to carry out his plans. In order to ensure that there should be no shortage in that respect, he cut down to the lowest limit the supplies sent to every other field of operations. That was the only strategic notion he ever contributed to the conduct of the War. Mr. Asquith, once upon a time, is related in one of his rare fits of emotional ecstasy, to have extolled Robertson as "the greatest living strategist." It was a ridiculous appreciation, but as neither of them had strategical minds, the giver and the recipient of the compliment were equally well fitted for their part in the tribute.

Sir William Robertson, in the book he wrote some years after the War, gives an account of the difficulties with which he was confronted in ascertaining the real truth about this ghastly battle.

He there states the reason why the operation continued for so long. It was due largely to "the belief at G.H.Q. that the strain imposed upon the enemy was being so severely felt that it might soon reach breaking-point." He and his Staff thought this view "appeared a little too sanguine." He seems to have expressed his doubts to the Commander-in-Chief. Sir Douglas Haig on that occasion asked him to interview his Army Commanders and ascertain for himself whether they agreed with him. Sir William Robertson then adds: "That, of course, I could not well do." He was then invited to meet these Commanders at a conference which he was about to hold on the matter, and he proceeds:

> I was not prepared to carry my doubts to the extent of opposing him, and thereby obstructing the application of that little

extra pressure upon the enemy which experience has so often shown may convert an inconclusive battle into a decisive victory.

It is difficult to deny that the campaign was protracted beyond the limits of justification, but a correct decision was not so easy to make at the time as it appears now. . . .[1]

He recalls the oft-quoted passage from Ludendorff about the anxiety the Germans felt up to the middle of September. He also pleads that:

It should be remembered from the first the prospects of success had depended upon the British Armies being kept up to strength, whereas, owing to an inadequate man-power policy, they fell greatly below it.

He forgot that at the Cabinet Council when the Flanders project came up, one of the arguments I advanced against it was that we had almost reached the limit of man power and that we could not increase the flow of recruits without causing damage to other essential war services and provoking serious labour troubles. The reply given then was that the losses would not be heavy. Sir William Robertson knew all about the difficulties we were experiencing in the matter of man power because of the imperative necessity of countering the submarine danger, and wrote Haig as far back as May to warn him of the fact. I have already dwelt upon the practical difficulties we were experiencing, in the chapters on Submarines, Man Power and Labour Unrest.

Although Sir William Robertson was practically in the position of a *Generalissimo*, since he had the authority of the Government behind him, he felt that he could not ask the Army Commander any question which implied that he had doubts as to the estimate formed by G.H.Q. on the progress of the attack. Had he done so they probably would not have given any opinion adverse to the then Commander-in-Chief.

[1] My italics.

Although we know now that several of the general officers who took part in the fight had grave doubts as to the wisdom of proceeding with it, not one of them uttered a murmur that reached me or any member of the Cabinet. So high is the standard of discipline amongst generals. "Theirs not to reason why: theirs but to send their troops to die" — if the Commander-in-Chief orders it.

I am bound to record the fact that although Sir William Robertson tells the public, in his book of criticism on statesmen, that he had misgivings about the reports emanating from G.H.Q. and that he thought "the campaign was protracted beyond the limits of justification", he never hinted to those who were dependent on his advice that any doubts had ever entered his mind on these points.

Had we intervened, what would have been the effect on public opinion? It would have been said: "Here is that great soldier, Sir Douglas Haig, supported by his fine Army, beating the Germans, chasing them from pill-box to pill-box — killing two of their men for every one he lost of ours — pulverising their divisions so that there were not many now left in a condition for renewing the fight. They are already squealing for peace. The reason is obvious: they are gasping with exhaustion. We shall soon sweep them off the coveted ridge. Then the Flanders coast will be within our grasp. The lair of the submarine will be captured. We shall be released from that terror and danger. But just as Haig is about to finish off the Germans and achieve the greatest triumph of the War, here come these nervous and meddlesome politicians, who know nothing about war, and snatch victory out of the grasp of our gallant soldiers, throwing all our sacrifices away." Public opinion could only have been set right by telling the whole gruesome tale of failure and slaughter. We should also have had to reveal how everybody had been misled by the dispatches and reports concocted and inspired at Headquarters. What would have been the effect in France, Italy, Russia? What would have happened here at home? The French crisis based on acknowledged disaster in May, would have been followed by a British crisis founded on a still bloodier disaster in the autumn. Confidence in military leadership — in military veracity — would have gone. With Russia on the brink of going out and Italy sagging and France unstrung, we could not have faced the necessary revelations. The heart of the Allies would have been depressed, maybe beyond stimulation — the spirit of the Central Powers would have been renewed and reinvigorated. I decided that the risk was too great and that it was better to take measures in time that would prevent the recurrence in 1918 of the blunders to which we had been committed in 1917 by the Chantilly decisions of November, 1916.

Perhaps I was wrong. I state the facts so as to enable others to judge fairly.

I considered that Sir William Robertson had signally failed to realise what his duty was as an independent adviser of the Imperial War Cabinet on military matters. He was not under Haig and therefore he owed him no obedience. There was no disciplinary obligation to prevent him from expressing an opinion which did not conform to that of the Commander in France.

What the Cabinet had to consider if they meant to dispense with the services of Robertson, was whether they should replace him with a man who was equipped for the task of thinking out and directing the strategy of the Allied campaign, or whether, if such a man were obtainable, it would not be better to put him in a position where he could act in more direct and constant coöperation with the military brains of the other Allies. If the Cabinet came to the latter conclusion, then Robertson might be left at the War Office. He was capable of directing efficiently all the administrative activities which would be brought into play by the policy adopted.

When the battle was finally called off, the Cabinet reviewed the results, and came to a decided and unanimous conclusion that it was a ghastly failure. Sir William Robertson was called into these consultations, and if he did not categorically agree with all that was said about the blunders perpetrated, he certainly expressed no dissent. He attributed the mistakes committed primarily to General Charteris' over-optimistic reports which misled Haig, and to General Kiggell's deficiencies as Chief of Staff. He was also disposed to blame General Gough for persisting in the attacks after it had become evident they could not possibly succeed. From his attitude at the time, I assume that he was not then aware of Gough's protests. It was decided that the Commander-in-Chief should be called upon to remove these three Generals from the positions they then held. Sir William Robertson and Lord Derby were asked to proceed at once to G.H.Q. and communicate these decisions to Sir Douglas Haig. The Commander-in-Chief agreed to dismiss Charteris and Kiggell, but demurred to the Cabinet request for the removal of Gough. On this point he was obdurate. He did not assign the real reason for his refusal to dismiss Gough. Both Lord Derby and Sir William Robertson urged the Cabinet to accept the compromise, as we were assured that Gough's Army was to be taken away from the salient and placed in a quiet part of the line! So Kiggell and Charteris disappeared and Gough remained. This action was a practical admission by the C.I.G.S. that the Battle of Passchendaele was a grave blunder. History will decide whether he placed the responsibility for it on the right shoulders. I have already recorded the admission of Sir Douglas Haig that his great plan was a dangerous failure.[1]

[1] Page 427.

In considering whether we should have gone further and taken more drastic action by replacing Haig and Robertson, I had always to bear in mind the possibility that such a step would inevitably have given rise to political complications. Both had a considerable backing in the Press and the House of Commons and inside the Government. The Asquithian Opposition were solid behind them. Northcliffe strongly supported both. They could also count on the support of a large contingent of influential Conservatives, of whom some were members of the Ministry. It was an incongruous combination, but too formidable to challenge at this stage. I never believed in costly frontal attacks either in war or politics, if there were a way round. In this case I sought and found one which in the end achieved the purpose.

CHAPTER XII

THE CAPORETTO DISASTER

Allied Armies fail to coöperate — Bissolati visits England to reopen discussion — Robertson asked to examine Italian position — Growing dread of German attack — British heavy artillery sent to Italy — French generals propose Allied offensive in Italy — Sir William Robertson's opposition — Impossible to stop Nivelle offensive — Lack of ammunition ends Italian offensive — Cadorna asks for heavy guns — His telegram to Foch — French Command sends six batteries — Allied Military Conference; Robertson refuses to budge — London Conference of August 7th — Foch supports Italian offensive — Robertson's message to Cadorna — My appeal to Robertson — My letter to Bonar Law — Cadorna postpones offensive; his reply to Robertson — Military position in October, 1917 — Germans strike on Italian Front — Magnitude of the peril — My dash to Italy — Quality of Italian generalship — How would Italian people face disaster? — Bravery of Italian troops — Awe of German Army — French and British troops to check panic — Conference of Allied Premiers arranged at Rapallo — French and British soldiers prefer Italy to Flanders — Returning confidence — Courage of Italian statesmen — Sonnino's lack of war mind — General Porro makes poor impression — Change in Italian Command; Diaz appointed; State of Italian Armies — My assurance of Allied aid — Conditions demanded by us — Problem of closer strategic unity — Meeting with King of Italy — Record of Conference at Peschiera — The King's confidence — Italians pray for snow — Plumer goes to Italy.

THE Italian campaign of 1917 furnishes a complete illustration of the difficulties experienced by a military alliance of independent nations in formulating any common plan of action which must necessarily involve giving priority to one national front at a time. These difficulties are greatly enhanced, and are almost insuperable if it is found necessary to change plans already agreed to by the commanders of all the national armies. It is next to impossible to persuade the majority of these generals to abandon operations on their own front for which they have made considerable preparation and of the success of which they are confident, in order to concentrate part of their strength on another front under another commander. The fetters riveted on at Chantilly in November, 1916, ruined the Allied campaign in 1917. If any still doubt this after reading the story, faithfully told, of the Chemin des Dames and Passchendaele, let him peruse the following account of the Allied dealings with Italy.

Early in 1917, soon after the Rome Conference in January, there were indications that the Italian War Direction were feeling uneasy at the display of timorousness and indecision which had lost their country the best opportunity yet afforded to its armies to win a resounding triumph. Rumour as to what had occurred about the offer of the heavy guns spread through the Italian capital.

A popular young Socialist Deputy of the name of Bissolati heard of the proposal made to Cadorna by the British delegation and how he had shrunk from the guns offered to him, as if they had been pointed at his own breast.[1] Bissolati had won popularity amongst all sections of opinion by his transparent sincerity, his ardent patriotism, his fine oratorical gifts, and his exceptional charm of manner. He had fought in the War and had been badly wounded. When he heard how the Italian representatives at the Conference, political and military, had allowed themselves to be intimidated into a stammering hesitancy when Italy had been offered a fine equipment of the best heavy artillery on any battlefield, he stirred opinion in Rome to recapture the lost chance. When the story reached the ears of the King of Italy, he was not too well pleased.

Signor Bissolati was sent over to England at the end of February on an informal mission to urge an Allied offensive against Austria and to sound the British Government on the probability of their renewing the offer made at the Rome Conference. But by that time we were so committed to the

[1] See Vol. III, Chapter X.

projected offensive in France that it was deemed inadvisable to withdraw any weight from the attack by sending a large consignment of heavy guns to Italy. In the middle of March, Sir William Robertson was sent by the Cabinet to Italy to carry out the decision of the Rome Conference as to arrangements for sending troops to the Italian Front in the event of a combined attack by Germans and Austrians. Before he started, a communication was received from General Cadorna indicating his opinion that the Germans might at any time set free sufficient troops for a decisive attack on the Italian Front. In the event of their adopting such a plan, a combined force of ninety German and Austrian Divisions could, according to him, be concentrated on the Italian Fronts. General Cadorna doubted whether, in such a contingency, the Anglo-French offensive on the Western Front would have sufficient effect to relieve the military difficulties on the Italian Front and urged that a scheme should be prepared for the direct reinforcement of the Italian Army from the West *by twenty divisions.*

From the extreme of reluctance to welcome any assistance he had dashed to the other extreme of asking too much. In practice it answered the same purpose. Nothing was done. I have seen the same device practised in other cases by military leaders who had an understanding with each other, when a certain section of civilian opinion had to be propitiated, but where at the same time the generals were anxious to prevent any steps being taken which would involve a departure from plans of a different character already agreed to amongst themselves.

The Italian appeal was discussed at the War Cabinet. I recalled the proposals I had made at the Rome Conference urging the preparation by the Allied Staffs not only of a defensive on the Italian Front, but also for a combined offensive, and I pointed out that "General Cadorna and the

Italian Government had then received these proposals in a somewhat lukewarm manner." However, the G.I.G.S., Sir William Robertson, undertook to give special attention to the whole question during his forthcoming visit to Italy.

Later on in March, I received a pressing letter from the British Ambassador in Rome, describing the very grave apprehension of Baron Sonnino as to the probability of a heavy attack by the Central Powers on the Italian Front, and expressing Baron Sonnino's regrets "that the proposals made by the Prime Minister at Rome for Allied coöperation on the Italian Front had not been carried out." I replied to Sir Rennell Rodd that the War Cabinet fully shared Baron Sonnino's apprehension, and that Sir William Robertson had already been sent to Italian Headquarters for the express purpose of going into the matter. When Sir William Robertson returned from Rome he reported that there was undoubtedly a possibility of a German attack on the Italian frontier. It is worthy of passing comment, in view of the gibes at "civilian strategy", that the Military Conference at Chantilly, in making plans for 1917, had undertaken no preparations to meet the possibility of a joint enemy offensive against Italy. That contingency was pointed out by a politician at the Rome Conference, and he was responsible for the proposal to take immediate steps to prepare transport and other arrangements to counter such an offensive. Upon a full consideration of all the communications which had been received from Italy, the War Cabinet decided to offer to lend the Italian Government ten batteries of six-inch howitzers with their personnel, and a suggestion was made that the Italians should apply to the French for field guns. Our guns were to be sent to Italy forthwith and were timed to arrive there to help General Cadorna in the offensive operations which he had planned.

Early in April, M. Painlevé, the French Secretary of

State for War, spoke to me about my plan of a combined offensive on the Italian Front. He informed me that General Pétain and other French generals had expressed doubts about the offensive planned by General Nivelle and that as an alternative they suggested the sending of eight divisions, four British and four French, to Italy. He said that not only was he personally of opinion that a combined attack on the Italian Front might have the effect of inflicting such a defeat upon Austria as would induce her to withdraw from the Central Alliance, but that the distinguished generals whom he named were also of opinion that such an attack delivered by the Italians with substantial help from the French and the British might produce decisive results. General Nivelle, who was then Commander-in-Chief of the French Army, had however not been consulted, and M. Painlevé's own colleagues in the Government, including his Chief, had expressed no opinion on the subject. It was not an authoritative offer upon which I was entitled to take action. Moreover, the British attack on the Arras Front had already actually commenced. I felt it was too late then suddenly to change our plans and I indicated that we might discuss the project later, after we had seen whether the offensive which had just been launched had succeeded or failed. Later on, when it had proved to be a disappointment, and General Nivelle had been dismissed from the High Command and General Pétain put in his place, the latter did not feel that he was in a position to renew the proposal. He was too much occupied in quelling the mutinies in the Army and restoring the morale of his troops. I reported the Painlevé conversation to the War Cabinet. Sir William Robertson was present and gave it as his opinion that it would be a mistake to send these divisions to Italy, as General Cadorna had all the infantry he wanted. No doubt he had at that time an overwhelming preponderance of men. The Italians had then a million and a half men at the front as against only six hundred and fifty thousand Austrians ranged against them. The Russian Army was still in being, and therefore the Austrians could not weaken that front. What the Italians lacked in order to make their offensive a real success was not men but guns and ammunition. The C.I.G.S. reported to us that he understood the "French military authorities were opposed to sending troops to Italy." That meant that General Nivelle and his Staff were opposed to the proposal. Pétain and Micheler certainly favoured the idea. The whole story of the war dealings with Italy shows how difficult it was in a coalition of far-flung nations and armies to get away from plans to which they had all agreed and for which they had all prepared. Had the French Government supported the proposal when the British delegates submitted it to the Rome Conference, and committed themselves in January to a spring offensive against Austria as their main strategical plan, instead of one which was merely a supplement to an attack on the German lines in France, the whole military situation would have been transformed. The new Austrian Emperor was anxious for peace, and as I have already recorded, had communicated in March with the French Government, through his brother-in-law, Prince Sixte, suggesting separate negotiations with the Allies.

But, at the very hour when I was reporting the Painlevé interview to the Cabinet, our troops were storming the Vimy Ridge. Could we have wired them to stop their victorious advance and ordered them to take the train for Italy, because one French Minister and two generals had, without consultation with their superiors, suggested dropping an offensive for which the French were primarily responsible and to which they had committed us much against our own judgment? Painlevé was an influential Minister, and the generals he quoted in support of his plan were among the ablest and most important in the French Army, but both the Minister and the generals made the suggestion without any authority from their respective chiefs.

Sir Rennell Rodd, in a letter he wrote to me, gave it as his opinion that pride would never permit the Austrians, even if Cadorna's offensive had been a success, to make any concessions to Italy, but if their defeat had been the result of an attack by an offensive in which British and French troops as well as Italians had been engaged, they would have taken a completely different view of the situation, and might then have been induced to surrender part of their territory as a condition of peace.

The promised howitzers were duly dispatched to the Italian Front. Our gunners received a great ovation when they reached Milan. The Italian Prime Minister reported that their arrival had a very good political effect. Even as a gesture of friendship and good will this contribution from the British Army had its moral value. The forty howitzers left France the second week in April, they arrived on the Italian Front in a few days, and they were all in position and ready to take part in the offensive on the Carso before the end of April. So they would have been had we sent three hundred guns instead of forty. It would not have taken much longer. All the talk about the time it would take to send artillery with its quota of ammunition was deliberately exaggerated in order to excuse inaction. What happened after Caporetto abundantly demonstrated that fact.

The offensive started well. The Italians stormed formidable positions and captured a considerable number of prisoners, but unfortunately they had to suspend a promising operation for "lack of heavy artillery ammunition." The same deficiency all round was responsible for an inadequate bombardment which caused heavy losses to the Italian Army. It was the same old story. The British and French heavy guns with a lavish expenditure of shell were insufficient to storm the elaborate German fortresses in France, defended as they were by the best troops of the greatest army in the field, supported by an abundant reserve of troops and by an equal, if not superior, artillery to that of the assailants. But a few hundred of these guns with an adequate supply of ammunition sent to Italy — especially if the Italians had been assisted to make up the deficiency in the supply of ammunition for their own guns — would have broken a front held by troops inferior in numbers, training and equipment, and possessing insufficient reserves upon which they could rely. The break might have been exploited before the Germans could have rushed sufficient reinforcements to the assistance of their defeated allies. The Germans were expecting a serious attack in France. Allied guns could have been transported to Italy without their knowledge. The enemy engineered a surprise on the Italian Front in October with considerable artillery and troops, sending six German divisions and artillery thither, without our suspecting the movement. Why was it impossible for us to execute the same manœuvre in May? There is no explanation, except the fanaticism of the Western Front. This infatuation prevented the experienced military leaders of France and Britain giving any thought to the possibilities of the Italian Front and how they might best be exploited in the general interest of the Allies. At least no thought was given to the question until it was too late to act effectively.

The Italians promised to renew their offensive in August, but they now realised thoroughly that their artillery equipment was unequal to the task of recapturing the Austrian entrenchments, and General Cadorna appealed to the French and ourselves for heavy artillery. In July, Cadorna communicated confidentially to us his views of the military position:

He thought that if the Russians maintained their pressure, this with the Italian offensive would lead to the disintegration of the Austrian Army.

He had, he said, always considered this to be the strategical object which the Allies should strive for, as if attained it would automatically cut off Bulgarians and Turks from their conjunction with Germany and make it possible to act with overwhelming effect against Germany. He said he doubted the possibility of defeating Germany on the Western Front, as even if pushed back further, the Germans could still take up a line resting on River Meuse and their fortresses and for a long time to come continue to defy any enemy.

It may be said that his view of the possibilities on the Western Front was falsified by events. It is true the German line was broken in the autumn of 1918, but the British and French troops had lost another two and a half million men in the efforts made since the Rome Conference. They had the help of a million American troops. Even then the Germans were never driven beyond the Meuse and the Armistice was signed on French soil after a revolution had taken place in Germany.

It was for this reason, he said, that he had always urged to be supplied with more heavy artillery, as it was heavy artillery which was most important for the offensive and it is the arm in which unfortunately he is most deficient.

Why did he not talk like this at the Rome Conference, where something might have been accomplished on these lines? Had he spoken up for his ideas then, the Conference would have taken a different turn. When I suggested in his presence the very strategical plan he now urged in writing and afterwards, he never uttered a word in support of the idea. He now proceeded to give our representatives his explanation of the French reluctance to assent to a combined offensive on the Italian Front.

He said he thought the French desired to concentrate all interest on the front in France and were reluctant to give much artillery to Italy, as *speaking frankly, they were rather jealous of any military success that Italy might achieve.*

Cadorna's appeal reached us about the middle of July, when Haig was giving the last finishing touches to the preparations for his rash venture in Flanders. He had been given a reluctant and conditional sanction for his attempt by the War Cabinet. The guns for which Cadorna pleaded were already placed and pointed at the German entrenchments in front of Ypres, and shortly afterwards started the ghastly process of churning up the mud in which so many of our devoted soldiers sank for ever.

At the same time Foch received the following telegram from Cadorna:

16th July, 1917.

The successful development of Russian offensive justifies suppositions foreseen by us that in the near future a situation similar to that which I foresaw in my telegram of 26th June (in which we asked France and England to supply 25 batteries and 13,200 rounds) may arise on the Front of the Julian Alps. I may state too, that from information received and by direct observation of movements behind the lines, the first symptoms of this are already visible. Consequently, the necessity of putting forward the date of our offensive as much as possible is evident, and on the other hand, on account of *our munitions crisis which the recent help from France and England reduced but did not solve, it seems as if the offensive in question cannot be begun before the end of August.* In my telegram quoted above I have already shown you that 100 guns with 1,000 rounds each are absolutely necessary to make up deficiency of munitions. But if General Pétain cannot spare the batteries which have been asked for and considers they can be better employed on the Franco-British Front, I must point out the serious consequences which the common cause of the Allies may suffer by not taking advantage of the particularly favourable strategical situation now developing on the Front of the Julian Alps and by giving up the advantages of a simultaneous attack with necessary means on both Austrian Fronts. In any case, if decision of the General Staff is irrevocable, kindly communicate above message to General Foch and ask him to use his influence with General Robertson to accept responsibility of finding at least part of the batteries which we have asked for and of the supplying of which to my certain knowledge the British Government is in favour.

On this our Military Attaché at Paris reported:

I am informed by General Weygand that General Foch and General Pétain consider the matter to be of the greatest importance. The latter, who is extremely short of artillery, nevertheless, decided to send six batteries at once.

General Foch looks upon the matter as follows:

"It is necessary to take Cadorna at his word so as not to give him an excuse for not attacking. If Cadorna considers the moment favourable for attack everything should be done to help him, especially in view of the fact that a separate peace has been openly discussed in Hungarian Parliament and because all information from Russia tends to show that when attacks at present in preparation have taken place, they will not be renewed. Therefore a very favourable situation now exists, which might not be renewed for a year. General Weygand asked me to urge upon you very strongly the great importance of sending to Italy as much artillery as could be spared."

The Cabinet instructed the C.I.G.S. immediately to get in touch with the French and Italian experts. A conference of Generals Foch, Cadorna and Robertson was held in Paris on the 24th of July. Cadorna appealed to Foch and Robertson for ten divisions and four hundred heavy guns and claimed that with that help he could inflict a decisive defeat on Austria. Foch was inclined to listen to this proposal. He had a poor opinion of the Flanders attack and would have preferred sending to Italy the divisions and guns he had promised us for that enterprise. But Robertson dug in his toes and refused to budge. He doggedly held the Cabinet to its assent. He had given our undertaking to Haig that he should be permitted to launch his attack. If it succeeded, the results would be greater than any we could expect in Italy. If it failed, then we could try Italy. But it was agreed that Ostend must come first and then Italy. The consequence was that we never came in sight of Ostend and we never reached Italy, except in November, to support an Italian Army broken by the "demoralised and exhausted" German divisions that had come from holding us up at Passchendaele until our feet were thoroughly stuck in the Flemish bog.

Once more Cadorna gave in. As to whether he was a good fighter in the field I cannot express an opinion. In conference he abandoned his positions at the first counter-attack. The conclusions reached at this Conference of Allied Generals in Paris were that:

> In view of *the primary importance of this objective of finally defeating Austria,* it was decided to examine, when the operations now in progress are finished, the situation which will result therefrom, as well as the desirability and possibility of placing at the disposal of Italy the forces necessary to enable her to attain this objective.

As the operations then in progress did not finish until November, the Germans struck first on the Italian Front.

The Conference illustrates the difficulty under which the War Cabinet laboured in the conduct of the War, owing to the Chantilly commitment. Foch, Pétain and Cadorna were good soldiers with actual experience of this War and the conditions under which it was fought. They were convinced of the primary importance of finally defeating Austria. But Robertson said that this must wait on Passchendaele. In practical experience of fighting under modern conditions, Robertson did not approach these three men. But he beat them all in a rigid and unreasoning stubbornness that was not open to argument or persuasion. He flourished the Chantilly agreement in their faces and held them to their bond, which was just as binding but more comprehensive than that of Shylock, for it included the spilling of blood. To all the appeals of Cadorna and the calm reasoning of Pétain, he had but one answer:

"I'll have my bond; I will not hear thee speak:
I'll have my bond; And therefore speak no more. . . ."

His sole concern was for the Flanders offensive to which he had committed himself. He was not there to confer or to consider. He went there to say "The Bond." He said it, and stuck to it, and got it. As long as he was C.I.G.S. we could not send anyone else to represent us at an Inter-Allied Military Conference — except Sir Douglas Haig. That would not have improved matters. His thoughts also were fixed on what he was assured would be the crowning victory of the War.

We had therefore either to proceed with the Ostend operation or to dismiss both Robertson and Haig and appoint generals who were not so committed. The Cabinet were not prepared for so sensational a change. I have already dealt candidly with the reasons. The guns had already opened fire on the slopes of Passchendaele and in a few days the infantry would advance to attack the German trenches. The first assault achieved a measure of success which, if it did not vindicate the project, at any rate did not justify its immediate abandonment. The first check came when we made our next efforts to break through. Early in August it became more and more evident that the great break-through to the coast could not be accomplished, certainly not without colossal losses. The fight was developing into a second and more hopeless Somme.

On the 7th and 8th of August there was an Inter-Allied Conference in London. Amongst other subjects that came up for discussion were the possibilities of an offensive on the Italian Front. Baron Sonnino raised the question. The discussion will show that by that date the Italians were getting discouraged. After the last failure of Cadorna to persuade Robertson, he had gone back to Italy with his ardour cooled for an offensive this year. His chill had been caught by his Government and his Staff. They had reverted to their January attitude. In introducing the subject, Sonnino said that at the present moment the British Army was making a big effort on the British Front in France, but the Italian General Staff were convinced that one of the weakest enemy fronts was that on the Carso and that it was the one where a strong attack would pay best. An Italian offensive would shortly begin, but Italy was not strong enough in guns and munitions to press the offensive to a decision, even if it started well. He dwelt on the advantages of really crushing Austria and suggested that if the Allies could help, especially in the provision of heavy guns (four hundred had been suggested as being required) something really effective might be done.

General Foch thought that it might be to Austria's interest, after a partial defeat, to make a separate peace. A great attack on the Carso might lead to the fall of Trieste, and Austria might then be willing to treat. But this was not by any means certain. It was, however, a serious possibility, and the military means of bringing it about deserved consideration. He was of opinion that if we could not expect to achieve a complete defeat of the enemy, at any rate we might bring about a situation in which either Austria or Turkey might be glad to come to terms.

When it became apparent that the Allies were prepared seriously to consider a combined offensive in Italy, as usual the Italian Staff began to waver and hesitate. General Albricci represented the Italian Army in the absence of Cadorna. Whilst professing to welcome any support the Allies could accord to the Italians, he said in reply to a question I put to him as to when their Army could launch an offensive:

"The latest season was the end of August, after that an offensive must wait till the end of the spring, say 15th May."

The answer, of course, disposed of any idea of a combined Allied attack in Austria during 1917. General Albricci stuck to his view, even though he was strongly pressed on all sides.

I observed that I had always thought myself that the best policy was for the Allies to try really to crush Austria. I had made the suggestion in Rome, and it was then considered too early. I made it now, *and it was apparently considered too late.* I contrasted the method of the Central Powers in pooling their resources, which enabled them to drive back and break up great armies and to hold a vast extent of enemy territory, with the Allies' efforts which, gallant though they were, only chipped a few bits off a granite rock. I considered it a great misfortune that the Allies could not deliver one big smashing blow. I criticised the methods hitherto adopted for settling Allied military plans, and urged that in future the strategy of the Allies should be determined not by soldiers meeting separately and independently of statesmen, but at gatherings where the points of view and the experience they each represented could be pooled.

The Generals examined the proposition put before them by the Conference and decided it would be too late to send any batteries to Italy after Haig had attained his first objective. The lure of Passchendaele and the timidity of the Italian Staff had effectively done in — not the politicians, but Italy, the Allies and most grievously of all, the chances of a favourable peace in 1917.

That was the end of the project of a combined offensive in Italy. Unfortunately, the Germans took a different view of the possibilities of that front in the late autumn and the early winter. They knew that an offensive late in October was a feasible operation.

As the futile massacres of August piled up the ghastly hecatombs of slaughter on the Ypres Front without achieving any appreciable result, I repeatedly approached Sir William Robertson to remind him of the condition attached to the Cabinet's assent to the operation. It was to be abandoned as soon as it became evident that its aims were unattainable this year and our attention was to be concentrated on an Italian offensive. He was immovable. He attributed the slowness of our progress to the exceptional rains. As soon as the weather improved we should sweep onward. As we know now, ten weeks more fighting with huge casualties gave us two more miles and then the furthest point was reached, without the achievement of any strategical result. But Robertson still believed in the possibility of great things after we had worn down the enemy's strength. According to him everything pointed to the growing exhaustion of the German Army. Why give in when we might be near a real triumph for our arms? I especially recollect a conversation with him, when he came down at my request to a house in Sussex where I was taking a few days' rest qualified by papers and interviews. (One of these interviews had been with Baron Sonnino.) From the lawn we could hear the thud of the guns of Passchendaele. To all my pleadings Robertson tendered a sullen negative. His final answer to my plea I only read long afterwards. It was a long message to Cadorna, making it clear that he must expect no help from us. The Passchendaele offensive was to be pressed for several more weeks and we could spare neither guns nor men for Italy. The communication is so characteristic of his general attitude that it is worth reproducing:

"War Office,
Whitehall, London, S.W.
17th August, 1917

"To:
His Excellency Lieut.-General Count L. Cadorna, G.C.B.

"My Dear General,

"You are probably aware that at the recent Allied Conference in London, of 8th August, 1917, the following resolutions were agreed to:—

"(1) The representatives of the three Governments agreed that the British, French and Italian General Staffs should be directed:

(*a*) To consult as to the operations which should be initiated with a view to striking at Austria and as the best time to begin such operations;

(*b*) To advise as to the theatres where, during the winter months, substantial results can be achieved, and as to the best methods of obtaining those results;

(*c*) To consider how to provide more heavy guns for an Italian offensive, either out of existing stocks, or by the creation of new stocks;

(*d*) To advise the Governments at their next informal meeting as to the result of their consultations.

"(2) It was decided that a further meeting of representatives of the principal Allies should be held in Paris between 10th and 15th September.

"(3) My views on the points upon which the Allied Governments require information are as follows:

(*a*) I understand the term "striking at Austria" to mean dealing Austria such a decisive blow as would induce her to make peace. It is clear that the only front from which there is any prospect of the Allies being able to strike such a blow at present is the Italian Front. I am of opinion that to make such a blow possible from the Italian Front it is necessary that the Austrians should be prevented from reinforcing their troops now opposed to you to any considerable extent, and that at the same time Germany must be prevented from coming to the aid of her ally. The first of these conditions can only be met if the efficiency of the Russian Armies is restored to an extent which will compel Austria to keep on the Eastern Front approximately the number of divisions she now has there. The second condition can only be met if Germany is prevented from moving her reserves from the Western Front to the Italian theatre.[1] Unless this is done the great superiority of the enemy's communications over those between the Western Front and Italy will always enable Germany to counter effectively any reinforcement of the Italian Armies by the British and French Armies. This makes it necessary that the blow to be struck from the Italian Front should be combined with operations on a large scale, carried through with determination on the Western Front. Unless the two conditions above mentioned are fulfilled it does not, at present, seem possible to deal Austria a decisive blow.

As to the best time to begin operations against Austria, you alone are in a position to decide, and I shall be glad to hear whether you have in any way modified the views that you expressed at the Conference in Paris on the 24th July, 1917. In this connection I cannot say when the operations now in progress in Flanders may be concluded, but they will certainly continue for many weeks, and until the result of them is known, and the development of the situation on the Russian Front can be more clearly forecasted than at present, it will not be possible for me to say whether it may, or may not, be desirable to transfer any troops or guns from that theatre to the Italian Front or when such a transfer, if desirable, can begin.

[1] What about the German divisions sent to Riga and Caporetto, whilst we were attacking with all our strength in Flanders?

Further, it is also necessary to consider the contingency that the enemy, if he is enabled to withdraw troops from the Eastern Front, may concentrate them against the Franco-British Front and that it may be impossible for that reason to weaken our forces in France. Meantime, as you are aware, such preliminary arrangements as are possible regarding the movements of troops from the Western Front to Italy have been prepared by our Staffs in consultation.

(*b*) *As to the possibility of obtaining substantial results during the winter, I think we should each speak for the theatres in which our troops are employed.*

As to the Western Front, the conditions of weather and ground during the winter do not make substantial results possible, but I am of opinion that the methods adopted last winter on the British Front in France should be continued this winter, and that every possible effort should be made to take advantage of our superior resources in guns and ammunition, and of the superior morale of our troops, to harass and wear down the enemy.

As to the Salonika Front, I adhere to the opinion which I have already expressed to you more than once, that no substantial results can be achieved either during the winter or at any other time except in combination with a decisive attack delivered on Bulgaria from the north, and I see no prospect of this maturing during the coming winter. The extent to which substantial results can be attained in Mesopotamia and Palestine depends upon the situation on the Russian Fronts in Asiatic Turkey, and I shall be prepared to explain when we meet, the arrangements I have made for operations in these theatres.

(*c*) As to the question of providing you with more heavy guns, those from existing stocks can only come from the British Armies in France, and, as I have already stated above, *it is not possible at present for me to say how many batteries can be made available, or indeed if they can be sent at all.* As to the possibility of providing you with guns from new stocks, I am making enquiries of the British Minister of Munitions and will have the information when we next meet, but you will understand that this also depends upon the requirements of the British Armies in France, which in turn depends upon the development of the operations now in progress.

"I shall be obliged if you will give me your views on the questions raised by our Governments, and will inform me when and where it will be convenient for us to have a meeting with General Foch, so that we may prepare a joint reply to be presented to the Allied Conference which is to assemble in Paris between 10th and 15th September, 1917.

Yours sincerely,

W. R. ROBERTSON."

This letter was shown to me. It might otherwise have been couched in different terms. It emphatically stamped on Cadorna's faint hopes of receiving any effective assistance in men or guns from the British Army.

Cadorna was about to launch another attack. It was not a stimulating letter to be sent to a general on the eve of a battle. This onslaught shared the usual fate of Italian offensives. It started well, promised considerable results, but had to be abandoned for lack of ammunition. General Delmé-Radcliffe wrote, imploring us to send help. I wrote to the C.I.G.S.:

"26th August, 1917.

"My dear Chief of Staff,

"The Italian attack seems to me to be developing well, and judging by the reports that come from Delmé-Radcliffe, there are great possibilities in it if fully and promptly exploited. I can, of course, only judge by what he says, but his account of the Austrian demoralisation and of their lack of reserves — both confirmed by the number of prisoners and guns captured and the extent of the ground occupied — seems to me to indicate immediate prospects of a signal military victory on that front. I need hardly point out that the overthrow of the Austrian Army might produce in the present condition of Austrian public opinion decisive results on the whole campaign. *I was therefore very distressed to find from one of Delmé-Radcliffe's reports that Cadorna apprehended that these brilliant possibilities might be rendered unattainable owing to the imminent exhaustion of the Italian reserves of ammunition.* Do you not think that a new situation has arisen there which requires immediate action on the part of the Allies to support the Italian attack, make up their deficiencies and enable them to convert the Austrian retreat into a rout? It would indeed be a severe reflection upon us all if later on it were discovered that we missed a great chance of achieving a signal and far-reaching military success for the Allied cause, through lack of readiness to take advantage of an opening made for us by the Italian Army.

"I feel confident that you are watching events with anxious scrutiny. If you think that the Italian victory is capable of being pressed to important conclusions would it not be worth while your paying an immediate visit to that front to judge for yourself and to form an independent opinion as to what might be accomplished if the French and ourselves were to make sacrifices which would enable Cadorna to press on until the Austrian Army completely breaks?

"Once more I would impress upon you and the War Cabinet the enormous responsibility that rests upon us not to allow the most promising opening which events have thrown in our way in any Western theatre to come to nought for want of opportune support.

"I should be obliged if you would mention this communication to the Cabinet this morning. I am writing to Mr. Bonar Law on the same subject.

Ever sincerely,

D. LLOYD GEORGE."

As I was still in the country, I wrote at the same time to Bonar Law to beg him to bring pressure to bear on Robertson:

"27th August, 1917.

"My dear Bonar,

"I enclose letter which I am sending by special messenger to the C.I.G.S. I have followed Delmé-Radcliffe's reports very closely and unless he is over-sanguine the events which are taking place on the Italian Front indicate overwhelming possibilities if promptly exploited. There are undoubted signs of demoralisation in the Austrian Army, and if it is pressed hard and continuously for another fortnight or three weeks there seems to me to be a very fair chance of a rout, with consequences which no one can foresee. As you know, Austria is anxious for peace. A great military defeat would supply her with the necessary excuse. Cadorna says his heavy ammunition will not last much longer, and that you ought to call for Delmé-Radcliffe's report on this point, and this corresponds with the information we had before the action. We should never be forgiven if we allowed such an opportunity to go by for lack of prompt action, and we should not deserve to be forgiven. It may be said that it is too late now to send guns and ammunition. But it must be borne in mind that if Cadorna is informed that guns and ammunition are being sent he can then afford to draw on his reserves and fire his last cartridge, whereas if there is nothing more coming he will have to stop in order to have the necessary supply of ammunition to meet the inevitable counter-attacks. I cannot believe that transport difficulties would stand in the way if a real effort were made. I understand that the Taranto Route is actually carrying some hundreds of tons a day already, and can carry more. But, in addition to that, special efforts might be made which would take guns and ammunition to the Italian Front in a few days.

"I beg the War Cabinet to take this matter into serious consideration, and specially to urge the Chief of Staff to pay an immediate visit to the Italian Front with a view to form an independent judgment as to the possibilities. That is, of course, in the event of his not being satisfied with the reports that come from Delmé-Radcliffe. If Sir William Robertson cannot see his way to go, what about asking General Smuts to go at once to Italy to report?

"If you wish it, I could come up for the afternoon to discuss this matter.

Ever sincerely,

D. LLOYD GEORGE.

"P.S. — If the Allied Armies from the North Sea to the Adriatic were under one command, I have no doubt as to the course which would be pursued. Surely our strategy ought to be based on the assumption that it is all one front."

Bonar Law failed to make any impression on Robertson. Cadorna, finding there was no help forthcoming, gave up the ghost of his starved offensive.

Having read and assimilated Robertson's discouraging missive of the 17th of August, the Italian Commander-in-Chief had made up his mind that there was no hope of securing adequate assistance from his Allies and that therefore he must postpone his offensive until May, 1918. Here is his reply to Robertson's message:

"Comando Supremo,
Royal Italian Army.
29th August, 1917.

"I thank you for your note and am glad to find myself in complete identity of views with you on all questions which are so clearly set forth in it. First of all, on that from which all the others depend, on the necessity of striking Austria so heavy a blow on the Italian Front as to prostrate her and induce her to make peace.

"(*a*) I recognise also — following the sequence of the questions put to the General Staffs by the representatives of Governments at the conference in London — that the condition indispensable in order successfully to translate into fact the strategical plan of beating down Austria, is that the Austrian forces should be held fast on the Eastern Front and the Germans held on the Western Front. Should Russia remain in arms (the opposite hypothesis is provided for in the plan agreed upon in Paris during the sitting on the 26th July) the first condition is fulfilled at once, in so far as it is not likely that Austria would be induced to weaken considerably in the Eastern theatre the number of divisions engaged to-day, which is hardly sufficient to hold the extensive Russo-Roumanian Front for which she is responsible.

"As regards the second condition, there can be no doubt as to the necessity for preventing Germany from moving her strategic reserves towards the Italian theatre, by means of operations on a large scale by the British and French Armies on the Western Front.

"Still the contribution of the Allies to Italy, as to which a preliminary agreement was made at the conference in Paris, cannot, in any way, prejudice the putting into effect of this programme because, on the one hand, the contribution itself is small as compared with the powerful Anglo-French masses which have operated this year, and because it will be amply compensated for by the ever-increasing efficiency of your means of offence, and, above all, by the progressive intervention of the United States.

"Allied aid to Italy and operations on a large scale on the Western Front are therefore two points in the same question which, judged in their proper relation to each other, appear to be perfectly compatible.

"As regards the most suitable time to launch the Inter-Allied offensive, I indicate — in accordance with views expressed by me at the conference in Paris — next May; and this taking into consideration that our offensives, still in full course on the respective fronts, certainly do not permit of undertaking another, and still greater offensive effort within the current year.

"(*b*) As regards the attitude to be taken up during the winter, excluding by reason of the season, the possibility of carrying on operations which might yield substantial and decisive results, I am in agreement with you in thinking that each of our armies should look to its own front, holding and wearing down the opposed enemy forces and economising its own for future and decisive struggles.

"As regards the Salonika Front, I have nothing to add to your point of view.

"(*c*) As regards the question of the supplies of heavy artillery I thank you and take note of what you tell me and will await the communications which you inform me you will make.

"Having thus set forth in detail my ideas which, I repeat, are in principle in conformity with yours, I do not consider necessary for the moment, another meeting between us, which, apart from taking us away, if even only for a short time, from the operations in which each of our armies is at the present time intensively engaged, could not, in view of the present indefinite situation and at such a distance in time from the period in which the operations will take place, render more concrete the undertakings which have already been established.

"I am sending a copy of this letter to General Foch in order to establish between us as complete and exhaustive an exchange of views as possible; and, with the same object in view, I am forwarding to you a copy of the letter which I have to-day addressed to General Foch, in which I have expressed some of my ideas on the constitution of the Allied contingent.

"Please receive, my dear General, the assurance of my warmest feeling and accept my cordial greetings.

L. CADORNA."

I have in my possession Cadorna's reply to Foch, from which it seems that the French were prepared to send troops to Italy to assist in the contemplated offensive. The continuation of the Flanders attack frustrated this project, for Foch could not spare divisions unless they were withdrawn from the fatuous attacks on the Houtulst Forest to which French G.H.Q. were committed by their agreement with Haig. Passchendaele was effectively preparing the ground for Caporetto.

One must consider the military position at that moment in order to appreciate what a disaster befell the cause of the Allies at Caporetto. Russia, with its innumerable millions of men, in quality equal to the finest fighting material in the field, was completely and finally out of the reckoning. As the revolution developed, the disintegrating influence became more apparent amongst the Russian Armies at the front. Germany and Austria were thus in a position to withdraw some of their best divisions from the East. The armistice of Brest-Litovsk was signed on December 17th, 1917, and then what was left of the choicest divisions of the German and Austrian Armies on that frontier were liberated from their stern vigil. 1918 demonstrated that Germany could treat her armies on the front as a depot for filling up depleted units on the Western Front. Russia had ceased to be a military anxiety for her. The Serbians were hardly an army — merely a few shrivelled divisions, recruited from gallant refugees who had escaped the great debacle and maintained their spirit in spite of it. Roumania had been ruthlessly crushed and was not a source of supply to the enemy. America was as yet only nominally in the War. She was not represented in the fighting line anywhere by a single platoon. By the following spring she had only one division in the line and three in reserve. The rest were still performing their equivalent of "forming fours." The French Army had not yet recovered from the terrible exhaustion of blood and nerve which culminated in the breakdown of April, 1917. It was still resting under General Pétain's careful nursing. Now and again its recovering health was tested in carefully prepared and well executed "limited offensives." The Italians had abandoned their attacks and were looking forward to a winter of rest and recuperation. The British alone were fighting on land and sea with the whole of their might. Their valiant Army was plunged by its leaders into the swamps of

Passchendaele, where its strength was exhausted and its fine spirit damped by that muddy enterprise. The fatuous muddle of Cambrai showed that the Army could not sufficiently extricate its strength from the slime to enable it to strike an effective blow in any other direction. Altogether a propitious moment for the great coup against Italy; and it would have succeeded completely had it not been foreseen as a probability and provided against as the result of the Rome Conference. Let me tell the story as I saw it.

Holding the Allied Armies in France with its right, the German Army, late in October, hit out with its left at the head of the Italian Army in the Styrian Alps. The Teutonic blow fell with staggering effect. The Italian Army reeled backward, stunned and confused. In sixteen days it retreated seventy miles, losing six hundred thousand in dead, wounded and prisoners and missing (including those who threw away their arms in the debacle and were scattered over the face of Northern Italy). Of the deficient Italian equipment in guns, 3,152 were captured by the enemy. The ground lost was considerable but it was not nearly as serious as the loss in men and guns and ammunition. In both these respects the Allies were already at a disadvantage in comparison with the Central Powers. The Italian disaster increased the discrepancy to an alarming extent.

Was the disaster irreparable? On important parts of the front the Italian Army still held; on others the retreat was conducted in an orderly manner, the enemy advance being skilfully delayed and embarrassed; in some places the retreat was a headlong rout of broken units, leaving behind a litter of guns, waggons, ammunition and even rifles. Would the panic spread? The fate of Italy, peradventure of Europe, depended on the answer given by the next few days. If the Italian Army were destroyed as an effective force, the great cities of the North, which constituted the main arsenals of

Italy, would fall into Teutonic hands, and once more the road to Rome would be open to the triumphant Goth. The cracks in the Austrian conglomerate would be cemented by the prestige of a resounding victory. The war party in Italy would be discredited by the catastrophe it had brought on their country. The peace party in Italy would emerge from its hidden fastnesses and perhaps succeed in persuading the victorious enemy to grant, and their defeated countrymen to accept, moderate terms of peace; and thus Italy would be beached on the strand where lay the wrecks of Russia, Roumania, Belgium and Serbia. Austria, with all four enemies on her frontier broken, would be free to assist Germany to overcome the last two resisting elements of the Great Alliance which once threatened to overwhelm the Central Powers with their incalculable resources of men and material. If Italy fell out, then, of the six powers that once confronted Germany, Austria and Turkey, there would remain only France and Britain. America would not count for much for at least another eight or nine months. For the first time the overwhelming advantage in numbers would have been on the side of the Central Powers and their artillery preponderance would be emphasised. It was a shrewd blow well timed, and if expeditiously, resolutely and skilfully exploited, calculated to bring final victory to the Teuton. I decided that the situation was so grave that it was desirable that not only the Chiefs of the French and British Staffs, but the French Premier and myself should hurry off to Italy, to concert measures with the Italian Government for coöperation between the Allied Armies to restore the position.

There were two elements, both of them to a certain extent incalculable, upon which the turn of events largely depended. One was the quality of the Italian leadership, civil as well as military. On the military side the generals in supreme command, General Cadorna and his Staff, were good officers of the kind to which recent years had accustomed us (with one notable exception) on the Allied side. They were highly trained, conscientious, courageous soldiers of average intelligence, but devoid of all the attributes of genius, imagination, originality of conception or fertility of resource, and quite unequal to the calls of a great emergency. When regulation plans carefully devised according to Staff College precepts were smashed in by an unforeseen irruption, they had no gift or initiative for improvisation to set up a new front which would prove more baffling than the old. Two or three Italian generals on this occasion displayed conspicuous gifts of leadership, and their generalship and the confidence it inspired in the troops along their own fragments of the front helped to arrest the panic. But the Higher Command was overwhelmed by the catastrophe. All the accounts I received alike from Sir William Robertson, Sir Henry Wilson and from French sources gave me a picture of a Staff suffering from the mental concussion of a great shock, issuing bewildering orders to units of whose whereabouts they were in complete ignorance and as to the very existence of some of which they entertained doubts. When I reached Italy, these were the reports brought to me by British officers. Divisions had dissolved into fugitive atoms swept by the storm like dust over the plains of Lombardy. How many divisions were destroyed and how many survived and which were the divisions which belonged to one or other of these two categories, no one could tell with any precision or certainty. There were divisions still holding together without artillery or baggage, as it were, by bits of string. Which? Who could tell? Not the Italian General Staff. Then there were two divisions somewhere on the critical front. Where were they? The last one heard of them was that they were fighting gallantly against great odds in the

Alpine foothills. Were they still fighting or had they also been overpowered? It was no use asking the Italian General Staff. They had no information on the subject. I am simply condensing the reports I received from reliable British and French officers, and subsequently confirmed by Sir Henry Wilson, of the dismay and disorder which followed Caporetto. General Cadorna was an able soldier, but of his Chief of Staff, General Porro, I formed a poor opinion. To this aspect of the question I will revert when I come to the meeting at Rapallo. These men proved quite unequal to the facing of a great and sudden crisis. This constituted one of the danger points of an already dangerous situation. In a crisis inadequate men convert peril into catastrophe. They constitute a peril in themselves.

There was a still more incalculable element to reckon with. How would the Italian Army and the Italian people face this unexpected disaster? As to their courage there could be no doubt. The Italian people had entered boldly into a doubtful war at a moment of exceptional doubt in its varying fortunes. They had supported losses, burdens and privations of unexampled magnitude with calm and fortitude. But they had the brilliant achievements of their army to sustain them. They were inspired to fresh efforts by some of the exploits in which their soldiers were wresting from their ancient foes fortresses hewn out of the towering and snow-clad rocks which sheltered their frontiers. But now came the sudden shattering of high hopes, and the armies victorious in many battles for two years were hurled back into the plains, leaving cannon and equipment which had cost the poor Italian peasants so dear, in the hands of an enemy they had thought beaten beyond apprehension. Italy had always a more potent peace party than France or Britain. It was led by Italy's wiliest and most formidable statesman, the veteran Giolitti. The higher priesthood of the Catholic Church was never friendly to the War. Would Italian zeal for the War survive a great defeat?

Then what about the Army? No one has ever cast a doubt on the bravery of the Italian soldier. Should a doubt exist, let him visit Italian battlefields and the last remnant of his scepticism will be shamed out of his heart. No one but brave men, and supremely brave men, could have stormed these gigantic fastnesses in the teeth of Austrian cannon and Austrian rifles, and at the weary end of the perilous climb, Austrian bayonets, wielded by courageous and trained soldiers, well led by competent generals. Napoleon, explaining the rout of his picked veterans at Waterloo, said there was a moment when panic was apt to grip the most seasoned troops and then they became a rabble. No one doubts the courage of French, British, Russian, Austrian or German troops. The world has never yet nourished more courageous races than those engaged in this horrible War, and yet at one time or another they have all turned and fled from the battlefield with a victorious army in pursuit, picking up their abandoned wounded, artillery and equipment and sweeping up hordes of beaten men who preferred exile in foreign cages to further resistance.

But the dangers of a retreat are not so great amongst the stolid races of the North as in the armies of a quick, imaginative, susceptible people such as the Italians. Panic is fed more by fear than by fact, and fear is fed through the channels of the imagination. Let us put ourselves in the plight of the sensitive and imaginative Italian soldier at and after Caporetto. To him the German warrior was a creature of report. The Germans had not hitherto appeared on the Italian Front and the Italian soldier knew nothing of his measure as a fighter. The Austrians he knew. He had faced and beaten him at many points. There was no mystery left about him. It had been probed by Italian bayonets and its quality inspired no dread. All he knew about the German was that he had overrun Belgium in a fortnight; that he had conquered the richest provinces of France, driving the great army of France and the picked troops of England pell-mell almost to the gates of Paris; that the combined efforts of England and France with a stupendous armament had failed to tear the captured land free from the bloodstained claws and that the unavailing effort to do so had cost the assailants millions of dead and wounded; that, whilst Germany was doing all this with her right arm, with her left she had smashed Russia, Roumania, and Serbia. Having accomplished their destruction, she was now sending her triumphant legions down to the Italian valleys against an army with not one tenth the equipment of the British or French. No wonder the stoutest Italian soldier felt a shiver of apprehension. The arrows of fear would have quivered in the bravest heart under the same conditions. The Italian Army only knew from report, and report always exaggerates, and the quick Italian fancy worked on these legends. Had the first onset been resisted, all would have gone well, and Italian courage would have been doubly reinforced by the knowledge that it was quite equal to Teutonic efficiency. But Caporetto went wrong. The reports were proved to be true. The Goth was invincible. So that when I went to Italy at the beginning of November, I found soldiers without their rifles who had fled hundreds of miles from the battlefields. Such is the effect of panic on the sturdiest soldiery — for these were the same men who had fearlessly stormed the steep heights of Monte Cristallo, bristling with Austrian guns and rifles, and inch by inch had driven the Austrians out of the rock-hewn trenches of the Carso.

The Italian Army had lost heavily in men, and its equipment was seriously impoverished, but it had reserves of men sufficient to fill all gaps and the Allies had the means to reëquip the Italian Army and to spare. All, therefore, depended on stopping the panic, ere it became too late to arrest the process or achieve any substantial results by doing so. It was in the achievement of this object that France and Britain could render the most immediate and effective service. Obviously the most useful means of restoring morale was to pour at once into Italy contingents of the troops that had held up the redoubtable German and even beaten him out of superbly constructed trenches for three years in France and Flanders. It is no disparagement of Italian courage to say that they were heartened by the sight and comradeship of the men who held Verdun for months against the most intense hail of high-explosive shell that was ever concentrated on any battle area, and of the men who held the narrow Ypres salient for years against the most protracted bombardment to which any fortress has ever been subjected; the men who, on the Somme, the Chemin des Dames and Passchendaele had walked through the terrible hailstorm of the German machine guns in order to come to a deadly grip with those very Germans, were now pouring across the passes to reinforce the Italian Army.

As soon as the news of Caporetto was brought to me by Sir William Robertson, I suggested that he should immediately arrange to send the necessary assistance. He demurred at first, but under pressure afterwards communicated with the French and Italian Staffs in order to put into operation without delay the plans which had been carefully prepared in anticipation of this event. They worked without a hitch. The Rome Conference saved Italy.

On my suggestion, Sir William Robertson proceeded at once to Italy to place himself in communication with the Italian Staff and ascertain from them what further assistance they required from us. In order to enhance further the impression that the Allies were behind the Italians, and that

GENERAL LUIGI CADORNA

Commander-in-Chief of the Italian Army, 1917

they did not stand alone in their trouble, I suggested to M. Painlevé, the French Premier, that we should both go to the Italian Front and invite the Italian Premier to meet us there. I certainly attached no exaggerated importance to our presence on the spot, but where the object was above all to reëstablish morale and to reinforce the national will for continuing the War, every gesture of friendship and comradeship had its effect in promoting that restoration of confidence which is the best antidote for panic. I decided to take General Smuts with me, also Sir Henry Wilson.

My intention was to leave General Wilson at the Italian Headquarters to keep in touch with the Italian Commander-in-Chief and ascertain from him what further coöperation or help was needed, and to keep us informed generally on the situation. M. Painlevé readily concurred in my suggestion that we should visit the Italian Front. As the result of a communication addressed to the Italian Government we were informed that Signor Orlando and Baron Sonnino would meet us at Rapallo to confer on the situation. M. Franklin Bouillon, who was the most strenuous vocal member of M. Painlevé's Cabinet, accompanied him. General Foch had already left with Sir William Robertson and they were both already in contact with General Cadorna. During our halt at Modane, trainload after trainload of French guns and cheerful French soldiers passed through on their way to meet the foe on battlefields where their ancestors had won undying fame. Frenchmen had fought and worsted the Austrians in many notable campaigns under the sunny skies of Italy and they took no account of the fact that their old adversaries were now reinforced by still older foes from the Rhineland. Three years' hard fighting had given them the measure of German prowess and they were not afraid to meet on the Piave the soldiers they had fought with success on the Marne and the Meuse. I never saw a more joyous crowd of young men hurrying to meet danger. The sulky depression that followed the Chemin des Dames had completely passed away. As we climbed the steep pass that led to the Mont Cenis tunnel, we caught glimpses of a road thronged with French *camions* loaded with materials of war, and when we emerged from the tunnel there were still miles of lorries trailing along towards the plains of Lombardy. The plan was working well. What a contrast was presented by those tranquil valleys blazing with the tints of autumn and the endless procession of waggons carrying material charged with death and mutilation that wended their way under the shadow of the hills! After we passed Turin we came upon the British troops that had arrived by way of the deserted Riviera to join hands with the French expeditionary force that was pouring through the Alps. The British soldiers were happy to exchange the sodden fields of Flanders for the smiling valleys of Lombardy. Their delight was written on their rugged and good-tempered faces. As we saw them, we knew in our hearts that the danger of a complete debacle was over. The Austrians were no match for these British and French veterans and the Germans were not numerous enough to make the difference.

Whatever the disorder in the Italian Army — and as yet we were not in a position to judge its full extent — we felt confident that the combined divisions of France and Britain could hold up the German invading force and we were hopeful that the unbroken divisions of the Italian Army could arrest the Austrian advance until the combined Allied forces could be reorganised into an invincible army. In this respect we had some faith in Austrian dilatoriness.

That was our first sketchy impression of the situation after crossing the Alps and viewing the successful development of our relief plans. At every wayside station we witnessed dejected fragments of the shattered Italian divisions, many without rifles. This gave us some idea of the extent of the defeat and of the demoralisation that had followed defeat. But we were reassured by accounts we received of the Duke of Aosta's army and of the forces under the command of General Diaz.

One little episode brought vividly to our minds the vastness of this war. Before we left Genoa, the wooden shutters were clamped down on the sea side of our railway carriages to shut out the light, lest we provide a target for stray German submarines cruising in the Mediterranean off that coast. The following day, we witnessed a spectacle that filled us with pride, a convoy of British tramps steaming in perfect order under the protection of a couple of British destroyers. It was a faultlessly marshalled answer to scoffing admirals who ridiculed the notion of tramps keeping station.

At Rapallo, where we arrived on November 4th, we met Signor Orlando and Baron Sonnino, and we were to judge the value of the civilian leadership enjoyed by Italy in her testing hour. They were seriously disturbed by the gravity of the position, but they were both men of undoubted courage, and never have they displayed that courage more conspicuously than at this crisis in their country's fate. Baron Sonnino was more responsible than any individual Italian statesman for bringing his country into the War and disaster meant for him the eternal reproach of having led Italy to her ruin. He must have realised all that as he entered the conference chamber at Rapallo. Nevertheless, I found him as resolute as ever to fight to the end of the issue he had forced by his personality. Never a word of surrender or of compromise did this dour and unbending diplomat utter. I discovered at the Rome Conference that he was entirely destitute of the war mind. His whole thought was centred in the aims and manœuvres of the diplomat. He had no understanding of war, its requirements, appliances or necessities. He left these entirely to others. He disliked being forced to apply his mind to this branch of the problem. In this respect he was a man after the professional soldier's own heart. They could not have invented a more ideal statesman. He was unhappy because the generals in whom he had placed implicit trust had failed him. At the Rapallo Conference he therefore seemed to look for guidance on the war situation entirely to others who had devoted more time and thought to its study. His sole concern seemed to be that the fight should continue and the position be restored with that purpose in view. I found Signor Orlando equally resolved that the fight should go on. Italian G.H.Q. was representer by General Porro, General Cadorna's Chief of Staff. I knew nothing of his qualifications as a soldier but he made the poorest impression on every mind at that conference. He presented a very inadequate account of the situation. He seemed to be ignorant of the most salient facts of the rout. He could tell us nothing that would enable us to form any true estimate of the military position of the Italian Army. He was the most unhelpful ingredient in that conference except in so far as his futility gave us at least one important clue to the disaster. He seemed to lack knowledge, energy and zeal for the discharge of his important duties and when we saw and heard him, we were not in the least surprised at the report given us by General Foch and Sir William Robertson of the chaos and confusion at Italian Headquarters.

It was obvious that the first step to be taken in order to restore confidence was to make a complete change in the Supreme Command. Apart from its patent shortcomings, the Army had lost confidence in it. This change we urged on Signor Orlando and Baron Sonnino and they agreed that it was inevitable. The appointment of a successor to General

Cadorna presented great difficulties. The most popular appointment in the Italian Army would have been the Duke of Aosta, who had the reputation of being a fine soldier. He commanded the confidence and had won the enthusiasm and affection of the whole Army. Unfortunately, there were insuperable difficulties of a dynastic kind in the way of his appointment and it became clear that the only alternative was General Diaz. He had done well throughout the War and acquitted himself with great credit during these last critical days.

A few notes made at the time will afford some idea of the course of the discussion and of its atmosphere.

At the conference on November 5th, General Foch reported that the 2nd Italian Army was absolutely broken, but the 1st, 3rd and 4th Armies remained intact. It was subsequently reported by Signor Orlando that the 2nd Italian Army was the most important of their four Armies, and that a panic had been spread throughout the whole of this Army, only twenty-four battalions remaining in proper military order. The gravity of the event, therefore, could not be dissembled. General Foch proceeded to report that the Armies still numbered some seven hundred thousand men and ought easily to be able to hold the shorter line of the Piave. The necessary condition, however, was that the Higher Command should be capable of issuing proper orders to the subordinate commanders. His impression was that the Higher Command was at present characterised by inertia. Orders were given, but no one saw that they were carried out. In fact, there was practically no Higher Command.

Signor Orlando, on behalf of the Italian Government, took an even graver view of the situation. He considered that the line of the Piave was a good line of defence except at one point, but in the present state of the 2nd Italian

Army the other Italian Armies were hardly sufficient to defend this line. There were two perils which had to be faced:

(1) The possibility of an attack in force in the Trentino, which would probably be made with increased German forces. The Italian troops now guarding the Trentino were not sufficient to resist this attack.

(2) The Italian Army was only just sufficient to defend the line of the Piave, and there remained no general reserve wherewith to support the shock of an attack on any other point.

Therefore, the help of the Allies, if it was to be effective, must be not less than fifteen divisions, which should be transported as rapidly as possible, and should be concentrated in positions where they could be moved to the various threatened points. If the military support of the Allies were given in these conditions of number, distribution and quantity, the Italian Government was convinced that it could meet the situation so far as was humanly possible. If, on the contrary, these conditions were not fulfilled, all the indications were in the opposite direction. Then it would not be possible to maintain the line of the Piave, and it would be necessary to retire. This would be a military disaster, and the political consequences would be of the gravest character. At the present moment the country was calm; it had resigned itself to the loss of territory and had discounted the retreat to the Piave. For the present, the Italian Government could guarantee internal order, unless the line of the Piave was abandoned. Hence the future of Italy depended upon the decision which the Allies took now. The Italian Government asked the Allies to consider that, in order to save the situation, it was not sufficient merely to render some assistance, but essential that that assistance should be adequate.

I said that I agreed with Signor Orlando that the Allies

were bound to do all in their power to assist their ally, Italy, in her difficulties. It was not merely that we had passed our word of honour to do so, but that it was the obvious interest of Britain and France to do all in their power to keep Italy in the War, even though her strength was employed more against Austria than against Germany.

Signor Orlando interpolated at this point with quivering passion that this was what Italy intended to do at any cost, even at the expense of retirement to Sicily. (He is a Sicilian.)

To this I replied that there were certain considerations which must be carefully weighed before our decision was taken, and I thought it necessary that we should talk frankly to each other. It was the common interest of all three peoples that we were fighting for. If Germany and Austria were to triumph, Europe would be a very different place from what it was at present. We were fighting for freedom, and hence we were bound to put all our resources into the common stock. France had already sent out four of her very best divisions, most of which were already in Italy. We also were sending two of our best divisions. We intended to send two more divisions, which would make a total of eight British and French divisions in as short a time as the railways would permit their transport. I laid stress on the fact that these eight divisions were about the best in the British and French Armies. When General Robertson had come to me I had asked him to select thoroughly reliable divisions, and the choice had been made on that basis.

I then came to the consideration of the conditions under which alone it was possible for us to render assistance. It was useless to pour troops into Italy unless we were assured of efficient leadership, that is to say, efficient leadership of the Italian Army. Otherwise, the British and French divisions might find themselves left in the lurch. A great disaster might then occur which would destroy not only the Italian Army but the best British and French divisions. I felt convinced from inquiries I had made that at present the leadership of the Italian Armies was not such as to justify us in entrusting to it the British and French divisions. On that point I felt it necessary to speak with great frankness. The Italian Prime Minister had said that part of the Italian Army had been seized with panic, and that history had shown that this was no reflection on their bravery. I reminded Signor Orlando that Napoleon at St. Helena had said that this might happen to the very best troops, and that then nothing could stop them. The Italian Army needed no defence of its valour. During the last few years it had shown itself equal to any troops in the world in gallantry and in confronting dangers of all kinds. Therefore, there was no question of any reflection on brave men. But I had to say frankly that there was some doubt of the capacity of the Higher Direction. I believed that brave men had been led to their doom through lack of proper organisation and staff work. In saying this, I was not talking at random, but on the high authority of Generals Foch and Robertson, and these great generals were the last men in the world to say such a thing unless they felt bound to. There was a *camaraderie* among officers that prevented their saying such things, especially to politicians, except in great urgency. All the information we had showed that leadership and command were lacking in the Italian Army. Exception had been made in the case of the Duc d'Aosta, who was understood to have directed the movements of his army with coolness and capacity. Our information, however, was that the General Headquarters had been in a worse panic than the troops and had lost control of the situation. When we sent troops we should be glad to entrust them to the gallantry of the Italian Army, and in that respect our confidence was not in the slightest degree impaired by recent events; but frankly speaking, we could not trust them to the present High Command.

M. Painlevé assented fully to the statement which I made. After referring to the fact that the French nation, after the Battle of Charleroi, had also experienced some sombre days, but after the retreat had known the glorious days of the Marne, he said that the triple army which was about to oppose the invaders of Italy must not fail for lack of good command. The check would have been terrible and considerable reaction on the three countries. He urged therefore that it was necessary to have a specially good and reliable command.

Both Signor Orlando and Baron Sonnino pressed hard for a promise of fifteen British and French divisions. General Porro urged that the Germans and Austrians together had a total of 811 battalions, whereas the Italians had only 377 battalions in all with which to resist this overwhelming force. General Foch scouted these estimates and treated them as a ridiculous exaggeration, as they ultimately turned out to be. The fact that such an estimate had been put forward was only further proof of the panic which had seized the General Staff. Our military advisers were of opinion that eight divisions would suffice, especially as they were eight of the best quality, provided that the High Command were changed and the Staff reorganized. Later in the day the Italian Prime Minister acceded to this suggestion.

We then proceeded to discuss the general question of a closer coöperation and greater unity of strategy and action between the Allied Armies. These discussions and the decisions we came to will be set forth in detail in the chapter on the Versailles Council and Unity of Command. It was then arranged to proceed to the Italian Front to meet the Italian King and to renew discussion with him. Progress was very slow as we neared the front and we passed trainloads of civilians and refugees flying from the invaded districts. It was a rainy day and dismal at that. The weather, the report from the front, the groups of runaway soldiers from the 2nd Army who had thrown away their arms to accelerate their flight, the huddled refugees in the railway carriages, and on the platforms, old men, women and children frightened and tearful at leaving their homes — all conspired to produce an atmosphere of terror and dejection. We had to wait at Brescia for some time to enable trainloads of French guns and gunners to pass through to the front. When we reached Peschiera, we were taken to a gloomy-looking building under the shadow of the old Austrian fortress of the Quadrilateral. Upstairs we met the King of Italy. Physically he is not a commanding figure but I was impressed by the calm fortitude he showed on an occasion when his country and his throne were in jeopardy. He exhibited no signs of fear or depression. His sole anxiety seemed to be to remove any impression that his Army had run away. He was full of excuses but not of apologies for this retreat; so much so that General Foch showed signs of impatience. This became manifest in the grunting protests from him which were intelligible to those who knew him well.

The record of the proceedings at our Conference at Peschiera on November 8th is so full of historical interest that it is worth while reproducing the *procés-verbal* of the discussions:

The King of Italy, at the outset, expressed his great regret that the advice of Mr. Lloyd George had not been followed and that the Allies had not made use of the Italian campaign to crush Austrian resistance. He had fully shared the view of Mr. Lloyd George and regretted deeply that, whereas a few months ago Austria was on the point of breaking down, she had had the opportunity, with German assistance, of turning the tables on Italy.

Mr. Lloyd George regretted that His Majesty was not present at the Rome Conference, where he had strongly urged his views in favour of a combined move on the Italian Front.

The King of Italy agreed with Mr. Lloyd George's remarks, and added that he did not always have the opportunity of having his own views carried out. The King then went on to give an account from his personal observation of the breakdown of the Italian Army under the combined Austro-German attack. The main causes of the Italian failure he attributed to:

(*a*) A very thick fog which prevailed on the day of the attack on the northern flank of the Italian Army, and which made the use of the artillery impossible.

(*b*) The absence of highly trained professional officers who could properly manœuvre the Army when the retreat commenced.

He said that the Italian Army had lost approximately thirty thousand officers during the War, and that the younger officers had not been properly trained and could not handle their men under the difficult conditions which arose with the retreat. The men again were also insufficiently trained, and were really only fit to hold trenches and to make a simple advance. They had not been sufficiently instructed to manœuvre for purposes of retreat, and when the retreat took place it soon degenerated into confusion. He had observed the same experience with the Austrian Armies. As soon as the Italians had broken through the Austrian line in their recent advance, the Austrian soldiers, who were also inadequately trained, could not conduct a proper retreat, and fell a prey to the advancing Italian Army. He thought that undue importance had been attached to the extent to which the pacifist movement had progressed in the Italian Army. No doubt a certain amount of mischief in isolated cases had been done by the preaching of priests, and to a smaller extent by the influence of Socialists; but on the whole he did not think that the Italian morale had been seriously undermined by these influences. He attributed more importance to the effects of the duration of the War, which made the men tired and depressed, and he remarked that it was generally observed that men who came back from leave were depressed and disheartened by the state in which they had found their families and their small affairs. Although charges of treachery had also been made, not a single case had been proved, and he was convinced that the Italian Army had not been successfully tampered with by the enemy.

With regard to the retreat itself, he said that the retirement of the 3rd Army had been quite successfully conducted, and that even the very large number of wounded of this Army had been successfully evacuated during the retreat. The 2nd Army had largely broken up in the retreat, but hundreds of thousands of men had been collected in the rear, and would again be organised into proper units as soon as possible. He did not think that the morale of the men had been very seriously affected by the retreat, and he spoke from personal observation of these men during their retirement.

With regard to the three divisions that were further north in the Cadore, one had successfully retreated, but two had not been heard of for some days, and it was still uncertain whether they had been cut off by the enemy, or whether they were retreating successfully through the foothills of the Alps in a westerly direction.

With regard to the future: the King thought that the Piave line could certainly be held; four hundred siege guns and other heavy guns were already mounted on the right bank, as well as six hundred field guns. Trenches were being made and the embankments of the river also afforded excellent cover. If this line was not held, the situation would become serious, not only because Venice would be lost — and that in itself was a serious matter — but because the loss of Venice would mean the retreat of the Italian Fleet to Brindisi and Taranto, as there was no suitable base further north on the Italian coast. With the Austrian Fleet and submarines dominating the Adriatic, the naval position would become very much worse. Therefore, in his opinion, every effort should be made to hold the Piave line. The real danger to this line, in his opinion, was in the north along the head waters of the Piave River, to which the German forces on the right flank of the Austrian Army were rapidly pressing forward. Should the Germans succeed in crossing the Piave higher up and seize Monte Grappa between Asiago and the Piave River, the position along the Piave would be turned, and a further retreat might become necessary. Monte Grappa was now being occupied, and everything was being done to check the rapidity of the German advance, but there was no doubt that grave danger was threatening on that sector.

Mr. Lloyd George then spoke very strongly about the state of the Italian High Command. He said the accounts which had reached the British and French Governments were such as to make them press strongly for a complete change. They were all the more entitled to make these representations, not only in the interest of the Italian Army itself, but of the British and French Armies, which were now appearing in Italy, and which would come under the supreme direction of the Italian High Command.

The King of Italy replied that, although he did not in every respect agree with the criticisms which had been made against General Cadorna, yet he thought that great weight should be attached to the representation that had been made, and his Government had already decided to remove General Cadorna from the command, and to appoint in his place General Diaz, who, although a comparatively junior officer, had been on the General Staff both before and since the War, and was generally recognised as the brains of the Italian Army and a profound student of the science of war. He himself (the King of Italy) had very great confidence in General Diaz, who certainly would be his own choice from among the officers of the Italian Army. To strengthen the Staff still further, the Government had decided to appoint General Giardino, the former Minister of War, as assistant to General Diaz. General Giardino was stated to be a man of great executive energy and would usefully supplement the work of General Diaz.

Mr. Lloyd George explained, with reference to the situation on the Piave and Trentino Fronts, that the British and French Governments and military advisers were not certain that the best use was being made of the four French divisions in moving them west of Lake Garda along the Val Giudicaria, especially in view of the considerations already referred to by His Majesty that the real danger was threatening between the Asiago Plateau and the Upper Piave. Both the British and French Government were therefore agreed, in view of the great urgency of the situation, that complete discretion should be given to Generals Wilson and Foch to move the six Allied divisions now in Italy to sectors of the Italian Front where they thought the best use could be made of them.

It was agreed that Generals Wilson and Foch should proceed forthwith, with Signor Bissolati, to the Italian headquarters at Padua, and there consult with General Diaz on the military situation, and thereafter move the six Allied divisions to the points of greatest danger on the Italian Front without further reference for instructions to their Governments. They were, however, requested to consult with the British and French general officers commanding these divisions.

(At this stage Generals Robertson, Foch and Wilson were called to the Conference and the above instructions explained to them.)

The King of Italy appeared cheerful throughout the Conference and said that he would do his best to continue working for victory for the Allied cause. He felt that more might have been made of the Italian campaign, and now more than ever he thought that the Italian campaign might assume very large and important proportions in the immediate future, and he expressed his great pleasure and gratitude that his British and French Allies were prepared to support the Italian Armies to the full in the phases of the campaign which were now opening.

We were not free from anxiety when we left Italy. Would the line of the Piave hold? Could it be turned by an attack from the Asiago, the great rocky spearhead that threatened the brain of industrial Italy and might at any moment be driven into it if skilfully wielded by Teutonic craft. This would have been a formidable move and if successful would have laid Milan and Northern Italy prostrate at the feet of the victor, but we felt we had done all we could to avert this disaster. As we left, the French were hurrying through Brescia to face any attack from the Asiago bastion. The snows were later than usual in falling on the hills, but soon they must come and any advance from that direction would be blocked. Throughout Italy that week there were millions of earnest prayers for the coming of the autumnal snows. The British were hurrying up as fast as Italian trains would bring them to take their positions on the Upper Piave and for some reason the Austro-German advance was tarrying. The knowledge that help had arrived was spreading far and wide. It heartened the Italians. It induced more caution in their enemies, for they knew that they had no longer to reckon with a broken and dispirited foe, but with a section of the Italian Army that had never faltered and was now supported by veteran divisions from the terrible battlefields of the North. We were hopeful that the great irruption had been stemmed. We soon knew that our hopes were well founded. Preparations made as a result of the Rome Conference had foiled the German blow. On my return to Paris, I met General Plumer, who was on his way to Italy to take command of the British Expeditionary Force. He did not conceal his satisfaction at the prospect of exchanging the Flemish swamp where he had been fighting a characteristically stubborn battle for the more genial surroundings of his new command. His delight, I felt certain, was not prompted merely by climatic reasons. He had no responsibility for initiating the campaign in Flanders and it was quite evident that his heart was not in it. In Italy he won the respect and good will of all with whom he came in contact, and justified to the full the reputation he had already won as one of the best soldiers in the British Army.

CHAPTER XIII

THE UNITED FRONT: THE INTER-ALLIED COUNCIL

Strategy of 1917 lacking in new ideas — Briand's efforts end in talk — Concentration on French Front — Excuses for attitude of Nivelle and Haig — Cadorna in honour bound to Chantilly policy — No new strategy without change of military leaders — No justification for change in December, 1916 — Soldiers' attitude to Brass Hats — Chiefs of Staff overborne — Disasters due to lack of united strategy — My decision to set up Inter-Allied Advisory Staff — Naval representation — Robertson's reply: importance of non-military factors — My letter to President Wilson — Haig's views on military prospects — Robertson supports Haig's view — I seek independent advice — Lord French and Sir Henry Wilson consulted — French's memorandum — Wilson's memorandum — My letter to Painlevé — Project accepted by France — Cabinet adopts the plan — Painlevé's letter: scheme approved — Rapallo Convention — Supreme War Council set up — Versailles selected as its location — Italian situation referred to new Council — Robertson initiates agitation against Council — My speech at the Paris luncheon — Organised criticism in England; Mr. Asquith's question — My reply — President Wilson supports Rapallo agreement — Mr. Asquith's criticisms in Commons debate — Question of naval representation — Mr. Asquith content with existing system — Pringle organiser of the attack; its failure — The *Times* changes its tone — Unity of strategy and unity of command — Inter-Allied Staff fundamental.

REVIEWING the campaign of 1917 on land, I realised that it was, on the whole, such as the military staffs in London and France had ordained it to be. The Government succeeded in forcing on the Admirals their ideas as to the best methods of fighting the enemy at sea. Had they not overruled the Sea Lords the submarines would have won, and the Allies would have been beaten. On land the High Command had its way. As far as the general strategy of the land fighting was concerned, it was their policy. The only exception was the campaign in Palestine which they deprecated. The difference between the Nivelle and Joffre offensive schemes was tactical. But the principle had not been changed. It was that of hammering on the strongest bastion in the enemy's fortress, hurling millions of shells and hundreds of thousands of men at this formidable stronghold whilst the weakest parts of the enemy's ramparts were neglected. In it there was "neither device nor wisdom."

Whenever I invited an examination by the C.I.G.S. or Haig of methods for getting at the enemy on his weakest rather than on his strongest side, I was put off with military axioms about "the decisive front", and engaging your principal enemy on that front. My experiences of this war, and may I also say, of politics, encourage me to venture on another axiom — you should never do what your leading foe would like best to see you expend your energies upon. To concentrate almost exclusively on the Western Front, where your enemy had exercised his utmost engineering skill to construct formidable entrenchments, where the transport system behind was perfect, where he had more cannon and machine guns than we had, and where consequently we lost three men in fruitless attack for every two he lost in successful defence — suited the foe. On the other hand, the neglect to equip Russia, which ultimately deprived us of the support of millions of first-class fighting men — the failure to exploit the Balkan opportunity for organising a great federation which would attack Austria on her weakest frontier and cut Turkey off from her sources of supplies — all that was just what the Germans would have wished us to do. And we did it every time and all the time. When the generals were forced by Governments to attempt other methods, like the Dardanelles and Gallipoli, they did it so half-heartedly as to make failure a certainty. They dispatched just enough men and material just late enough to make these side shows a drain on our resources without giving them a chance of achieving justification by results.

As soon as I formed my Ministry, I strove to induce the Allies to reconsider this policy. I was encouraged to think it might be possible to effect a complete change because of Briand's great speech at the Paris Conference on the "one front." Guns, ammunition, even men were to be pooled. I did not realise then that as soon as Briand descended from the rostrum he took no further interest in his speeches. For him speech was the same thing as action. At least, his contribution to action ended with his perorations. It was for others to do the rest. If they neglected to do so, he was not to blame. He had done his part and knew he had done it well, better than anyone else possibly could.

When we had our first Inter-Allied Conference in 1917, Briand made it clear that by the "one front" he meant the French Front. He was all for another great offensive on the Western Front and for concentrating the whole French and British strength upon a victory on French soil. In spite of all his oratorical flights about the Allies pooling their resources, he was not ready to spare a single gun for Italy. Nivelle had captivated his fancy and fired his imagination. I had arranged the Rome Conference in order to have an opportunity for persuading the Allies to reconsider the Chantilly programme. But once the programme was settled and all the Allied Staffs had accepted and started working on it, then it was impossible to change it radically without securing the whole-hearted coöperation of all the Governments concerned. Apart from the reluctance to upset plans already worked out with great elaboration and care by the General Staff, there was the insuperable obstacle that any change in the front of concentration would mean that the British and French Staffs on the Western Front would necessarily have to play a secondary part in what might be the final victory. If the Italian Front were chosen, Cadorna must be Commander-in-Chief, and Nivelle and Haig would have to be satisfied either to remain on the defensive in France, or to confine their activities to comparatively minor operations. There would be no triumphant break-through to Laon for one, and no clearing of the Flemish coast for the other. It would be expecting too much of human nature to hope that they would view such a prospect without a sense of disappointment. It would be a bad psychological blunder to imagine that this would not unconsciously influence their judgment. They had greater confidence in the possibilities of French and British troops than in those of the Italian — that was a natural and commendable patriotic bias. They had also greater faith in their own capabilities as military leaders than in those of Cadorna. That was not conceit but the outcome of that self-confidence, without which no leader can inspire confidence in others. As far as the French were concerned, there was also the dislike of giving to Italy the lead in victory. Whatever the cause, both Nivelle and Haig were utterly opposed to any combined Allied offensive except on their own front. Robertson was on all questions of military policy just Haig's man. On all occasions he said in effect, "I say ditto to Sir Douglas Haig." He never expressed a military opinion which differed from Haig's. Any fundamental change of plans therefore involved overriding the immutable opinion of the military leaders of the two most powerful Allied Armies. That could not be done unless both Governments agreed to do so. Briand and Thomas were zealous Nivellites. So the French Government stood by the Chantilly version, revised and enlarged by Nivelle. What about Italy? If Cadorna and the Italian Government had played up, something might and would have been accomplished. If the British Government had decided against the French offensive in favour of an attack on the Italian Front, the situation would have been changed. The French *Generalissimo* could not have carried out his plans without the full support of the British Army. Even with it he failed. Without it, he could not even have tried. But an active and zealous initiative on the part of the Italians was a condition precedent to any such change in the strategy of the year. This was not forthcoming. Why? Cadorna had agreed to the Chantilly plans, and he felt he could not go back on them without a breach of faith with his professional comrades. The coolness with which he received the proposal of a combined offensive on the Italian Front was not attributable to strategical doubt. It was prompted by his deference to professional etiquette. Robertson rubbed it into him. He collared him before he ever entered the Conference room and told him he could not go back on his bargain and sell his brother officers to the politicians for his own advantage. Cadorna was a man of sensitive honour. It was a cruel choice — between his bond and his country. Where such gigantic issues were at stake, he ought to have resigned rather than sacrifice the chance offered not only to Italy, but to the Alliance, of achieving a victory which might have led to an honourable peace and saved millions of lives. There was no real dishonour involved in a change of plans. The circumstances were changed completely by the change in the attitude of the British Government and by their offer of material support for an Italian offensive.

Looking back on the events of 1917, I ought to have foreseen that a change of strategy was impossible without a thorough change in our military leadership. With Robertson and Haig, both men of an abnormally stubborn character, remaining in the commanding position they held, a new policy was not attainable. No policy can be worked effectively through reluctant instruments. A general direction may be given, but the entire machinery by which it is to be carried out is in hostile hands. Between direction and execution there is endless scope for manipulating details in a way which baffles every purpose. Both Haig and Robertson working together were adepts at that game. All information came through their hands. It was selected and prepared for our consumption. I have shown how over the preparations for the Passchendaele campaign it was handled in such a way as to guide the Cabinet inevitably to the desired conclusion. Some facts and figures were exaggerated or overemphasised, others understated or suppressed altogether. The professional conscience is a mystery which defies every ethical system ever yet inaugurated. Historically, we know of instances where the most exalted Christian ethics have bowed before the inexorable plea of its agents that the end justifies the means. Both Haig and Robertson were genuinely convinced that victory was only attainable on fronts under their direct control. Every scheme for diverting endeavour elsewhere, in their honest opinion, placed the ultimate triumph in jeopardy and must be thwarted by every device. I had to judge these eminent soldiers as I found them at the end of 1916. They were both able, conscientious and hard-working men who stood high in the esteem of all in their profession. Those who are in charge of a great concern know that there is no more difficult question to solve than the dismissal or retention of men under their command who are competent, upright and experienced, with a thorough knowledge of the details of their business, and working without stint to the best of their ability for the success of the business, but who are obstinately attached to old methods when a change of policy is desirable. If they deliberately disobey an order, then one's course is clear. But if they are clever enough just to avoid that indiscretion, then the question of how to deal with them is the most embarrassing that confronts any business man. It often needs a smash to make a change of personnel practicable without creating a sense of injustice to worthy men. If it is done when the reports that come in from them show that the concern is prospering and beating its rivals, then to the interested public a dismissal of such men at such a moment constitutes a scandal and an outrage which are difficult to explain away. There is a suspicion of personal motives which can only be dispersed by an independent investigation that is in itself a reflection of the capacity and integrity of the management, and involves a full revelation of facts which will undermine confidence and damage the whole business of the firm — maybe irretrievably.

That was the position in which the Cabinet were placed at the end of both the 1916 and the 1917 campaigns. The air throbbed with the drums of victory beaten lustily in Parliament and Press and on every platform.

The talk about the admiration, trust and affection felt by the men in the trenches for their leaders is utter nonsense. There were no legends of the *Petit Caporal* kind attached to any of the generals. The soldiers never saw and cheered before a battle an impressive figure on a white horse. They hardly ever caught a glimpse of their commanders except when a vision of burnished brass flew past in a motor car. That is all they saw of the men who spoke the word that sent them to fight in the drowning mud. To the fighting men they were not even individuals. The men in the trenches never spoke of Haig or Gough. To them these exalted personages were "G.H.Q.", "Fifth Army", or more often "the brass hats." The press messages, when they were read in the lines, were a cause of scoffing merriment. The legend of the men's faith in their leaders only flourished in the warmth and comfort of the home front; it never struck root in the trenches. But I had to deal with opinion behind the lines and carry it with me at every step. That there should be no change in our commanders was stipulated by an influential contingent of Conservative leaders ere they joined the Government. I ought never to have accepted that condition. It hampered and baffled my plans at every turn.

It was necessary therefore to find some method of altering the war direction which would not involve the shock to public opinion resulting from the abasement of men who had won a larger measure of confidence at home than they had amongst the survivors of the men whom they had driven into the Flemish charnel house.

We had to remove the fundamental cause of the failures of 1915, 1916, and 1917. What was it? The blind and stupid refusal to accept the principle of the single front. Theoretically and rhetorically the united front was boomed; in practice it was ignored. Each G.H.Q. concentrated on its own front. They gave no conscientious or coördinated thought to other flanks which were equally important and at a given moment might be more vital to the fortunes of the Alliance. When from another side of the immense battlefield, our Allies sent a cry of despair, then a little assistance was scraped together — always belated. The full platters were for the trenches where they were commanding; for the real need there were only scraps. Russia, France, Britain and Serbia were just Allies; they were not comrades fighting the same battle for a common cause. Joffre, Haig and Cadorna were entitled to say, "We have been entrusted with the conduct of the fight on this particular sector. The business entrusted to us is to beat the enemy in front of us. In order to do so we must secure as many men and as much material as can be spared for our enterprise. It is for the statesmen, with such advice as they can command, to survey the battle area as a whole on land and sea, to examine the needs and possibilities, to make their plans and to dispose of their resources to the best advantage." That was nominally the position. In practice, there was no such distribution of functions. All Governments had their expert military counsellors attached to their War Ministries. But in ability and especially in prestige, they were so far inferior to the Commanders-in-Chief of the principal Army in the field that the opinions of the former were ridden down.

In France even Gallieni had not been able to stand up to Joffre. Robertson was terrified of Haig and never dared to utter or mutter a doubt as to his strategy. He himself has admitted that he had serious misgivings about Passchendaele, but not one word of scepticism passed his lips. The first Chief of Staff who was able and influential enough to give independent guidance to his Government was Foch. But taking the position as a whole, Governments were at the mercy of the Commanders-in-Chief. That is why it came to pass that the War was conducted sectionally. How disastrous were the consequences of this we realised before the end of 1917. The failure to help Russia in 1915 and 1916 with guns, munitions and transport when she had overwhelming reserves of men, ultimately forced her out of the War — crushed, and angry with the allies who refused to equip her brave peasants with the means to defend themselves. The French and British Commanders-in-Chief wanted all the men and material to win victories on their own fronts. It would not be just to say that they were prejudiced even unconsciously by the thought that feathers in Russky's and Brussiloff's hats did not look nearly as well as they did in their own; but they were influenced by the knowledge that their particular job was to beat the Germans in the swamps of Flanders and not in the Pripet Marshes, and they concentrated mind and will on the duties assigned to them. To the same cause may be ascribed the fatal betrayal of Serbia, which gave Bulgaria and the Balkans to the Central Powers, saved Austria from the danger of being speared on her most exposed side, revived the military powers of Turkey and prolonged the War by two years, endangering ultimate victory.

The Commanders-in-Chief needed all the men and machinery to break through in France, so the greatest chance of the War, being elsewhere, must be neglected. We had the same experience in 1917. An offensive against Austria which would have converted her desire for peace into an urgent necessity, was turned down in favour of colossal attacks in France and in Flanders, both of which were colossal fiascos ending in colossal losses. The only Allied military successes of the year 1917 were won in the despised East, where two of the most famous cities of the world, Jerusalem and Baghdad, fell into Allied hands, and the Turkish military façade was smashed in and the hollowness behind exposed. Had this been done in 1915 or 1916, Turkey would have been out of the War. Access to Russia and the Danube by sea would have been opened and hundreds of thousands of men hitherto locked up in sham fights with the Turk — childish exhibitions of the prod and run-away sort — would have been available for other fronts.

The only operation where the common front had been the basic principle was the organisation and dispatch of a combined French and British Expeditionary Force to Italy after Caporetto. That had been a decisive success. It redeemed a desperate situation. But the preparations had been suggested and urged by British Ministers at the Rome Conference. The generals had reluctantly acquiesced.

A mere change in commanders and War Office advisers would not alter the intrinsic defect which led direct to these failures in Allied strategy. The French had changed their Commanders-in-Chief, but Nivelle was only Joffre writ small. They changed their Chiefs of Staff repeatedly and nothing happened except a change in the signature appended to War Office documents. I came to the conclusion therefore that the removal of Haig and Robertson would not touch the real problem, but that there must be a more thorough and essential change in the whole method of conduct of Allied strategy if we were to win. I was of opinion that the only way out of the *impasse* was to set up an authoritative Inter-Allied body which would have its own Staff and its own Intelligence Department who, working together, would review the battlefield as a whole and select the most promising sector for concentrated action. The essential conditions for the efficacious working of such a body would be:

(1) That whilst it would be necessarily in constant touch with the various G.H.Q.'s it should be entirely independent of their control.

(2) That the experts should be men of unquestioned ability and mastery of their respective professions.

(3) That Ministers should be represented on that body so that they should be consulted on questions of policy whilst plans were being considered. Hitherto the plans of campaign had only been submitted to the Governments after they had been formulated and fashioned and agreed to by the Military Staffs in every detail. It was the Governments alone who could decide such vital questions as the available man power, shipping, finance, blockade and diplomatic expedients. But hitherto plans had been prepared to the last details without their ever being consulted. No sound plans could be formed by such methods.

(4) Naval experts must also constitute one integral element in the composition of the Inter-Allied Staff. Sea power turned out to be the decisive factor in the end. Up to 1917 there had not even been an Inter-Allied Naval Conference. It is amazing that with a full knowledge of the importance of sea power, statesmen and naval experts had not up to this date been called into effective consultation when campaigns for the coming year were being settled by the military chiefs. They were consulted when a particular operation was de-

pendent on the active coöperation of the Navy — for instance, Gallipoli and the battle for clearing the Flanders coast. But that was taking much too narrow a view of the vast battle area of the War. The sea front was as essential to victory as the Western or any other front, and it was impossible rightly to judge the wisdom or otherwise of the general campaign without understanding thoroughly how the command of the sea would affect the military situation and especially the economic conditions which determined the equipment and morale of the various belligerents.

Campaigns must therefore be prepared which would take the naval situation into account as an essential element.

These points are admirably elucidated by Sir William Robertson in a paper he submitted to the Cabinet — alas, only at the end of 1917.

> . . . Further, the question of the Entente outlasting Germany to such an extent as to be able to dictate terms of peace to her is obviously affected by many political, social and economic conditions of the different Entente countries with which I am imperfectly acquainted, and regarding which, indeed, no one can give an accurate forecast. Of no less importance are the naval and shipping situations, as to which also I can express no opinion. It is therefore quite impossible for me to give a definite and comprehensive reply to the question, and I accordingly wish it to be understood that what is said below is not intended to be a complete answer, but to be considered in conjunction with the other numerous considerations of a non-military character.
>
> If we were engaged in a war in which the British Army alone was fighting a single belligerent, and in which considerations other than those of a purely military nature were of little or no account, the General Staff ought to be able to give an opinion with reasonable accuracy. But nothing resembling these conditions obtains in the present stupendous struggle, which is not a war merely of armies, but of some twenty or more nations, and draws

into its vortex every branch of national life. *The chief factors about which I am necessarily ignorant* and which prevent me from being more explicit in my replies, are the extent to which the Royal Navy expect to cope with the submarine menace and generally to secure our sea communications, the shipping position, the rate at which American troops will be put into the field, the staying power of the Entente, and the number of men to be supplied to the British Army during 1918. . . . Nor do I know what personnel the Navy requires, what it has got, how it is employed, what number or class of ships are needed, what are being constructed, what labour is required in the shipyards, and whether it could be further diluted. Nor do I pretend to know the possibilities of offensive and defensive naval action. . . . I suggest, with every respect and deference, that the allotment and employment of our resources of all kinds merit further investigation. When this has been made it will, I think, be possible for the War Cabinet to reach a safer and clearer conclusion as to our prospects of winning the War than they are able to reach from the restricted and indefinite replies I have been compelled to give. . . . Our task is to do our utmost to ensure holding our own until America arrives, and meanwhile make every endeavour to expedite her arrival. . . .

Why was he "necessarily ignorant" of these vital factors? They were all accessible to him at any time. Up to the present he does not seem to have sought them. He had formed his judgments and advised the Government on strategy, whilst he admits that he "did not pretend" to know, and had not taken the trouble to investigate facts and conditions which were essential to a sound opinion.

The civilian and naval experts who alone could give reliable advice on all these "chief factors" had never been called into council in the planning of campaigns, the success of which depended on these considerations. The failure of the Chantilly strategy in 1917 convinced me there must be a fundamental change in the method of settling our military policy.

The real weakness of Allied strategy was that it never existed. Instead of one great war with a united front, there were at least six separate and distinct wars with a separate, distinct and independent strategy for each. There was some pretence at timing the desperate blows with a rough approach to simultaneity. The calendar was the sole foundation of Inter-Allied strategy. Let us each hit as we like, where we choose, and with such weapons as we each have at our disposal — but all hit at the same time. There was no real unity of conception, coördination of effort or pooling of resources in such a way as to deal the enemy the hardest knocks at his weakest point. There were so many national armies, each with its own strategy and its own resources to carry it through. Neither in men, guns or ammunition was there any notion of distributing them in such a way as to produce the greatest results with the available resources of the Alliance as a whole. There had been no genuine endeavour to pool brains with a view to surveying the whole vast battlefield and to deciding where and how the most effective blows could be struck at the enemy. Before 1917 no general that mattered in the East had ever met a military leader who counted in the West. The two-day conferences of great generals which were held late each autumn to determine the campaign for the ensuing year, were an elaborate handshaking reunion. They had all of them come to the meeting with their plans in their pockets. There was nothing to discuss.

It was essential that a body should be set up for common thinking for the next campaign.

As soon as I was convinced that it was essential that the future of the War must be subject to advice given by an independent body, organised on these lines, I took steps to sound the Allies on the point. I first of all communicated with President Wilson:

"3rd September, 1917.

"Dear President Wilson,

Views on the Conduct of the War

"I am taking advantage of the visit of Lord Reading to Washington to lay in front of you certain views about the conduct of the War which I have formed in the light of my experience during the last three years. We are approaching a very difficult period in which it will be necessary to take far-reaching decisions which will be of the utmost importance as regards our future campaign — decisions which will be of vital moment to all the Armies in the field. In arriving at these decisions I think it is essential that the heads of the British and the United States Governments should fully understand one another's views. I avail myself of this method of communication because I do not wish my remarks to have an official character. I am only anxious that you should, as far as that is possible without direct conversation, be in full possession of my views.

"First of all as to the general strategy to be followed in the prosecution of the War during the winter of 1917–1918 and the spring and summer of 1918. The hard fact which faces us to-day is that in spite of the efforts of the Allies to raise and equip armies and to manufacture munitions, in spite of their superiority in men and material and the perfection to which they have brought their offensive arrangements, the Germans at the end of 1917 as at the end of each of the previous years' campaigns, find themselves in possession of more and not less Allied territory. By the end of 1917, the Allies had confidently expected to have produced very serious inroads on the German military power, even if they did not succeed in overthrowing it altogether. Their failure is, of course, mainly attributable to the military collapse of Russia. It is also true to say that in every other respect, politically and economically, the Germanic combination is far weaker than it has ever been. But I am convinced from my experience of the last three years that *the comparative failure of the Allies in 1917 is also in some measure due to defects in their mutual arrangements for conducting the War.*

"As compared with the enemy, the fundamental weakness of the Allies is that the direction of their military operations lacks real unity. At a very early stage of the War, Germany established a practically despotic dominion over all her allies. She not only reorganised their armies and assumed direction of the military strategy, but she took control also over their economic resources so that the *Central Empires and Turkey to-day are to all intents and purposes a military Empire with one command and one front. The Allies on the other hand have never followed suit.* The direction of the War on their side has remained in the hands of four separate Governments and four separate General Staffs (namely those of France, Great Britain, Italy and Russia) each of which is possessed of complete knowledge only of its own front and its own national resources, and which draws up a plan of campaign which is designed to produce results mainly on its own section of front. The defects of this system have not been lost sight of. From time to time of late with greatly increased frequency, there have been International Conferences to discuss the Allied war plans. But up to the present these Conferences have done little more than attempt to synchronise what are in reality four separate plans of campaign. *There has never been an Allied Body which had knowledge of the resources of all the Allies and which could prepare a single coördinated plan for utilising those resources in the most decisive manner, and at the most decisive points, looking at the front of the Central Powers as a whole and taking into account their political, economic and diplomatic as well as their military weaknesses.*

"*At the forthcoming Conferences,* which will assemble as soon as the results of the present offensives have become clear, *I shall urge the imperative importance of establishing more effective unity in the Allied strategy.* The policy we have pursued hitherto has been to concentrate all our attacks on Germany, on the ground that Germany is the mainspring of the hostile alliance, that it is therefore sound policy to try and knock out her army first, even though it is the strongest with which we are confronted, because if we succeed, all the rest will collapse with it. In consequence, for more than three years, the armies of the main Allies have been engaged each summer in a series of terrific and most costly offensives against the strongest part of the enemy line — offensives which have never yet produced any decisive results in breaking down the enemy military organisation. He still opposes a solid and hitherto impenetrable defence. That we have continued to pursue it so long despite the great changes which have come over the general character of the War, is, I believe, mainly due to the fact that there has been no body in existence on the Allied side which could consider the military problem as a whole regardless of the traditions which have grown up in each army, and of the national prejudices and prepossessions of the several Allies in the use of their forces.

"Before committing ourselves to a repetition of these frontal assaults, I feel that we are bound to study the position, especially with the view of determining whether there is not an alternative plan of campaign. For some time past, it has seemed to me that we ought to consider very carefully whether we cannot achieve decisive results by concentrating first against Germany's allies. In favour of this latter policy it can be urged that the opposing armies are now on parallel lines from one end of every front to the other, and that the War is now practically a siege of the Central Empires, to which must be applied the principles of siege warfare. In a siege you do not seek out the strongest part of the enemy line, but the weakest, in the hope that if you break down the defence there, the position as a whole will be turned. To-day, the weakest part of the enemy line is unquestionably the front of Germany's allies. They are weak not only militarily but politically. They are also very anxious for peace, so that a comparatively small success might produce far-reaching results. Moreover, just inasmuch as their armies have been controlled and their resources organised by Germany as part of the defence of their new Empire of Mittel-Europa, to attack them is to strike at Germany to a far greater extent than was the case in the early days of the War. It is to knock away the props upon which the German military power now increasingly depends.

If this were once done, if the inability of the Prussian military machine to defend its allies were thus proved, and the dream of Eastern dominion thus destroyed by the defection of one of these allies, the whole enemy military edifice might fall rapidly in ruins.

"There is another aspect of the case. In Northern Europe it is only possible to carry on an intense campaign for six, or at most seven, months of the year. It so happens that these winter months are the best campaigning season in Southeastern Europe and Turkey and Asia. It seems to be doubtful if we have ever made really adequate use of the Allied forces to achieve decisive results in the Southeastern theatre during the periods when they could not be employed on the main fronts.

"I need not go further into the strategical question at issue. What I have said will be sufficient, I think, to make it clear that if we are to make the best possible use of the forces at the disposal of the Allies, it is of supreme importance to establish effective unity in the direction of the War on the Allied side. If we are to avoid wasted effort and wanton loss of life, those who draw up the plan of campaign must have full knowledge of the resources of all the Allies, not only in men and munitions, but in shipping, railway material, and so forth, so as to determine how they can best be employed against the enemy organisation. *In my opinion it will be necessary to establish some kind of Allied Joint Council, with permanent military and probably naval and economic staffs attached to work out the plans for the Allies, for submission to the several Governments concerned.*

"This brings me to the second question to which I would like to draw your attention. It relates to the representation of the United States at the councils of the Allies. I fully appreciate the objections which the American people feel to being drawn into the complex of European politics. The British people have always attempted to keep themselves aloof from the endless racial and dynastic intrigues which have kept Europe so long in a state of constant ferment, and even to-day their main desire is to effect a settlement which will have the elements of peaceful permanence in itself, and so free them and the rest of the world from the necessity of further interference. These feelings must naturally be far stronger in America. I have not, therefore, the slightest desire that the United States should surrender the freedom of action which they possess at present.

"At the same time, there are, in my opinion, very strong reasons why the United States should consider whether they ought not to be represented at the conferences of the Allies. To begin with, I think the presence of a representative of the United States at the conference which will determine the future strategy of the War, would be of the utmost value to the Allied cause. I do not say this merely because the decisions will vitally affect the American Army in Europe. I attach great importance to it for this reason. But another reason weighs still more strongly with me. I believe that we are suffering to-day from the grooves and traditions which have grown up during the War, and from the inevitable national prejudices and aspirations which consciously or unconsciously influence the judgment of all the nations of Europe. I believe that the presence at the deliberations of the Allies of independent minds, bringing fresh views, unbiased by previous methods and previous opinions, might be of immense value in helping us to free ourselves from the ruts of the past, and to avoid having our armies drawn into a strategy which is bound to be immensely costly, and which may not be that calculated to give us the best results.

"There is another reason. We have now reached a point when it is becoming more and more difficult to maintain, not only the national unity of each of the Allies, but unity among the Allies themselves in the vigorous prosecution of the War. Every nation in Europe is becoming exhausted. The desire for peace in some quarters is becoming almost irresistible. The argument that any kind of peace is better than a continuation of the present suffering and carnage is daily increasing its appeal. At the same time people are beginning to ask themselves whether victory is obtainable at all and this question will be asked with all the greater insistence in a few weeks' time if the end of the campaigning season shows that the whole campaign of 1917 has made no decisive impression upon the German military position. There is no question that victory is within our power. It may be nearer than any of us can reasonably calculate. But if it is to be obtained, it will only be because the free nations exhibit greater moral unity and greater tenacity in the last desperate days than the servants of autocratic power. The preservation of that moral unity and tenacity will be our principal task during the forthcoming winter, and I believe that it depends more and more upon the British Commonwealth and the United States. This does not mean, of course, that our Allies are not fighting as vigorously and as valiantly as ever. It rather means that for one reason or another they have mobilised their national resources to the utmost point of which they are capable without having overthrown the enemy, and that consciously or unconsciously they rely upon the British and the Americans to supply that additional effort which is necessary in order to make certain of a just, liberal and lasting peace. As you may be aware, the appearance of the vanguard of the American Army has produced a tremendous effect, especially in France. I would ask you to consider, therefore, whether it is not of the utmost importance that the purpose and ideals as well as the wisdom of America should be manifested in the Council Chamber as well as the battlefield, if we are to preserve unshaken during this difficult winter season the resolution of the Allies to go on with the War until Prussian military despotism over Germany and her allies is broken, by revolution from within or defeat from without. I recognise, of course, that there are grave difficulties in the way, but I feel that I ought to put in front of you the immense importance to the success of our cause which I believe attaches to the manifestation at the Conferences of the Allies of the determination of America to prosecute the War with her whole strength, and of her confidence in ultimate victory.

"In conclusion may I say how much we all here have appreciated the speeches you have made about the War. If you will permit me to say so, I believe that your statements have been not the least important of the contributions which America is making to the cause of human freedom. They have not only been a profound and masterly exposition of the Allied case. They have recalled to many the ideals with which they entered upon the War, and which it is easy to forget amid the horrors of the battlefield and the overtime and fatigue in the munition shops. They have given to the bruised and battered peoples of Europe fresh courage to endure and fresh hope that with all their sufferings they are helping to bring into being a world in which freedom and democracy will be secure, and in which free nations will live together in unity and peace.

Sincerely yours,

D. LLOYD GEORGE."

How President Wilson responded to this appeal will be seen when we come to the action he took to give practical support to the Inter-Allied Council which was set up in November, on the lines indicated in this letter.

Before coming to any final decision as to the course which I should recommend to the Cabinet and to the Allies for the future conduct of the campaign, I invited Sir Douglas Haig's views on the subject. Unfortunately when he dictated his review of the military prospect, he was absorbed in the conduct of one of the greatest and most prolonged battles ever fought. In spite of the huge armies engaged on both sides it was fought on a narrow front. He had just captured a small Flemish village and his whole mind was now concentrated on reaching the next hamlet half a kilometre further on. The inevitable visual compression involved in such a task, together with the mental ferment of battle, were not conducive to a broad and calm survey of the stupendous problem of carrying on a struggle in three continents and over immense seas. You feel that throughout this document his mind is stuck in the mud. He never gets out of it from the first paragraph to the last. His review of the World War is limited by the Passchendaele Ridge a few hundred yards above his front line. That is his horizon. If you storm that, all the rest will be added unto you. Beyond that range of vision you can gallop through easily to a final triumph.

In his appreciation of the military situation, he started with the very obvious proposition:

. . . that if the power of resistance of the German Armies were once broken down completely, or even manifestly on the point of breaking down, Germany and her allies would gladly accept such terms of peace as the Allies might offer.

We now know that all Germany's allies had broken down completely before her own Armies gave in, and accepted the humiliating terms dictated to her. Had Austria, Turkey, and Bulgaria kept on fighting, Germany would not have been the first to surrender, and she certainly would not have submitted to such conditions of peace.

The Haig memorandum then proceeds not so much to review the military prospects, as to justify the continuation of his Flanders offensive.

The first question to be answered, therefore, is: Are we justified, under the conditions postulated by the Prime Minister, in basing our plans on a belief in the feasibility of overcoming the resistance of the German Armies by direct attack before the endurance of the British Empire, and its Allies remaining in the field, breaks down?

If the answer to that question is in the affirmative, our course is clear. If it be in the negative, the next question is, — what better course is open to us and our Allies?

He says he will deal, briefly, with the second question first. He does not so much deal with as dispose briefly — very briefly — of all the various alternative courses which were then open to us. He brushes aside scornfully the various plans proposed for gaining "some success against the Turks, or possibly, against the Austrians." His main argument against them is that "every addition to our strength in the East entails a corresponding weakening of our efforts in the West", and in another phrase, "my armies might be reduced to the defensive." Following an example which had been repeatedly set by Sir William Robertson, he uses two quite contradictory arguments. One is that the Germans might follow us to other theatres and check us there. And the other is that the Germans would remain in France and assume the offensive against our weakened forces there. He is alarmed about "the effect on our Allies (including America), on the peoples of the British Empire, on public opinion throughout the world, and not least in the East, and on the enemy", of a cessation "of offensive operations in the Western Theatre."

The implication is that if he discontinued his muddy campaign at Passchendaele it would seriously disconcert and depress the Allies. So he dismisses contemptuously "the various indirect means which have been suggested to sap Germany's power by operating against her allies."

He makes the admission that "there are conditions under which such indirect action is wise, and offers the best chance of success in war: but those conditions do not obtain for us in this war."

Therefore there was no alternative but for us to go on with the offensive in front of Ypres, which he assures us "continues to make good progress."

There are the familiar assurances that:

> . . . the enemy is undoubtedly considerably shaken, and the ground we have already gained gives us considerable advantages and renders us less dependent on weather in following up our success further. Our troops are elated and confident: those on the enemy's side cannot but be depressed, and we have good evidence of it.
>
> In these circumstances it is beyond question that our offensive must be pursued as long as possible.

The output of optimistic slosh was at this date at its maximum in quantity and quality. The looms of the victory mills were then working overtime at G.H.Q. The radiant fabrics turned out by the Intelligence Factory were dazzling the deluded public who saw nothing of the terrible conditions of the battle.

The Commander-in-Chief was the most important of those who were taken in. This document reveals his condition. I have already exhibited some patterns of the glittering stuff sent across the Channel from the Château of Beauquesne. Here are a few more samples, and as they have a bearing upon the campaign of 1918 I put them down here.

> The considerable wastage imposed on the enemy by a continued offensive (this he explains will take a few weeks more), may be expected to leave at the end of the year but a small balance, if any, of the five hundred thousand men in the reserves he now has available.

That is a fair illustration of the state of morbid exaltation into which Haig had worked himself. Between October 8th and the end of the Passchendaele campaign, he anticipated wiping out nearly half a million Germans! He is elevated by his triumph above all comprehension of the grim facts. He ignores completely the fact that he was wasting his own fighting men and reserves at the rate of five to three of the enemy. The German Army would be decimated and enfeebled: the British Army would be stronger than ever. He assures us that the defection of Russia would make no appreciable difference to his chance of success. He bases his confidence on his belief, not only that the enemy reserves would be exhausted, but that the German troops that survived Passchendaele would be such poor material that they could be held in 1918 by mutinous Russians and discouraged French soldiers, whilst he continued his smashing offensive up to the final scattering of the tattered remnants of Germany's great Army. He takes no account of the immense losses sustained in his own Army in picked men and experienced officers, and the exhaustion and resentment created in the survivors by this delirium of unbridled authority which had tortured them almost to the limits of human endurance. His assurance is undimmed by the fact that:

. . . though the French cannot be expected to admit it officially, we know that the state of their armies, and of the reserve man-power behind the armies, is such that neither the French Government nor the military authorities will venture to call on their troops for any further great and sustained effort.

He continues:

Though they are staunch in defence and will carry our useful local offensives against limited objectives, French armies would not respond to a call for more than that, and the authorities are well aware of it.

Then he adds a sentence which is very ominous of the intoxicated state of his mind, when he protests that the French dare not call on their troops for any such further effort "at any rate before it becomes evident that the enemy's strength has been definitely and finally broken."

He was not daunted "even though Russia should collapse entirely and despite the weakened state of France and Italy."

As he puts it: ". . . the British army alone can be made capable of a great offensive effort."

Without any help from crumbling or crouching Allies, he would, before this battle was over, have reduced the German Army to a state where they would have their best men put out of action, their reserves destroyed and their spirits broken so that they could easily be disposed of next year by the victorious British Army rested and replenished with such assistance as the French, the Americans and Portuguese might be able to afford by holding up the Germans on their respective fronts.

There were certain stipulations which, he said, were conditions precedent to this achievement by his Army. The first was that we must take over no more French line. The French troops were good enough to hold trenches, but they were incapable of a great offensive. That must be left to the British, but they must not be wasted in mere defensive tasks. Therefore, if the French pressed us to take over more line, it was "necessary to refuse . . . and to adhere resolutely to that refusal, even to the point of answering threats by threats if necessary."

The second stipulation was that we must supply him with all the men, munitions and aeroplanes he asked for. The difficulties we were experiencing at home in finding men to fill the appalling rents caused by the slaughter in Flanders he completely ignored. He must have the men. It was our business to find them. His was only to use them up. The third condition was that he was to have the final say in the strategy of 1918. Such failures as had occurred had been entirely attributable to the fact that we had been overruled in military policy by the French. "We must insist upon occupying the predominant position in the Councils of the Allies to which our strength entitled us."

In fact, the crashing victory of Passchendaele justified us in demanding the military hegemony of the Alliance. French, Americans, Italians and Russians would have to bow to the will of the only victors in the fight.

The concoctions of Haig's Intelligence Staff had clearly gone to his head, and he was therefore not in a state of mind to give us sober advice. We then turned to Sir William Robertson for his views. He was in substantial agreement with the conclusions arrived at by Sir Douglas Haig, although he does not commit himself to the exultant views of the Commander-in-Chief as to the triumphs of Passchendaele. At that time, he was beginning to be troubled with hesitancies about the Flanders campaign. He loyally kept them from the Government he served. He only revealed them to the British people years after the disclosure had ceased to be of any service to them or their valiant sons. In his paper reviewing the military position, he completely overlooks the great battle that was then raging as if its outcome would not affect the position either way. He relies rather on accepted commonplaces such as that "no country ever has had, or probably ever will have, sufficient resources to seek a decision in two theatres at the same time."

. . . .

"The first rule of all wars is to concentrate in the main theatre all forces that can be supplied. Any departure from this rule has invariably proved to be disastrous."

I wonder what Grant would have said to this rule when Sherman was sent marching through Georgia in order to turn the Confederate flank!

When there are several theatres, a decision ought to be sought where it is most likely to be found. In any war or battle the decisive theatres vary according to fluctuating conditions. It is only the generals who see the flank on which opportunity has arisen and take it without hesitation that win victories.

Robertson is very bitter about the French:

> Politics have there largely taken the place of patriotism. French Ministers are thinking mainly of the rear, and not of the front of their Armies — that is, of the pressure likely to be put upon them by Deputies who are interested in releasing this or that class of men from the Armies, and not of the great military problems which face the Entente.

This is rather hard on a people who had made such tremendous sacrifices and who had called to the Army one out of every seven of the population. He is just as contemptuous about the Americans:

"The people moreover are beginning to be sceptical of the Americans winning the War."

Then comes the inevitable conclusion:

"For the above and many other reasons, it seems to me most unwise to weaken our efforts on the Western Front."

As to any idea of a campaign in Palestine, he had never been able to regard it as a sound military measure:

> The right military course to pursue is to act on the defensive in Palestine and the East generally, and to continue to seek a decision in the West. . . . It entails, of course, that all resources should be sent to the West Front, other than those which are absolutely required for the defence of our Eastern positions.

He is very suspicious about the idea of Unity of Command:

"The principle of 'Unity of Command' and 'one front' must be cautiously applied. In theory it is attractive, in practice it has not been encouraging."

He insists that we should give the Allies a strong military lead. Here he follows Sir Douglas Haig's hint. Unity of Command must mean that the Commandment must be ours. He then ends with the demand that there should be more men, and he has left us in no doubt that they are wanted to continue the offensive on the one and only front where the altars were adequate to the immensity of the sacrifice.

In order to enlighten the Cabinet on the military position and to test and fortify my own judgment on the action which I was inclined to take, I decided to seek independent expert opinion. I saw that Robertson, if he had views independent of Haig's opinions, was stubbornly bent on keeping them to himself, and that he would do nothing to stop throwing our men into the Flemish shambles until Haig was ready to give up. Of that there was no hope until the winter set in. Haig was constitutionally incapable of changing plans he had once prepared and set his mind on carrying through. I therefore followed a precedent set in August, 1914, when Mr. Asquith called into his first War Council not only the Commander-in-Chief of the Expeditionary Forces and the Chief of Staff but other distinguished soldiers like Lord Roberts, Sir Douglas Haig and Sir Henry Wilson. I decided to ask the opinion of Lord French, then commanding the Home Forces, and Sir Henry Wilson. They were invited to attend a meeting of the War Cabinet on October 11th, which was also attended by Sir William Robertson, and asked to give their considered opinion on the military outlook in view especially of the Russian collapse, and also on the best methods of solving our difficulties in the face of that collapse. They naturally asked for time to frame their replies to such grave questions and they also asked whether the War Office would furnish them with all the information at its disposal which would enable them to form an accurate judgment as to the position. Sir William Robertson promised to see that this was done. Haig had been asked to attend but stated that he had already given his views in writing.

After a thorough examination of the information submitted to them by the War Office, including the document written by Sir Douglas Haig, from which I have quoted, both Lord French and Sir Henry Wilson each submitted a memorandum to the Cabinet on October 20th. These memoranda contain a very elaborate and highly interesting survey of the whole military position. A few extracts will give an idea of their substance. Lord French, in dealing with a statement by Sir Douglas Haig that his attacks in Flanders would have a greater effect upon our prestige in the East than any operations on the Eastern or Southeastern Fronts, says:

Sir Douglas Haig's estimate of the effect produced upon the minds of "the leading men in the East" by the operations on the

Western Front is in my view largely illusory. I do not believe that the people of India or Egypt, or the Middle East generally, or even of the Far East, take such interest in the Western Front. I should say that India is perhaps interested to a limited extent in what has happened internally in Russia, and that it takes a general interest in the welfare of the Allies; but I should also imagine that India and the East took more interest in the capture of Baghdad than in all the battles on the Western Front after the first definite setback of Germany in September, 1914, which was a thing they could understand. The Mohammedans probably do not look much beyond Turkey. In any case, fighting battles on the Western Front to impress the East, or even to impress the German people is not a good military reason, and I am sure that with the possible exception of any action which is very far-reaching and decisive, the East will always be far more impressed by what happens at its own doors, in which I include Palestine.

He then proceeds to deal with the Field Marshal's summary of the position on the Western Front:

He draws a vital distinction between 135 divisions which have been "broken by their losses" and are therefore of low fighting value, and 12 which he presumably considers to be good.

On what evidence does he draw this distinction or make this assumption? Have not many of our own divisions at certain points in the line been "driven from their position, or withdrawn, broken by their losses, since April, 1917"? Have not many, if not all of them, gone on again and succeeded? And do we not still count all alike as effective units in the line of battle?

He then casts a doubt upon Sir Douglas's statement about the great wastage suffered by the German Army, and on his estimate that the Germans had suffered fifty per cent. greater casualties than we had. He talks of Sir Douglas Haig's optimism as to the effect produced by his various offensives:

Up to a very short time ago Sir Douglas Haig's own utterances in public: his statements to people who interviewed him: his secret messages to the War Cabinet: and his assurances to the troops under his command, all expressed the firm conviction which had complete possession of his mind that he could break the enemy's line in such a manner as to pour large bodies of cavalry through the gap he had made and compel a great German retreat.

As a matter of fact, masses of cavalry were actually brought up to points close behind the trenches, in this hope and expectation.

He summarises in the light of accomplished facts the results which have been achieved by the various offensives:

Taking a complete clearance of Northern France and Belgium as the least objective to ensure a military defeat of the German Army, we find that in 15 months' fighting (July 1st, 1916, to October 1st, 1917), 200 square miles have been gained out of an area of 13,500 square miles which are directly in front of the British forces.

These results have been attained at a cost of upwards of one million killed, wounded and missing.

The answer will, of course, be: "We have put a great many more Germans *hors de combat,* and their morale and fighting efficiency have been heavily damaged."

I submit that there is not sufficient evidence to justify such a conclusion.

As to a paper showing comparative casualties which had been shown to him by the General Staff, and where it was computed that the enemy had lost 255,000 men on the Ypres Front alone between July 31st and October 5th, he says:

If this is really so, and the pressure we exert is so enormous, why are they able to embark on their present Russian activities, or form two new divisions for service in Asia Minor, as we have been informed by the General Staff they are in process of doing?

Personally, I entertain grave doubts as to whether we have not been playing the German game throughout the whole of our operations in the last year and a half.

It seems to me very possible that they have made the most of the greatly enhanced power of the defensive, amongst which the element of "deception" is perhaps the most important. It is quite open to question whether they have not deliberately led us on to the capture of ground which is, in the long run, of little military importance to them, and which they know they never want to keep even if they could. It is by no means unlikely that their object throughout has been to hold us on the Western side, and to do so in such a manner as to invite our attack and impose enormous casualties upon us, with a minimum loss to themselves.

This possibility has been strengthened in my mind by numerous conversations I have had from time to time with officers from the front and from other sources.

He then quotes the "rule of war"[1] which Sir William Robertson had laid down as a principle which ought to guide the decision of the Cabinet:

In Para. 2 he lays down a "rule" of war, which he says must guide the decision of the War Cabinet, and which furnishes the basis of his subsequent argument.

In regard to this, Lord French says:

In some aspects I disagree with the C.I.G.S. The immense line held by the Allies from the Persian Gulf to the North Sea embraces several alternative theatres of war; and whilst it may be right to say that all our energies should be concentrated on *one at a time,* it does not by any means follow that the principal theatre should be always the same. This is particularly so when climatic conditions favour operations in one theatre, while they absolutely preclude them in another.

The history of Napoleon's campaigns affords many examples of this.

[1] See extract from Sir W. Robertson's memorandum, p. 529.

It appears to me that Sir William Robertson calls upon history to bear out his contention that, by every "rule of war", we should adopt the first alternative adumbrated by the Prime Minister.

I do not think that military history will support this view.

It is probable that after the experiences of the War, our ideas of strategy will undergo considerable modification.

The increased power conferred on the defence by modern weapons and inventions postpones a decision for so great a length of time that war, in a far greater degree than formerly, affects the innate resources and the vital power of a nation. The immense size of modern armies and the extent of territory over which they fight brings of necessity many different races and nationalities within the orbit of war influence. The submarine and the aeroplane bring new and untried factors into the problem.

For all these reasons political considerations enter much more than formerly into the problems of strategy. Many of the older "rules of war" are no longer applicable.

The C.I.G.S. further draws attention to the danger of "gambles" at this stage of the War, and he characterises as such the suggested operations in Syria. To my mind, the idea of staking the remainder of our resources on one desperate blow after another on the Western Front has become much more of a "gamble" than anything else we have undertaken in the War. This method has been given a very long and patient trial under the most favourable conditions. It has entailed enormous loss and produced comparatively little result. We might be justified in trying it further if we had an unlimited number of men, but we are not justified in risking in such a process, and after such a long trial, the very limited balance of our resources. Such an attempt, after the experience we have gained, would be a "gamble" of the very worst kind.

He has an interesting paragraph about the Nivelle offensive and the deprecatory reference made by Sir William Robertson to what he called "the Nivelle era and its consequences":

It is sought to depict the French attack of April in a very unfavourable light as compared with our own results at Ypres. Such a comparison is misleading.

General Nivelle made as long, if not a longer, advance than we have yet accomplished in the Ypres area. By his capture of the Chemin des Dames Ridge, the important railway communication between Soissons and Rheims was opened up and is now of the utmost value to the French.

If General Nivelle can be accused of failure, it could only be on the ground that he expressed himself too confidently as to what he could accomplish, and that he absolutely underrated the enemy's power of resistance. Have we not all been more or less guilty of such faults?

After very severe fighting, which had lasted since July 31st, and very heavy losses, we are not yet in complete possession of Passchendaele Ridge, but only of its southern extremity. This ridge extends some miles north of Passchendaele.

The further statement that "we can beat the Germans every time we fight them and inflict heavier losses than we ourselves suffer", is, in my judgment, somewhat optimistic.

He points out that, although Sir William Robertson condemns the principle of "unity of command" and "one front", when the idea is to centre them in the hands of a French or other general, it seems to be highly approved of if we can "acquire it for ourselves."

He then makes some searching comments on the functions of the C.I.G.S.:

Far be it from me to say that the Field-Marshal is not justified in feeling the utmost confidence in himself and his troops. But I think this most natural and commendable state of mind has somewhat warped his judgment in appreciating the situation on the Western Front. Confidence in themselves and their own troops, even though somewhat extravagant, is not to be deprecated in Commanders who are ever in close contact with their enemy. But when it is a question of directing a war which is going on over half the world, offering, for this reason, so many alternative possibilities, the conclusions arrived at and the recommendations made by any individual Commander in the field, must be subjected to the crucial test of exhaustive examination by the General Staff. Their functions are to take a deliberate and dispassionate survey of the whole situation, to form *their own* estimate of the results attained, to balance those results most carefully with the price paid for them in the shape of losses, expenditure of ammunition and wearing out of guns, and to keep ever in mind the limitation of the national resources in man-power and in every other respect. Finally, and above all, it is their duty to give completely independent advice to the Government.

Every statement, every estimate and every forecast made by the Commander-in-Chief in France, should be put to the most crucial test.

After making a close examination of the papers submitted to me, I have, rightly or wrongly, formed the opinion that this has not been done. Statements from the front have not been sufficiently tested as to their accuracy, and have, to a great extent, formed the basis of the war plan and schemes which are put forward for sanction by the War Cabinet.

He is careful to say that he does not wish anything in his memorandum to convey the impression that he underestimated the splendid work done by the Army in France:

They have delivered tactical blows under which the enemy has reeled: but this magnificent performance has led to no strategic result, and our limited resources in man-power will not allow us to reach a strategic end by tactical slogging alone.

He comes to the conclusion that:

. . . our strength, so far as our own forces are concerned, is being gradually sapped by the enemy in indecisive attacks which attain inadequate results and entail undue loss. If such results can ever become possible, they can only be brought about by husbanding our strength and resources with the greatest care, by awaiting a much fuller development of the fighting forces of the United States, and by careful coördination of the strategic possibilities and economising of resources of all the Allies on the Western Front. For these and other reasons mentioned before I do not think a *purely military* climax can be reached in 1918.

[This prediction was verified in the ultimate result. It was the Revolution behind the lines, attributable to the privations endured by the German population, coupled with the collapse of Germany's allies, that precipitated the end.]

It is my fixed belief that such coördination and economy can only be obtained by establishing a common coördinating authority over the whole front from the Adriatic to the North Sea.

As to the idea of making Syria for a time the theatre of war, he would have favoured the project, had time allowed:

Without underestimating these manifest drawbacks to making Syria for a time the main theatre of war, I would have favoured the project had time allowed.

If plans had been considered and the necessary arrangements made some months ago, I believe this alternative would have been the right one to adopt, and that the coming of the spring might have found us at peace with Turkey and Bulgaria.

As to an attack on the Italian Front, that would depend on the coöperation of France and the whole-hearted cooperation of the Italian Government. His main conclusion is that there ought to be a Superior Council of the Allies immediately set up:

I would therefore emphasise the extreme desirability of establishing at once a Superior Council of the Allies. It is only such a body that can thoroughly examine a joint scheme of action in all its bearings. The weight and influence of such a council must carry conviction to the minds of the several Allied Governments.

. . . That the representatives of the Allied Powers should meet together without delay to discuss the immediate formation and establishment of a Superior War Council . . . I think this body should be composed of the Prime Ministers or their selected representatives, and one or more Generals from each Allied country.

That the Supreme Council at once proceed to appreciate the general situation and to formulate plans.

I quite realise the difficulty in including Russia in these arrangements, but I do not regard her representation as absolutely essential.

Sir Henry Wilson's memorandum practically came to the same conclusion. He reviewed the military position from the standpoint of a confirmed Westerner:

If I may be allowed here to interpose a remark about myself, it is to say that I have always been (even years before the War broke out) and I shall always remain, an ardent "Westerner", for the simple reason that it is along the West Front that the bulk of the forces of our principal enemy is disposed and the death grapple must always be with those forces; but, on the other hand, I hold that this death grapple must be engaged in at the time and place and in the manner best suited to our cause.

It is no use throwing "decisive numbers at the decisive time at the decisive place" at my head if the decisive numbers do not exist, if the decisive hour has not struck or if the decisive place is ill-chosen.

We seem to be as confident of success when Russia and Roumania have collapsed and France is temporarily weakened as we were when all these three countries were capable of heavy offensive actions.

The German has done otherwise.

Finding in the winter of 1914 and 1915 and during the course of 1915 that he could not gain a final decision in the West or in the East, he at once turned his attention to other theatres and tried, sometimes successfully, sometimes unsuccessfully, for decisions in those theatres; thus, he failed in Mesopotamia and again in Egypt, but he succeeded in the Balkans, in Roumania and now in Russia. His underlying thought being that he would weaken his enemies in all theatres and strengthen himself, not only in territory, in food, in raw material, etc., but also in morale, and put himself in the position to mass a much larger number of troops in the decisive theatre (*i.e.*, in the West) when the time for the death grapple came.

It is incontestable that the German position is better to-day with all the gains I have mentioned above (*vis-à-vis* terms of peace) than it would be had they not gained Turkey and Bulgaria as allies, had they not effectively occupied Roumania, Poland, and part of Russia; had they in fact, during the last two years, restricted themselves to attempting a final decision, as we have done, in the main theatre, *i.e.*, the West.

I have made these comparisons of the application of a precept not in order to prove that the West is not the decisive front — because it is — but because it seems to me that the final decision can only be reached where decisive numbers are applied at the decisive place and at the decisive time, and the numbers and the place and the time are not yet, and the Germans are trying their best that they never shall be.

Curiously enough, our constant thought of a decision in the West — a frame of mind amounting almost to an obsession — has led us to consider only that part of the Western Front which is held by ourselves, and partly because of this and partly from other causes the tendency for the whole line from Nieuport to Trieste to be cut up into three sections — British, French, Italian — has become more and more accentuated. This is noticeable in Sir Douglas Haig's memorandum of October 8th, 1917, and the Chief of the Imperial General Staff's memorandum of October 9th, 1917, although the latter very wisely remarks that "the British Army alone cannot win the War. Our Allies must be made to fight."

He then leads up to the same conclusion as Lord French:

The superior direction of this war, has, in my opinion, been gravely at fault from the very commencement — in fact, it is inside the truth to say that there has never been any superior direction at all.

Up to the time when Marshal Joffre was removed from the Chief Command of the French he tried, with poor results indeed, but still he tried, to assume and exercise a kind of benevolent control over all the Allies, but his position was not sufficiently exalted, his powers were not sufficiently great to admit of success.

Since then we have tried many expedients but always with most disappointing, sometimes even with disastrous results. We have had frequent meetings of Ministers, constant conversations between Chiefs of Staff, deliberations of Commanders-in-Chief, mass meetings of all these high officials in London, in Paris, in Rome. We have tried the experiment of placing one Commander-in-Chief under the orders of another and all these endeavours have failed to attain any real concerted coördinated effort in diplomacy, in strategy, in fighting or in the production of war material. . . . I do not wish to exaggerate, but human nature being what it is and our Commanders-in-Chief and Chiefs of Staff being what they are — all men of strong and decided views, all men whose whole energies are devoted to their own fronts, and their own national concerns, we get as a natural and inevitable result a war conducted not as a whole, but as a war on sections of the whole, *i.e.*, a war on the British Front, a war on the French Front, a war on the Italian Front; and the stronger and the better the various Chiefs, the more isolated and detached the plans.

It seems to me that all this confusion, overlapping and loss of collective effort are due to the same causes which throughout the whole war have led to a narrow vision, and too limited outlook over the whole colossal struggle; and the better the sectional Commanders-in-Chief are, the more loyal and responsive the Chiefs of the Home Staffs, the more we see the whole of the national effort restricted to the national fronts.

The net result seems to me to be that we take short views instead of long views, we look for decisions to-day instead of laying out plans for to-morrow, and as a sequence we have constant change of plans, with growing and increasing irritation and inefficiency.

This is the picture that I see and that I have seen for a long time.

What can be done to remedy a state of affairs which is undoubtedly prolonging the War to an unnecessary, even to a dangerous extent?

The answer to this question lies in the establishment of an intelligent, effective and powerful superior direction. And by this I mean a small War Cabinet of the Allies so well-informed, and above all, entrusted with such power that its opinion on all the larger issues of the War will carry the weight of conviction and be accepted by each of the Allies as final. There is no question here of overruling the Home Cabinet, since the Supreme War Cabinet, or Superior Direction, as I have called it, will represent the Home Cabinets; nor is there the least danger of any interference with the soldiers in the field, since the Chiefs of Staff in each country will remain as to-day.

Such a Body will be above all Sectional Fronts, it would view the War as a whole, it would treat the line of battle from Nieuport to Mesopotamia as one line, and it would allot to each of the Allies the part which it would play. Perhaps I can make myself clearer if I take one or two concrete instances.

Such a Superior Direction would, two years or a year ago, have come to the conclusion as to whether we should have sought for a final decision *then,* on the Western Front, or whether the time for such an attempt should be postponed until a favourable decision had been reached in some of the minor theatres, thus enabling a larger force to be concentrated at a later date for the death grapple in the West.

Such a Superior Direction would *now* lay out the broad line of action for the next twelve or twenty-four months. It would show when and under what conditions and in which part of the main theatre the final decision should be attempted and reached.

This done, it would be in a position to settle the pending and vexed question of our taking over more line from the French — a question impossible to solve to the satisfaction of both parties if no plans for the future have been agreed to, but quite easy to solve when the broad lines of next year's campaign have been arranged.

It would lay out the broad policy for our joint aeroplane campaign of the future, and would adjust construction to obtain the end in view, allotting to each Ally the task for the future.

In short, such a Superior Direction would take over the Superior Direction of the War — a thing which has not yet been done, and for the lack of which we have suffered so grievously in the past and without which we shall, as certainly, suffer even more in the future.

The strain of this war increases day by day, and as the strain increases, so any mistakes that are made become increasingly dangerous, and the tendency for each of the Allies to fight for its own hand becomes more and more marked. I see no other way of drawing the Allies together and of keeping them together, of gradually enlarging the outlook and of showing the crying necessity for long views instead of short views, except by the creation of such a body. I see no other way by which a real plan of campaign for the future can be drawn up. Such a plan of campaign must be based on all the factors which go to make up this gigantic war. The greater part of these are unknown and necessarily and rightly unknown, to the Commanders-in-Chief in the field who, up till now, have dictated the strategy of the campaign, each on his own front.

Without such a body the tendency for the Allies will be to concentrate each on his own front, each on his own production, each on his own war, each thus drifting further and further from his neighbour, while all the time the enemy, under one governing authority, will be able to concentrate and to defeat each of the local efforts.

We (the Allies) hold all the cards in our hands — men, munitions, guns, aeroplanes, food, money *and* the High Seas — there remains only the question of how to play them and when to play them, and my absolute conviction is that there is no other way than by the creation of a Superior Direction.

On finding that my views as to an Inter-Allied War Council were supported so unreservedly by two of the ablest Generals in the British Army, I proceeded to sound French

Ministers on the point. I had several conferences on the theme of a United War Direction with M. Painlevé, the French Minister of War, to whom the same idea had occurred. On October 30th, I wrote him as follows:

"Dear M. Painlevé,

"I have been discussing with my colleagues for some time past the future strategy of the War. I have come to certain provisional conclusions which I am anxious to communicate to you without delay. I am, therefore, sending you this letter in the hope that after you have had time to consider it, we may be able to discuss together the matters to which it refers.

"The hard fact which stares us in the face to-day is that at the end of three years' strenuous war and after the utmost exertions on the part of the Allies, the German Government is still militarily triumphant. Despite all the battles won by the Allies this year — and these victories are undoubtedly brilliant — and the perfection of the equipment and training which the French and British Armies have reached and their valour in the field, the Germans have been able to end the year, not only with a military and naval success against Russia, but with a strategic victory of considerable magnitude over the Italians, a victory which has compelled us to send strong reinforcements to their assistance, and which may profoundly alter the face of the War.

"Even without this final disaster the campaign of 1917 would unquestionably have been a bitter disappointment to the Allies. At the outset they were confident that, as the result of a great converging movement directed against Germany, they would make a decisive impression upon the military position of the enemy alliance, if they did not overthrow its military organisation altogether. The failure to do so, has, of course, been mainly due to the collapse of the Russian Armies. It is also true that, as the result of the shortage of food and other essential supplies, the longing for peace among the peoples of the Central Empires has reached an intensity which threatens the disintegration of the whole combination. None the less, I am convinced from my experience of the last three years that the fact that the result of the third year's war is a definite military success for Germany and a definite military reverse for the Allies is in great measure also due to defects in their mutual arrangements for conducting the War.

"As compared with the enemy, the fundamental weakness of the Allies is that the direction of their military operations lacks real unity. At a very early stage of the War Germany established a practically despotic dominion over all her allies. She not only reorganised their armies and assumed direction of the military strategy, but she took control also over their economic resources, so that the Central Empires and Turkey are to-day, to all intents and purposes, a military Empire with one command and one front. The Allies, on the other hand, have never followed suit. The direction of the War on their side has remained in the hands of four separate Governments and four separate General Staffs, each of which is possessed of complete knowledge only of its own front and its own national resources, and which draws up a plan of campaign which is designed to produce results mainly on its own section of front. Attempts have been made to remedy the defects of this system by means of Inter-Allied Conferences, which have lately been of increased frequency. But up to the present these conferences have never been fully representative, and at best have done little more than attempt to synchronise what are in reality four separate plans of campaign. There has never been an Allied body which had the knowledge of the resources of all the Allies, which could prepare a single coördinated plan for utilising those resources in the most decisive manner, taking into account the political, economic, and diplomatic as well as the military weaknesses of the Central Powers.

"The crushing of Serbia and the opening of the road to the East in 1915, the total defeat of Roumania in 1916, and now the break-through in Italy in 1917, may be largely, although not entirely, traced to the attempt to conduct the War in a series of water-tight compartments. It is very remarkable that each winter the Central Powers have been able to make a crushing attack on the weakest member of the Entente with complete success while no adequate counter-preparation has been made by the Allies to meet the danger, and that during these same winters no corresponding serious efforts have been made by the Allies to weaken Germany by concentrating against her weaker allies and so destroying the props upon which her power depends. These results, which mean that the enemy has steadily deprived us of the preponderance of men and resources we would otherwise have possessed, while compelling us to squander our resources all over the globe without achieving decisive results anywhere, would probably never have happened, had there been any such unity of direction on the Allied side as exists in the case of the Germanic Alliance. If we are to win the War, it will only be because the Allied nations are willing to subordinate everything else to the supreme purpose of bringing to bear upon the Central Empires in the most effective manner possible, the maximum pressure military, economic, and political which the Allies can command.

"There is, I am sure, only one way in which this can be done, and that is by creating a joint council — a kind of Inter-Allied General Staff — to work out the plans and watch continuously the course of events, for the Allies as a whole. This council would not, of course, supersede the several Governments. It would simply be advisory to them, the final decisions, and the orders necessary to give effect to them, being given by the Governments concerned. But it would be a council possessed of full knowledge of the resources of all the Allies, not only in men and munitions, but in shipping, railway material and so forth, which would act as a kind of General Staff to the Alliance to advise as to the best methods of winning the War, looking at the fronts and the resources available as a whole. Its composition might be settled later. But provisionally I would suggest that it should consist of one, or perhaps two, political representatives of first-rate authority from each of the Allies, with a military staff of its own and possibly naval and economic staffs as well. The military representatives would remain in continuous session at whatever place was chosen as the scene of the Council's labours and could therefore not be the same people as the chiefs of the several national General Staffs, though they would have to be in the closest touch with them. It would also be the same with the naval and economic staffs if it were found necessary to attach them also.

"This brings me to the second point. I do not think it is possible to decide about the taking over of more line by the British without regard to the plan of campaign for next year. The question of who is to hold the line during the winter is inseparable from that of the character and extent of the offensive next year and the respective parts to be played by the various allies in that offensive, because the Armies which are to take the offensive must spend the winter in hard training. This is exactly the sort of question which would be referred to the Allied Council. I therefore consider that it is of the utmost urgency that a decision should be come to about the Council without delay, and if the proposal is approved that it should be constituted as soon as possible.

"I would, therefore, be greatly obliged, if you would let me know at your early convenience whether the French Government would support this idea and coöperate with us in giving effect to it.

Ever sincerely,
D. Lloyd George."

M. Painlevé came over to London to discuss the proposal set forth in that letter. On November 2nd, I reported to the Cabinet that I had seen him and that the French Government accepted the scheme for the establishment of a Supreme Inter-Allied Council and Permanent Advisory General Staff. General Pétain, whom I had also seen, cordially approved the scheme, and had expressed the opinion that, in view of the very serious position on the Italian Front, the new organisation should set to work as soon as possible.

After some discussion, the War Cabinet decided:

(*a*) To accept in principle the proposal for the establishment of a Supreme Inter-Allied Council consisting of the Prime Minister and one other Minister, who would meet at frequent intervals together with a Permanent Inter-Allied Advisory General Staff composed of one General Officer from each of the principal Allies.

(*b*) That Lieutenant-General Sir Henry Wilson should be appointed the British General on the Inter-Allied Advisory General Staff, and that it should be a recommendation to the Secretary of State for War that the appointment should carry with it the temporary rank of General. The Secretary of State for War expressed his approval of General Wilson's appointment.

(*c*) That the Secretary should formally communicate the two above decisions to the Secretary of State for War, who would notify his appointment to Lieutenant-General Sir Henry Wilson and arrange details as to his pay and staff.

(*d*) That no announcement in regard to the Supreme Inter-Allied Council and General Staff, or in regard to General Wilson's appointment, should be made until the attitude of the Italian Government towards the scheme had been ascertained.

(*e*) That the Secretary of State for Foreign Affairs should telegraph to the Italian Government the general lines of the scheme.

At the same meeting it was decided that owing to the gravity of the position on the Italian Front, arising out of the Caporetto disaster, I should at once leave for Italy to confer with the Italian Government. I communicated my intention to M. Painlevé and suggested that we should settle the draft of our plan for a Supreme Inter-Allied Council at Paris on our way to Italy, and take immediate steps to set it up. I sent on to him the draft we had prepared in order to give him time to study it carefully, and he replied to me as follows:

"Paris,
4th November, 1917.

"Dear Prime Minister,

"I have the honour to acknowledge receipt of your letter of 30th October, which I have passed on to the French War Committee, who are in full agreement with its leading ideas.

"The ideas are furthermore in complete accord with those which, on behalf of the War Committee, M. Franklin Bouillon and myself had the honour of expounding to you at our interviews of 9th–13th October. For a long time past the French Government and Parliament have been pressing for such a coordination to be established between the Allies. To bring about the collaboration and interlocking of the Allied War Committees, we proposed to you in particular, in our conversations at the beginning of October, that each War Committee should delegate in a permanent manner two of its members, to take part in the work of War Committees of the other countries. To this conception would naturally be attached the creation of an Inter-Allied General Staff.

"Thus the proposals which you are so good as to lay before us fit in perfectly with those which we were commissioned to present to you. The events on the Italian Front can only make their realisation more desirable and more urgent. At the same time, the scheme which accompanies your letter, and defines the future supreme war council, seems to us to call for certain modifications, which will not in any way alter its spirit, but will define certain details in such a way as to avoid any misunderstandings in the future.

"I have accordingly the honour to enclose you herewith the modified scheme, with the certainty that we shall without difficulty reach a mutual understanding upon an authoritative text which will express our common ideas.

"Begging you to be assured, Mr. Prime Minister, of my high regard, and of my feelings of cordial devotion.

PAUL PAINLEVÉ."

At the Rapallo Conference the final draft for the constitution of a Supreme Inter-Allied War Council was settled and agreed to as follows:

I. The representatives of the British, French and Italian Governments assembled at Rapallo on the 7th of November, 1917, have agreed on the scheme for the organisation of a Supreme War Council with a Permanent Military Representative from each Power, contained in the following paragraph.

SCHEME OF ORGANISATION OF A SUPREME WAR COUNCIL

II. (1) With a view to the better coördination of military action on the Western Front a Supreme War Council is created, composed of the Prime Minister and a Member of the Government of each of the Great Powers whose armies are fighting on that front. The extension of the scope of the Council to other fronts is reserved for discussion with the other Great Powers.

(2) The Supreme War Council has for its mission to watch over the general conduct of the War. It prepares recommendations for the decision of the Governments, and keeps itself informed of their execution and reports thereon to the respective Governments.

(3) The General Staffs and Military Commands of the Armies of each Power charged with the conduct of military operations remain responsible to their respective Governments.

(4) The general war plans drawn up by the competent Military Authorities are submitted to the Supreme War Council, which under the high authority of the Governments, ensures their concordance, and submits, if need be, any necessary changes.

(5) Each Power delegates to the Supreme War Council one Permanent Military Representative whose exclusive function is to act as technical adviser to the Council.

(6) The Military Representatives receive from the Government and the competent Military Authorities of their country all the proposals, information and documents relating to the conduct of the War.

(7) The Military Representatives watch day by day the situation of the forces, and of the means of all kinds of which the Allied Armies and the enemy armies dispose.

(8) The Supreme War Council meets normally at Versailles, where the Permanent Military Representatives and their Staffs are established. They may meet at other places as may be agreed upon, according to circumstances. The meetings of the Supreme War Council will take place at least once a month.

III. The Permanent Military Representatives will be as follows:

For France .... General Foch
" Great Britain .... General Wilson
" Italy .... General Cadorna

Rapallo, 7th November, 1917.

The only difficulty or disagreement that occurred in the course of the discussion arose as to which would be the most suitable place for the establishment of the Council. The French representatives were anxious it should be Paris. I was very insistent that it should be located somewhere outside in order that it should not only be entirely independent of the French Government, but that the fact of its independence should thereby be emphasised. At last Mr. Painlevé agreed to Versailles.

The question of an Inter-Allied Naval Council was left to be determined later.

Sir William Robertson ostentatiously declined to attend the discussions of the Supreme Council. His general sulkiness was apparent to all. He left the room with a flaunting stride the moment the idea of a Supreme Inter-Allied Council was mentioned, just stopping on the way for an instant to instruct Sir Maurice Hankey to make a note of the fact that he was not present during the discussions. He wished Sir Maurice to send for him when the Conference passed on to other subjects. He said: "I wash my hands of this business." His whole attitude during the Rapallo Conference was sullen and unhelpful, and it was ominous of acute trouble to come in our future relations. He meant to fight the Inter-Allied Council.

The first question referred to the new Council was the situation on the Italian Front. It was directed to report immediately on the position:

In consultation with the Italian General Headquarters they should examine into the present state of affairs, and, on a general review of the military situation in all theatres, should advise as to the amount and nature of assistance to be given by the British and French Governments, and as to the manner in which it should be applied.

The Italian Government undertakes to instruct the Italian

Supreme Command to give every facility to the Permanent Military Representatives both in regard to documentary information and movements in the zone of operations.

The Military Members of the Inter-Allied Council proceeded immediately to the Italian Front to examine the position. I accompanied them as far as Peschiera on my visit to meet the King of Italy. This meeting I have already described. Robertson returned to England to reorganise his broken front. The articles and paragraphs which appeared in the anti-Government Press soon after his arrival showed that the preliminary bombardment had commenced, and I knew the parliamentary attack would follow. It would be a formidable offensive. Mr. Asquith was to lead the assault in person. He had a large personal following amongst the Liberals. He could also count on the Irish and the pacifist section of the Labour Party. A number of influential Conservatives were disposed to back up military authority against civilian criticism. It was a powerful if ill-assorted confederacy. If the Staff could rally a sufficient number of these Conservatives in support, the Government might very well be beaten. For that I was quite prepared. I preferred this rather than remaining responsible any longer for a military policy that was dissipating the strength of our fine Army in carrying out the fatuous and wasteful schemes of purblind and obdurate sectionalism. Our greatest peril, the submarine attacks, was in a fair way to being overcome. Our food supply was assured for another year. We had gone through most of the period of waiting for the Americans, in spite of Russian defection, without being overwhelmed. As a free lance I would be able to talk more freely about the military leadership and thus rouse public opinion to correct its shortcomings. I knew the soldiers in the field were not behind the Staffs and would be only too glad to find someone giving expression to their dissatisfaction. I therefore made up my mind to take up the challenge of the War Office junta and its friends.

It was arranged that the setting up of the Council should be announced by M. Painlevé at a luncheon in Paris, to which all the Deputies and Senators should be invited. At that function I delivered a speech in which I explained the reasons for taking this step. In the course of my speech I placed before the distinguished assembly of French politicians and publicists a candid survey of the military position as it appeared to me. I pointed out that we had failed up to that date to make the best of the advantages we possessed by sea and land, that the fault had not been with the armies: it had been entirely due to the absence of real unity in the war direction of the Allied countries. From there I proceeded:

"As my colleagues here know very well, there have been many attempts made to achieve strategic unity. Conferences have been annually held to concert united action for the campaign of the coming year. Great generals came from many lands to Paris with carefully and skilfully prepared plans for their own fronts. In the absence of a genuine Inter-Allied Council of men responsible as much for one part of the battlefield as for another, there was a sensitiveness, a delicacy about even tendering advice, letting alone support for any sector other than that for which the generals were themselves directly responsible. But there had to be an appearance of a strategic whole, so they all sat at the same table and metaphorically took thread and needle, sewed these plans together, and produced them to a subsequent civilian conference as one great strategic piece; and it was solemnly proclaimed to the world the following morning that the unity of the Allies was complete.

"That unity, in so far as strategy went, was pure make-believe; and make-believe may live through a generation of peace — it cannot survive a week of war. It was a collection of completely independent schemes pieced together. *Stitching is not strategy.* So it came to pass that when these plans were worked out in the terrible realities of war, the stitches came out and disintegration was complete.

"I know the answer that is given to an appeal for unity of control. It is that Germany and Austria are acting on interior lines, whereas we are on external lines. That is no answer. That fact simply offers an additional argument for unification of effort in order to overcome the natural advantages possessed by the foe.

"You have only to summarise events to realise how many of the failures from which we have suffered are attributable to this one fundamental defect in the Allied war organisation. . . ."

I then summarised the successes which Germany had achieved owing entirely to the fact that we had not realised the importance of treating the whole front as one and indivisible. As to the Italian disaster, I said it was no use minimising its extent. If we did, then we would never take adequate steps to repair it:

"When we advance a kilometre into the enemy's lines, snatch a small shattered village out of his cruel grip, capture a few hundred of his soldiers, we shout with unfeigned joy. And rightly so, for it is the symbol of our superiority over a boastful foe and a sure guarantee that in the end we can and shall win.

"But what if we had advanced 50 kilometres beyond his lines and made 200,000 of his soldiers prisoners and taken 2,500 of his best guns, with enormous quantities of ammunition and stores? [1]

"What print would we have for our headlines? Have you any idea how long it would take the arsenals of France and Great Britain to manufacture 2,500 guns? . . ."

I told them that I believed we had at last learnt the lesson of the essential unity of all the Allied fronts. If I was right in my conjecture, the new Supreme Council would be given real power and the efforts of the Allies would be coördinated and victory would await valour. We should then

[1] I understated the total losses of Caporetto.

live to bless even the Italian disaster, for without it I did not believe it would have been possible to secure real unity. I then read a very remarkable message from Washington, which had appeared in the *Times,* and said that shrewd men in America, calmly observing the course of events from a distance of thousands of miles, had come to conclusions which we would have done well to make ours years ago. The message ran:

> " 'It is realised here that delicate questions of prestige exist between the great European nations engaged in the War, and that this militates against quick decisions and effective action when these are most needed. It is believed by some of President Wilson's closest advisers that Germany owes much of her success in this war to her unity of control, which permits the full direction of all Teutonic efforts from Berlin. Indeed, it is felt here that unless the Allies can achieve a degree of coördination equal to that which has enabled Germany to score her striking, though perhaps ineffectual successes, she will be able to hold out far longer than otherwise would have been believed possible. American military experts believe that if the Allied help rushed to General Cadorna's assistance to stem the tide of invasion had been thrown into the balance when Italy's forces were within forty miles of Laibach, the Allies would have been able to force the road to Vienna. Victory at Laibach would have spelled a new Austerlitz, and the magnitude of the prize almost within its grasp is believed here to have justified General Cadorna in taking the risk of advancing his centre too far and temporarily weakening his left flank. The lack of coöperation between France, Great Britain, and Italy is blamed here for the disaster which ensued, and which it is believed would not have occurred if one supreme military authority had directed the combined operations of the Allies with the sole aim of victory without regard to any other considerations.'

I continued:

"You may say the American estimate of the possibilities of the Italian Front for the Allies is too favourable. Why? It is not for me to express an opinion. I am but a civilian; but I am entitled to point out that the Austrian Army is certainly not better than the Italian. On the contrary, whenever there was a straight fight between the Italians and the Austrians, the former invariably won. And the Germans are certainly no better than the British and the French troops. When there has been a straight fight between them we have invariably defeated their best and most vaunted regiments. And as for the difficulties of getting there, what we have already accomplished in the course of the last few days is the best answer to that."

It might be said that the Americans at that distance from the battle area were not competent to form an opinion on the military possibilities. On the other hand, there lies much truth in the saying that outsiders see most of the game, and they certainly could judge it more calmly and impartially.

I said that national and professional traditions, prestige and susceptibilities had hitherto all conspired to render nugatory our best resolutions, but now we had set up this Council our business was to see that "the unity it represents is a fact and not a fraud." I apologised for having spoken with perhaps brutal frankness at the risk of much misconception here and elsewhere, and the risk perhaps of giving temporary encouragement to the foe.

"We shall win, but I want to win as soon as possible. I want to win with as little sacrifice as possible. I want as many as possible of that splendid young manhood which has helped to win victory to live through to enjoy its fruits.

"Unity — not sham unity, but real unity — is the only sure pathway to victory. The magnitude of the sacrifices made by the people of all the Allied countries ought to impel us to suppress all minor appeals in order to attain the common purpose of all this sacrifice. All personal, all sectional, considerations should be relentlessly suppressed. This is one of the greatest hours in the history of mankind. Let us not dishonour greatness with pettiness. . . ."

When I returned to England there were a great many signs of arranged and coördinated criticism and I think I can say intrigue, against the new move. Papers which had hitherto received their inspiration from the War Office were particularly hostile. For instance, one paper had an article headed "Hands off the Army." The *Times* was chilly. Mr. Asquith sympathised with the criticism and was prepared to make himself the spokesman of the General Staff. On the day I returned, he asked a question in Parliament which clearly indicated the attitude he had assumed. One paragraph out of that question will illustrate what I mean:

Whether it is proposed that the Council is, if so advised by its Staff, to have power to interfere with or override the opinion on matters of strategy with the General Staff at home, and of the Commanders-in-Chief in the field.

My answer gave the view of the British, French, and Italian Governments as to the general nature of the functions which we proposed that the Inter-Allied Council should discharge. I quoted the terms of the Rapallo agreement, the text of which I have given already on pages 549–550. I proceeded:

"From the foregoing it will be clear that the Council will have no executive power, and that the final decisions in matters of strategy and as to the distribution and movements of the various armies in the field will rest with the several Governments of the Allies. There will be, therefore, no Operations Department attached to the Council. The Permanent Military Representatives will derive from the existing Intelligence Departments of the Allies all the information necessary in order to enable them to submit advice to the Supreme Allied Council. The object of the Allies has been to set up a central body charged with the duty of continuously surveying the field of operations as a whole and, by the light of information derived from all fronts and from all Governments and Staffs, of coördinating the plans prepared by the different General Staffs, and, if necessary, of making proposals of their own for the better conduct of the War. Should the House desire an opportunity of discussing this important subject and my Paris speech, the Government would propose to set aside Monday next for the purpose."

A debate was arranged to take place in the House of Commons on November 19th. On the day the discussion took place, President Wilson issued a message indicating that he was in complete accord with the action taken by the Allied Governments, and that he was prepared not merely to associate himself with the Council but to take an official part in its deliberations:

"Colonel House, Head of the American Mission and Special Representative of President Wilson in Europe, has received a cable from the President stating emphatically that the Government of the United States considers that unity of plan and control between all the Allies and the United States is essential in order to achieve a just and permanent peace.

"The President emphasises the fact that this unity must be accomplished if the great resources of the United States are to be used to the best advantage, and he requests Colonel House to confer with the heads of the Allied Governments with a view to achieving the closest possible coöperation.

"President Wilson has asked Colonel House to attend the first meeting of the Supreme War Council with General Bliss, Chief of Staff of the United States Army, as the Military Adviser. It is hoped that the meeting will take place in Paris before the end of this month."

In the debate Mr. Asquith was critical, but not as censorious as those who supplied his brief would have wished.

He defended the action of the High Commands over Serbia, Roumania and Russia by saying:

"The experts may have been wrong. I do not claim any infallibility for them. I myself think they were right. That is a point that only history can decide."

As far as Serbia was concerned, the best answer to this defence of the military leaders and the head of the Government of that day was given by Mr. Noel Buxton (now Lord Noel-Buxton) later in the debate. Mr. Buxton was the greatest authority on the Balkans in the House of Commons. He gave illustrations from his own knowledge of the fatal delays of 1915 in dealing with the Balkan situation, owing to the lack of coördination amongst the Allies.

His view was that had the Inter-Allied Council been in existence at that date, these delays would not have arisen and he expressed the opinion that:

> "There cannot be the slightest doubt that if by hook or crook, coördination could have been brought about as early as that in the War, the whole situation would have been different and obviously the War would have been over long ago."

Mr. Asquith dwelt at length on the absence of naval representation on the new Council. I replied that provision had already been made for a permanent naval representative to keep the military advisers at Versailles informed on all naval questions which bore on their tasks. I also indicated that we were considering setting up another Inter-Allied Council to coördinate naval strategy. That was done a few weeks later. Mr. Asquith deprecated strongly the idea of unity of command. I agreed with him to the extent of saying that the appointment of a *Generalissimo* of *the whole of* the forces of the Allies was impracticable.

There was an underlying suggestion of interference by the Government with the soldiers in the discharge of their functions. Mr. Asquith hinted at it. The War Office Press accused us openly of meddling. I dealt with this accusation by saying:

". . . I will lay down two propositions, and I defy any man to challenge them. The first is this: No soldiers in any war have had their strategical dispositions less interfered with by politicians. There has not been a single battalion, or a single gun moved this year except with the advice of the General Staff — not one. There has not been a single attack by British troops ordered in any part of the battlefield except on the advice of the General Staff — not one. There has not been a single attack not ordered. The whole campaign of the year has been the result of the advice of soldiers. Never in the whole history of war in this country have soldiers got more consistent and more substantial backing from politicians than they have had this year. What do I mean by 'backing'? I do not mean 'backing' in speeches. I mean backing in guns, backing in ammunition, backing in transport, shipping, railways, supplies and men. Speeches are no substitute for shells.

"I have only twice during this War acted against the advice of soldiers. The first occasion was with the gun programme. I laid down a programme which was in advance of the advice of soldiers and against it. They thought that I was manufacturing too many and was extravagant. They thought that they would not be necessary, and that they could not man them. I took a different view, and there is not a soldier to-day who will not say that I was right. I was told that I was mad. That, I think, was the word used. There were the same attacks in the Press. What was the second occasion? The second case where I pressed my advice on soldiers against their will was in the appointment of a civilian to reorganise the railways behind the lines — my right honourable friend (Sir Eric Geddes) — and I am proud to have done it. . . ."

Mr. Asquith's supporters in the debate made clear the source of their inspiration. The gravamen of their charge was that the new Council was intended to supersede Sir William

Robertson and they urged that he should be our principal military representative at Versailles. I could not have assented to that proposition without stultifying the whole aim and purpose of the scheme. He would have obstructed and thwarted at every turn. Independent examination of strategy on the basis of a united front would have been a farce, had he been the chief military representative of the British Government.

Mr. Asquith was very insistent that in his day the Inter-Allied Conferences supplemented by liaison officers secured the necessary coördination of policy and strategy between the Allies. To this claim I answered:

> "The present system is a sporadic one, where you have meetings perhaps once every three or four months, barely that — there is only one meeting a year between the whole of the staffs; that has been the rule — for the purpose of settling the strategy of the Allies over the whole of the battle front, which extends over thousands and thousands of miles of front, with millions of men in embattled array upon those fronts. A single day, with perhaps a morning added! No generals, however great their intuition, no generals, whatever their genius, could settle the strategy of a year with a sitting which will only last over five or six hours. Utterly impossible! Therefore, it is an essential part of the scheme that this body should be permanent, that they should sit together day by day, with all the information derived from every front before them, with a view to coördinating the plans of the General Staffs over all the fronts."

As an attack on the Government, the debate was an utter failure. Mr. Pringle, who always prepared and organised these raids against the Government, in the course of his speech disclosed its main object. It was to bring about the fall of the Government.[1] This was to be done by rallying the friends of Sir William Robertson from every quarter. Had it

[1] Mr. Pringle also in the course of this speech predicted that I should be making an exactly similar speech twelve months from that date. The Armistice was signed a week before the term of the prophecy had expired.

succeeded, the war direction would have passed entirely into his hands. Whoever would be nominal Prime Minister, the C.I.G.S. would be a military dictator. The extent of the failure of this parliamentary manœuvre was revealed by the change in the attitude of the *Times*. Before the debate its tone was hostile. It now said:

> The Prime Minister achieved a great personal triumph yesterday. . . . He completely vindicated to the satisfaction of a crowded and excited House the essential soundness in its broad principles of the scheme he has devised and championed for the closer union of the Allies, and therefore for the better conduct of the War. Mr. Asquith, who opened the debate, carefully marshalled the familiar objections to the Rapallo plan and the obvious criticisms upon the Paris speech. But his reasoning was confined to secondary points. He never for a moment grappled with its leading features or ventured to contest the principles on which it rests. . . .

Now that the organised attack on the project for an Inter-Allied War Council had thus conspicuously collapsed, the path was clear for the setting up of the new machinery.

Why did the Government concentrate on Unity of Strategy rather than on Unity of Command?

Unity of Command had already been attempted in this year's campaign on the Western Front. In the spring offensive the combined French and British attack had been placed under the general control of General Nivelle. In the Flanders offensive the French contingent was under the direction of Sir Douglas Haig. In neither operation did the arrangement work satisfactorily. In the first the explanation is largely personal. The two commanders did not hit it off — consequent lack of zeal on one side and of tact on the other led to misunderstandings, and misunderstandings to delays, where rapidity of action was of the essence of the strategy. Whatever the reasons might be, in neither offensive was there any unity or agreement on policy. The result was that, although there was apparent coöperation, it was not real and whole-hearted in either case. Thus Unity of Command was for the time being discredited by the failure of the two experiments made in 1917 — one with a French *Generalissimo* and the other with a British. They failed, partly because there was no joint Staff to work out the basis of united action.

The first step in the attainment of Unity of Command-ment was to secure real agreement on strategy and to have an Inter-Allied Staff directly responsible to the Commander-in-Chief, which would not be thwarted by the Staffs attached to and dependent upon the ideas of the Commander-in-Chief of each national army.

A genuine Unity of Command was ultimately evolved out of this move. Even then, so great were the prejudices to be overcome, it had to be achieved by two separate steps and as a necessity, arising out of the consequences of overwhelming disaster. At Doullens, Foch was called upon to "coördinate" the effort of the two armies. But he was not given the authority to command. That did not constitute a united leadership and in practice it failed to achieve one common direction. Unity of Command was only established later on at Beauvais, where Foch was made Général-en-Chef of the two armies. But Versailles was the first step; Doullens was the second; Beauvais was the final achievement of Allied Unity on the Western Front.

When a Commander-in-Chief of the Allied Armies on the Western Front came to be appointed, he had behind him the ablest Staff in the field, which he could always call upon to assist him in developing his plans. His orders could not therefore be delayed or frustrated if any individual general under his command proved refractory and interposed obstacles on questions of detail, as Haig and Robertson did in the Nivelle enterprise. Thus Versailles assured the success of the Beauvais decision.

CHAPTER XIV

SUMMARY AND RESULTS OF 1917 CAMPAIGN

Twofold methods of belligerents — Time on the Allied side — Success of national organisation — Central Powers victorious on land — Bitter legacy of Chantilly — Russia's final collapse — Losses and discouragements of Western Allies — British victorious in Asia and Africa — Importance of Baghdad — Versailles Inter-Allied Staff — Tanks at Cambrai — America's entry into the War — Crucial part played by British Navy — A war of endurance — Success of anti-submarine organisation — Declining morale in Germany.

WHAT was the net result of the fourth campaign in this world struggle of infuriated nations? At the end of it some of them were prostrate and never rose again to continue the fight. Others were staggering in the ring. Even those who stood firmly on their feet and were able still to hit reeling blows were gashed with wounds and visibly becoming exhausted from loss of blood. The Allied group sought to gain the ascendency by two general methods. For one the military chiefs were responsible. The other was left to the Navy and the Civil Administration. The military idea was to force an immediate decision by hitting with the whole strength of their armies at the most formidable but least vulnerable parts in the enemy's defensive system — the Governments had to ensure that, if these onslaughts failed to take effect, the reserve of national power should be sustained and stimulated, so that it might outlast that of their adversaries. In the prosecution of the first aim of this double policy, the Western Allies undertook tremendous attacks on the German entrenchments in France, Flanders and Italy, with a view to breaking through their defences and defeating the most redoubtable enemy of the Alliance. In pursuit of the second aim of this common war policy, the Allies took steps to strengthen their position in respect of food and war materials whilst tightening the blockade on the enemy countries in order to weaken their striking power. In both the blockading of the enemy and the organisation of the national resources, Britain took the lead. The blockade at sea became more ruthless than ever and the enemy countries felt its stranglehold telling on their vitality. The British Government, by a series of unprecedented measures, led the way in a reorganisation of the national assets in man power, in food production and distribution, and in transport. The Government proceeded on the assumption that the Allies had been manoeuvred, by the improvident and short-sighted war direction hitherto adopted, into a position where the issue had become mainly a question of staying power. Hence the gigantic efforts put forth during this year in the development and mobilisation of all the available resources of our country.

As to the Central Powers, they gave up any idea of attempting to force a decision this year by a great military *coup* against the most powerful of their surviving enemies. They had practically shattered the military strength of four of the nations in battle array against them before the end of 1916. By the end of this year they had almost completed their overthrow and had also broken the battle front of another of their foes. As to the French and British Armies, Germany was content to repel their assaults on her fortifications. Her deadliest effort to overcome the Allies and compel them to sue for peace was made not on land but at sea. Ultimate victory or defeat depended on the success or failure of that effort. She attacked Britain, which was now the most resourceful of her remaining foes in Europe, by a well-organised and devastating campaign to sink her shipping. Had she succeeded, the Allied countries, their people, and their armies would have been at her mercy and 1918 would have witnessed the greatest military and naval triumph in the history of the Teuton.

Time was on the side of the Allies. This year was Germany's last chance to win, for America would be in next year. Germany, therefore, had this year either to defeat the Allied Armies or destroy the means of transporting war material, food and reinforcements, whether from America or the British Empire.

Each of the belligerents endeavoured to handle against their opponents the grim weapon of famine. If the war went right on through 1918, stark hunger would drive the population and armies of one or other of the two rival groups into surrender. Which of them would starve first?

Those were the problems of 1917. How did it all work out? There were victories on both sides and also defeats and disappointments. There can be no doubt that by December 31st the balance of advantage was decisively on the Allied side. In a war of this kind, where fighting was by no means the only factor in decisive victory, organisation behind the lines ultimately determined the event. But even so far as actual blows were concerned, the history of 1917 is one of our winning the War on sea in spite of the Board of Admiralty, whilst our Generals were doing their best to lose the War on land in spite of the Government. The sea campaign went in our favour decisively — and that determined the final issue of the struggle. The land campaign went definitely against us — and that jeopardised the advantage gained by the efforts of our fine seamen and our great organisers and also enormously increased the cost in life and treasure of our final triumph.

The fighting on land in 1917 went heavily in favour of the Central Powers. It is impossible for any impartial observer of the events of 1917 to come to any other conclusion.

The military chiefs had already, in the winter of 1916, planned their campaigns for 1917 on the same rigid and arid lines as they had pursued in 1915 and 1916, achieving nothing but a horrifying carnage unparalleled in the annals of war. This time they felt certain that their one great idea must succeed at last. They had made a few changes and improvements to correct little mistakes they had discovered last time in the action of their great plan. Moreover, they were confident that the German troops had deteriorated in quality since last year. So first the French were to conduct a great hurtling offensive with masses of their troops on a wide front, with the help of a diverting attack in the north by the British on a narrower front. Then if these operations did not finally succeed in driving the German Army out of their entrenchments, the British Army were to undertake another attack, and propel hundreds of thousands of their best troops against the German fortresses in Flanders, in order to expel the Germans from the Flemish coast, and then fall on their exposed flank with masses of cavalry. It was all based on the dynamics of the butting head against a tremendous wall — in this case a wall bristling with machine guns. It is only fair to the military intelligence to state that the British were not enamoured of the French plan, and the French were at first quite indifferent and eventually contemptuous of the British project. Haig did not believe in the Nivelle strategy and Pétain and Foch scoffed at Haig's "duck march" in Flanders. They judged wisely of each other's plans if not of their own. That is a common attribute in all human affairs. They nevertheless agreed, in that spirit of fraternal toleration and accommodation that ought to prevail amongst partners, to try both — in turn. Neither of the two schemes had a reasonable chance of succeeding, for reasons which I gave before they were ever attempted. But the military staffs clutched at their respective projects. With fierce tenacity they stubbornly refused to let go and declined angrily even to consider any alternative. Italy was left to her own devices. What was worse, she was left to carry them out with what was obviously — even to civilians — an inadequate equipment. Russia was entrusted with tasks which she was no longer fitted to discharge. Every front where there was any chance of obtaining a signal victory which would have threatened the security of the Central Powers was treated as a "side show."

The mildewed strategic ideas that had wasted away the large margin of advantage in resources and chances that once appertained to the Alliance, had once more been furbished up and presented as fresh projects of action at Chantilly and endorsed by all the Allied Governments at Paris in November, 1916. These schemes were left to the new British Government as a legacy of inevitable disaster. The tragedy of the year's land struggle lay in the fact that the Allied Governments could not arrive at an agreement amongst themselves to insist on new methods being considered. The efforts of the British Government to alter these schemes were rendered ineffectual, owing to the resistance or inertia of the other Allied Governments. France only changed her mind about the butting strategy after the Nivelle defeat had almost destroyed what was left of her fine Army, that is, what was left after the Joffre-Nivelle tactics had worked their will on the great Army of France for two and a half years. But even after the French Command had finally thrown over the old strategy, there was no agreement between the Allied Staffs as to what should be substituted. An alliance between independent political parties for effective joint action to attain a common aim is difficult enough to achieve and still more difficult to work satisfactorily, but when it is attempted between independent nations, it is a baffling proposition and often unattainable. The great offensive designed at Chantilly in November, 1916, had therefore to be laboriously plodded through at a ruinous cost, without reference to any exposure of basic assumptions by events, or to any complete alteration which had been effected by these events in strategic conditions.

Each Army, French, British and Italian, in its turn was forced to stop through sheer exhaustion. Russia and Roumania had already been finally defeated by the end of 1916. The Russian soldiers as well as the Russian people had both had enough of the fighting. That means they were thoroughly beaten and knew it. To continue in the War meant useless slaughter. Desperate efforts were made by the Duma leaders and by Kerensky once more to rouse and revive the combative spirit of the Army. It was all in vain. A great offensive was staged in the summer. But you cannot attack effectively with an army which has already given up all hope of winning. Once this offensive had definitely failed — as it soon did — the Russian Army ceased to be a serious menace to the Central Powers. Their military and political leaders had only to consider whether it was better to go forward and push over the crazy fabric, or allow it to disintegrate and crumble. The latter process was steadily and perceptibly going on. The cords which just held the military power of Russia together were rotting before our eyes, owing to the corrosive elements with which they were drenched by revolutionary propaganda. The Russian and Roumanian defeat transferred the favourable balance of man power immediately available from the Allies to the Central Powers. American man power was not a military factor in 1917. Pétain and Foch grasped the change in the military situation due to the paralysis of one Ally with its immense army, and the accession of another great country with a great army not in being, but only in the making. They also realised that the temporary collapse in the spirit of the French troops caused by the slaughter of the Chemin des Dames was an element with which they must reckon. Haig and Robertson went on as if there had been no alteration in the fundamental facts that determined strategy. Every time the altered circumstances were urged upon them, they treated them as irrelevancies. What mattered to them was that the French Generals had been given their chance and had missed it, and that the British Generals must not now be robbed of theirs. They meant to have it and show the French how to use it. But frankly on this subject the Government was so divided that it could not overrule its military experts. They were fully aware of that division and took full advantage of circumstance to stick to their plan. We know what a ghastly fiasco it all turned out to be.

The Eastern Allies had been for all practical purposes finally overthrown and France, Britain and Italy had all of them done badly on the Western Front — from the North Sea to the Adriatic. The spring and autumn offensives captured some ground and a number of prisoners and guns, but in substance they both failed conspicuously in their objectives. The losses in officers and men were much heavier amongst the Allied Armies than those they succeeded in inflicting on the Germans. In morale the French Army was reduced to a condition in which it could not be trusted to do any sustained fighting on a great scale. We had yet to discover how seriously the spirit of the British troops had been shaken by the Flanders offensive. The German Army still maintained its offensive intrepidity. On the Italian Front opportunities were thrown away and passed on gratuitously to the enemy. It is lucky that it was rather late in the season when he took advantage of his chances on that front. The early summer offensive of the Italian Army achieved nothing owing to lack of guns and ammunition which their Western Allies could easily have spared. The effort made by the British Government at the Rome Conference subsequently to help the Italians to what would have been an assured and probably a decisive victory, was frustrated by military obtuseness and selfishness. The disastrous rout of Caporetto was the inevitable climax of such narrow strategy. Hundreds of thousands of Italian troops were put out of action and thousands of guns were lost. The offensive power and spirit of the Army were not restored during the rest of the War. On the Salonika Front the elaborate show of an Allied offensive was a prearranged fiasco. The British and French troops there were deliberately deprived by their respective General Staffs at home of the artillery and ammunition which alone could have enabled them to smash through the obstacles with which the infantry were confronted. It was a sham, a preordained sham, but a costly sham, and after this experience there was no heart left in either generals or men for further fighting on that front. Thus in the East and the West the war of attrition in men, in guns, in territory, and in morale had gone emphatically in favour of the Central Powers. They claimed that their armies were victorious on all European fronts, and their claim could not be challenged.

The only bright spots in the military campaign were the genuine victories won in the Far East and the clearing of the Germans out of East Africa. The progress made in these spheres was due to the direct intervention and insistence of the Government. The defeat of the hitherto victorious Turkish Armies in Palestine and Mesopotamia and the occupation of the world-famous cities of Jerusalem and Baghdad were a patch of blue sky which lightened the gloom that hung over the battlefield as a whole. The psychological effect — and that counts in war — was immense. The name of Baghdad counted for more throughout the Mussulman world than did Passchendaele, with all the notoriety it had acquired.

Jerusalem meant more to hundreds of millions — Christian and Mussulman alike — than Ostend. The calling of the Turkish bluff was not only the beginning of the cracking-up of that military impostorship which the incompetence of our war direction had permitted to intimidate us for years; it was itself a real contribution to ultimate victory. The encouragement it gave to the Allies at a moment of depression was useful, but the decided blow it gave to German prestige amongst their confederates was of still greater service. It was the first time the Germans exposed to their Allies their utter inability to give them effective aid in defeat when they were at last intelligently and resolutely attacked, and to protect them from impending disaster. It made a definite impression on the Turkish mind, and it was not without its influence on Bulgaria — probably also on Austria.

Field Marshal von Hindenburg in his autobiography bears out the impression which the loss of Baghdad made both in Germany and amongst her Allies. He says:

> The loss of Baghdad was painful to us, and as we well believed, still more for all thinking Turkey. How often had the name of the old city of the Caliphs been mentioned in Germany in previous years. . . . We had guaranteed the Turkish Government its territorial integrity of the Empire, and we felt that, in spite of the generous interpretation of this contract, our political account was heavily overdrawn by this new great loss.

So much for the charge that the British Government were wasting our resources on useless side shows. No wonder Hindenburg, in discussing the weakness of the military position of the Turkish Empire beyond the Taurus, and our failure to take advantage of it says:

> If ever there was a prospect of a brilliant strategic feat, it was here. . . . Why did England never make use of her opportu-

nity? . . . Some day history will perhaps clear up this question also.[1]

There were three other events which were of good omen for the future. The first was the setting-up of the Inter-Allied Military and Naval Staff at Versailles. This was a completely new departure. Its object was to put an end to the disjointed and haphazard methods of particularist strategy which had prevailed hitherto. For the first time in the War the mere pretence of unity of action was to be discarded, and a genuine effort was to be made to consider the vast battlefield as one front with several flanks, to survey and assess the opportunities and possibilities not only of each flank, but of the whole front on sea and land, and adjust the general strategy of the Allies accordingly. There was now sitting at Versailles a body of very able generals from each Allied country and assisted by a brilliant staff of experienced officers drawn from each Allied Army. They were engaged in making a thorough study of the position and prospect on all the fronts. They had placed at their disposal all the information gathered by the Staff of each Allied Army and Navy. The process of examination and coördination was going on.

The second was the demonstration at the Battle of Cambrai of the great possibilities of the tank in trench warfare. This action was grossly bungled and the tank success was thrown away through the ineptitude of the High Command. Nevertheless, the tank attack showed clearly what an effective use could be made of these machines in overcoming the most formidable entanglements and entrenchments. This discovery was one of the principal factors in the German defeat of 1918. Stimulated by the knowledge gained at Cambrai, the efforts made to manufacture more and more of these weapons of offensive warfare were redoubled and, profiting

[1] "Out of My Life", Field Marshal von Hindenburg, pp. 295 *et seq.*

by the mistakes made, new methods were devised for using them to the best advantage.

When I was Secretary of State for War, in September, 1916, I ordered one thousand tanks to be manufactured. Sir William Robertson countermanded the order without my knowledge. Thanks to Sir Albert Stern, I discovered this countermand in time, and gave peremptory instructions that the manufacture should be proceeded with and that the utmost diligence should be used in executing the order. We had now a large fleet of these land battleships already completed and many more in course of construction.

But infinitely the greatest warranty of victory which came to the Allied side — apart from the defeat of the submarine — was the accession of the great Western Republic to the Allied side. I place it second to the checking of the havoc of the submarines, because if the U-boats had triumphed in their purpose, no American forces of any magnitude could have reached the battlefield. But once a safe passage across the Atlantic was ensured, America, with her enormous resources in men, money and material, was bound to have a decisive influence on the fortunes of the War. The Russian strength had dwindled from campaign to campaign. The American would grow as time went on. In a war of exhaustion which had already lasted three years, America, coming in fresh with her mighty strength untouched, would be a determining factor, provided her power could be brought into action before the Allies cracked. The reorganisation of the resources and energies of the British Empire carried the Allies over the interregnum between the American declaration of war and American readiness for war. The discomfiture of the submarines by British marines enabled that readiness to be made effective before it was too late to profit by it.

Although as a whole things had not gone well on land

where the military staffs had their way, the whole situation had been redeemed by our victories at sea, where the experts were overruled by the Government. In addition to this, our reorganisation of the home front by the business men called in by the Government had an enormous effect in strengthening our prospects of endurance in the war of attrition to which we had been committed. Had it not been for these activities, it is doubtful whether the Alliance could have stayed the course.

The part played by our sailors in gaining ultimate victory for the Alliance has not been sufficiently acknowledged. Even British histories accord infinitely more space to battles that did not get us any nearer a decision and ended in nothing but heavy losses. The conflict at sea was not one of a kind which lent itself to diurnal publicity. For that reason, not even a paragraph could be accorded to the achievements of our sailors in the daily Press. There were no special correspondents in the vicinity to describe the unceasing conflict waged daily and nightly on the trenchless sea — a conflict on which the fate of great nations hung. Even the British public with its traditional understanding of the importance of sea power had no clear conception of the predominant influence which these individual manœuvres and fights, enacted where the visibility was not clear to the eyes of the most discerning journalist, were having in determining the question of final victory or defeat. Some of the British histories and memoirs of the War show no clear apprehension of the importance of the struggle for mastery on the High Seas. The Dogger Bank, the Dardanelles bombardment, the Falkland fight and Jutland are given a prominent place. They were spectacular, but these battles constituted a small part in the prolonged struggle which determined the issue. French and Italian histories ignore almost altogether the maritime contests that pulled them through in the end. The details of the struggle were rightly kept secret at the time, and yet in the aggregate these individual deeds of sustained courage and skill won the War.

The real conflict resolved itself into many occasional combats, but more often into manœuvres to escape attack. There were a myriad heroic incidents and episodes, none of them reported, where only a handful of men were engaged at a time. The story as a whole is the greatest epic in our history, but each line was composed separately by different men at diverse times. The battle on land was pyrotechnic — and therefore made good copy. A convoy of tramps gave a thrill when you saw it, but there was none of the shuddering drama of the great tragedies enacted on land. Here thousands of great cannon were firing millions of shells until the reverberations could be heard across the Channel by multitudes well within our shores: masses of men dashed along in the face of shot and shell: here was indeed the lightning and thunder of war: crowded hospitals scattered all over the land advertised the immensity of the devastation: and yet nothing happened that finally determined the event of the War. Even the air bombing of London and the destruction of a few Zeppelins attracted more attention than the silent fight with the U-boats. During the night whilst London, with its teeming millions, was stricken with nervous fear by the throbbing sound of German aëroplanes hovering in the moonless sky and by the thud of the explosive bombs they dropped on the darkened city, a number of humble steamers would be navigating in formation, escorted by two or three torpedo boats flitting around to watch over their flock like faithful shepherd dogs. It was almost a noiseless procession, whose movement was not heard above the breaking of the waves or the sough of the winds. The enemy was hidden under the waters. He might be waiting for the heavy-laden packhorses of the sea — the tramp steamers — to hurl his crashing torpedo at the unresisting plates. One detonation and a ship disappeared in the deep. The noisy land battle and the exciting air raid occupied pages of the morning paper. The struggle at sea, of which not a sound reached the shore or any ear remotely connected with Fleet Street, passed without any detailed notice being taken of it; because of the details nothing was ever heard by the public. The wolves that prowled through the jungles of the deep were more of a peril to the great city, its pride and its people, than the clattering menace of the clouds. And yet the latter had no influence whatever on the course of the War, whereas the former was an essential part of the process that settled it.

It had become a war of endurance. The strategy on both sides was unimaginative and commonplace. There was no military genius on either side to devise, execute and exploit a stroke that transformed the course of the War and determined the result. Castelnau's penetrating observation about Napoleon still held good. "Had he been here he would have thought of the something else." No general had yet discovered it. It was therefore entirely a question of which combination would be the first to get tired of the War, and to fall from exhaustion or retire because unnourished nerves could stand the strain no longer. Here the command of the sea became the dominant factor. A half-starved Britain and France would inevitably have followed a hunger-stricken Russia. Had the submarines succeeded, then by the end of 1917 the Allied populations would have been fortunate to secure half rations. The soldiers would also have had their food allowance reduced. Coupled with the discouragement and losses of the land campaign, the withdrawal of the Russian colossus, the dwindling chance of carrying American troops to Europe, the effect of the Russian Revolution on the working class would have been intensified by a hundredfold, and no Government could have hoped to carry their ill-fed people and their stinted and shrinking armies through another campaign.

The unmistakable success of the anti-submarine measures taken by the Government — taken, as far as the maritime arrangements were concerned, against the advice of their chief naval experts — changed the whole situation. These measures included a great shipbuilding programme, a complete reorganisation of our shipping, our docks, our rail transport and the resources of our soil. There was also a mobilisation of the whole adult population with a view to a more efficacious use of the labour reserves of the nation. Tonnage was saved by diminishing the sinking and increasing the building — by making a more businesslike use of the available ships — by cutting down nonessential imports and by a great programme of increased home production. Our imports of essential supplies, war material and food were maintained — our home yield of food, timber and ore was substantially increased. There were restrictions on consumption but they did not deprive the nation of sufficient food to provide nourishment for all. The apprehension that we would not be able to reinforce, feed and equip the armies of the Alliance, that we might not be in a position to transport the huge American Army across the seas and that we might not be able to keep our population from starvation, vanished altogether like a bad dream. The disaffection which threatened trouble early in the year gradually disappeared and by the end of December it was giving the Government no anxiety. Before 1918 arrived we knew that we must win if we could constrain the High Command not to repeat the prodigious military errors of 1917.

What was the state of things in enemy countries? The food shortage was becoming acute. It was telling on the physique of the population, and consequently on its temper. The food deficiency was causing a sense of general irritation amongst the industrial population whose zealous coöperation was so essential in the mines and works. The difference between the frame of mind of the German worker and that of his opposite number in Britain and France will be better appreciated when one recalls that a resolution demanding that an effort should be made to negotiate peace was carried by an overwhelming majority in the Reichstag but rejected by an even larger majority in both the British Parliament and the French Chamber of Deputies. The bulletins issued to the enemy public about German victories in France, Russia and Roumania, although in substance authentic, did not appease the cravings of incipient and unsatisfied hunger amongst those who returned the German deputies. Even the soldiers in the trenches were becoming increasingly conscious of the fact that the blockade was tightening. As long as the submarine campaign was thriving and the figures of ships sunk were swelling week by week, the suffering inhabitants of the Central Alliance felt that the enemy who stopped their supplies would soon be in a worse plight than their own, and that they would be starved into submission before German and Austrian cupboards became quite bare. That prevented disaffection from fermenting into revolution. Even by the end of the year they had still hopes of the submarine. The check which had been put on its ravages had not been generally realised in Germany. A time was coming when it could not be concealed. Then any nation, however brave, would know that it was useless to continue the struggle. All would depend on the German Admiralty finding some means of circumventing the new methods successfully applied by the British Government for the protection of their ships. So far the British were winning in the tremendous conflict going on by day and by night in this decisive sphere of action. That is why I regard the success of the steps taken to counter the submarine attack as the most important contribution made to victory during the year 1917.

APPENDIX I[1]

Memorandum by Sir William Robertson,
20th June, 1917.

1. I HAVE not attended most of the recent meetings of the Cabinet Committee on War Policy, but I understand that, amongst other things, they are considering whether, unless success in the North can be practically guaranteed, we ought not to abandon the plan now being carried out by the *War Cabinet instructions,*[2] in order to reserve our men for next year, and meanwhile send a large amount of artillery to Italy in the hope of defeating Austria.

2. Personally, I have been sceptical of Austria making a separate peace, as her whole future depends upon her relations with Germany, to whose wheels she is tied in a variety of ways, economic, industrial, political, etc. Assuming, however, that she would make a separate peace if fairly *heavily punished, the question is can she be so punished?*

3. In the recent Italian offensive a fairly important advance was made on one flank and a smaller one on the other. The losses on both sides appear to be approximately equal. The Austrians fought well and showed no sign of collapse and have, in fact, taken back some of the ground they lost.

4. It would, of course, be a great advantage if we could completely dispose of Austria, but Germany knows this as well as we do and she may be depended upon to try and support Austria, if and when she is in danger, in the same way as she did in the Bukowina.

[1] See Chapter IX.
[2] As I have pointed out already, no such "instructions" were ever issued.—D. LL. G.

5. I understand that the dispatch of some 75 batteries of heavy artillery from our front in France to Italy is being considered. *The time required to withdraw these batteries and get them ready for battle there would probably not be less than six weeks.* The passage of this number of guns through Italy *could not be concealed* and the enemy might be expected to have the best part of a month for counter-preparations.[1] I have many times pointed out the advantages enjoyed by the enemy in having the interior position, which enables him to move his troops more quickly than we can move ours. We have but two railways into Italy, one of which — the Mont Cenis — is not very good, whereas the enemy have five — one leading to the Trentino and four to the Isonzo. The enemy can therefore always hope to beat us, if he wishes to, in concentrating superior forces on the Italian Front.

6. As regards the number of troops Germany might send to Italy, General Cadorna stated on the 14th of March last, *i.e.* before the Russian Revolution, that if the Germans decided to attack Italy they could with the Austrians bring 90 divisions and a very superior artillery against him. These reinforcements would, he said, be so overwhelming that he would need reinforcements from us in order to enable him to defend himself.

The Allied offensive on the Western Front has prevented the Germans from undertaking any offensive operations in Italy. If Germany is relieved from serious pressure on the Western Front she will be in much the same position for attacking Italy as she was last March, but plus the advantage she may get from the weakening of the Russians, and therefore, if she decided to reinforce the Italian Front to the extent regarded as possible by Cadorna, not only could

[1] Our military representative at the Italian Front, General Delmé-Radcliffe, was of opinion that guns and ammunition could be transferred to the Italian Front without attracting the attention of the enemy.

he not defeat Austria but he himself would need support.

7. So much for the prospect of Austria being defeated. As regards our postion, if the 75 batteries were sent *we must necessarily pass to the defensive for all practical purposes,*[1] and be prepared to suffer losses similar to those suffered by the Germans while on the defensive this summer. *Also, we abandon all hope of making either our air or sea situation more secure* so far as the Belgian coast is concerned, *and, in fact, the Germans might conquer us by an attempt to take Dunkirk,* and if they succeeded the situation would become even worse than it is now. I do not say that they would succeed, as this would depend to some extent upon the reinforcements that Germany might be able to bring over from the Russian Front and upon the power of her artillery. *This power has not been great recently,* and as the number of heavy guns she has on the Western Front are approximately equal to the Allies, her failure must be due to other reasons — for instance, the declining morale, inferiority in the air, inefficient employment of the guns, or want of ammunition. I do not pretend to say which; it may be a combination of all. But as a shortage of ammunition has been alleged I would point out that if left to her own devices Germany might be able to accumulate a sufficient stock for offensive purposes. *I think we should follow the principle of the gambler who has the heaviest purse and force our adversary's hand and make him go on spending until he is a pauper.* As a matter of fact, we are not very sure about this shortage of ammunition. Von Arnim commands the Fourth Army in the North opposite the Belgians where a small amount of ammunition would suffice, while all that could be made available may have been sent to Arras and Champagne where heavy fighting was in progress at the time he issued his order.

[1] This is an assumption that Germans attack, *i.e.,* do not take their men to Italy. — D. Ll. G.

8. Germany would bring over heavy reinforcements if Russia continues to do nothing or if she drops out of the War altogether. The best chance we have of keeping her in the field is to continue our activity, *for if we stop being aggressive she may think that we admit our failures.* Further, the Russians are themselves supposed to be preparing for an offensive early next month and have asked us to keep up our pressure.

9. The conclusion I have arrived at, taking the broadest possible view of the general situation, is that our chances of obtaining good results are certainly no greater in Italy than they are in the North, while the risks involved are much greater in the former place than in the latter. *I deprecate as strongly as anyone our incurring heavy casualties without a corresponding return,* BUT THE PLAN AS OUTLINED BY THE FIELD MARSHAL SHOULD SECURE US AGAINST THIS MISTAKE. *I have shown, and I understand the War Cabinet agree, that we must continue to be aggressive somewhere on our front, and we ought of course to do this in the most promising direction.* The plan provides for this and will enable us to derive a real advantage till the enemy shows signs of weakening, *while at the same time it permits of our easing off if the situation so demands.* No doubt the enemy will fight as hard as he possibly can, and he will use as many troops and guns as he possibly can, but he will also do these things on the Italian Front rather than see Austria decisively defeated. I do not for one moment think that Germany is as yet near the end of her resources in men or material. I think she may yet take a great deal of beating, and that it is necessary France should be aggressive as well as ourselves. On the other hand, Germany may be much nearer exhaustion both on the fronts and at home, than we imagine, and there are many indications of this. Doubtful situations such as the present one have always arisen in war, *and great mistakes*

have been made by endeavouring to find a fresh way round as soon as the strain begins to be felt.[1] *We should be on our guard against this mistake.*

10. I am therefore in favour of continuing our present plan on the chance of getting a success in the north, not only because of the military situation but also because of the necessity of trying to improve the air and sea situation, and I am consequently averse from diverting any of our resources to Italy. We should, however, do all we can to provide Italy with means for increasing her ammunition supply, as she already has far more guns than she can keep employed, and in this connection I would remind the War Cabinet that there is no reason why Italy should remain inactive throughout the winter, as operations can continue on the Isonzo up to the end of January.

[1] Where? Scipio — Sherman — Wellington.

APPENDIX II[1]

Memorandum by Sir Douglas Haig on the strategical situation with special reference to the comparative advantages of an offensive in Northern Belgium as against an offensive from Italy against Austria.

THE railway capacity of Northern Belgium is sufficient for the maintenance of some 40 German divisions north of the river Lys and possibly even more.

But given our present superiority in the air, we could almost certainly cause such serious interruptions and consequent disorganisation in the railway working (by bombing important junctions) as to upset all calculations.

In any case the limiting factor may be taken as the number of German divisions available rather than as a question of railway capacity.

On the 17th of June, Germany had *156 divisions on the Western Front*. Of these, 25 were in the army entrusted with the defence of Northern Belgium, leaving 131 for the defence of the remainder of the German line.

Of this 131, 96 are in line and 35 in reserve.

Judging by past experience of her methods, Germany would not reduce this number of 96 in line, opposed as they are by a considerably larger Allied force (at present about 140 divisions). She must also retain her reserves behind them.

Of the 96 divisions in line, not less than 63 have been seriously engaged lately, and of the 35 in reserve, 25 have

[1] See Chapter IX.

INDEX

been seriously engaged, so that, of the 131 divisions available for defence on the long front (roughly 400 miles) from the Lys to Switzerland, only 43 are fresh.

The present allotment works out at over three miles of front per division for the whole front south of the Lys — which may be taken as a minimum for reasonable security, especially as German divisions have a low establishment and as no less than 17 Landwehr divisions of comparatively poor quality are included in the figures given.

It is highly improbable, therefore, that the Germans would reduce appreciably the 131 divisions available on this front.

Of the 25 divisions allotted to the German Army garrisoning Northern Belgium, 13 are in line between the Lys and the sea, a distance of 32 miles, of which 13 are protected by flood. The number of divisions in reserve in this army is 11, all of which could be made available north of the Lys. This is a high allotment for this area even allowing for the fact that it includes the coast garrisons.

One division in line to about two miles of front on which attack is expected is as much as we need expect to be employed against us; and, allowing for the flooded area, 14 or 15 divisions may be taken as the largest force that will be placed in line between the Lys and the sea. The reserves at first available behind that front are unlikely — for the reasons given above — to exceed ten divisions, and there may be two or three divisions in addition placed on the coast itself.

If fresh divisions can be brought from Russia we may confidently expect them to be centrally placed, at some distance back, until the situation is clear; or they may be used to relieve exhausted divisions at special points, the latter being drawn into central reserves.

At present, Germany's reduction of her forces on the

Russian Front is practically limited to exchanging fresh troops there for tired ones from the West. *But the number of her good divisions in the East is limited and moreover, it is estimated that her transport facilities will only suffice to move ten divisions a month from the East.*

For all these reasons we are justified in calculating that the Allies will have a considerable superiority in infantry on the front of attack — probably not less than two to one. And our capacity for exchanging tired divisions for fresh ones along our defensive line will not be less than that of the Germans.

In guns and ammunition, judging by experience and information from captured orders, etc., our superiority will be even greater; while in the air we may regard our superiority as still more assured. The last-mentioned factor is of immense importance from the points of view of artillery efficiency, information, damage behind the enemy's lines, and general morale.

As regards the alternative to an attack in Belgium, namely, attacking Austria from Italy, the arguments against this are overwhelmingly stronger than those in favour of it.

It has always been accepted as the most effective form of war to attack and destroy the enemy's strongest forces as soon as possible IF THERE IS A REASONABLE PROSPECT OF SUCCESS. *If there is not a reasonable prospect of success the next best course is to weaken the enemy by holding his main forces and attacking his weaker ones, if that be possible. The possibility depends, however, firstly on being able to hold his main forces, and secondly, on being able to defeat his weaker ones.*

If we were to detach largely to Italy it is probable that we could still hold the Germans on the Western Front, *but it is not certain* and it would depend much on the French.

It is at very best very uncertain that we could defeat Austria.

If the Germans elected to send divisions round to meet us on the Italian frontier, their railway facilities are better than ours *in the proportion of five to two;* and as it is Germany's interest to uphold Austria just as much as it is ours to overcome Austria, it is practically certain that she would endeavour to do so either by attacking the French violently, or by transferring divisions to the Italian Front.

The Italian frontier is difficult to attack from. It would take us so long to transfer troops and prepare an attack that it is doubtful if we could complete preparations this summer.[1] *The main part of the forces employed in the attack would be Italian,* and even if the Allied offensive gained some success at first, Germany's reply might be to counterattack the Italians as soon as possible. If they gave way our force might — and probably would — be seriously compromised. The danger of this would be far greater than the danger of any counterattack against our offensive in Belgium, where all the troops employed in our offensive will be trustworthy.

A decision to transfer troops to Italy would mean abandonment of our offensive in Belgium. A consequent gain of time to Germany; *very dangerous disappointment in France* and to some extent in Russia; small prospects of success against Austria supported in all probability by German troops; a possibility of reverses on the Western Front; and a possibility of still more serious reverses on the Italian Front.

Against all this we have a reasonable chance of success in Belgium which may have greater results than even a bigger success against Austria, and which at least may be expected to open the way for greater results subsequently.

[1] The Germans prepared the attack which broke through the Italian Army some weeks later than this date.

It is *not impossible that Germany aims at inducing us to detach from the Western Front — that is a very usual form of war, often employed with telling effect*. But whether she is deliberately trying so to induce us or not, there seems no doubt that our wisest and soundest course is to continue to wear down the German forces on the Western Front, as we are undoubtedly able to do.